Farm, Factory and Fortune:
New Studies in the Economic History
of the Maritime Provinces

Edited by
Kris Inwood

Acadiensis Press

Fredericton
New Brunswick

1993

Canadian Cataloguing in Publication Data

Main entry under title:
Farm factory and fortune

    Includes bibliographic references.
    ISBN 0-919107-38-9

    1. Maritime Provinces — Economic Conditions.
    I. Inwood, Kris E., 1951-

HC117.M35F37 1993   330.9715   C93-098520-6

Cover Design: Brenda Steeves for Goose Lane

Acadiensis Press is pleased to acknowledge the support of the New Brunswick Department of Municipalities, Culture and Housing and of the Writing and Publishing Section of the Canada Council.

The paper used in this publication meets the minimum requirements of the American National Standard for Information Sciences — Permanence of Paper for Printed Library Materials, ANSI Z39,48-1984.

Farm, Factory and Fortune:
New Studies in the Economic History
of the Maritime Provinces

Edited by Kris Inwood

Acknowledgements

The origin of this volume was a conference held in Halifax during September of 1990. Support from Saint Mary's University and the Social Sciences and Humanities Research Council of Canada (SSHRC) defrayed some costs of the meeting and of the volume. I gratefully acknowledge this assistance. During the preparation of this volume I have had congenial and always-helpful assistance from the editorial staff including Phil Buckner, Beckey Daniel, David Frank, Ruth Vallillee and Charles Stuart. Elizabeth Ewan in Guelph made the important contribution of suggesting the title.

It is particularly appropriate to acknowledge the efforts of people who reviewed manuscripts for this volume. Each paper was read by at least three and as many as eight reviewers in the course of its evaluation. These readers must remain anonymous but their considerable commitment of time and expertise is reflected in the quality of the collection as it now stands. It has not been possible to publish all of the papers presented at the 1990 conference, but I am pleased to be able include additional work by Professors Craig, Forbes, Gerriets, MacNeil and Muise.

Most of all I wish to thank the authors whose effort and imagination have brought us the fine papers which appear in this volume.

Kris Inwood
Guelph
October 1992

Introduction

At the mid-point of the 19th century one in every 50 North Americans lived in Nova Scotia or New Brunswick; by 1911 this figure had declined to one in 100. To a large extent the slow growth of the Maritime population reflected the reluctance of European migrants to settle in Nova Scotia or New Brunswick and the propensity of the native-born to leave for greener pastures elsewhere.[1] Since most people moved in search of secure employment and higher incomes, we can restate the problem as one of explaining why employment opportunities and income were lower in the Maritimes than in most other parts of the North American continent. In different ways and for different periods the papers in this volume examine the determinants of regional income and employment growth. The locations of communities and railways discussed in the various papers are represented on the accompanying map on p. ii.

The paper by Jim Irwin and Kris Inwood indicates that as early as 1870 per capita commodity income was relatively low in Nova Scotia and New Brunswick.[2] The early appearance of low incomes naturally directs attention at agriculture which accounted for roughly one-half of all employment. Although it is notoriously difficult to generalize about agriculture, the summary evidence presented by Inwood and Irwin indicates that on average agricultural income was lower in the Maritimes than in the rest of the country on a per acre and a per household basis. Not surprisingly agriculture looms large in a recent literature which focuses on growth with inequality in the pre-Confederation countryside.[3]

---

1   Alan Brookes, "Outmigration from the Maritime Provinces, 1860-1900: Some Preliminary Considerations", *Acadiensis*, V, 2 (Spring 1976), pp. 26-56 and "The Golden Age and the Exodus: The Case of Canning, King's County", *Acadiensis*, XI, 1 (Autumn 1981), pp. 57-82; Patricia Thornton, "The Problem of Out-Migration from Atlantic Canada, 1871-1921: A New Look", *Acadiensis*, XV, 1 (Autumn 1985), pp. 3-34.

2   Kris Inwood and Jim Irwin, "Canadian Regional Commodity Income Differences at Confederation", below pp. 93-120.

3   Rusty Bittermann, "Middle River: The Social Structure of Agriculture in a Nineteenth Century Cape Breton Community", M.A. thesis, University of New Brunswick, 1987, and "The Hierarchy of the Soil: Land and Labour in a 19th Century Cape Breton Community", *Acadiensis*, XVIII, 1 (Autumn 1988), pp. 33-55; Robert McKinnon and Graeme Wynn, "Nova Scotian Agriculture in the 'Golden Age': A New Look", in Douglas Day, ed., *Geographical Perspectives on the Maritime Provinces* (Halifax, 1988), pp. 47-60; Alan MacNeil, "Cultural Stereotypes and Highland Farming in Eastern Nova Scotia, 1827-1851", *Histoire sociale/Social History*, XIX, 37 (May 1986), pp. 39-56, and "Society and

i

Map 1

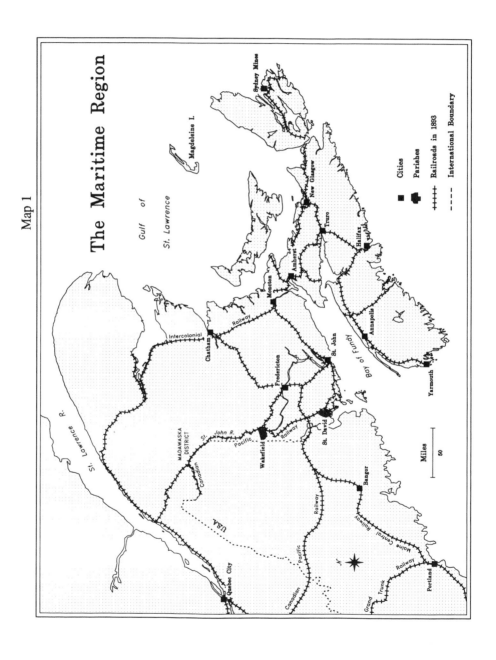

Three papers in this volume directly address the state of pre-Confederation agriculture. Alan MacNeil examines the community of Annapolis as it emerged after the last Acadian expulsion.[4] Although the expulsion created a powerful and tragic discontinuity in regional development, MacNeil explores the inheritance by subsequent populations of capital originally accumulated by Acadian communities. Implicit in the argument is a counterfactual assertion that 18th-century Annapolis would have developed more slowly in the absence of an Acadian legacy.

Annapolis benefited from its location near tidewater in the Bay of Fundy region. By contrast, the agro-forestry settlement on the upper St. John River was situated far from the major urban markets of the Atlantic seaboard. This community, examined by Béatrice Craig, developed slowly until the lumber boom of the 1820s in part because a border dispute made it impossible for landowners to acquire clear title.[5] During the 1830s the farming population was a heterogeneous and commercially-minded lot who as a group produced a significant surplus. The precise character of the surplus depends on assumptions made about the composition of local consumption and livestock feeding practice, but it would seem that food production during the 1830s and 1840s expanded absolutely and relative to the population.

T.W. Acheson in this volume blends local and aggregate evidence about New Brunswick agriculture on the eve of Confederation.[6] Acheson finds considerable variation in butter surpluses; in two sample parishes he uses family histories and the census reports of commodity production to identify the broad outline of rural social structure. He emphasizes the diversity and efficiency of New Brunswick agriculture and concludes that "most farmers were engaged in the market economy, that many farmers had the capacity to accumulate capital from the output of their agricultural activities, and that many less

---

Economy in Rural Nova Scotia, 1761-1861", Ph.D. thesis, Queen's University, 1991; Graeme Wynn, "Exciting a Spirit of Reform Among the 'Plodholes': Agricultural Reform in Pre-Confederation Nova Scotia", *Acadiensis*, XX, 1 (Autumn 1991), pp. 5-51; Debra McNabb, "Land and Families in Horton Township, N.S., 1760-1830", M.A. thesis, University of British Columbia, 1986 and "The Role of Land in Settling Horton Township, Nova Scotia", in Margaret Conrad, ed., *Making Adjustments: Change and Continuity in Planter Nova Scotia, 1759-1800* (Fredericton, 1991), pp. 151-60.

4   Alan MacNeil, "The Acadian Legacy and Agricultural Development in Nova Scotia, 1760-1861", below pp. 1-16.

5   Béatrice Craig, "Agriculture in a Pioneer Region: The Upper St. John River Valley in the first half of the 19th Century", below pp. 17-36.

6   T.W. Acheson, "New Brunswick Agriculture at the End of the Colonial Era: A Reassessment", below pp. 37-60.

productive farmers would have been forced to participate in a wide-ranging network of exchange in order to survive".

Nova Scotia coal-mining is examined in this volume by Marilyn Gerriets, who resurrects a 19th-century argument that the acquisition of all mainland coal by a single British company raised the local cost of coal, reduced opportunities for capital accumulation by Nova Scotians and impeded the development of the colonial economy.[7] It is argued that the General Mining Association used the protection afforded by transportation cost to maintain prices higher in Nova Scotia than was possible in American port cities. She also argues that different government policy could have produced a more pluralistic pattern of ownership, which in turn could have brought lower mining costs and prices.

The agriculture and mining papers in this volume remind us that the pre-Confederation economy consisted of more than shipping, shipbuilding, fishing and related activities. Nevertheless, the relatively slow growth of these "wood, wind and water" activities after 1870 provides one possible explanation for a post-Confederation lag in the growth of regional population and industrial activity.[8]

A rich and influential literature about industrialization has emerged in response to T.W. Acheson's seminal 1972 paper.[9] My survey paper in this volume reveals two important facts about Maritime manufacturing.[10] The low level of output and productivity in 1870 would appear to reflect patterns and

---

7 Marilyn Gerriets, "The Impact of the General Mining Association on the Nova Scotia Coal Industry, 1826-1850", *Acadiensis*, XXI, 1 (Autumn 1991), pp. 54-84, reprinted below pp. 61-92.

8 Scholars continue to examine the "wood, wind and water" economy. Recent, and for most part, non-traditional treatments of the so-called traditional economy include several fine volumes. See Rosemary Ommer, *From Outpost to Outport: A Structural Analysis of the Jersey-Gaspé Cod Fishery, 1767-1886* (Montreal and Kingston, 1991); Eric Sager with Gerry Panting, *Maritime Capital: the Shipping Industry in Atlantic Canada, 1820-1914* (Kingston and Montreal, 1990) and L. Anders Sandberg, ed., *Trouble in the Woods: Forest Policy and Social Conflict in Nova Scotia and New Brunswick* (Fredericton, 1992). An interesting approach to the problem of transition from merchant to industrial capitalism is outlined in Ian McKay, "The Crisis of Dependent Development: Class Conflict in the Nova Scotia Coalfields, 1872-1876", in G.S. Kealey, ed., *Class, Gender and Region: Essays in Canadian Historical Sociology* (St. John's, 1988).

9 T.W. Acheson, "The National Policy and the Industrialization of the Maritimes, 1880-1910", *Acadiensis*, I, 2 (Spring 1972), pp. 1-28.

10 Kris Inwood, "Maritime Industrialization from 1870 to 1910: A Review of the Evidence and its Interpretation", *Acadiensis*, XXI, 1 (Autumn 1991), pp. 132-55, reprinted below pp. 149-70.

structures inherited from the pre-Confederation era.[11] A second important fact is that Maritime industry did not share in the acceleration of growth experienced elsewhere in Canada after 1900. The origin of the 1900-1913 national growth spurt lay in Prairie agricultural expansion and an accompanying investment boom.[12] One explanation for the Maritime lag, therefore, is that the "wheat boom" originated too far west for strong linkage effects to be felt east of Montreal. Evidence in support of this view may be found in the fact that Maritime manufacturing continued to grow as quickly from 1890 to 1910 as it had in the period from 1870 to 1890. The problem was not a decline in Maritime industrial output or a change in its rate of growth, but rather a failure to share in the acceleration experienced by industry in the Great Lakes-St. Lawrence corridor.

Other explanations focus on particular industries, such as steel and coal production which expanded to become an important source of employment during the second half of the 19th century. After 1900, these industries experienced little new investment, rising extraction costs and complications related to the quality of raw material.[13] Further deterioration during the war years led in 1920 to a controversial re-organization which is thought to have made matters worse.[14] The precise impact of the 1920 merger is unclear in the context of widespread unemployment in coal and steel regions around the world at this time.[15] Whatever the reason for it, the region's steel and coal in-

11 There is some evidence that Maritime manufacturing growth was relatively slow even before Confederation; see Kris Inwood and John Chamard, "Regional Industrial Growth during the 1890s: The Case of the Missing Artisans", *Acadiensis*, XVI, 1 (Autumn 1986), pp. 101-17, Table 4.

12 M.C. Urquhart, "New Estimates of Gross National Product, Canada, 1870 to 1926", in S. Engerman and R. Gallman, eds., *Long-Term Factors in American Economic Growth* (Chicago, 1986), p. 9-88; M. Altman, "A Revision of Canadian Economic Growth: 1870-1910 (a challenge to the gradualist interpretation)", *Canadian Journal of Economics*, XX, 1 (February 1987), pp. 86-113; Kris Inwood and Thanasis Stengos, "Discontinuities in Canadian Economic Growth, 1870-1985", *Explorations in Economic History*, vol. 28, no. 3 (July 1991), pp. 274-86.

13 Kris Inwood, "Local Control, Resources and the Nova Scotia Steel and Coal Company", *Historical Papers/Communications historiques*, 1986, pp. 254-82.

14 Acheson, "The National Policy"; David Frank, "The Cape Breton Coal Industry and the Rise and Fall of the British Empire Steel Corporation", *Acadiensis*, VII, 1 (Autumn 1977), pp. 3-34, and "Class Conflict in the Coal Industry: Cape Breton 1922", in Ian McKay, ed., *The Challenge of Modernity: A Reader on Post-Confederation Canada* (Toronto, 1992), pp. 258-85.

15 Barry Supple, "The Political Economy of Demoralization: the State and the Coal-mining Industry in America and Britain between the Wars", *Economic History*

dustries after 1900 failed to fulfill their early promise as a leading sector in the regional economy.

The railway and financial industries have also attracted attention for their alleged failure to support regional economic development. For more than a century Maritime advocates have protested that the Intercolonial Railway was not managed in the interests of the regional economy to the extent that would have been possible.[16] Ken Cruikshank sheds new light on this grievance by demonstrating that the government railway carried little through-traffic and that operating costs were high as a result of the railroad's routing and low traffic density.[17] Cruikshank finds no evidence of a significant impact resulting from controversial rate changes beginning in 1905; he explains the lack of impact on the grounds that Intercolonial freight rates were largely influenced by competition from water and other rail carriers, by a dependence on other railways to complete delivery beyond Montreal and by the Intercolonial's high operating costs. Taken together with his earlier work Cruikshank's paper provides a masterful survey of the political economy of railway operation and points toward a re-evaluation of regional transportation systems.[18]

The revised view of transportation accompanies new insight into financial flows affecting the regional economy. The pioneering research of James Frost documented a post-1900 flow of funds out of the region through the banking system.[19] Neil Quigley and his coauthors argue persuasively that capital outflow was a result rather than a cause of regional underdevelopment.[20] Through a detailed examination of lending by two large banks they argue that Maritime borrowers did not face adverse discrimination and that the character of the banking system did not impede Maritime growth. In a related paper

Review, XLI, 4 (November 1988), pp. 566-91.

16 E.R. Forbes, *The Maritimes Rights Movement, 1919-1927: A Study in Canadian Regionalism* (Montreal and Kingston, 1979), and "Misguided Symmetry: The Destruction of Regional Transportation Policy for the Maritimes", in David Bercuson, ed., *Canada and the Burden of Unity* (Toronto, 1977), pp. 60-86.

17 Ken Cruikshank, "The Intercolonial Railway, Freight Rates and the Maritime Economy, *Acadiensis,* XXII, 1 (Autumn 1992), pp. 87-110, reprinted below, pp. 171-96.

18 Ken Cruikshank, "The People's Railway: The Intercolonial Railway and the Canadian Public Enterprise Experience", *Acadiensis,* XVI, 1 (Autumn 1986), pp. 78-100.

19 James Frost, "The 'Nationalization' of The Bank of Nova Scotia, 1880-1910", *Acadiensis,* XII, 1 (Autumn 1982), pp. 3-38.

20 Neil C. Quigley, Ian M. Drummond and Lewis T. Evans, "Regional Transfers of Funds through the Canadian Banking System and Maritime Economic Development, 1895-1935", below, pp. 219-50.

Greg Marchildon chronicles the development of the Royal Securities Corporation and its principal figures, including the imaginative financiers John F. Stairs and Max Aitken, the future Lord Beaverbrook.[21] Marchildon's narrative of this important company and its principal figures demonstrates the vitality of regional entrepreneurship at the outset of the 20th century.

Del Muise's paper examines the human dimensions of industrial change.[22] Muise uses census manuscript information to document the changing participation of women in the economy of three communities between 1871 and 1921. The data indicate an increase in the participation of women relative to men from 1871 to 1891, and no change from 1891 to 1921. The apparent increase in female participation in the employed labour force during the 1870s and 1880s probably is an artifact created by improvements in occupational census enumeration and changes in the nature of women's work. The more reliable 1911 to 1921 data provide a fascinating glimpse of life-cycle and occupational differences in the work of men and women. Girls in the Yarmouth cotton mills earned as much as boys, while young (16-21 years) women earned almost as much as young men. However, adult women earned much less than adult men. Muise explains the gendering of the life-cycle within the context of patriarchal family organization and accompanying market patterns.

The papers by Muise and other authors may be read as a collective investigation of regional underdevelopment during the formative years before the First World War. Equally important questions surround the course of public policy in subsequent decades. A great deal has been written about regional policies since the Second World War, but the paper by Ernie Forbes in this volume is one of the few investigations of government policy before the 1940 Report of the Royal Commission on Dominion-Provincial Relations.[23] Forbes points out that during the 1930s the federal government allocated various funds in direct proportion to local spending, even in low-income regions of the country. This principle of matching grants ruled out inter-provincial redistribution of a sort that has become significant since the Second World War.

---

21 Greg Marchildon, "John F. Stairs, Max Aitken and the Scotia Group: Finance Capitalism and Industrial Decline in the Maritimes, 1890-1914", below pp. 197-218.

22 D.A. Muise, "The Industrial Context of Inequality: Female Participation in Nova Scotia's Paid Labour Force, 1871-1921", *Acadiensis,* XX, 2 (Spring 1991), pp. 3-31, reprinted below pp. 121-48.

23 E.R. Forbes, "Cutting the Pie into Smaller Pieces: Matching Grants and Relief in the Maritime Provinces during the 1930s", *Acadiensis*, XVII, 1 (Autumn 1987), pp. 34-55, reprinted below pp. 251-73. See also E.R. Forbes, *Challenging the Regional Stereotype: Essays on the 20th Century* Maritimes (Fredericton, 1989).

The papers published in this volume constitute a small sample of current research about Maritime economic history. The concentration of papers on the inland economy of this coastal region reflects a growing interest in the distinctive patterns of Maritime rural economy and industrialization.[23] These papers also illustrate how far the literature has come since S.A. Saunders prepared his pioneering survey for the Rowell-Sirois Commission in the 1930s.[23]

Important research challenges and opportunities are before us. One topic in need of greater attention is migration. Alan Brookes and Patricia Thornton have established the broad dimensions of regional outmigration. Articles such as those in the present volume advance our understanding of income generation in various sectors of the economy. A further and promising stage of research will be to situate the migration decision within the context of individual and family strategies to acquire income and accumulate wealth. But this is only one topic among many in the economic history of the Maritimes. It is my hope that the publication of this volume will support and encourage further research along these lines.

KRIS INWOOD

---

24 S.A. Saunders, *The Economic History of the Maritime Provinces* (Fredericton, 1984 [1939]). For recent approaches to regional economic development, see David Alexander, *Atlantic Canada and Confederation: Essays in Canadian Political Economy* (Toronto and St. John's, 1983), Ralph Matthews, *The Creation of Regional Dependency* (Toronto, 1983), and Donald Savoie, *Regional Economic Development: Canada's Search for Solutions* (2nd edition, Toronto, 1992).

The Acadian Legacy and Agricultural Development in Nova Scotia, 1760-1861

A.R. MacNeil

One of the remarkable aspects of New England's northward expansion into Nova Scotia in the second half of the 18th century was the speed with which its newly formed agricultural settlements in the Bay of Fundy region were transformed into productive farming communities. Between 4,000 and 5,000 New Englanders migrated to this area during the 1760s,[1] and the agricultural gains they made within the first years of settlement, as shown by the census of 1767, were considerable.[2] Few areas of settlement in North America achieved such a rapid growth within so a short period of time. Although a number of factors such as the well-organized character of the New England immigration associations,[3] the assistance provided by the Nova Scotia government and the "new world" farming experience of the New Englanders made these gains possible, one of the most important considerations was the acquisition of Acadian farms and livestock. Indeed, it is widely acknowledged that one of the major inducements lieutenant-governor Charles Lawrence offered to New England settlers in encouraging migration to Nova Scotia was the promise of free Acadian land.[4]

I thank Gerald Tulchinsky, Marvin McInnis, Graeme Wynn and Allen Greer for their helpful comments on an earlier version of this paper.

1   In 1767 there were 4,872 people in the region. See census of 1767, c.o. 217, vol.22, Public Archives of Canada [PAC].

2   Settlers produced 45,581 bushels of grain, and 5,855 bushels of peas and beans; they kept 9,686 cattle, 1,006 horses, 6,649 sheep and 2,484 swine. The large number of cattle is particularly impressive. The rapid growth of the Bay of Fundy settlements can also be seen in the early fragmentary returns for Cornwallis and Horton townships. See John Frederic Herbin, *The History of Grand Pré* (Saint John, 1911), p. 49; and Debra Anne McNabb, "Land and Families in Horton Township, N.S., 1760-1830", M.A. thesis, University of British Columbia, 1986, Table IV, p. 66.

3   For an excellent discussion of this aspect of the settlement process, see Elizabeth Mancke, "Corporate Structure and Private interest: The Mid-Eighteenth Century Expansion of New England", in Margaret Conrad, ed., *They Planted Well* (Fredericton, 1988), pp. 161-77.

4   See Arthur Wentworth Hamilton Eaton, *The History of Kings County* (Salem Mass., 1910), pp. 83-4; John Bartlet Brebner, *The Neutral Yankees of Nova Scotia* (Toronto, 1969), pp. 21-4; R.D. Longley, "The Coming of the New England Planters to the

Although some authors have pointed to the use of Acadian labour and diked land, there has been no attempt to survey the extent of the legacy of farm improvements and livestock and how it influenced settlement and rural development. In fact, it has been generally assumed that considerable loss and waste of Acadian property occurred during and immediately following the deportations. For example, John Bartlet Brebner suggests that large numbers of animals were withdrawn from Nova Scotia by the fleeing Acadians, thereby further reducing the animal population.[5] Naomi Griffiths emphasizes the looting and burning of Acadian villages and the expenses the colonies incurred during the expulsions.[6] Many writers are sceptical about the state of Acadian dikes and lands after five years of inattention following the deportations and the damage caused by a large storm that occurred in 1759.[7] Some scholars also contend that New England settlers lacked the necessary expertise to repair and/or operate the abandoned Acadian dikes, which in turn impeded the growth of the settlements.[8]

The dissipation of Acadian farm capital through negligence, natural forces and the loss of Acadian labour, creates considerable uncertainty for scholars about the extent and significance of the Acadian legacy. This paper surveys the available evidence, which leads to the conclusion that New England Settlers benefited handsomely from a windfall of Acadian farm improvements and livestock. In the short term, this facilitated the farm-making process, permitting a more rapid transition from pioneer to commercial agriculture. In the

Annapolis Valley", in Conrad, ed., *They Planted Well*, p. 18; W.S. MacNutt, *The Atlantic Provinces: The Emergence of a Colonial Society, 1712-1857* (Toronto, 1972), pp. 60-3; George Rawlyk, *Nova Scotia's Massachusetts: A Study of Massachusetts-Nova Scotia Relations, 1630 to 1784* (Montreal, 1973), p. 218; Bernard Bailyn, *Voyagers to the West: A Passage in the Peopling of North America on the Eve of the Revolution* (New York, 1988), p. 363; and Graeme Wynn, "Late Eighteenth-Century Agriculture on the Bay of Fundy Marshlands", *Acadiensis*, VIII, 2 (Spring 1979), pp. 80-9 and "A Province Too Much Dependent on New England", *The Canadian Geographer/ Le géographe canadien*, 31, 2 (1987), p. 100.

5   John Bartlet Brebner, *New England's Outpost: Acadia before the Conquest of Canada* (New York, 1973), p. 255.

6   Naomi Griffiths, *The Acadians: Creation of a People* (Toronto, 1973), p. 59.

7   Herbin, *Grand Pré*, pp. 148-9; Brebner, *The Neutral Yankees*, pp. 26-7; Ian F. Mac-Kinnon, *Settlements and Churches in Nova Scotia, 1749-1776* (Montreal, 1930), p. 23; Longley, "New England Planters", p. 24; and Robert Rumilly, *Histoire des Acadiens, Vol. 2* (Montreal, 1955), p. 579. Wynn suggests that the damage caused by the storm of 1759 was "not general": Wynn, "Late Eighteenth-Century Agriculture", p. 84.

8   Brebner, *The Neutral Yankees*, p. 97; R. Cole Harris and John Warkentin, *Canada Before Confederation* (Toronto, 1974), p. 200.

long term, however, most of the effects of the legacy were diffused with the arrival of subsequent immigrants. The paper focuses chiefly on the development of Annapolis Township between 1760 and 1861, which contained a large and productive Acadian farming population before the deportations and subsequently became one of the more significant areas of New England settlement.

The early development of Annapolis resembled other New England settlements on the Bay of Fundy. The deportations, however, did not leave the area entirely unoccupied. A small garrison was based in Annapolis Royal, which provided a local market for agricultural surpluses. In addition, a few farms were established outside the fort by officials and individuals who were probably affiliated with the garrison.[9] In 1760 the township was granted to an association based in Massachusetts (see Map 1).[10] By the end of the decade the locality contained about 400 settlers.[11] As was the case in the other township grants, each member of the association was entitled to at least one full share of land (500 acres) and no more than two shares, as well as some of the more valued marshland.[12] Later, the settlers were joined by Loyalists and other groups who purchased land or obtained grants adjacent to and behind the New Englanders.[13] This process of land alienation was typical of the New England settlement experience in the region.[14]

A number of sources allow us to investigate the settlement process in Annapolis, among which the numerous censuses are particularly important. Indeed, this area is one of the best documented townships in Nova Scotia; it has some surprisingly rich census data for the 1760s and 1770s, rarely available at that time for other areas of recent settlement in British North America and New England. Six censuses were carried out during the first decade of settlement: in 1762, 1763, 1767, 1768, 1770 and 1771. The first two contain

---

9   Annapolis Royal became a significant administrative centre after the conquest of 1710, but declined substantially following the establishment of Halifax.

10 Longley, "New England Planters", pp. 24-5; and MacNutt, *The Atlantic Provinces*, pp. 60-1.

11 See censuses of 1767, 1768, 1770, and 1771.

12 For a discussion of land-granting practices and settlement patterns, see A.R. MacNeil, "Society and Economy in Rural Nova Scotia, 1761-1861", Ph.D. thesis, Queens University, 1990, ch. 2.

13 MacNeil, "Rural Nova Scotia".

14 The land may have been less fertile than in other Bay of Fundy settlements. The Annapolis uplands are composed chiefly of Class 4, 5, 6 and 7 soils, suitable merely for pasture. The river lots, however, are quite fertile. See J.I. MacDougall and J.L. Nowland, *Soil Survey of Annapolis County, Nova Scotia* (Truro, 1969).

MAP 1: NOVA SCOTIA AND ANNAPOLIS

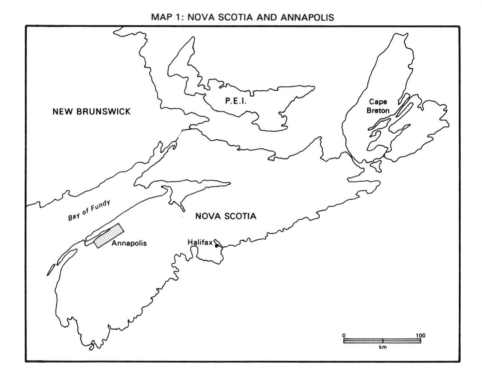

aggregate statistics on population and improved acreage; the last four collected data on many agricultural items (see Table One).[15]

The subsequent censuses in 1827 and 1861 provide useful benchmarks with which to examine farm productivity over the long term.[16] The latter enumeration is particularly valuable because it was conducted during the winter.[17] In order to make the most effective use of the large number of individual returns surviving for 1861, a sample of one in every four was drawn from this census.

One of the major difficulties in determining the scope and short term effects of the Acadian legacy in Annapolis is the degree to which we must rely on circumstantial evidence and hypothetical estimates. Unfortunately, there are no documents which specifically show that New England settlers benefited directly from Acadian farm improvements and animals. Nevertheless, the evidence gathered is compelling and it is hoped that deductions and hypothetical estimates presented in the paper will convince others to begin looking more closely at the settlement process in other parts of the region. But, before considering the Annapolis experience, it is necessary to review in more specific terms the character of the legacy.

The legacy of farm improvements comprised important and valuable elements such as the dikes and diked lands, cleared uplands, orchards, buildings and other farm structures. Indeed, vague references exist regarding the discovery and use of Acadian farmhouses and apple orchards in several of the New England settlements.[18] Moreover, even if such improvements were in a poor state or even partly demolished when the settlers began arriving, it is likely that some of these could have been repaired with less labour and at a lower cost than building anew.[19] The legacy also included livestock, particularly cattle. Before 1760 most of the animals not slaughtered or lost were probably in the hands of a small group of farmers or speculators who were associated with the garrison and owned land near Annapolis Royal. Later, the livestock were likely sold to the New Englanders. A final consideration, which should not be overlooked, was Acadian labour. A small number of Acadians resided in the township during the 1760s, though most had left by the end of

---

15 All of these censuses were made in the month of January, so we can assume that the size of the animal population would be downwardly biased since most of the farmers slaughtered or sold their livestock in the fall.

16 The 1861 returns for Annapolis cover a slightly smaller area than those that were made in 1827; the 1861 polling districts do not correspond exactly with township boundaries.

17 The census of 1827 was made in the month of September.

18 Longley, "New England Planters", p. 21.

19 Rumilly, *Histoire des Acadiens*, p. 567.

Table One
Land, Crops and Livestock in Annapolis Township, 1767-1861

Item	1767	1768	1770	1771	1827	1861
Arable Land (acres)	n.a.	n.a.	304	276	n.a.	n.a.
Mowing Land "	n.a.	n.a.	1,298	1,166	n.a.	n.a.
Pasture Land "	n.a.	n.a.	591	643	n.a.	n.a.
All Improved Land "	n.a.	n.a.	2,193	2,085	9,485	16,684
Woodland "	n.a.	n.a.	37,446	39,994	n.a.	n.a.
Wheat (bu.)	600	591	449	315	1,225	3,711
Other Grain "	649	1,089	1,242	930	7,270	18,964
Total Grain "	1,249	1,680	1,691	1,245	8,495	22,675
Corn "	n.a.	n.a.	n.a.	n.a.	n.a.	3,430
Peas and Beans "	53	80	104	149	n.a.	919
Potatoes "	n.a.	n.a.	n.a.	n.a.	65,415	77,890
Turnips "	n.a.	n.a.	n.a.	n.a.	n.a.	21,527
Other Roots "	n.a.	n.a.	n.a.	n.a.	n.a.	3,367
Apples "	n.a.	n.a.	n.a.	n.a.	n.a.	26,298
Hay (tons)	n.a.	n.a.	n.a.	n.a.	5,182	7,430
Cattle	832	855	770	768	2,713	4,241
Horses	76	90	57	48	314	606
Sheep	589	716	552	558	8,315	3,458
Swine	108	103	95	121	1,291	611
Butter (lbs.)	n.a.	n.a.	n.a.	n.a.	n.a.	54,835
Cheese "	n.a.	n.a.	n.a.	n.a.	n.a.	82,742

*n.a.= not available

Sources: Censuses of 1767, 1768, 1770, 1771, 1827 and 1861.

the decade.[20] In sum, the potential benefits of such a legacy could be considerable.

Regrettably, few details exist regarding the state of Acadian agriculture in Annapolis before the deportations.[21] The last agricultural census was carried out in 1707 and the Acadians reported having 400 arpents of cleared land (excluding diked marshland) and 952 cattle.[22] Andrew Hill Clark estimates that there were perhaps 3,000 acres of diked land and 3,000 cattle in the locality by the late 1740s.[23] We have no way of determining the condition of both the diked land and cattle at the start of New England immigration, though we do have some information about the settlement process.

The settlers began arriving in 1760 and farm-making moved forward at a rapid pace. Indeed, there is fragmentary evidence regarding the use of land and cattle during the first years of settlement suggesting their early experience was unlike that of most North American pioneers. In a letter to the Lords of Trade dated 11 January 1762, Jonathan Belcher, the lieutenant-governor of Nova Scotia, reported that Annapolis "contains about sixteen hundred acres of Marshland and 1200 acres of cleared upland" distributed among 60 New England families.[24] Although we cannot ascertain how much of this marshland was diked, the locality did possess a substantial amount of cleared upland for a settlement that was less than two years old. Nor was the township's experience unusual. In Horton and Cornwallis townships, for example, settlers began arriving in 1760. Within three years, there were 154 families residing in Horton and 128 families in Cornwallis; the average family possessed 19 and 15 acres

---

20 There were 68 Acadian inhabitants in the township in 1767. They owned no improved land and kept few animals; some reported having boats and were involved in the fishery. Most of the people moved into the southwest district of Nova Scotia where they eventually acquired title to land. See censuses of 1767 and 1768.

21 For information about Acadian agriculture, see Andrew Hill Clark, *Acadia: The Geography of Early Nova Scotia to 1760* (Madison, Wis., 1968), chs. 5, 6; Aurel Young, "The Acadian Economy, History and Development", in Jean Daigle, ed., *The Acadians of the Maritimes: Thematic Studies* (Moncton, 1982), pp. 197-218; and Naomi Griffiths, "The Golden Age: Acadian Life 1713-1748", *Histoire sociale/Social History*, XVII, 33 (May 1984), p. 21-34.

22 This area included the lands occupied by Acadians on both sides of the Annapolis River. The west side would later become Granville Township.

23 Clark, *Acadia*, p. 236.

24 Jonathan Belcher to the Lords of Trade, 11 January 1762, MG 11, vol. 67, Public Archives of Nova Scotia [PANS]. It appears that Belcher obtained his figures from the census of 1762. Belcher employed the term "cleared upland" whereas the census used "under culture". Although the two terms may have referred to the same type and quantity of land, it is important to note that "under culture" implies "in use" rather than the broader and more likely heading of "improved land", which refers to any land cleared of trees or obstacles.

of improved land (excluding diked lands) respectively.[25] How much of the cleared upland in Annapolis was part of the Acadian legacy?

Peter A. Russell's investigation of the land-clearing process in early-19th-century Upper Canada provides us with some useful figures with which to set some reasonable upper limits regarding hypothetical land clearing rates in Annapolis.[26] His findings show that there were in fact two different rates of land clearing depending on local circumstances. If a man and his family devoted all of their energies to felling trees and nothing else, then they might clear as many as five acres a year. But few settlers could sustain this pace for very long. Once they began attending to other chores, such as breaking the soil and building fences, the rate dropped sharply to between one and two acres. Working at this pace, it would have been virtually impossible for the 60 New England families to have cleared 1,200 acres of upland in less than two years (while presumably repairing damaged dikes). Moreover, the use of hired labour would have been quite costly; it is doubtful that many could have borne this expense even if the necessary labour was available, which is unclear. Even if we doubled the hypothetical land-clearing rate for each household to allow an extra Acadian hand, the settlers would still have fallen short of the reported acreage by about 50 per cent. Thus, we must conclude that much, if not most, of the land was part of the Acadian legacy.[27]

What did this legacy represent in terms of saved labour? Using a generous land-clearing rate of five acres in the first year and two acres in each year thereafter, it would require a minimum of six years of labour to produce 15 to 20 acres of cleared upland. If the New Englanders also found some of the dikes and buildings salvageable, then the savings in labour, not to mention capital, would have been even greater.

The early settlers also acquired a large number of cattle. This is evident from a report made in 1763.[28] It was observed that the townships of Annapolis and Granville, which then had a total population of 140 families, carried 1,500 cattle through the previous winter, or approximately 11 head per family. Cattle represented a considerable investment in capital and it is surprising to find

---

25 Herbin, *Grand Pré,* p. 149 and McNabb, "Horton Township, N.S.", Table IV, p. 66.

26 Peter Russell, "Forest into Farmland: Upper Canadian Clearing Rates, 1822-1839", in J.K. Johnson and Bruce G. Wilson, eds., *Historical Essays on Upper Canada* (Ottawa, 1989), p. 139.

27 A small proportion of the cleared acreage may have been owned by the handful of pre-1760 farmers/speculators.

28 See "State and Condition of the Province of Nova Scotia with some observations etc.", reprinted in *Report of the Board of Trustees of the Public Archives of Nova Scotia* (1934).

such large herds at this early stage in the settlement process.[29] Although we have no way of confirming the accuracy of the 1763 report, it is not unrealistic given that the area near the Annapolis basin (Annapolis, Granville and Wilmot) supported 1,746 cattle in 1766.[30] The presence of a large number of livestock also implies that the settlers from the very beginning must have had access to considerable quantities of improved acreage just to keep those animals fed. Unfortunately, we have no information regarding how they may have obtained Acadian livestock. As discussed earlier, they were probably purchased from officials or military personnel connected to the local garrison. Graeme Wynn cites the account of a Captain Huston who ran a herd of 70 cattle in the Chignecto Marshes in the 1750s before the arrival of New England settlers to that part of the province.[31]

Although it is impossible to show conclusively that a direct link existed between the settlement process and the Acadian legacy, the early gains of the settlers were impressive and unusual by North American standards.[32] Further evidence of the rapid development of the settlement and the productivity of recently established farms can be found in the censuses of 1768, 1770, and 1771 (see Table One). Table Two presents a useful profile of New England farms and average output.[33]

Annapolis contained about 400 settlers by the end of the decade; it possessed, however, more than 2,000 acres of improved land (about 5 acres per capita). Between 77 and 82 per cent of the households reported having some improved land, of which the average holding was 38 acres. Some individual

---

29 According to one account, the New Englanders brought only a small number of livestock to Annapolis. The *Charming Molly* transported 31 oxen, 17 cows, 24 young neat cattle, 9 horses, 56 sheep, and one swine in two trips. W.A. Calneck, *History of the County of Annapolis* (Toronto, 1897), p. 151.

30 Census of 1767.

31 Wynn, "Late Eighteenth Century Agriculture", p. 83. Later Huston acted as an agent for absentee landlords in Cumberland County. See MacNeil, "Rural Nova Scotia", ch. 4.

32 See, for example, Percy Wells Bidwell and John Falconer, *History of Agriculture in the Northern United States, 1620-1860* (Washington, 1925); Paul W. Gates, *The Farmer's Age: Agriculture 1815-1860* (New York, 1960); Howard S. Russel, *A Long Deep Furrow: Three Centuries in New England* (Hanover, 1976); and Robert Leslie Jones, *History of Agriculture in Ontario, 1613-1880* (Toronto, 1946).

33 All of the estimates for agricultural output found in Table Three are made on a household and producer/owner basis because it is not entirely clear at this early stage who was a "farmer". The census takers did not record occupations. A small number of households were connected with the garrison and were not new arrivals. By including all of the households in the computations, the estimates understate the average output of farmers.

holdings were much larger. In 1771, for example, Phineas Lovet owned 150 and Obed Wheelock 90 improved acres.[34]

Grain production was never very great in Annapolis, and it was fairly modest during the first decade. The gross harvest ranged from 1,200 to 1,700 bushels per season; the average household produced approximately 20 bushels.[35] One of the interesting developments revealed by the data was the declining importance of wheat. Not only was the size of the harvest dropping, but fewer farmers were planting it. This drop should not be interpreted as a sign of poor farming practices or even a withdrawal from markets into self-sufficiency. Rather, it was a sensible adjustment to local conditions, which were better suited to animal husbandry. As wheat cultivation fell, more attention was devoted to coarse grains. Hay was the most important crop. Unfortunately, census takers did not record output, though the large quantities of mowing land owned by farmers would indicate that the harvest was substantial. The average hay producer possessed approximately 22 acres of mowing land. A conservative estimate, based on a hypothetical yield of one ton per acre would result in a minimum harvest of 22 tons per producer.[36] If this is a reasonably accurate calculation, then hay cultivation greatly exceeded local requirements and therefore constituted a major market crop.[37]

The settlers raised a variety of animals, but the emphasis was clearly on cattle. Nearly 90 per cent of households reported having them. Although the overall number found in the township appears to have declined somewhat between 1767 and 1771,[38] the average herd remained fairly stable at 12 head.[39]

34   Census of 1771.

35   In 1770 wheat production was comparable in Amherst-Cumberland and twice as great in Horton. McNabb, "Horton Township, N.S.", Table IV, p. 66; and MacNeil, "Rural Nova Scotia", Table 4-3, p. 128.

36   Hay yields vary greatly depending on the kind of land in use. Yields on diked lands ranged from two to four tons per acre; on cleared upland the yield was about one ton per acre. Abraham Gesner, *The Industrial Resources of Nova Scotia* (Halifax, 1849), p. 202; Eaton, *The History of Kings County*, p. 187; and Harris and Warkentin, *Canada Before Confederation*, p. 203.

37   For a discussion of livestock feeding practices, see MacNeil, "Rural Nova Scotia", ch. 5.

38   This may simply reflect growing stability and therefore higher slaughter ratios/sales. The effects of slaughter/sale can seriously influence census taking and the reported size of herds. For a discussion, see Frank D. Lewis and R. Marvin McInnis, "Agricultural Output and Efficiency in Lower Canada, 1851", *Institute for Economic Research* (Kingston, 1981); Rusty Bittermann, "Middle River: The Social Structure of Agriculture in a Nineteenth Century Cape Breton Community", M.A. thesis, University of New Brunswick, 1987; and MacNeil, "Rural Nova Scotia", ch. 4.

39   In 1770 cattle-raisers in Amherst-Cumberland averaged 13 head per herd.

Table Two

Agricultural Output per Household in Annapolis Township, 1768-1771

Item	1768	1770	1771
Households	83	70	73
Population	396	398	399
Arable land per Household (acres)	n.a.	4.3	3.9
Arable Land Per Owner "	n.a.	7.3	6.2
Per cent Owning Arable Land	n.a.	61.4	62.8
Mowing Land per Household (acres)	n.a.	18.5	16.6
Mowing Land per Owner "	n.a.	22.7	22.4
Per cent Owning Mowing Land	n.a.	81.4	74.2
Pasture per Household (acres)	n.a.	8.4	9.1
Pasture per Owner "	n.a.	19.0	18.9
Per cent Owning Pasture	n.a.	44.2	48.5
Improved Land per Household (acres)	n.a.	31.3	29.7
Improved Land per Owner "	n.a.	38.4	38.6
Per cent Owning Improved Land	n.a.	81.4	77.1
Wheat per Household (bu.)	7.1	6.4	4.5
Wheat per Producer "	13.1	13.2	12.7
Per cent Producing Wheat	54.2	48.5	35.7
Other Grains per Household (bu.)	13.0	17.8	13.2
Other Grains per Producer "	22.5	31.2	12.7
Per cent Producing Other Grains	57.8	57.1	62.8
Peas and Beans per Household (bu.)	0.9	1.4	2.1
Peas and Beans Per Producer "	4.4	4.3	6.2
Per cent Producing Peas and Beans	21.6	34.2	34.2
Cattle per Household	10.1	10.6	10.9
Cattle per Owner	11.5	11.6	12.0
Per cent Owning Cattle	87.9	91.4	87.1
Horses per Household	1.0	0.8	0.6
Horses per Owner	2.0	1.9	2.0
Per cent Owning Horses	51.8	42.8	32.8
Sheep per Household	8.6	7.5	7.9
Sheep per Owner	14.9	12.0	12.4
Per cent Owning Sheep	57.8	62.8	61.4
Swine per Household	1.2	1.2	1.7
Swine per Owner	1.9	1.9	2.1
Per cent Owning Swine	63.8	62.8	77.1

Sources: Censuses of 1768, 1770 and 1771.

Some farmers kept surprisingly large herds given the recency of the settlement. In 1771, for instance, John Harris owned 60 and Phineas Lovet 51 head. It is also important to note that cattle-raising by its very nature was a market-driven pursuit; there is no incentive for farmers to maintain large herds merely for subsistence purposes. Approximately 60 per cent of the Annapolis households kept sheep and owners typically had 12 to 15 head. By contrast, there was only a small number of horses in the township. One-third to one-half of the households possessed horses, and most of these maintained two animals. During the first decade horse ownership declined steadily. This probably reflected a growing dependence on oxen, which were hardier and required less feed.[40] Swine-keeping did not figure prominently and the average herd had only two animals. Even allowing for the effects of slaughter, which would reduce the size of the herds, the number of swine was modest, possible reflecting feed limitations.

The considerable gains made by early New Englanders can be readily appreciated by looking briefly at the rough outlines of productivity established by the American economic historian Jackson Turner Main in his work on colonial Connecticut.[41] His estimates are useful because they measure productivity in agricultural areas where livestock-raising was important. Levels of productivity are determined on the basis of the average number of animals per farmer. Main suggests that a farmer could achieve "subsistence" with six cattle and a few sheep and swine, and "subsistence plus" with ten cattle, one mare, one colt and a few more sheep and swine. More than this would have placed the farmer in what Main calls the "comfortable" category. At this level a farmer could not only meet the needs of his family, but also send significant surpluses to market. By this standard, the average Annapolis farmer had already attained a "comfortable" level of productivity and was in a position to sell surplus animals within a decade of his arrival.[42]

Much of this success can be attributed to the Acadian legacy. This becomes strikingly apparent when one examines the state of agriculture in other early Nova Scotia settlements. Take, for example, the initial development of St. Andrews Township. Situated in the eastern part of the colony, it would eventually become one of the most productive districts of that region. The main focus was on livestock-raising and most of the agricultural surpluses were exported to Newfoundland and other markets in the Gulf of St. Lawrence.

---

40   Bidwell and Falconer, *History of Agriculture*, p. 227.

41   Jackson Turner Main, *Society and Economy in Colonial Connecticut* (Princeton, NJ, 1985), Appendix 3J.

42   In 1771, 25.8 per cent of the farmers had fewer than six cattle, 20.6 per cent owned between six and nine, and 53.6 per cent possessed more than nine.

Loyalists and Highland Scots began settling in the locality in the 1780s.[43] When the settlement was less than a decade old and still quite small, a poll tax collector passed through the area and gathered statistics concerning the ownership of cattle and sheep.[44] His data are instructive because they illustrate the "slow" pace of growth in new and undeveloped areas of settlement. Of the 47 adult males enumerated, approximately one-half possessed cattle, and one-fifth kept sheep; owners averaged two and five heads respectively.[45] By contrast, early Annapolis cattle-raisers acquired five times as many animals per owner within the same length of time. Although one should be careful about pushing such comparisons too far given the different settlement experiences of the two townships,[46] there is little doubt that Annapolis developed rapidly during its first decade of New England settlement.

The stimulus provided by the Acadian legacy, however, was of short duration and largely limited to the early New England settlers. There is no evidence indicating that it influenced the long-term development of Annapolis. Indeed, a brief examination of the censuses of 1827 and 1861 (see Table I) reveals that although the area's agricultural base expanded greatly since the 1770's, the relative gains in productivity were fairly modest. Table Three offers some insight into average farm output in 1827 and 1861.

Considerable growth occurred in Annapolis during the 19th century. By 1861 the population had increased nearly ten-fold. More than 16,000 acres of land had been brought into an improved state. Despite the overall growth there was little change in the average size (improved acres) and output of Annapolis farms since the first decade of New England settlement.[47] Between 1771 and

---

43 For information about immigration, settlement and economic development in St. Andrews, see D. Campbell and R.A. MacLean, *Beyond the Atlantic Roar: A Study of the Nova Scotia Scots* (Toronto, 1974); J.M. Bumstead, *The People's Clearance, 17770-1815* (Winnipeg, 1982); Neil MacKinnon, *This Unfriendly Soil: The Loyalist Experience in Nova Scotia, 1783-1791* (Kingston and Montreal, 1986); MacNeil, "Cultural Stereotypes and Highland Farming in Eastern Nova Scotia, 1827-1861", *Histoire sociale/Social History*, 19, 37 (May 1986), and "A Reconsideration of the State of Agriculture in Eastern Nova Scotia, 1791-1861", M.A. thesis, Queen's University, 1985, ch. 1.

44 See RG 1, vol. 444 1/2, PANS.

45 The low figures cannot be simply attributed to "poor" farming skills on the part of the disbanded troops at St. Andrews. In the adjacent township of Arisaig, which was settled entirely by Scottish immigrants, 68 cattle and 49 sheep were distributed among 65 polls in 1793. This reinforces the point that it took time to build up the size of herds in early settlements. RG 1, vol. 444 1/2, PANS.

46 It was probably more difficult and costly to ship animals to St. Andrews during this period as well.

47 Apple cultivation became increasingly important. Unfortunately, early census takers do not record output, so no comparisons are possible.

1827 the number of improved acres per farm fell from 38 to 32. Thereafter, the typical holding rose to only 34 acres by 1861. Wheat production remained low with little apparent change. A modest gain was realized in the cultivation of coarse grains; the average harvest grew from 13 to 34 bushels between 1771 and 1861. Farmers kept about the same number of cattle throughout the period. One area in which there was a significant change was in the case of sheep-raising. In 1771 the typical sheep owner possessed 12 animals. By 1861 the figure had risen to 21. The increase can probably be attributed to a growing demand for wool and a greater access to carding machines. It is difficult to make a firm assessment regarding swine-keeping because of the effects of slaughter on the returns, but it appears there may have been a small increase in the number of animals reported. Horse-raising had never been a serious concern in the township on account of the number of oxen present, which were cheaper to maintain. However, the proportion of farmers with at least one animal (67 per cent) had risen by 1861. The data suggests that the greatest gains in farm output were realized during the first decade of settlement.[48] This differed sharply from the pattern of development in agricultural districts outside the Bay of Fundy region.

This can be seen, for instance, by looking briefly once again at the experience of St. Andrew's Township. The same censuses show that dramatic increases in farm output were realized in the locality throughout the period. Here, only four examples will be cited. Between 1827 and 1861 the average number of improved acres per farm grew from 32 to 53. Coarse grain production rose five-fold from 26 to 131 bushels per farm. The quantity of hay cut increased from 10 to 14 tons. Lastly, the typical cattle herd expanded from 11 to 16 head. Clearly then, the Acadian legacy did not result in any long-term permanent advantage for Annapolis, at least in comparison with other farming districts in Nova Scotia.

The Annapolis evidence suggests that the New England settlers benefited greatly from Acadian farm improvements and livestock. The record, however, is not complete and it is possible that the New Englanders may also have received some assistance from the pre-1760 inhabitants. As a result, New England settlers were able to largely circumvent the harshest and most demanding aspects of pioneer life. Within a remarkably brief period of time, they managed to create — on the very foundations of the old Acadian community — large, well-stocked and productive farms. Furthermore, the benefits

---

48   Some diversification did occur in the agricultural economy. By mid-century, more emphasis was placed on garden crops, cider, poultry, and eggs. Unfortunately these items were not surveyed by census takers in 1827 and 1861. See MacNeil, "Rural Nova Scotia", ch. 4.

of the legacy appear to have been largely limited to the New Englanders, whereas other groups that settled in the area had less attractive grants and greater obstacles to overcome.

Table Three
Agricultural Output Per Farm in Annapolis, 1827-1861

Item	1827	1861*
Returns	409	178
Improved Acres	32.7	34
Wheat per Farm (bu.)	4.1	7
Wheat per Grower "	12.4	14.5
Per cent Growing Wheat	33.5	48.8
Other Grains per Farm (bu.)	24.4	34.1
Other Grains per Grower "	32.8	44.7
Per cent Growing Other Grains	74.4	76.3
Potatoes per Farm (bu.)	221.2	157.8
Potatoes per Grower "	241.5	169.5
Per cent Growing Potatoes	91.6	93.1
Turnips per Farm (bu..)	n.a.	51.3
Turnips per Grower "	n.a.	83.0
Per cent Growing Turnips	n.a.	61.8
Hay per Farm (tons)	16.9	15.6
Hay per Grower "	18.1	18.5
Percent Growing Hay	93.6	84.7
Cattle per Farm	9.1	10.9
Cattle per Owner	9.5	11.9
Per cent Owning Cattle	95.9	91.6
Horses per Farm	0.9	1.1
Horses per Owner	1.5	1.7
Per cent Owning Horses	64.4	67.2
Sheep per Farm	11.1	12.8
Sheep per Owner	17.8	21
Per cent Owning Sheep	62.4	67.2

* continued on following page

Item	1827	1861*
Swine per Farm	4.2	2.4
Swine per Owner	5.1	3.4
Per cent Owning Swine	82.5	70.9
Butter per Farm (lbs.)	n.a.	107
Butter per Producer "	n.a.	134.8
Per cent Producing Butter	n.a.	79.3
Cheese per Farm (lbs.)	n.s.	176.6
Cheese per Producer "	n.a.	701.2
Per cent Producing Cheese	n.a.	25.1
Apples per Farm (bu.)	n.a.	60.2
Apples per Producer "	n.a.	133.7
Per cent Producing Apples	n.a.	45

* sample of 1861 returns. All of the livestock figures have been adjusted to account for the effects of slaughter. For more information, see A.R. MacNeil, "Rural Nova Scotia", ch. 5.

Sources: Censuses of 1827 and 1821.

Agriculture in a Pioneer Region: The Upper St. John River Valley in the first half of the 19th Century

Béatrice Craig

Prince Edward Island excepted, the Maritime provinces are not famous for their agriculture, either in the present or in the past. Nineteenth century New Brunswick, for instance, is perceived as a "timber colony" that had to import foodstuffs. Nova Scotia evokes images of shipping, shipbuilding and fishing. In general, the maritime farmer is assumed to have been self-sufficient and uninvolved with the market.[1] However, recent studies of agriculture in the Maritimes have challenged this stereotype. Alan MacNeil's doctoral thesis demonstrates that Nova Scotia agriculture performed at a wide variety of levels, ranging from subsistence farming complementing other activities such as lumbering and fishing, to market-oriented ventures, such as the exporting of goods to New Brunswick, Newfoundland and St Pierre and Miquelon. In the better areas, farms were as productive as those in Upper Canada.[2] This wide range of productivity could be found even within the limits of a single community, as Rusty Bittermann's study of Middle River demonstrates.[3] T.W Acheson's survey of New Brunswick farming suggests that the "timber colony" was not that different from Nova Scotia: 25 per cent of farms in the parish of Wakefield, Carleton County were definitely commercial in 1871.

Wakefield was located in the St. John River valley; almost the entire length of the river was suitable for agriculture, and it supported properous farms throughout the 19th century. The lower valley was the site of several small settlements even before the arrival of the Loyalists. The middle valley was settled by disbanded soldiers. Further up, the valley attracted migrants from Britain, especially from Ireland, who spilled into the adjacent Aroostook River valley, in Maine.

The section of the upper St. John River which is the subject of this article was opened to settlement in 1785 by a handful of Acadian families from

---

1   For a survey of opinions concerning Maritime agriculture, see T.W. Acheson "New Brunswick Agriculture at the End of the Colonial Era: A Reassessement", in this volume.

2   Alan MacNeil, "Society and Economy in Rural Nova Scotia, 1761-1861", Ph.D. thesis, Queens's University, 1990.

3   Rusty Bittermann, "Middle River: The Social Structure of Agriculture in a Nineteenth Century Cape Breton Community", M.A thesis, University of New Brunswick, 1987.

southern New Brunswick, and by French Canadians from Rivière Ouelle and Kamouraska. At the time, the governors of Quebec and New Brunswick were trying to protect the Halifax-Fredericton-Quebec mail route, which used the valley in winter. The Acadians and French Canadians, led by Louis Mercure, a government courier, settled above the Grand Falls, where the river was lined with intervale land. Half-pay officers were established along the portage route on the highland separating the St. John and St. Lawrence valleys, where they supplemented their income with a few animals and a garden patch. No land grant was issued after 1794, on account of the boundary dispute between the British and the Americans. The two countries could not agree on the exact location of the northeastern boundary, and both claimed the upper St. John Valley (also refered to as "Madawaska territory"). The disagreement was not settled until 1842, when both parties split the disputed territory lengthwise: the northern bank of the river remained British; the southern bank became American.

Diplomatic quarrels notwithstanding, the population grew steadily, fed not only by a high birth rate, but also by immigration from the St Lawrence valley. There were 331 settlers in 1799, 1,200 in 1820, 2,500 in 1830, 6,200 in 1850 and 15,000 in 1870.[4] Until 1842 the newcomers, as well as the children of the founders, squatted on the land of their choice, which they cleared, improved, sold or bequeathed as they saw fit. Under the terms of the 1842 treaty, bona fide settlers were to receive a grant of the land they occupied. The state of Maine issued 563 such grants in 1845, and the province of New Brunswick 505 in 1848.[5]

Agriculture was the sole economic base of the community until the winter of 1823-4, when lumber camps opened in the vicinity.[6] The St. John Valley was, and still is, blessed with land that is unusually fertile by regional standards. Distance and poor communications, however, had an adverse effect on initial economic growth. There was a potential market at Rivière du Loup, 70 miles away on the St Lawrence, but to reach it travellers had to boat up the Madawaska River and Lake Temiscouata, then walk the rest of the way

---

4 Lettres des prêtres missionnaires du Madawaska à l'évêque de Québec, Archives de l'Archidiocèse de Québec, Québec; U.S. census, 1820 and 1830, US census, 1850, M432, roll 248; New Brunswick provincial census, 1851, C996, Public Archives of Canada.

5 "Maps of the Madawaska Survey conducted by Land Commissioners J.A. MacLaughlan and John C. Allen to settle the claims arising under the treaty of Washington, 1844-1848", Crown land office, Province of New Brunswick; "Report of the Commissioners Appointed under the Resolve of February 21, 1843 to locate grants and determine the extent of possessory claims under the late treaty with Great Britain", Special Collection, Fogler Library, University of Maine.

6 Graeme Wynn, *Timber Colony* (Toronto, 1980), p. 36; Lettres des prêtres missionnaires, 27 March 1824.

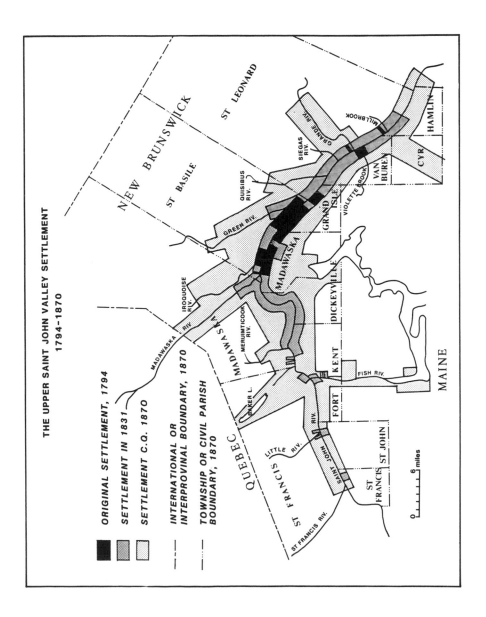

THE UPPER SAINT JOHN VALLEY SETTLEMENT
1794–1870

ORIGINAL SETTLEMENT, 1794

SETTLEMENT IN 1831

SETTLEMENT C.Q. 1870

INTERNATIONAL OR
INTERPROVINAL BOUNDARY, 1870

TOWNSHIP OR CIVIL PARISH
BOUNDARY, 1870

through the portage route — a distance of 12 miles. This route was adequate for people and mail, but not for bulky agricultural products. According to an 1831 report by surveyor Joseph Bouchette, the Madawaska settlers had never tried to sell products in Lower Canada.[7]

Another potential market was the more accessible, but more distant, town of Fredericton, 170 miles downriver, or the even further port of St. John. The road, when and where it existed, was in poor condidtion. But the whole length of the river was navigable five months a year, broken by only one serious obstacle: the Great Falls, just below the French settlement. Distance, and the additional costs incurred portaging goods around the falls, often made sending goods downriver uneconomical. Monsignor Plessis, Bishop of Quebec, noted during his 1813 pastoral visit:

> Les habitans ont plus de 30 lieues à aller au fleuve St Laurent et 60 à aller à Fredericton. Voila néanmoins leurs seuls débouchés. Comment tirer parti de leurs denrées? Les frais de voyages n'en absorbent-t-ils pas presque tout le profit?[8]

In 1831, surveyor Bouchette reported that the valley was blessed with an abundance of natural meadows, which enabled the inhabitants "to keep numerous flocks and herds, and these would, if they had any means of getting them to market, be a source of great wealth to the settlement".[9]

Low-priced or perishable products could not bear the transportation costs to Fredericton. But high-priced agricultural goods could be profitably sold there. American agents John G. Deane and Edward Kavanagh mentioned in 1831 that the valley exported large quantities of maple sugar.[10] Peter Fisher mentioned a more important market commodity in his 1825 history of New Brunswick: wheat.[11] Bouchette also reported that the inhabitants milled their

---

7   Joseph Bouchette, *The British Dominions in North America or a Topographical and Statistical Description of the Provinces of Lower and Upper Canada, New Brunswick, Prince Edward Island, Newfoundland, Nova Scotia and Cape Breton Island, and a Topographical Dictionary of Lower Canada* (New York [London], 1968 [1831]).

8   "Le journal des visites pastorales de Mgr Joseph Octave Plessis, Evêque de Québec en Acadie, 1811-12-15", *Société Historique Acadiennes*, Cahiers, 11, 1-3 (mars/septembre 1980), p. 25.

9   Bouchette, *The British Dominions in North America*, p. 104.

10   W.O. Raymond, ed., "State of the Madawaska and Aroostook Settlements in 1831, Reports of John G.Deane and Edward Kavanagh to Samuel E. Smith, Governor of the State of Maine", New Brunswick Historical Society, *Collections*, 9 (1914), p. 455.

11   Peter Fisher, *History of New Brunswick, as Originally Published in 1825, with a Few Explanatory Notes* (St. John, 1921), p. 53. According to Deane and

wheat into flour and sent "considerable quantities to the market in Fredericton, where it meets with a ready sale at an abundantly renumerating price".[12]

Unfortunately for the Madawaska settlers, wheat-growing was struck a fatal blow in the early 1830s. It was killed by the same pest that destroyed it in New England and Lower Canada, and as in New England and Lower Canada, the farmers gave it up. By the 1850s the farmers were buying wheat flour in the local stores, like their colleagues in New England. In 1848 the St. John Valley was described as shipping out timber, "small quantities of wheat", fur and maple sugar.[13] But the failure of the major cash crop did not force the settlers into self-sufficiency. Lumbering seems to have created a substitute market for local products. The local priest wrote to his bishop (27 March 1824), "Les effets ont assez bon cours à présent parce que des faiseurs de bois de tonne ont ouvert cet hiver des chantiers dans nos endroits", whereas as late as 1821, he was complaining he could not sell the products collected as tithes ("les effets").[14] Visitors also identified the lumber camps as a market and source of employment for local people. Ward stated in 1841 that the valley boasted several substantial farmers, who raised large quantities of oats and grains "with which they supply the lumbering parties in their immediate vicinity".[15] J.F. Johnston also noted in his remarks on the agricultural capabilities of New Brunswick that lumbering offered "a more ready market for farm produces. It kept prices up and gave employment to idle hands".[16]

Visitors failed to notice another market for the local farmers: people clearing land for their farms. According to Danhoff, it took five to ten years to develop a farm.[17] The St. John Valley does not seem to have been different.[18] Newcomers therefore constituted a genuine market for several years, and there were many of them in the valley. All through the 19th century, the

---

Kavanagh, there were three grist mills in the upper St. John Valley in 1831, two of which were in operation.

12 Bouchette, *The British Dominions in North America*, p. 104.

13 Abraham Gesner, *New Brunswick, with Notes for Emigrants* (London, 1847), p. 180.

14 Lettres des prêtres missionnaires.

15 Edmund Ward, *An Account of the St. John and Its Tributary Rivers and Lakes* (Fredericton, 1841), p. 86.

16 James F.W. Johnston, *Report on the Agricultural Capabilities of the Province of New Brunswick*, 2nd ed. (Fredericton, 1850), p. 51.

17 Charles Danhoff, *Changes in Agriculture, The Northern United States* (Cambridge, Mass., 1969), p. 120.

18 A land agent report for 1831 gives the date when most pieces of land were initially taken by their first owner; this report can be linked with an 1833 agricultural survey taken by a New Brunswick official. In 1833, half of the eight to ten year old

St. John Valley attracted a steady stream of immigrants. Immigration was particularly important in the few years after the opening of the lumber camps. The population more than doubled between 1820 and 1830, and 41 per cent of this increase was the result of immigration. The year 1826 alone saw the arrival of 30 new families. The newcomers were not merely following the lumber camps: they took land, and most became permanent residents. By 1850 those people were identified as farmers by the census taker. Immigration explains why at any time in the 1830s, 1840s and 1850s, between 50 and 60 per cent of the farms were at the clearing stage. Their owners and their families had to be fed somehow. The men could work in the woods in winter, and use their wages to buy seeds, stock, and food. In a simpler fashion, they could barter their services with a farmer-lumberer in exchange for various agricultural products. In any given year, then, about every other family in the valley had to rely on the market to secure its subsistence.

We do not have a lot of data on the St. John Valley agriculture prior to 1850, besides the fragments of information conveyed by visitors. Sources are scarce: a few tithing records, grain bonus lists from New Brunswick, an American land agent report for 1831, an agricultural survey taken in the winter of 1833, aggregate figures from the New Brunswick census of 1851, and the 1850 agricultural census for the American side of the river. Only four tithing records exist: two for the whole settlement (in 1799 and 1804) and two for its western section (1832 and 1841). All four were sent to the Bishop of Quebec by the local people, who tried to convince him they could support a priest for the whole settlement (1799 and 1804), and that a new parish should be erected in the west of the territory (in 1832 and 1841). Parishioners (and in those years almost everyone was Roman Catholic) were expected to give 1/26 of their grain, peas and potatoes to the priest.[19] The grain bonus lists were established by the New Brunswick government. In 1818 the New Brunswick legislature passed a bill providing for bonuses ranging from 4d to a shilling per bushel of grain raised on new land. The last bonus list for Madawaska is dated 1830.[20]

---

farms had crops as opposed to 29 per cent of the six to seven year old farms and 20 per cent of the farms five years and younger. Twenty-nine per cent of the farms five years and younger had neither crop nor animals in 1833, but only 20 per cent of the six to seven year old and ten per cent of the farms eight years and older were in this situation. This seems to indicate that on the average, it took seven or eight years to make a farm on the upper St. John River Valley.

19   Tithing records for 1799, 1804, 1832 and 1842. Lettres des prêtres missionnaires.

20   Papers of the Legislative Assembly, Schedule of Persons entitled to the Bounty for raising Grain on New Land, 1818-1830, Provincial Archives of New Brunswick [PANB].

The 1831 report was written by agents Deane and Kavanagh, who were sent by the state of Maine to investigate if the people of the St. John Valley people had rights on the land they occupied, and which the state claimed as its own. The report is a nominal list of residents, indicating the number of people in each household. It contains fairly detailed information about property size, number of acres cleared, land improvement, duration of tenure and names of the previous owners for about half the settlement. Deane and Kavanagh's investigation was restricted when James A. MacLauchlan, the British "warden of the disputed territory", stepped in, warned the two Americans he considered them trespassers, and discouraged settlers from answering their questions. The information relating to the rest of the settlement is generally limited to the name of the occupant and what the two agents could observe. Deane and Kavanagh made some comments about crops and husbandry practices; they also reported the tithes collected that year.

The 1833 agricultural survey, taken by MacLauchlan, is an extremely rich document. The crops failed in the Madawaska district in the fall of 1833 because of a wet summer and an early winter. The hard-pressed inhabitants petitioned Fredericton for relief. Before taking action, the provincial government requested a report from MacLauchlan, who had lived in the area for several years and was likely to be well informed about local conditions. Maclauchlan proved extremely zealous. His report consists of a census of all the local families, naming the heads of household, indicating the number of people living with them, listing all the stock they owned, how much they had sowed in the spring, how much they had harvested, the quality of the crops, and how much they used to harvest, on the average, in the past few years. The document is extremely valuable because nominal agricultural censuses were not taken until 1850 in the U.S. and 1861 in New Brunswick.[21]

The last useable document is the 1850 census. By that time the valley was divided, and censuses cover only one bank of the river or the other. Only the aggregate figures published in the *Journal of the Legislative Assembly* are available for New Brunswick in 1851.[22] The agricultural schedule of the 1850 U.S. census on the other hand still exists, and entries can be linked most of the time with the corresponding ones in the population schedule.[23] Unfortunately, only the 167 farms above a certain value (officially $500, in fact $300) were enumerated. Despite the fact the other heads of household were enumerated as "laborers" in the population schedule, there were more than 167 farms on the

21 "Report of the Commissioners of Affairs at Madawaska, 1834, Papers of the Legislative Assembly relating to the Settlement of Madawaska", PANB.

22 *Journal of the Legislative Assembly of New Brunswick, 1851-1852*, pp. xxvi-xxvii.

23 The population schedule is available from U.S. Census, 1850, M432, roll 248, National Archives (Washington, D.C.). The agricultural census is available from the Maine State Archives in Augusta, Maine.

U.S. bank of the river. In 1845 the state had granted 565 farm lots — and they had not been massively abandoned. The 1845 grantees (or their children) were still living in the valley five years later. By 1860 those lots were included in the agricultural census, and reported crops. They were therefore genuine farms. But in 1845, two-thirds of the lots granted had been recently taken, and were reported by the land agents as not yet improved.[24] The proportion of unimproved farms was similar in 1833 at 60 per cent. The farms enumerated in 1850 represented 36 per cent of the 1845 land grants. It is therefore plausible that the 167 farms listed in the 1850 agricultural census were all the productive farms on the American side of the valley, and those left out by the census taker were still at the clearing stage, and had little or no stock or crop to report. (Productive farms are here defined as those growing crops.)

Tables One and Two summarize the information contained in these different sources. The households counted here are the separate co-residential groups which are identified by the various documents; the households listed in the 1831 and 1833 reports occasionally included other relatives, some servants or some boarders, besides the conjugal family. The "farms" included in Table Two are productive farms. At first glance, some of the figures seem anomalous. The average production per household in the early 1830s is much higher than that reported in the tithing lists, or in the Deane and Kavanagh report (which is based on tithing figures). The early 1830s figures are calculated from the "average yield in past years" column of the MacLauchlan report. Although high, these figures are not unrealistic. One can, for instance, estimate the acreage under cultivation from the quantities of seed sown. Most are under 20 acres. One can also estimate from the same seed figures the anticipated yields for the fall of 1833 and compare these figures with the ones for the past years; they are very close. One can estimate the yield per acre by dividing the past year crop average by the acreage sown in 1833. Not only are the resulting yields not excessive, but they fall below the yields reported by Deane and Kavanagh:

	Wheat	Barley	Oats	Buckwheat	Peas	Potatoes
Estimated yields (bu.)	11.9	14.6	17.5	8	13	132
D. and K.'s figures	20	25	30	no data	n.d.	250

In short, the Madawaska settlers could easily have grown the quantities they reported. The document is internally consistent. The question then is: why only in the early 1830s? Why are the MacLauchlan figures conflicting with those derived from the tithing records?

---

24 "Report of the Commissioners appointed under resolve of February 21, 1843, to locate Grants and determine the extent of Possessory Claims under the Late Treaty with Britain", Special Collections, Fogler Library, University of Maine, Orno, Maine.

Tithing records are likely to underestimate agricultural production as residents did not tithe as much as they were supposed to. Tithes were an object of perpetual quarrels between priests and parishioners, if we can believe the letters the priests sent their bishops. The MacLauchlan figures on the other hand may overestimate production; the settlers may have exaggerated their past production to make their plight seems worse. But it is doubtful that Mac-Lauchlan would have taken unrealistically high figures at face value. And if one compares not average production per household, but average production per farm, the early 1830 figures are not excessive compared with those for the 1850s.

Despite their apparent lack of consistency, the data in Tables One and Two seem fairly reliable. The figures suggest that the upper St. John Valley was prosperous and normally capable of feeding its entire population. In addition, a comparison between the state of agriculture in the early 1830s and in 1850 not only confirms the shift from wheat to other crops noted by visitors, but also suggests that changes in the natural, economic and political environment led farmers to switch to a different type of husbandry altogether. In the early 1830s settlers harvested trees, grew wheat for sale out of the upper valley, and foodstuffs for their use and that of their neighbours. In 1850 local residents were primarily farmers engaged in mixed agriculture. In both cases they sought to provide for their needs both from subsistence farming and market-oriented activities. Beginning in the 1850s, they were not loath to purchase some of their food either.

In the early 1830s only a minority of farms (40 per cent, or 159) were operational, that is reporting any crops. Nonetheless, those 159 farms were capable of feeding the entire permanent population, and still have some surplus to sell to lumber camps or out of the valley. To estimate this surplus, we must first evaluate the food and feed needs of this population. Deeds of maintenance offer useful information about food needs.[25] When elderly people decided to retire, they often exchanged all or part of their property for maintenance until their death. The deeds of maintenance very often listed in great detail everything the retiree expected to receive. In some parts of North America, widow's portions — which were forms of deeds of maintenance — seem to have significantly exceeded needs, and historians have claimed that part of the supplies was meant to be sold.[26] This does not seem to have been

---

25 Deeds of maintenance are found at the Northern Registry of the Deeds (opened in 1845) in Fort Kent for the Maine side, at the Victoria County registry Office (1850-73) for the New Brunswick one. Records of land transactions prior to 1845 are very rare. The few that exist can be found in the York County registry (1785-1831) and the Carleton County registry (1831-50)

26 Bettye Hobbs-Pruitt, "Self-Sufficiency and the Agricultural Economy of Eighteenth-Century Massachusetts", *William and Mary Quarterly*, 3d. ser., XLI, 3 (July 1984), p. 348.

Table One
Production per Household, 1799-1851

Year	1799	1804	1831	1832	1830	1833	1841	1850[a]
Number of Households	56	100	475	113	400	400	140	466
Wheat	51	42	29	29	45	15	15	3
Buckwheat	0	0	0	0	1	1	10	51
Oats	10	11	6	10	30	11	22	46
All grain[1]	64	nd	nd	nd	80	30	57	111
Peas	8	8	9	10	16	5	11	9
Potatoes	67	75	41	88	143	90	123	61
Hay[2]	nd	nd	nd	nd	nd	8.8	nd	8

a U.S. side only

1 Includes wheat, barley, oats, buckwheat, corn and rye. All quantities in bushels.

2 Quantities in tons.

Table Two
Production per Farm

Year	1830	1840	1850
Number of Farms	159	159	167
Wheat	112	37	8
Buckwheat	3	3	142
Oats	74	29	134
All Grains	202	75	310
Peas	39	12	24
Potatoes	359	226	171
Hay	nd	16	21
Horses	nd	1.96	1.8
Oxen	nd	1.96	1.23
Cows	nd	3.78	3.62
Cattle	nd	3.4	3.4
Sheep	nd	14.6	19
Pigs	nd	5.21	3.62

Sources: 1799 and 1804, tithing records for the parish of St. Basile; 1831, Deane and Kavanaugh Report; 1832, tithing records for the parish of St. Luce; 1850, U.S. census, population and agricultural schedule.

the case here. On the one hand, retirees often requested small amounts of cash in addition to their supplies. Many deeds of maintenance also contained a clause specifying that unused supplies were to revert to the younger couple. On the other hand, the quantities requested provided people with a diet that was both quantitatively and qualitatively adequate, although bland and monotonous. A typical retiree would consume weekly at least seven pounds of potatoes,[27] nine pounds of bread or wheat based products, two pounds of mess pork, one pound of beef or mutton, one and a quarter pounds of dried peas, one and a half ounces of rice or barley, half a pound each of sugar, dried fish (after 1855), and butter, half an ounce of tea (this is the weight of six modern tea bags, with their bags) two ounces of lard, as well as milk, eggs, poultry and vegetables in season. (All these are modal values.) Some families stored onions and cabbages as well as salted greens for winter use, but the practice was not universal. These various food items, in the quantities listed above, could provide each retiree with a generous, but not excessive, amount of calories for an active person living in a cold climate. There is therefore no reason not to rely on deeds of maintenance to estimate consumption patterns and levels.

The 1833 survey reports a population of 426 men, 394 women, 844 boys and 854 girls. If we count every two children as equivalent to one adult for consumption purposes, this population was equivalent to 1669 adult consumers.[28] Modal allowances of wheat, potatoes and peas were nine bushels of wheat, six bushels of potatoes and one and a half bushels of peas yearly. Grain, peas and potato requirements and surpluses would have been the following:

	Production	Consumption	Seeds	Total	Surplus
Wheat (bu.)	17,946	15,021	2,332	17,353	593
Peas (bu.)	6,243	2,503	624	3,127	3,116
Potatoes(bu.)	57,141	10,014	5,714	15,728	41,413

Farmers, after satisfying the needs of their neighbours, would have had not only a small surplus of wheat to export out of the valley, but also a mountain

---

27 The distribution of potato requirement is bi-modal, with a peak at six bushels, and a slightly smaller one at ten. The elderly could also grow potatoes on the garden plot that most of them requested.

28 "Adults" are here defined as people 16 or older. Most historians prefer to distribute the population in narrower age categories, and assume increased consumption with the increased age of children. To test the accuracy of the simpler method, I calculated the number of adult equivalents in two control townships using first Atack and Bateman's formula in *To Their Own Soil*, then McInnis's formula in "Marketable Surplus in Ontario farms", and finally the equation of two children = one adult. The results were virtually identical. For instance, in the township of Eagle Lake, I counted respectively 75.5, 77.5 and 75.5 adult

of peas and potatoes. Potatoes were not worth shipping out, being cheap, bulky and perishable. It is doubtful farmers would have eaten their cash crop and let others rot away. It is also doubtful Bouchette would have referred to the valley as a flour producer, if it could send only 100 barrels of flour a year to outside markets. It is plausible the bulk of the population ate less bread and more peas and potatoes than their elders (at any rate, it would have have made more business sense). Nine bushels of wheat was enough to feed each adult consumer one and a quarter pounds of bread every day — a generous allowance for people who had potatoes and peas in abundance.

St. John Valley residents could have lived easily on three-quarters of a pound of bread a day (one barrel of flour or six bushels a year), if they had increased their potato consumption to two or three pounds a day (12 or 18 bushels a year).[29] Requirements and surplus would have been the following:

	Food	Seeds	Total	Surplus
Wheat (bu.)	10,014	2,332	12,342	5,604
Peas (bu.)	2,503	624	3,127	3,116
Potatoes(12 bu./yr)	20,028	5,714	25,742	31,399
(18 bu./yr)	30,042	5,714	35,756	21,385

The valley was therefore in a position to send a substantial quantity of wheat or wheat flour to external markets, without hardship to its human residents; in this case a total of 934 barrels of flour, which averaged 35 bushels of wheat per operating farm.[30]

Even in a year of famine such as 1833, the quantity of grain was sufficient — unfortunately, two-thirds of it was labelled "bad" by MacLauchlan — and the potatoes, struck by the blight, were rotting in storage. The 159 established farmers could make ends meet, but likely had nothing left that year for their newer neighbours, who wintered over on meal supplied by the provincial government.

---

equivalents. As I find the expression "adult equivalent" positively awful, I will use "adult consumer" instead. Jeremy Atack and Fred Bateman, *To Their Own Soil: Agriculture in the Antebellum North* (Iowa, 1987); and Marvin McInnis, "Marketable Surplus in Ontario Farms", *Social Science History,* VIII (Fall 1984), pp. 395-424.

29 This consumption pattern would also have been similar to the one reconstructed by Frank Lewis and Marvin McInnis for Canada East in 1861 (seven bushels of wheat and 14 bushels of potatoes). F. Lewis and M. McInnis, "Agricultural Output and Eficiency in Lower Canada", *Research in Economic History,* 9 (1984), pp. 45-87.

30 According to Deane and Kavanagh, there were two operating and one disused grist mills in the upper valley in 1831. The disused mill had been built in the 18th century.

Surplus production was not evenly distributed among all the productive farms. All farms that were productive grew a surplus; none grew fewer than 35 bushels of wheat equivalent (the minimum needed for subsistance)[31] But 18 per cent grew between 250 and 1,000 bushels, and two-thirds grew more than 100. Milk and meat production were similarly impressive. The 723 cows enumerated in the survey could produce 325-350 gallons of milk a year, or two quarts a day per adult consumer.[32] The quantity of available meat can be calculated using the number of animals in the 1833 survey, the slaughtering ratio used by McInnis, and the animal weights reported by Johnston.[33] Total production would have been 151,012 pounds of beef, 209,912 pounds of pork and 36,290 pounds of mutton. This translated into 90 pounds of beef, 126 pounds of pork and 22 pounds of mutton a year per adult consumer — slightly more that the amount requested in the deeds of maintenance. Most farmers, if any, evidently did not try to produce a surplus of meat to sell outside the valley.

Meat production was also more widespread than grain production. Two-thirds of farms had animals, and about 20 per cent of the animals were on farms reporting no crops. Not surprisingly, farms reporting a high level of grain production also had a higher than average number of animals. Farms reporting a production of 250 bushels of wheat equivalent had twice the average number of cows and pigs and three time the average number of sheep. Two farms had 17 and 18 pigs, three had 50 sheep or more and three had 10 cows or more. Three farms had an extremely large number of animals: Joseph Hébert had 50 sheep, 15 pigs, and 10 cows; his brother Simonet had 50 sheep,

---

31 All bushels are not equal in weight (e.g., a bushel of oats weighs 32 pounds, whereas a bushel of wheat weighs 60 pounds). Consequently I converted all grain production to a common unit. My initial intention had been to use the same conversion rates as Atack and Bateman in *To Their Own Soil*, to facilitate comparisons. Unfortunately Atack and Bateman are rather vague about the ways they converted various grains into corn equivalents, and I could not get the same conversion ratios when I tried to replicate their calculations. Besides, it seems a bit silly to convert into corn the production of a region which could not grow that particular grain. My conversion rates, like Atack and Bateman's, are derived from Morrison, Feed and Feeding (20th ed.). They take into account both the different weight of each grain, and the difference in nutritive content. For instance, a bushel of wheat weighs 60 pounds, of which 84 per cent (50.4 pounds) is digestible matter. One bushel of barley weighs 48 pounds, of which 37.77 pounds is digestible matter. One bushel of wheat = 50.4 37.77 = 1.33 bushels of barley. It is also equal to 1.1 rye, 1.6 buckwheat, 2.2 oats.

32 The figure is based on an annual production of 450 gallons per cow, reported by Johnston in *Agricultural capabilities of New Brunswick.*

33 Johnston, *Agricultural Capabilities of New Brunswick*, p. 12; Frank D. Lewis and Marvin McInnis, "Agricultural Output and Efficiency in Lower Canada", *Research in Economic History*, 9 (1984) pp. 45-87.

10 pigs and 10 cows; Michel Martin had 64 sheep, 18 pigs and 9 cows. The three men produced among themselves 1,580 bushels of wheat equivalent, 1,900 bushels of potatoes and 400 bushels of peas. Farmers who grew very large quantities of grain also grew large quantities of peas and potatoes and had a lot of stock. They had more improved acres and more draught animals, and almost always had several sons. Increased production was conditioned by access to sufficient human and animal power to clear the land, plow, and harvest the crops. Those who had access to these resources obviously made the most of them. The 22 farms that produced at least 250 bushels of wheat equivalent were full-fledged commercial ventures, despite their lack of specialization. But it seems unfair to deny the label to their 137 colleagues. 159 farms could adequately feed 400 households, which means each farming family on the average fed two others. If a commercial farm markets 60 per cent of its production, most established farmers indeed deserved the title.[34]

Although the St. John Valley was more than self-sufficient in human food, it suffered an apparent feed deficit. The animals reported in the 1833 survey would have required 3,582 tons of hay and 41,305 bushels of oats to be properly fed.[35] Production was only 3,554 tons of hay in 1833, but the wet summer of 1833 may have caused a below average hay crop (there is no hay figure for the "years before"). The valley produced only 11,804 bushels of oats in the early 1830s. This was enough oats for 219 horses, however, there were 436 of them to feed, not to mention the oxen (it is assumed that sheep were never given oats). Horses and oxen could winter over on a poor diet if not required to work. But everything suggests that the St. John Valley farmers kept large number of draught animals to work in the woods in winter, and those alone would have required 32,713 bushels of oats (using the McInnis figures). Outside purchase of fodder seem unlikely at that time. The deficit then had to be made up from local resources. The two major ones were bran and peas. But those could, at best, cover two-thirds of the deficit:

---

34 This production level was also similar to that uncovered by Alan MacNeil in the Annapolis Valley in 1827.

35 I am using here the same figures as Marvin McInnis to estimate yearly animal consumption:

Horses	1.52 tons of hay, 53.7 bushels of oats
oxen	1.82 tons of hay, 26.8 bushels of oats
cows	1.8 tons of hay
young cattle	.86 tons of hay
sheep	.15 tons of hay, 3 bushels of oats.

Lewis and McInnis, "Agricultural Output and Efficiency in Lower Canada, 1851", p. 79.

Feed shortfall	22,088 bu. of oats or 706,816 lbs.	
Bran production (12 lbs./bu.)	187 bu.	368 lbs.
Peas surplus	186 bu.	960 lbs.
Deficit	10,390 bu. of oats, 332, 488 lbs.	

Less obvious types of feed could also supplement orthodox ones. An 1858 report of the Maine board of agriculture claims that 200 pounds of potatoes were equivalent to 59 pounds of oats for feeding purposes.[36] Oat straw, grain and pea chaff could also have been used for feed, according to the same source. There was no feed deficit in the valley then, although the quality of the animals' diet may have left much to be desired. Even the most productive farms, those growing more than 300 bushels of wheat equivalent, were not necessarily growing large quantities of oats. Three of them, out of 14, suffered a small shortage of hay, and half of them did not grow enough oats. Farmers who stepped up grain production invested their time and effort in wheat.

North American farmers adopted a casual approach to stock feeding, improvising their animals' feed rather than produce specifically for it. McInnis, MacNeil and Bittermann all found that feeding practices fell short of the standards recommended by the literature of the time. But in addition, New Brunswick farmers were encouraged to do so by government policy. In 1817 the province had passed "An Act to encourage the raising of Bread Corn on New Land".[37] The stated purpose of the act was to encourage grain growing in the province; it was also designed to encourage clearing, as the bounty could be claimed only for the first crop, which had to be planted within two years of clearing. The province paid one shilling for each bushel of wheat, rye, corn, buckwheat and barley (the latter two were dropped to 9d. in 1826), but only 4d. for each bushel of oats. Farmers who grew wheat on new land instead of oats not only could expect to earn three to four times as much from its sale, but also to collect three times as much in bounty.

The grain bounty was an additional incentive to clear land, even if this one was used only once or twice for wheat. A farmer who knew his business would have tried to clear a few acres every winter, perhaps planted some patches of peas and potatoes between the stumps until he could remove them

---

36 *Annual Report of the Secretary of the Maine Board of Agriculture* (Augusta, 1859), p. 194.

37 *Acts of the General Assembly of his Majesty's Province of New Brunswick from the Forty Seventh to the Fifty Seventh Year of the Reign of King George the Third* (Fredericton, 1817), p. 333; the act was extended in 1826 and 1829. *Acts of the General Assembly of his Majesty' Province of New Brunswick from the First to the Third Year of King George the Fourth* (Fredericton, 1826), p. 159; *Acts of the General Assembly of His Majesty's Province of New Brunswick Passed in 1829* (Fredericton, 1829), p. 71.

to plough, then put in wheat and, after one crop, use the new field for peas, potatoes or lesser grains. It did not make financial sense to plant wheat on old fields. Some farmers who appeared in the bounty lists year after year probably did just that. Hilarion Daigle (who grew 765 bushels of grain in the early 1830s) reported 200 bushels of wheat and 40 bushels of barley on new land in 1826, 210 bushels of wheat and 90 bushels of barley in 1827 and 265 bushels of wheat in 1830. Assuming a yield of 11 bushels per acre, he would have brought about 70 acres into cultivation in those three years alone. Deane and Kavanagh reported in 1831 that he had 128 acres cleared on three lots. He collected £40 in bonuses. Others, on the other hand, seem to have preferred to collect all at once, such as innkeeper David Cyr who received £25 in 1830 for 372 bushels of wheat, 165 of barley and 22 of oats.

Farmers could also have chosen to keep fewer draught animals. Operating farms reported a considerable number of horses and oxen. Fifty-six per cent of the farms had at least three horses or oxen; nine per cent had at least six draught animals. Horses, like sons, were a source of wealth. They were needed to clear the land on which bounty-earning grain could be grown. Land clearing was also a profitable operation in itself, because the trees could be sent downriver to be sold. Lumbering was theoretically illegal in the disputed territory, but both the British and American authorities tolerated the cutting of trees by farmers on their own land. There is, however, evidence that local people were passing off trees taken from public land as the product of land clearing.[38] Lumbering, especially deep in the woods, requires animals. Judging by the number of draught animals in the valley, it seems that anyone who could was busy harvesting trees.

In the early 1830s, Madawaska farmers obviously tried to take advantage of all the money-making opportunities they had access to. They grew large amount of foodstuffs (peas, potatoes, grain) which they could sell to newcomers; they grew large quantities of wheat, had it milled, sold the flour downriver, and earned bounties. They cleared land, which provided them with timber for the Fredericton market, as well as increasing the value of their holding. And they cut on public land when they could get away with it. But they stretched themselves thin. Animals were fed whatever was handy, and the yields were low. North American husbandry was sloppy by European standards; St. John Valley farming seems to have been worse. This was not extensive agriculture, but slash and burn! Yet this casual approach to farming was probably a rational choice. Farmers spent more time clearing land than tending their fields because they could get a higher return for their labour that way.

---

38 Lettre de M. Langevin, 20 October 1837, Sir John Harvey, Correspondence, MG 24 A17, vol. 4, PAC.

By 1850 on the other hand, farmers may have reversed the strategy. Fields probably came first. As in the early 1830s, only a minority of farms (36 per cent, or 167) seem to have been operational. If we assume that these 167 farms were the only ones with crops, the farmers on the U.S. side of the valley would have grown 9.12 bushels of bread grain (in wheat equivalent) per adult consumer (932 adults and 1864 children), 2.14 bushels of peas and 15.72 bushels of potatoes, as well as 46 bushels of oats and eight tons of hay per household (466 households were enumerated in the U.S. census).

Grain production was again sufficient to cover food needs. If families relied exclusively on their own production, their diet was nonetheless very different from that of their parents. Farms grew about 10 bushels of buckwheat, two-thirds of a bushel of wheat, two bushels of barley and less than a quarter of a bushel of rye per adult consumer (exclusive of seed set aside). This was probably what the poorer people were forced to eat. The ideal was different. Few people asked for buckwheat in the deeds of maintenance (11 out of 93 between 1845 and 1870), and only four of these did not ask for any wheat product. Other grains were seldom listed as alternatives to wheat, but one such was store-bought flour.

One can wonder why the St. John Valley farmers did not revert to wheat growing after the wheat midge epidemic burned itself out. Soil exhaution could not have been a factor in a settlement where two-thirds of the farms at any one time were less than 10 years old. But the inhabitants were frequently reminded of their vulnerability to the climate. The local growing season is a mere 110 days, with last frost around 30 May, and the first one around 15 September — barely enough to ripen 19th century wheat. Climate-induced crop failures struck again in 1840 and 1854-5. Buckwheat, often labelled a "distress crop", was better suited to this short growing season, and this may have been the major reason behind its widespread adoption. By 1850 wheat was a luxury crop, grown only in small amounts by substantial farmers.

However, the local population did not give up eating wheat bread altogether. Barrelled flour was available locally as early as 1845 and at a reasonable price. John Emmerson, who operated a store in what is now Edmundston, received 81 barrels of flour in November and December 1846, and 395 barrels in 1850 (not to mention those he ordered specifically for the lumber camps). From 1848 onwards, he also purchased barrelled biscuits (8 barrels in 1850).[39] Emmerson seems to have ordered his wheat products from Rivière du Loup, at or below St. John market prices. In September 1848, he was selling flour at 30s. a barrel, whereas it fetched between 30 and 32s. a barrel in St. John in the last two quarters of the same year.[40] In the last quarter of

---

39 Abraham and Simon Dufour Ledger Book, 1844-8, Madawaska Public Library, Madawaska, Maine; the Dufours were selling flour in 1845 and after. New Brunswick Museum, John Emmerson Receiving Book, 1845-73.

40 Johnston, *Agricultural Capabilities of New Brunswick*, p. 35.

1848, Emmerson also bought local oats and barley for respectively 2s. and 3s.6d. a bushel. Fifteen bushels of oats consequently purchased the flour equivalent of six bushels of wheat. It is not surprising that local farmers decided wheat growing was not worth their time and effort.

Individual farms were still very productive — grain production per farm increased by about 20 bushels of wheat equivalent since the 1830s. The proportion of very productive farms also increased. In the early 1830s, only three per cent of the operating farms grew 400 bushels of grain or more. In 1850 six per cent were in this category, and one farm reported crops in excess of 1,000 bushels of wheat equivalent (but none in 1830). Twenty-one per cent of the farmers, as opposed to 17 per cent a generation before, grew at least 250 bushels of wheat equivalent. The proportion of farms growing less than 100 bushels dropped from 34 per cent to 20 per cent.

The increase in production may have been the result of a different mix of crops. Wheat, which proved difficult to grow, had become a marginal crop; it had been replaced by higher yielding, and more reliable, oats and buckwheat. The quantity of potatoes grown also declined, freeing some acreage for grain production. This decline could have been a result of the potato blight, which discouraged farmers from planting the tuber on a large scale. Unfortunately, inadequate sources make it impossible to know if the average number of improved acres per farm had increased. Crops were also better balanced between food and feed. The production of animal fodder had increased absolutely and relatively. The south bank produced 3,431 tons of hay and 22,456 bushels of oats. It needed 24,601 bushels to feed all its horses and oxen, and have enough seeds for the next spring. This shortfall was less than 10 per cent of the needs, and could be covered with the now reduced bran production, with the peas surplus, and possibly with buckwheat as well as potatoes. There was a surplus of 524 tons of hay as well. But of course, Madawaska settlers could have continued to feed their stock odds and ends in order to sell more oats to the lumber camps.

Some oats and hay were sold to the shanties. The ledgers of the local store show evidence of purchases of local oats and hay, which were carted, boated or sleighed up the St. John River or to Lake Temiscouata.[41] A brother of the Dufour traders, Cyrille, took full advantage of the opportunities offered by the shanties. In 1850 he harvested 1,000 bushels of oats and 40 tons of hay. He needed only 262 bushels and 35 tons for his own animals. Nonetheless, the Upper St. John Valley could not satisfy the shanty demand for oats and hay. As early as 1844, Shepard Cary, a large-scale lumber operator based in Houlton, Maine, was cutting up the St. John Valley and importing oats and hay from Lower Canada. In January 1846 he bought 3,058 *minots* of oats and 30 tons of

---

41   Abraham and Simon Dufour Ledger Book, 1844-8. John Emmerson Receiving Book and Ledgers.

hay from Isaac Hutton in L'Islet.[42] It is doubtful this was an isolated case.[43] The shanty market, like the lumber trade, was very volatile. The prices paid the farmers reflected the fluctuation of the lumber trade: the Dufour brothers, general merchants, bought oats for 2s.6d. in 1844, but for only 1s.6d. in 1848, when the bottom fell off the lumber trade. Farmers could not afford sacrificing subsistence in order to produce more for the shanty market; this would have been a greater gamble than playing the stock market! Only very well-established farmers could take the risk. Cyrille Dufour's farm, for instance, was also self-sufficient in food and feed: he even grew 50 bushels of wheat. The shanty market probably made him wealthy (his farm was valued $900 in 1850), but he did not need it to provide for the basic needs of his family.

Another level of lumbering operations provided an outlet for oats and hay production. Some local farmers continued to run their own shanties. Some can be identified through the store accounts; either their purchases included shanty equipment, or they settled their accounts with lumber. For those men, farming and lumbering were two facets of the same family business — it was a form of vertical integration. But they were not numerous. The disastrous 1847-8 season, which left some of the small-scale entrepreneurs heavily in debt, may have convinced the more marginal farmer-lumberers to give up their involvment in the forest industry. Farmers in 1850 also had less stock and fewer draught animals than their fathers. In 1833, 56 per cent of the operating farms had three horses or oxen or more; in 1850, only 36 per cent had that many.

Per capita milk and meat production seems to have been less in 1850 than in 1830; the valley produced only 69 pounds of beef, 21 pounds of mutton and 55 pounds of pork per adult consumer in 1850. In 1833 though, 16 per cent of the bovines, 20 per cent of the sheep and 25 per cent of the pigs were on nonproductive farms. The real level of meat production in 1850 was therefore likely to be slightly higher than that calculated from census data. If the distribution of animals was the same as in 1833, beef and mutton production levels would have been the same as in 1833 and pork production about half. This could have been a consequence of the reduced potato crop, as pigs were customarily fattened on potatoes in areas where corn would not grow. In addition, the increased buckwheat production may have supported larger flocks of poultry. Unfortunately, sources never mention those birds. On the surface then,

---

42 Shepard Cary papers, in possession of M. Peltier, Houlton, Maine. Cary was the larger operator on the American side of the Upper St. John River, employing 100 men in 1850. The Glaziers were also bringing their supplies from Lower Canada, using John Emmerson as their purchasing agent.

43 For more details on the trade with Lower Canada, see Martine Coté, "L'exploitation des forêts publiques sur la Cote-du-Sud, 1830-1900: un exemple de la perméabilité de la frontière canado-américaine", paper presented at the Congrès de l'institut d'histoire de l'Amérique française, October 1991.

meat production did not seem to keep up with population growth, but we cannot know for sure.

Farmers in 1850 were different from their fathers. In 1830 farming and lumbering were tightly linked. The same people did most of the cutting and most of the growing. The local economy, oriented towards outside markets, could be very profitable, but was also extremely fragile. The failure of the wheat crop, the end of the provincial grain bounties, and the evolution of the lumber industry, which became legal and gradually controlled by large scale entrepreneurs after 1842, forced the St. John Valley settlers to reorganize their activities.

In 1850 more residents devoted their attention solely to husbandry. They shifted to a diversified agriculture catering mostly to local markets; crops were no longer grown primarily for outside markets. Foodstuffs could be imported to substitute for uncertain local production, even though some substitutes could, and were, grown on the farmstead. Some food imports seem to have had no other purpose than to improve the quality of the diet: the Dufour brothers began selling cod in 1845; Emmerson did the same in 1852, and a few years later began to sell herrings. Families setting up new farms still constituted a significant market for farm surpluses, a market that was apparently not mediated by the local stores. Lumbering also played an important role in the local economy, but not a direct one. It encouraged better-off farmers to grow specific crops for a specific market. Local stores acted as middlemen for at least part of this trade. This market was not stable and fluctuated with the lumber trade, which was controlled by forces outside the valley. When the lumber trade collapsed in 1848, so did the price of oats, and local people could not settle their accounts. Although the St. John Valley farmers had turned their backs on outside markets, they were not isolated from them.

The evolution of agriculture in the St. John Valley parallels the experiences in New England and Lower Canada. Crop failures and competition from cheap Canadian flour incited farmers to give up wheat growing as a commercial venture, seek markets closer to home and adjust production accordingly. T.W. Acheson suggests elsewhere in this volume that most New Brunswick farmers were rational men who were engaged in those economic activities which produced the best returns. Upper St. John Valley farmers do not seem to have been the exception. And like farmers in other parts of New Brunswick and Nova Scotia, they did not constitute a homogeneous class of self-sufficient households with tenuous relations to the market.

New Brunswick Agriculture
at the End of the Colonial Era:
A Reassessment

T.W. Acheson

In New Brunswick, as in every other part of North America, agriculture was the most important economic activity of the early- and mid-19th century. History, however, tends to be a game for winners, and the historiography of the colony is very long on timber and ships and manufacturing and very short on any discussion of the principal economic activity. Much of the reason for this state of affairs stems from the longstanding assumption that New Brunswick was not an agricultural community and that most colonists worked the woods in winter, drove logs in spring, cut lumber in summer and made ships on demand. Agriculture was, at best, a matter of subsistence: a truck garden, a potato plot, a pig for winter killing, and a draft animal for use in the woods. The colonial economy was perceived as driven by its export trade in staples, and its rural society was seen as an undifferentiated mass of part-time lumbermen living on their small undeveloped farm lots.

The traditional historiography suggested that the rural family lived in two interrelated economic worlds: the world of a cashless subsistence agriculture, and the commercial world of the timber trade and the public purse. Arthur Lower drew the classic portrait of the New Brunswick farmer-lumberer in his two studies on the Canadian forest frontier. He characterized such men as the "usual mixture of amateur farmer and timber cutter" who turned from the honest toil of farming to the "illusory promise of an easy cash return for a winter's work in the woods", and for whom the "neglect of their farms ended either in abandonment or in extremely slovenly farming". Even the food consumed in the lumber camps had to be imported from the United States, the Canadas and the West Indies.[1]

Lower's depiction of the province as one vast seasonal lumber camp was accepted and taken for granted a generation later by Stewart MacNutt. MacNutt's history of the colonial period — still the standard work on pre-Confederation political development — is in large measure a study of the politics of the timber trade. Although the great majority of the electorate of the

---

1   A.R.M. Lower, *The North American Assault on the Canadian Forest* (Toronto, 1936), pp. 78-9. See also Lower's *Settlement and the Forest Frontier in Eastern Canada* (Toronto, 1936), pp. 31-7. The author wishes to acknowledge the support of the Social Sciences and Humanities Research Council of Canada in the preparation of this study.

period were farmers and rural freeholders, the terms "agriculture" and "farming" do not appear in the index of the work. To Lower's image of the farmer-lumberman MacNutt added the vision of the economically dependent rural freeholder bound to the central government through the dole of public money. Most of the provincial revenues were dispensed through the medium of the local assemblymen for the construction of public roads and other undertakings. The cash income paid for this work in a hundred localities was an essential part of the rural economy.[2] In his 1982 study of the communities of the upper Miramichi River valley, William MacKinnon demonstrated that most freeholders in this timbering centre were active participants in the trade. Taking a theme hinted at in Lower, MacKinnon revealed a community of farmer-lumberer-entrepreneurs who mortgaged their farms to raise the capital needed to speculate in this potentially profitable undertaking.[3] The first suggestion that a prosperous and complex agricultural economy existed at mid-century was made by Graeme Wynn in his *Timber Colony*. He writes of an agricultural economy paralleling that of the forest, of farms sufficiently productive that they rented for as much as £50 a year in the early part of the century, of agricultural labourers making £25 and board each year. Béatrice Craig has found the same variety of agricultural enterprise in the upper St. John Valley in the first half of the 19th century.[4]

The evolution of New England and Canadian rural historiographies has followed a similar pattern. The traditional historiographies of New England and Canada, in different ways, portrayed early and mid-19th-century rural society in a similar fashion. On the one hand, the self-sufficient rural freeholder was seen as the glory of New England and the township as the basis of an egalitarian democracy. On the other hand the ubiquitous wheat farmer of Upper Canada was considered the principal instrument of prosperity, and the export of wheat provided a margin of prosperity that contrasted sharply with the economy created by the largely self-sufficient peasantry of Lower Canada, who thus contributed to the economic backwardness of that society. Recent studies have challenged both these views.

In 1961 Charles Grant challenged the interpretive framework of New England agriculture created half a century earlier by Percy Bidwell. Bidwell had argued that most New England farmers in the 18th and early 19th cen-

---

2   This is a continuing theme throughout MacNutt's work. For specific examples at critical junctures in the political process see W.S. MacNutt, *New Brunswick: A History, 1784-1867* (Toronto,1963), pp. 112, 243.

3   William MacKinnon, *Over The Portage: Early History of the Upper Miramichi* (Fredericton, 1984), ch. 4.

4   Graeme Wynn, *Timber Colony: A Historical Geography of Early Nineteenth Century New Brunswick* (Toronto, 1981), pp. 80-4. See also Béatrice Craig, "Agriculture in a Pioneer Region: The Upper St. John River Valley in the first half of the 19th Century", in this volume, pp. 17-36.

turies had been trapped in a narrow subsistence agriculture existing outside the market economy. Grant argued from his township study of Kent, Connecticut that there were, in fact, agricultural surpluses in the region — surpluses that implied the presence of markets. More important, Grant went on to postulate that, far from being a people caught up in an ideal of the perfect life as one of a self-sufficient, family-centred community, his New Englanders were entrepreneurs committed to achieving the material benefits that aggressive entrepreneurship could acquire.[5]

Grant's concept of a commercial mentality was in turn attacked in the late 1970s by several scholars of the New Left, including James Henretta and Robert Mutch, who argued instead for the existence of an agricultural mentality based on community, family production and mutual benefit.[6] In 1981 Winifred Rothenburg reiterated the presence of "a commercial *mentalité*, an entrepreneurial spirit, an individualist ethic of private gain" in her study of the marketing habits of a number of Massachusetts farmers working between 1750 and 1855.[7] The destruction of the traditional historiographical edifice was completed in 1984 when Bettye Hobbs Pruitt demonstrated that a significant proportion of Massachusetts farms did not possess the most basic farming needs. More than one-fifth of farmers, for example, did not own any draft animals and nearly 40 per cent were not self-sufficient in grain.[8] This suggests an economically divided society and the necessity for extensive local and provincial markets extending far beyond the reciprocal market relationships found in much of the literature of the 1970s.

5   Percy W. Bidwell, "The Agricultural Revolution in New England", *American Historical Review*, 26 (July 1921), pp. 683-702; Charles S. Grant, *Democracy in the Connecticut Frontier Town of Kent* (New York, 1961).

6   James Henretta, "Family and Farms: *Mentalité* in Pre-Industrial America", *William and Mary Quarterly*, 3rd Ser., XXXV (1978), pp. 3-32; Christopher Clark, "Household Economy, Market Exchange, and the Rise of Capitalism in the Connecticut Valley, 1800-1860", *Journal of Social History*, XIII (1979), pp. 169-89.

7   Winifred B. Rothenburg, "The Market and Massachusetts Farmers, 1750-1855", *Journal of Economic History [JEH]*, Vol. XLI, No. 2 (June 1981), p. 313. The dimensions of the debate are set out in the comments of Rona S. Weiss, Michael Bernstein and Sean Wilentz and the rebuttal by Winifred Rothenburg. See Rona Weiss, "The Market and Massachusetts Farmers, 1750-1850: Comment" , Winifred B. Rothenburg, "The Market and Massachusetts Farmers: A Reply", *JEH*, Vol. XLIII, No. 2 (June 1983), pp. 475-80; Michael A. Bernstein and Sean Wilentz, "Marketing, Commerce, and Capitalism in Rural Massachusetts" and Winifred B. Rothenburg, "Markets, Values and Capitalism: A Discourse on Method", *JEH*, Vol. XLIV, No. 1 (March 1984), pp. 171-8.

8   Bettye Hobbs Pruitt, "Self-Sufficiency and the Agricultural Economy of Eighteenth-Century Massachusetts", *William and Mary Quarterly*, 3rd Ser., XLI (1984), pp. 339, 352.

In contrast to the social democracy traditionally portrayed in New England, Canadian historiography has reflected the all-powerful influence of the staples theory. According to this interpretation the export of wheat was the driving force behind the economic development of Upper Canada. The revenues from this trade created a colony of consumers who generated a greater demand, which led to the development of a more diversified economy. By contrast, the inability to produce a surplus of wheat accounted for the comparative under-development of the economy of Lower Canada. The former proposition recently has come under sharp attack from Douglas McCalla, who argues that the development of Upper Canada (later Canada West) before Confederation cannot be explained in terms of the relatively small per capita wheat exports of the period. Instead, he argues, the commercial agriculture of the colony was much more diverse and significant and the domestic market a more important factor than we have been led to believe.[9]

What McCalla and Pruitt have in common is their affirmation of the significance of local and provincial markets in explaining both the nature of the colonial societies and the development of the colonial economies. McCalla confirms the essentially commercial and proto-capitalistic nature of the Upper Canadian rural economy while Pruitt asserts that Massachusetts rural society, while still clinging to the ideal of self-sufficiency, had to be something much more than a barter system based on a form of use-value. In the communities portrayed by both scholars the social distances among households are potentially far greater than those suggested in the traditional literature. The internal markets, in turn, were capable of generating wealth or at least considerable prosperity for significant elements of the rural community.

The traditional rural historiography of New Brunswick has fallen curiously between the New England and the Canadian traditions. On the one hand, New Brunswick farmers have been depicted as fully a part of the great staples enterprise; on the other, they have been seen as isolated, relatively self-sufficient agriculturalists functioning largely outside the market economy. Several major problems need to be addressed before any resolution of this contradiction is possible. There has been no systematic attempt to come to grips with the popular mentality or mentalities of the rural population of the province. Nor has there been any systematic treatment of the development of the agricultural sector over the course of the 19th century. The emphasis on the

---

9   Douglas McCalla, "The Internal Economy of Upper Canada: New Evidence on Agriculture Marketing Before 1850", *Agricultural History*, Vol. 59, No. 3, (July 1985), pp. 397-416. For the most recent restatement of the traditional thesis see John MacCallum, *Unequal Beginnings: Agriculture and Economic Development in Quebec and Ontario Until 1870* (Toronto, 1980). For an assessment of the historiography of Lower Canadian agriculture see R.M. McInnis, "A Reconsideration of the State of Agriculture in Lower Canada in the First Half of the Nineteenth Century", *Canadian Papers in Rural History*, Vol. III (1983), pp. 4-49.

timber trade in the writing of provincial history has resulted in the assumption that the province was a perpetual forest frontier, despite the obvious fact that by mid-century there were agricultural districts of new settlement, and of one, two, three and four generations standing.

This study seeks to explore the social and economic nature of New Brunswick agriculture at the end of the colonial era. It assesses the significance of the industry and the potential for the development of agricultural markets. This is accomplished through an examination of the structure of the industry in two parishes of the province. The general argument is that most New Brunswick farmers were rational men and women who engaged in those rural economic activities which produced the highest return for their efforts, whether they be farming, lumbering or weaving. Agriculture was the most valuable sector of the provincial economy, but while much of the output of this industry went to the subsistence of the farm family, there were few farms that could be seen as self-sufficient. Indeed, there was a wide range of producing farms and a significant degree of agricultural specialization. Many farm families saw agriculture as one of several activities. Younger men, in particular, participated in the timber trade when more money could be made through this avenue of endeavour, just as they sometimes went to sea for a time, or, when satisfactory opportunities were not available at home, they emigrated to foreign lands.[10] In contrast, a growing number of farm families at mid-century derived most of their income from the farm by producing surpluses of several commodities, which could be sold on the growing provincial market for agricultural produce.

There is nothing at all exceptional in this argument, except that it has so rarely been applied to the farmers of the period in New Brunswick. Contemporary commentators confirmed what historians would say of these colonial agriculturalists: that they were backward and slovenly, that they generally made the improvident decision to engage in seasonal woodswork instead of tending to what should have been the proper concerns of stable yeomen. This point is made most explicitly in the work of the British agronomist J.F.W. Johnston in 1850, and has been repeated in almost every discussion of the subject by both contemporary commentators and scholars.[11] Of 20th-century scholars only Vernon Fowke defends the offending farmers. He justifies their

---

10 See, for example, Eric Sager, *Seafaring Labour: The Merchant Marine of Atlantic Canada 1820-1914* (Montreal, 1989), pp. 50-7, 82-96, 137-8; Wynn, *Timber Colony*, pp. 82-6; Allan Brookes, "The Exodus: Migration from the Maritime Provinces to Boston During the Second Half of the Nineteenth Century", Ph.D. thesis, University of New Brunswick, 1978, chs. 4, 5.

11 J.F.W. Johnston, *Report on the Agricultural Capabilities of the Province of New Brunswick* (Fredericton, 1850), especially pp. 127-37. See also Abraham Gesner's assessment in *New Brunswick with Notes for Emigrants* (London, 1847), pp. 237-9.

non-agricultural interests on economic grounds. But he then goes on to argue that the province was not an agricultural colony and suggests that alternative opportunities were much more attractive at the time of Confederation.[12] Neither of these explanations is entirely satisfactory, both because they assume that the whole colonial period was pretty much of a piece during which no significant change occurred, and because they largely ignore the substantial agricultural industry that emerged in many areas of the province. And to the traditional debate must be added consideration of the issue that has been at the centre of recent discussions of New England antebellum agriculture: was the 19th-century farmer a community-minded peasant or an incipient capitalist?[13]

The nature and extent of any agriculture is intimately connected to the fertility of the soil. Fertility is a function both of the soil base and of the climatic conditions found in an area. A northern extension of the New England Appalachian region, New Brunswick contains an astonishing variety of soils interspersed to the point where a single hundred-acre lot may contain several varieties. Despite this distribution, series of adequate to very good agricultural soils often run through many miles of contiguous countryside. In his report on the agricultural capabilities of the province in 1850, James Johnston predicted that 13 million of the province's more than 18 million acres were capable of producing at least one ton of hay per acre each year (and more than a million acres could each produce two or more tons). Modern agronomy has settled for much more modest estimates of the province's soil capacity. The cool moist climate that characterizes the province through spring and autumn limits the potential for plant growth. It is clear that perhaps half the area of the province is unfit for any kind of productive agriculture. Moreover, many of the soils covering the other half have features that make them capable of sustaining only a limited and inefficient agriculture. These limitations and the importance of the timber industry have led most students of the 19th century, with Fowke, to dismiss the province's agricultural output and potential as largely unimportant. This perception is misleading. There are a number of soils

---

12 Vernon C. Fowke, *Canadian Agricultural Policy: The Historical Pattern* (Toronto, 1946), pp. 63-6.

13 See Henretta,"Family and Farms", pp. 3-32; J.T. Lemon and J.A. Henretta, "Comments on James Henretta's Family and Farms", *William and Mary Quarterly*, 3rd Ser., XXXVII (1980), pp. 688-700; Rothenburg, "The Market and Massachusetts Farmers 1750-1850", pp. 283-314; Weiss, "The Market and Massachusetts Farmers 1750-1850: Comment", pp. 475-8, and "Reply", pp. 171-3; and Bernstein, "Marketing, Commerce and Capitalism in Rural Massachusetts", pp. 171-8. For the Province of Canada see R.M. McInnis, "Marketable Surpluses in Ontario Farming, 1860", *Social Science History*, vol. 8, no. 4 (1984), pp. 395-416; McCalla, "The Internal Economy of Upper Canada", pp. 397-416; McInnis, "A Reconsideration", pp. 9-49; and MacCallum, *Unequal Beginnings*.

capable of producing good to excellent yields of certain crops. Sometimes these cover extensive areas; more often they extend like thick fingers of ore stretching along intervales or across country. These soils are suited to the growing of grains, potatoes, hay and fruits, and generally made good pasture.[14]

Under these circumstances 19th-century agriculture was almost always a local affair. The nature of agriculture differed so much even between adjoining parishes that it is impossible to speak of the province as a whole, or even of a significant part of it, as being a common agricultural community. Instead, economic specialization occurred rapidly in most parts of the province, typically within a generation of the initial settlement of the parish. In areas where agricultural resources were weak or where access to significant timber resources could be easily found, most farmers engaged in subsistence agriculture. In almost all cases, however, farm-based income was being supplemented by that received for off-farm operations either in the woods or in nearby villages. In older areas of settlement, in areas with good agricultural resources, and in almost any parish near a town or city, some form of commercial agriculture was an important element in the incomes of many and, depending on the time and circumstances, perhaps most farmers. In the earlier part of the century that "commercial" agriculture was often little more than a form of barter with neighbouring farmers and local storekeepers. That situation was changing by mid-century and while most business was still transacted by account, these increasingly showed cash payments on both sides.

It was the timber trade and the ancillary industries it produced that made possible the economic specialization characteristic of the economy of the province by mid-century. Evidence of large-scale trade among the regions of the province is found in the early part of the century. The Tantramar district of Westmorland County — the oldest area of continuous settlement in the province — was producing meat and draft animals for the great timber-producing region of the Miramichi well before 1810.[15] The major provincial market for agricultural produce was the city of Saint John, the principal timber port and shipbuilding centre of the British Atlantic colonies. The growing demands of that market organized the agriculture of the parishes in the valleys of the Kennebecasis and Petitcodiac rivers, as much as 30 miles away from the city, and large volumes of meat, hay, grain and butter made their way each

---

14 Most of this discussion is informed by the New Brunswick soil survey reports, especially the second report by P.C. Stobbe and H. Aalund, *Soil Survey of the Woodstock Area* (1944), Dominion Department of Agriculture Publication 757, and the fourth report by R.E. Wicklund and K.K. Langmaid, *Soil Survey of South Western New Brunswick* (1953), Department of Agriculture.

15 "Report on Agriculture", New Brunswick, *Journals of the Legislative Assembly* (1884), pp. 23-5.

week to the city markets.[16] By mid-century this hinterland extended into the Tantramar. As other significant commercial centres and mill towns developed in the first half of the century, nodules of commercial agriculture developed around them. Sometimes the great demand for foodstuffs in the timber camps and in the towns raised food prices to the point where profitable agriculture was possible in adjacent areas possessing only marginal agricultural capability.

The principal commercial agriculture was found in the parishes where large surpluses of hay and grain and potatoes permitted the raising of small herds of cattle. In part because of its proximity to the American border, the Carleton County area west of the St. John River provided the best illustration of this phenomenon. By the Confederation era these parishes provided large quantities of grain, meat, butter and hay to lumber camps, shipped grain, meat and butter to Saint John and to the fishing parishes of the Bay of Fundy islands 150 miles away, and exported cattle, sheep and oats for the markets of southern Maine and Boston.

Another factor which contributed to the growth of a market economy in the province was the large proportion of the population that either did not live on farms, lived on farm lots but did not consider themselves to be farmers, or lived on farms that supplied only a small part of their food requirements. While the concept of "farmer" was subject to self-definition, it is probable that, by Confederation, no more than 60 per cent of New Brunswickers lived on a piece of land containing at least ten improved acres.[17] In addition, there were a large number of families living on farm lots of more than one improved acre that possessed neither beasts of burden nor sufficient hay or grain to feed themselves and their livestock. This factor alone would have created an extensive market for food and firewood, most of which could not be met simply by way of local barter.

---

16 The regulated farmers market was provided for in the city charter granted in 1785. By mid-century more than 15 per cent of the population of the colony lived in the Saint John area. Feeding this population required a complex system of marketing consisting of farmers who brought their produce to market, and of shopkeepers who purchased their supplies outside the city. Farmers provided both food and firewood. See John S.. MacKinnon, "The Development of Local Government in the City of Saint John 1785-1895", M.A. thesis, University of New Brunswick, 1968, and T.W. Acheson, *Saint John: The Making of a Colonial Urban Community* (Toronto, 1985).

17 There were 31,202 occupants in 1871 but this number included 2,034 who occupied fewer than 10 acres. The population of the province at the time was 285,594. Given an average of six people to a household, this left about 40 per cent of the population in villages, towns, cities and on small country lots. These figures are drawn fron the first Canadian census of 1871. These estimates are confirmed by contemporary observers. See "Agricultural Report", New Brunswick, *Journals of the House of Assembly* (1867), p. 39.

Estimates of the comparative value of agriculture within the provincial economy are difficult to make since most agricultural produce did not enter into trade. Table One presents a rough statement of commodity output in the province in 1860 using census data, customs reports, weekly market reports and the reports of local agricultural societies. The results reflect the strength of the manufacturing sector — particularly that of the primary and secondary wood-processing industries — which remained comparatively strong when the first Canadian census was taken a decade later. Agricultural output accounted for somewhat less than half the potential market value of commodities produced in the province that year, slightly less than the proportion of the population engaged in agriculture. Perhaps half of the manufactured product — mainly lumber and ships — was exported, and most of the remainder was sold on the provincial market. If any significant portion of farm output entered the provincial market, then it was much more important than has generally been assumed. Table One measures the significance of farm output by assessing the value-added output of the major commodities in the New Brunswick economy. It omits poultry, eggs and hides, important items which were not measured in the census.

The mid-century evidence further suggests that, despite the comments of their critics, New Brunswick agriculturalists were at least as efficient and productive as were farmers in other jurisdictions having similar geographic circumstances. There seems to have been no significant per capita difference in the agricultural output of New Hampshire, Maine, Quebec, New Brunswick and Nova Scotia. As Table Two demonstrates, New Brunswick agricultural output compared favourably with that of all its landward neighbours. Though contemporary commentators complained of the necessity of importing grain, the provincial per capita output of all grains was nearly twice that of Nova Scotia, Maine and New Hampshire, and rivalled that of Quebec. Despite its considerable market value, the production of wheat was small. Soils that could sustain a productive wheat culture were found in several areas of the province, but moisture and growing season combined to make wheat a risky crop and it was grown only as an adjunct to other more reliable crops. Hay, oats, buckwheat, potatoes and roots were the crops of choice and they gave rise to an agrarian emphasis on livestock, dairy, meat and wool. Potatoes, buckwheat and butter were the distinguishing marks of the New Brunswick farmer's diet. And buckwheat, which rarely entered into trade, most distinguished the agriculture. It was found in all the major grain-growing areas of the province and particularly on the most productive farms. Elsewhere in this volume, Béatrice Craig shows that buckwheat constituted almost half of all grain output in the Upper St. John Valley by 1850. In 1870 New Brunswick farms produced enough buckwheat to provide 250 loaves of bread, or the pancake equivalent, for every man, woman and child in the province. Pancake was a dietary staple normally consumed several times a week on farms and in the

Table One
New Brunswick Commodity Ouput, 1860

Farm Output	($) Value of Outputs	—	Value of Inputs	=	Value Added
Hay (b)	3,241,000				
Meat (c)	2,076,000				
Potatoes (b)	1,697,000				
Oats (b)	1,062,000		Hay(bc)	2,884,000	
Butter/cheese (e)	955,000		Oats(bc)	743,000	
Buckwheat (b)	361,000		Seed(b)	400,000	
Wheat (b)	313,000		Wool	190,000	
Other crops (b)	334,000		Flax	29,000	
Wool (b)	190,000		Buckwheat(c)	72,000	
Cloth (af)	711,000		Turnip(c)	63,000	
Firewood (bd)	964,000		Potatoes(c)	170,000	
Total	11,904,000			— 4,551,000	= 7,353,000
Forest Output					
Timber exports (a)	356,000		Hay	226,000	
Other timber (j)	2,050,000		Oats	106,000	
Total	2,406,000			— 332,000	= 2,074,000
Manufactured Output					
Lumber exported (g)	2,920,000				
Other lumber (g)	490,000		Timber(j)	2,050,000	
Shipbuilding (h)	1,674,000		Lumber	486,000	
Other manufacturing (a)	2,619,000		Other(i)	1,000,000	
Total	7,703,000			— 3,536,000	= 4,167,000
Fisheries Output (a)	518,000				
Minerals Output (a)	380,000				

Sources: a) Figures from the 1861 New Brunswick Census, Provincial Archives of New Brunswick [PANB].

b) Calculated from 1860 outputs reported in the 1861 census on the basis of the following average market prices: oats .40/bu., wheat 1.12/bu., barley .73/bu., rye .91/bu., turnips .20/bu., potatoes .42/bu., butter .17/lb., wool .30/lb., buckwheat .40/bu., firewood $4/cord and hay at $10/ton. Timothy actually sold for $12 a ton, but the lower price is used to accommodate poorer quality hay. Inputs were deemed to be costs of hay and oats for horses and oxen, based on Lewis' and McInnis' calculation of 1.8 tons of hay per ox, 1.5 tons of hay and 54 bu. of oats per horse. See F. Lewis and R.M. McInnis, "Agricultural Output and Efficiency in Lower Canada 1857", *Research in Economic History*, vol. 9 (1984), p. 79. Ten per cent of the estimated value of grain and potatoes and one per cent of hay was included as lumber camps, and accounted for much of the 880,000 gallons of molasses that New Brunswickers consumed in 1860.

Discussions of the gross and per capita output of provincial agriculture tell us little of the nature of an industry which by 1870 was found in 29,000 complex local manifestations, gathered into more than a hundred parishes. The role that local circumstance played in the form of agriculture which emerged, and the significance of agriculture in various parts of the province, can be illustrated through an examination of parish butter production in 1860. Average parish output of butter per farm ranged from a high of nearly 400 pounds in parishes as diverse as Southampton, Westmorland and St. Stephen to less than 40 pounds in Caraquet, Saumarez and Hardwick. The largest ouputs were found in parishes with extensive grasslands and grain production, and/or those with significant town markets, and/or those in long-established river valley settlements. The smallest outputs were found in Acadian parishes — 13 of the 21 parishes produced fewer than 100 pounds of butter a year, in parishes where fishing was the dominant activity and in those where frontier timbering still predominated. Thus every North Shore and Miramichi River Valley parish, including those with high grain outputs, kept few cows or cattle and produced only marginal quantities of butter.

In his study of marketable surpluses in the mid-19th-century dairy industry of the northern United States, Fred Bateman demonstrated that farm families

seed input. Hay and oats consumption for horses and oxen were pro-rated over the field crops and firewood on the basis of output. Twenty per cent of the value of oats and 10 per cent of all hay output was assigned to off-farm purposes.

c) Pork outputs were reported in the 1861 census. Beef and mutton outputs were calculated from J.F.W. Johnston's 1850 estimates that one in six cattle were slaughtered each year yielding an average of 500 lbs. of meat. It is assumed that half of all sheep were slaughtered each year and yielded 50 lbs. of meat. All meat was calculated at .065/lb. Input costs included two-thirds of the cost of hay requirements for sheep (.15 ton per animal) and pigs, all of the hay costs for beef animals and 10 per cent of oxen and milk cows averaged at 1.5 tons per animal. In addition 10 per cent of the provincial oat and potato output, 20 per cent of buckwheat (which had to be boiled first) and 50 per cent of turnip output was assigned to these inputs.

d) Firewood was calculated at 10 cords per farm, the average reported in the 1871 census.

e) The only input assigned to milk cows was the cost of hay at 1.8 tons per animal.

f) Cloth inputs include the cost of wool produced in the province, and cotton and flax imports.

g) Lumber exports calculated from the 1861 Customs House Return. "Other lumber" shown here was used in the construction of sailing vessels, furniture and woodenware. Inputs are estimated costs of timber used in making lumber.

h) Inputs include the value of lumber at $9/m., canvas, cordage, stores, nails, sails and copper sheeting.

i) Inputs are complete and, apart from domestically produced lumber and leather, include only imports of copper, hides, sheet tin, cast iron, pig iron, steel bars, skins, leather, hops and iron bars. An obvious lack is the cost of imported cloth for manufacture in the colony.

j) Estimated value of timber subsequently made into lumber products in New Brunswick at $4.50/m. of spruce logs.

Table Two
Agricultural Commodity Output per Capita

	1850	1860	1870		1850	1860	1870
Hay (tons)				Wheat (bu.)			
N.B.	1.2	1.3	1.2	N.B.	1.1	1.1	.7
N.S.	1.0	1.0	1.1	N.S.	1.2	.9	.8
Maine	1.2	1.6	1.7	Maine	.5	.4	.4
Quebec	.8	.6	1.1	Quebec	3.5	2.4	1.7
Potatoes (bu.)				Barley (bu.)			
N.B.	14.4	16.0	23.0	N.B.	.4	.4	.2
N.S.	7.2	11.6	15.2	N.S.	.7	.8	.8
Maine	n.d.	n.d.	n.d.	Maine	.5	1.3	1.1
Quebec	4.5	11.5	15.2	Quebec	3.5	2.4	1.7
Oats (bu.)				Corn (bu.)			
N.B.	7.3	10.5	10.7	N.B.	n.d.	n.d.	.1
N.S.	5.0	6.0	5.7	N.S.	n.d.	n.d.	.1
Maine	3.7	4.8	3.8	Maine	3.0	2.5	1.7
Quebec	10.1	16.5	12.7	Quebec	n.d.	n.d.	.5
Buckwheat (bu.)				Cheese (lbs.)			
N.B.	3.6	3.6	4.3	N.B.	n.d.	n.d.	.5
N.S.	.6	.6	.6	N.S.	n.d.	n.d.	2.3
Maine	.2	.4	.7	Maine	4.2	2.9	1.8
Quebec	.6	1.1	1.4	Quebec	n.d.	n.d.	.4
Butter (lbs.)							
N.B.	15.8	18.2	18.0				
N.S.	13.1	13.7	18.5				
Maine	15.8	18.6	18.6				
Quebec	10.9	14.3	20.4				

Source: New Brunswick censuses of 1851 and 1861, Nova Scotia censuses of 1851 and 1861, Canadian censuses of 1851, 1861 and 1871, *Historical Statistics of the United States*.

in 1860 annually consumed nearly 25 pounds of butter per person.[18] Applying this same standard to New Brunswick at the same period, and assuming the farm household averaged six persons, it appears that the farms in 74 of the 109 non-city parishes of the province produced marketable surpluses of butter in 1860. These surpluses ranged from as little as 10 or 20 pounds on average per farm in parishes such as Canterbury to nearly 250 pounds in the more productive parishes such as Wakefield, where the total surplus of the parish's 368 farms amounted to more than 70,000 pounds of butter — enough to meet the

18 Fred Bateman, "The Marketable Surplus in Northern Dairy Farming: New Evidence by Size of Farm", *Agricultural History*, Vol. 52, No. 3 (1978), p. 354.

needs of more than 4,600 non-farm consumers, according to Bateman's calculations.

Studies of butter or other sorts of commodity output strongly suggest the existence of specialized market-oriented agriculture designed primarily to serve the provincial domestic market in 1860. Generalized parish studies do not allow us to see the range of outputs that occurred among the farms within a single parish, and this range was almost certainly wider than that which existed among the various parishes. This range of outputs at the local level is significant because it adds further support to the arguments that there was a significant domestic market for agricultural products, and that there was a growing body of commercial farmers emerging in the province. Two parishes are studied using the Canadian agricultural census of 1871: St. David's in Charlotte County and Wakefield in Carleton County.

St. David's Parish in southern Charlotte County was one of the older areas of settlement in the province. Most of the parish was covered by a soil identified as Carleton Shaly Loam. Beginning in the southern reaches of Carleton County and extending in an erratic sweep through western York and Charlotte counties, this soil covers 525,000 acres. It is a moderately fertile soil capable of producing good crops of grain and clovers and adequate crops of potatoes and hay. The area's original settlers were Irish-born Americans from New Londonderry, New Hampshire who arrived in 1784. Although nominally Loyalists, they were not favoured by the imperial officials at Fredericton, who suspected their motives, and they did not receive river-front lands on the St. Croix. The interior soils that they received were moderately productive. In the 1830s their offspring were joined by a number of Irish immigrants, mostly Protestant, who were granted lands on a recently opened Crown pine reserve. By 1870 the best lands in the parish had been farmed for four generations. Sustaining soil fertility was becoming increasingly difficult. The population

Table Three
Average Butter Surplus per Farm by Parish, New Brunswick, 1860

Butter Output	No. of Parishes
Deficit (under 100 lbs.)	21
Balance (100-150 lbs.)	14
Surplus (150-200 lbs.)	22
Surplus (200-250 lbs.)	19
Surplus (250-300 lbs.)	25
Surplus (over 300 lbs.)	8

Source: New Brunswick Census of 1861.

grew rapidly until 1840, shortly before the last of the agricultural lands were granted. By 1870 the population was stagnant, but the number of farms continued to slowly grow as families tried to provide farm holdings for more than one of their offspring. The people of St. David's had always been fecund and emigration had been heavy throughout the century.

The Parish of Wakefield in central Carleton County was completely landlocked. While a few Loyalists had come at the conclusion of the Revolution and some families from southern New Brunswick and Maine had settled in the area in the early 19th century, the major settling group were Irish Protestant immigrants who moved into Wakefield — which then comprised much of west-central Carleton County — between 1820 and 1850. Isolation and transportation problems at first hindered development of the parish, but by the 1860s the farmers of the parish were exporting significant quantities of surplus grain, butter, potatoes and livestock from their county. The leaders of the Wakefield farming community were in the forefront of the provincial movement to import purebred stock and seed. The most productive soil in Wakefield was Caribou. Caribou was typical of the better soils in the province, and spread in an erratic fashion over 141,000 acres of land in Carleton and York counties. Caribou produced excellent crops of potatoes and good crops of oats, barley, wheat, buckwheat, hay, clover and fruit.

Despite the presence of other soils in both Wakefield and St. David's, every settlement, and indeed almost every farm, was located on land largely covered by the Caribou and Carleton Shaly Loam. The sometimes erratic pattern of settlement in both parishes often reflected the location of these soils. The earliest surveys largely confined settlement to the best soils — a high tribute to the instincts of both surveyors and settlers, who generally managed to claim every island of potentially productive soil straight from the virgin state.

Table Four
Population of St. David's and Wakefield, 1840-1871

	St. David's	Wakefield
1840	1,609	n.a.
1851	1,681	1,854
1861	1,758	2,060
1871	1,880	2,321

Source: Canada, *Census of 1871*, III.

The per farm output of most commodities in St. David's placed the parish in the bottom half of those parishes in which agriculture was the principal activity. Wakefield, in contrast, ranked among the top dozen in the province. Both parishes were overwhelmingly agricultural. Of the 312 households in St. David's, 260 were headed by farmers and another 39 contained members who identified themselves as farmers. The comparable figures for Wakefield were 415 households, of which 324 were headed by farmers and 44 contained members identifying themselves as farmers. The analysis that follows is based on 299 farm units in St. David's and 368 in Wakefield. The two parishes were prototypes of two forms of rural New Brunswick community. Within Wakefield the distinction between farm and non-farm was clearly drawn. Wakefield non-farm households had little occupational connection with the farming community. The farm families, on the other hand, were entirely devoted to agriculture: virtually all working sons of Wakefield farmers were farmers, a reflection of the opportunities and labour requirements of the extensive farming operations in the parish. By contrast, the distinction between farm and non-farm in St. David's was very subtle. Nearly two-fifths of the gainfully employed population claimed not to be farmers, but the great majority of these — 79 out of 116 — were sons or other relatives of farmers and lived in farmers' households.

Table Five documents the results of this enquiry. It is based on the analysis of the outputs of the 299 households in St. David's Parish and of the 368 households in Wakefield Parish that contained farmers or more than one acre of improved land. The table measures the output of each product at the appropriate percentile of the farms in each parish. Two significant differences are obvious in this table, one reflecting the relatively high outputs that characterized Wakefield farms, and the other demonstrating the long distance between the most productive and the least productive farms in each parish. For while the percentiles shown in the table reflect the output of each commodity across all the farms in the parish, the output of the principal products, notably hay, potatoes, butter, oats and meat, remained quite consistent within each farm. The great majority of farms that had butter output falling above the 75th percentile of all farms in the parish, for example, also fell in the same range of farms in the production of hay, oats, meat and wood. Those that did not were almost always found in the 50th to 75th percentile range. Similarly, farms producing any major commodity below the 25th percentile normally produced all major commodities in that range and never fell above the 50th percentile of farms in the production of any commodity. The pattern is not as clear in the output of minor products such as wheat, barley, turnip, cloth, logs and apples. Most farms did not produce these products, so any farm that did so fell in the upper percentiles. At the same time, with the exception of cloth, these minor products were normally produced in conjunction with significant farming operations and were usually found in farms with major outputs ranging from

Table Five
Range of Agricultural Outputs, St. David's and Wakefield Parishes, 1870

Product		10th	25th	Percentile Median	75th	90th	100th	No.
Improved land	D	15	30	40	60	75	200	299
(acres)	W	4	30	50	80	100	250	368
Horses and oxen	D	0	1	1	2	2	6	
	W	0	1	2	2	3	5	
Hay (tons)	D	3	6	10	15	24	60	
	W	0	5	14	20	35	100	
Oats (bu.)	D	0	10	30	70	100	500	
	W	0	100	300	500	700	3,200	
Potatoes (bu.)	D	20	60	100	200	250	900	
	W	15	100	200	400	600	1,500	
Butter (lbs.)	D	50	100	200	250	400	1,000	
	W	0	100	250	400	600	1,300	
Wool (lbs.)	D	0	11	23	35	48	175	
	W	0	15	35	50	78	120	
Cattle kill (head)	D	0	0	1	2	3	13	
	W	0	1	3	4	6	18	
Swine kill (head)	D	0	1	2	2	2	100	
	W	0	1	2	4	7	49	
Sheep kill (head)	D	0	1	4	7	12	25	
	W	0	1	6	10	17	41	
Firewood (cords)	D	8	10	12	15	20	150	
	W	10	12	15	20	30	200	
Buckwheat (bu.)	D	0	0	8	20	30	85	
	W	0	30	100	150	205	1200	
Wheat (bu.)	D	0	0	0	6	15	33	
	W	0	0	13	35	55	159	
Barley (bu.)	D	0	0	0	0	20	50	
	W	0	0	0	0	0	40	
Turnip (bu.)	D	0	0	0	15	50	650	
	W	0	0	0	0	30	400	
Cloth (yds.)	D	0	0	0	0	30	1,384	
	W	0	0	0	70	140	800	
Apples (bu.)	D	0	0	0	6	20	150	
	W	0	0	0	15	30	400	
Logs (no.)	D	0	0	0	0	0	800	
	W	0	0	0	0	30	40,350	

Source: Canada, 1871 Manuscript Census.

the 50th to the 100th percentile. Large outputs of these minor commodities almost always corresponded to larger outputs of major commodities. This was generally true of cloth as well, although there are several instances where clothmaking was obviously the major activity on the farm.

The distances between the most productive and the least productive farms in both parishes are so obvious and pervasive that, by using the standards of Table Five and the outputs of individual farms, it is possible to identify several different kinds of farms and, by inference, several different kinds of agriculture and probable social statuses. As American agricultural historians have demonstrated, there was a high correlation between improved land and levels of agricultural output. In New Brunswick there was an even closer correlation with hay production — an understandable development in a community where hay often passed as a form of common currency. The farms have been grouped in terms of the degree of autonomy that they could provide for their operators. For the purposes of this discussion, four farm categories have been distinguished, ranging from those able to provide no more than a dwelling and a few basic commodities, to those large diversified agricultural enterprises producing significant surpluses of several products.

About 15 per cent of the farms of St. David's and Wakefield were little more than cottage operations, incapable of sustaining a significant agriculture because they possessed neither horse nor oxen. They are ideally depicted in the 10th percentile column below. These were farms producing only the most basic commodities seen as essential to life in rural New Brunswick: eight cords of firewood (enough to heat a modest dwelling) and 30 to 50 bushels of potatoes. It is interesting to note that the marginal St. David's farm was considerably more productive than its Wakefield counterpart — it usually produced some hay and supported a cow. Even the most rudimentary ploughing or woodhauling would require the assistance of others in the community, although at least one elderly St. David's farmer, the census-taker reported, ploughed the potato field and the truck garden for himself and his wife using their milk cow. The greater age of the St. David's community is reflected in the large quantity of improved land found on even the meanest farm. An old couple or a single young man or woman might eke out a living here. Most occupants, however, earned the greater part of their livelihood off the farm.

The greater diversity of output in St. David's reflects the more limited opportunities for employment off the farm. There is some evidence that the cottage farmers were younger than those on the more productive farms, but for many of middle age this category of farm was probably a way of life. Typical of this group was James Webber, a 36-year-old Irish New Brunswick Anglican, who lived with his wife and three children on 30 acres next to his father's farm in St. David's. Although he had neither horse nor oxen, nor waggons, nor ploughs, Webber kept a cow and a pig, raised 30 bushels of potatoes, and cut three tons of hay and 10 cords of firewood. His wife made 50 pounds of butter over the course of a year. His Wakefield counterpart was James Muldoon, a 40-year-old Irish Catholic who grew 100 bushels of oats, 80 bushels of potatoes and cut 15 cords of firewood. He kept no livestock. He lived with his wife and four daughters on 10 cleared acres. Farmers such as these had to make the most of their living by bartering or selling their labour.

The second category of farm, characteristic of perhaps 20 per cent of the farms in each parish, consisted of fully developed farming operations containing typically 20 to 30 cleared acres, a horse or oxen, a pig, a few cows and sheep, producing sufficient hay to feed the stock in normal conditions, and potatoes and firewood adequate for all farm household needs. There was one critical difference between the farms of this type in the two parishes: the Wakefield farms produced adequate quantities of oats and buckwheat to make them self-sufficient in grain, whereas St. David's farmers had to acquire part of their requirements. Wakefield farms at this level could be largely self-sufficient or could produce sufficient surpluses to allow the farmer to make modest off-farm purchases. Even under optimal conditions the St. David's farmer would require a small off-farm income. These were marginal farms capable of supplying most family needs at a modest level.

Wesley Robinson, 32, reflected the St. David's model of this group. Robinson lived with his wife, daughter and mother on 17 cleared acres, where he kept a horse, two milk cows, several meat cattle, sheep and pigs. To feed this stock he had only nine tons of hay, 12 bushels of oats and 16 of turnips, which meant that he either had to slaughter most of his meat cattle each fall or buy hay to keep them over the winter. He raised enough wheat (six bushels), barley (10 bushels), and buckwheat (two bushels) to produce three or four barrels of flour. The farm produced 150 pounds of butter, 12 bushels of apples and 12 cords of firewood, all of which would have been consumed by the family. His 13 pounds of wool could have been sold or exchanged for woollen cloth. Only the 100 bushels of potatoes and the 1,300 pounds of meat provided any clear surplus of output. Finally, the family's other vegetable needs would have been met from the acre-sized garden that Robinson kept. The farm provided a living, but only just. Robinson's material condition thus reflected that of nearly a third of the farm families in St. David's.

The farms of Robinson's Wakefield counterparts were less numerous — fewer than 15 per cent of all farmers — and their farms were generally less diversified. James Gardner, 64, kept a horse, two milk cows and several sheep and swine on his 20 cleared acres. He was certainly self-sufficient in grains (150 bushels of oats and 100 bushels of buckwheat), meat and dairy produce, had a small surplus of potatoes (100 bushels) and wool (30 pounds), and may even have had a small surplus of hay (13 tons). Six people lived on this farm, and the lack of waggons and ploughs strongly suggest that off-farm work would have been part of their lives.

The third and most common category of farm varied considerably in size —from perhaps 40 to 70 improved acres — and comprised one-third of the farms in Wakefield and considerably more than 40 per cent of those in St. David's. They possessed all of the resources of the farms described above, but in greater quantity. In addition, they also produced some quantities of the minor commodities. Typically, they contained one or two horses, three to six milk cows, beef cattle and a dozen sheep. In St. David's they generally produced enough grain to provide for their own needs and in Wakefield they produced grain surpluses. Farms in both parishes had surpluses of butter, wool and potatoes. Most of these farms were also more diversified than the smaller farms, often raising small quantities of fruit and sometimes manufacturing cloth. A number of them employed fanmills, rakes, mowers and threshers. Any off-farm income — when winter employment was available in St. David's — would have significantly raised the standard of living of these farm families.

A typical St. David's farmer from this group was George Young, 34, of Loyalist origins, a third-generation inhabitant of the parish. He and his wife Annie lived with their daughter and two other children on 90 acres of cleared land. They had two horses, were self-sufficient in hay, wheat, buckwheat, barley, turnip and apples, and raised small surpluses of potatoes and butter. Their butter output was smaller than most farms in this group, largely because they devoted the resources of the farm to meat production. They possessed extensive meadows and produced significant surpluses of meat and wood, slaughtering two cattle, 24 sheep and 11 pigs in 1870.

Young's Wakefield counterpart, William Tracy, produced similar quantities of hay (16 tons), wheat (60 bushels), buckwheat (100 bushels) and apples, but raised neither sheep nor beef cattle on his 50 cleared acres. Instead, he and his wife and one child produced significant surpluses of butter (400 pounds) and oats (400 bushels). The household meat and clothing needs were largely met from the slaughter of four pigs and from the 50 yards of woollen cloth made on the farm.

The most productive farms comprised about 35 per cent of those of Wakefield and 10 per cent of those of St. David's. In the framework of eastern North American agriculture in 1860-70 these were large farms, normally producing large surpluses of several commodities. Sometimes they were highly specialized in output, but more often employed both men and women in generating a variety of products for the market. They normally had at least two adult males working on the farm and usually employed some combination of hay-rakes, mowing machines, threshing machines and fanmills. These were large dairy and meat-producing operations. St. David's farms averaged the same number of cows that Bateman found on the farms of the northern United States of the same period. Wakefield farms averaged 30 per cent more cows than their American counterparts, and those farms with more than 49 cleared acres in particular would have been comparable to the most productive dairy townships in the northern United States.[19]

Farm machinery was extensively employed by this fourth category of farmers. This reflected both their extensive labour needs and their ability to purchase these important instruments. Machines were employed most extensively in Wakefield, where nearly two-thirds of all farmers owned fanmills, and one-third owned hay-rakes. Most of the fourth category of farmers, in addition, had mowers and threshers.[20] The proportion of farmers utilizing at least one of these instruments was of course larger than the proportions given here. One of the larger Wakefield farms, though with an operation similar in kind to that of a third of the farmers in the parish, was owned by Elijah Briggs. Briggs, 64, his wife, three daughters and two sons farmed 150 acres on which they produced 100 tons of hay, 1,100 bushels of oats, 300 bushels of buckwheat, 159 bushels of wheat, 800 bushels of potatoes and 100 bushels of apples. Their 12 milk cows produced 850 pounds of butter. In 1870 they slaughtered eight cattle, 18 sheep and 11 swine, made 200 yards of cloth from their own wool and cut 35 cords of firewood. They had very large surpluses of every commodity that they produced. To assist their extensive undertaking they employed five horses, five waggons, six ploughs, two mowing machines, a hay-rake, a threshing machine and a fanmill.

Briggs' St. David's counterpart, William Leaver, 51, had a smaller but still very extensive operation. Leaver, his wife, daughter and two sons used four horses to farm their 110 cleared acres. They produced large quantities of hay (35 tons), oats (300 bushels), potatoes (400 bushels) and small quantities of wheat, buckwheat and turnip. Like most St. David's farmers, Leaver specialized in livestock. His wife produced more than 1,000 pounds of butter a year, and used some of the very large wool output to make 100 yards of cloth. Leaver slaughtered 22 cattle, 22 sheep and one swine — perhaps 12,000 pounds of meat. In addition the Leavers cut and hauled 800 logs, making them the largest lumber producers in the parish. They too employed a mowing machine and a hay-rake.

Many factors seem to have accounted for the range of agricultural productivity both between the parishes and within each parish. Certainly, variations in soil fertility account for much of the difference between Wakefield and St. David's. Location within each parish was also a factor. Those St. David's farms nearest the prosperous urban areas of St. Stephen were highly productive despite being located on less fertile soils than farms in the interior of the

---

19 For example, Wakefield farms of over 100 cleared acres averaged 8.5 cows compared with the American average of 6.1. See Bateman, "The Marketable Surplus", p. 351.

20 Canada, Manuscript Census of 1871, Charlotte County, St. David's Parish, Schedule 3, and Carleton County, Wakefield Parish, Schedule 3, Provincial Archives of New Brunswick [PANB].

parish. The most productive farms were clustered together, even when soil and location were not the best, suggesting that emulation or relationships among a number of families in the area were important. Commentators of the period noted that the background of the farm families was important: British immigrants made better farmers than did the American Loyalists or the Acadians. The importance of background is confirmed in these parishes to a point, although much of the difference is reflected in strong preferences for certain crops.

If the structure of agriculture found in St. David's and Wakefield was at all representative of the agrarian province at large — apart from the fishing and frontier communities — then it seems clear that there was no single provincial agriculture or simple definition of farmer. The concept of the self-sufficient farmer, as Bettye Hobbs Pruitt demonstrated for Massachusetts, was probably a pervasive ideal, or ideology, rather than a reality. New Brunswick agriculture has traditionally been characterized as subsistence. There was a stratum of farms that fit that description, provided it is understood that subsistence farmers frequently engaged in small-market exchanges with local storekeepers. The second category of farms — about a third of the total — might, for this purpose, be considered "subsistence" in that more than 90 per cent of farm output was consumed by the farm household and the farm could provide most of the basic necessities of life and sustain the household in a "retreat from the world" during short periods of economic adversity. The first category of farmers, by contrast, secured their living off-farm either in woodswork or on the farms of their kinsmen or neighbours. Some had prospects if they were young men such as James Webber, developing their lots or anticipating the probability of an inheritance. Mature proprietors at this level, however, were farmers in name only. All members of this class participated in a market economy, consuming more than they produced and working out the difference through contractual relations with storekeepers, lumbermen and other farmers.

Half of the farms in St. David's and more than two-thirds of those in Wakefield produced surpluses — of a variety of products ranging from hay, oats and potatoes to meat. butter, firewood and cloth. In most cases they were clearly selling or trading more than half the output of one or two products; in many cases they were disposing of more than half their entire output off-farm. What were the motives behind the decision to produce these surpluses? Were they inspired by a desire for personal aggrandizement? Did it "just happen"? Or was it, as Daniel Vickers has recently suggested, inspired by a desire to create "competencies" — basically a respectable livelihood for their children.[21] Vickers argues a position between Henretta and Clark: that antebellum Americans pursued comfortable independence for their families and in the

---

21 Daniel Vickers, "Competency and Competition: Economic Culture in Early America", *William and Mary Quarterly*, 3rd Ser., Vol. XLVI, No. 1 (1990), pp. 1-28.

process of accumulation moved from household production into the world of capitalist relationships. A version of the competencies thesis has provided the principal explanation for the agricultural development of 19th- century Ontario.[22]

This is a persuasive argument and a possible explanation for the development of a market-oriented agriculture in mid-19th-century New Brunswick. It may not, however, have been a necessary precondition for many farmers. By 1870 the province had been the centre of a major, heavily capitalized trans-Atlantic timber trade for nearly 65 years. The critics of the mid-century trade were particularly concerned about its risk-taking nature and the poor values it taught. By mid-century, as well, the dominant element among New Brunswick farmers were not colonial Americans but British immigrants, and Irish Protestants were particularly well-represented among the larger producers. The progressive philosophy of the increasingly important agricultural societies bespoke the influences of the Enlightenment. Even more significant was the operational structure of the larger producers. These were complex organizations requiring a high degree of integrated and disciplined activity, as well as a conscious determination to produce for a market. Moreover, while children ordinarily inherited property on the demise of their parents, there is little evidence that the parents consciously attempted to provide for their children in their lifetime, or that the more productive farmers were more conscientious in this regard than the less prosperous. The notion that prosperity passed through the generations is not supported by close examination. One case study of this will suffice.

The Youngs had been one of the earliest settlers of St. David's. Three Young brothers had settled in the parish by 1797. In 1870 there were nine families containing 38 people in the clan. They owned almost contiguous farms in one of the more fertile areas of the parish. The Youngs came from a common colonial American tradition, and were all Methodists. The head of the clan in 1871 was 82-year-old Jacob Young, a long-time Justice of the Court of Common Pleas and one of the largest landowners in the parish. Significantly, while the clan was more prosperous than the population at large, they were scattered across all the social strata of the parish. Jacob and his unmarried son operated a fourth-level farm. George (60), Charles (52), William (71) and George (34) owned third-level farms. The brothers Levi (35), Amos (27) and Jacob E. (56) had second-level farms. Hill (28), the son of William, lived with his wife, two daughters and two brothers on an undeveloped piece of land beside his father's farm. Various explanations can be offered for the variety of holdings farmed by these second, third and fourth-generation family members, but it is clear that the provision of farm competencies for offspring was not among them. In 1851 the older Jacob, then 62, had three adult sons

---

22 See, for example, David Gagan, *Hopeful Travellers: Families, Land and Social Change in Mid-Victorian Peel County, Canada West* (Toronto, 1981).

and four younger daughters living at home. The two older sons, William, a trader, and Thomas, a sailor, married young women from St. David's (the third never married) and soon left the countryside altogether. Three of the four daughters followed suit. The seven Young families in St. David's in 1851 had 42 children living with them at that time; 12 of these remained in the parish in 1871.[23] Jacob E. Young and his wife Margaret had five children at home in 1851; by 1871 all five had left St. David's, and they had six more living at home. This rapid circulation of youth out of the community suggests that by mid-century parental and structural influences were perhaps not as clearly dominant as they might once have been.

Another factor that raises important questions concerning the motives behind the significant agricultural surpluses produced on certain farms was the use of wage labour by the leading farmers of the parish. Jacob Young normally kept a live-in labourer. In 1851 he employed a 46-year-old American. But the practice was common at least as early as 1813 when James Brown worked through a series of fixed-term contracts over a number of years in return for cash wages.[24] And to this must be added the explicitly market-oriented rhetoric of the agricultural societies from 1820 onward. At the very least, this evidence suggests the existence of a group of rural proprietors committed to trading relationships designed to yield profits and possessing a will to engage in any opportunity that furthered this prospect. The interesting question is why some of these men seem to have been so motivated while others were not.

There was, therefore, a growing capitalist agriculture dominated by men who resemble Winifred Rothenburg's farmers. And there was a class of relatively independent yeomen who had considerable choice about whether to concentrate their efforts on agriculture or pursue more profitable avocations while maintaining a secure livelihood on their own homestead. And there was a class of marginal agriculturalists who counted farming as one part of a team of undertakings and who were probably respectable but always a little poor and somewhat insecure. And there were groups for whom family and community support were critical to their decisions to remain and in their ability to survive. Finally, there were the cottars of the community, distinguishable from the odd hired hand only in that they possessed the gentility that attached itself to the ownership of land. But that did not fool anybody. They may have found themselves there as a result of bad luck, bad health, bad judgement or lack of opportunity. It did not matter. If they could neither improve their condition nor rely on kith or kin to help them, in a short time they became the unspoken underclass of the community, objects of mild contempt, not considered even a very effective reserve supply of labour. For while this rural people were

---

23 New Brunswick, Manuscript Census of 1851, Charlotte County, St. David's Parish, PANB.

24 James Brown Papers, MC 295, MS 2, PANB.

friends and relatives and part of a functioning community of informal relationships, they were also, at bottom, a people who held individuals accountable for the state in which they found themselves.

The intricate sets of relationships that are implied in these communities offered opportunities both for advancement for the individual and for exploitation of others, with the latter sometimes resulting directly from the former. The wide range of prosperity and poverty inferred from the study of individual farms suggests that most farmers were engaged in the market economy, that many farmers had the capacity to accumulate capital from the output of their agricultural activities, and that many less productive farmers would have been forced to participate in a wide-ranging network of exchange in order to survive. It is difficult to conceive of any large group of farmers by 1870 who were not drawn into the market economy as either producers or consumers, and usually as both. At the same time the present study tells little of the mentalities that motivated farmers at any strata of either rural society. It may well be that many farmers — especially from the first two categories of farms — were part of a closely knit community in which bonds of kinship and tradition produced a willingness to remain in a culture of "making do" and "getting by" with the farm, the woodlot and the odd job. Standards of living in most communities of the province had been rising in the 1850s and 1860s, a fact reflected in the sharp increase in provincial imports of fine wheat flour in the period.[25] The growth and diversification of secondary industry and transportation facilities produced a growing demand for food and drew more New Brunswickers into a cash economy.

New Brunswick farmers responded to the opportunities they perceived in the mid-19th century and exploited — sometimes quite efficiently — the natural and human resources they had at their disposal. Their exploitation of their agricultural resources compared favourably with that of their New England neighbours, whose circumstances most closely resembled theirs, and with whom they shared a common environment and often a common heritage.

---

25 A clear indicator of the relative prosperity of the colony is found in the quantity of wheat four imports. These fluctuated wildly from year to year, dependent, in large measure, on the state of the economy. Imports of flour and flour equivalents, assuming five bushels of wheat to a barrel, were 87,000 barrels in 1839, 116,000 barrels in 1845, 144,000 in 1851, and 210,000 in 1861. Only small amounts were exported in each of those representative years. The per capita consumption of fine wheat flour in New Brunswick rose from .56 barrels in 1840 to .83 barrels in 1861. See the New Brunswick Customs House Reports published each year in the *Journals of the House of Assembly.*

The Impact of the General Mining Association on the Nova Scotia Coal Industry, 1826-1850

Marilyn Gerriets

In the age of the industrial revolution abundant deposits of coal frequently attracted industry and led to vigorous economic growth; coal-rich regions of England, Scotland, and Belgium led neighbouring coal-poor regions in early industrialization. Similarly, the development of heavy industry accelerated in the United States only when good quality coal became readily available.[1] The correlation between industrialization and coal deposits is not surprising. Coal is a bulky commodity consumed in the production process, so that the high transportation costs of the early 19th century encouraged industry to move to coal deposits. Heavy industry, requiring heat, was particularly attracted to abundant supplies of coal.[2] It is true that wood and water power were important substitutes for coal, and where they were abundant they supported considerable growth, as in the textile industry of New England. However, in most cases continued industrialization was facilitated by the ability to substitute coal for wood. An early start in the use of coal gave local industry a great advantage later in the 19th-century when wood and water power became inadequate energy sources for industry.[3]

Nova Scotia was unique in the settled regions of early 19th century British North America in possessing extensive coal deposits located near ocean

1   Alfred D. Chandler, "Anthracite Coal and the Beginnings of the Industrial Revolution in the United States", *Business History Review*, 46 (1972), pp. 141-81, Peter Temin, "Steam and Waterpower in the Early Nineteenth Century" *The Journal of Economic History*, 26 (1966), pp. 187-205, and Peter Temin, "A New Look at Hunter's Hypothesis about the Antebellum Iron Industry", *The American Economic Review*, 54 (1964), pp. 344-51.

2   J.H. Dales, "Fuel, Power and Industrial Development in Central Canada", *American Economic Review*, 43 (1953), pp. 181-98.

3   I would like to thank Alasdair Sinclair of Dalhousie University and Satyadev Gupta of St. Thomas University for their helpful comments made on presentation of this paper to the Atlantic Canada Economics Association, 19-21 October, 1989. The suggestions of two editors of *Acadiensis*, Gail Campbell and David Frank and three anonymous reviewers have been most helpful in improving the paper. I would also like to thank Neil MacKinnon of St. Francis Xavier University for his careful reading of the typescript, R. Roger and the staff at the Beaton Institute for their particularly friendly and helpful assistance, and Ahmed Garriba and Marci Baker

transportation. From 1828 to 1858 the right to exploit this resource was controlled by a London-based firm, the General Mining Association, which held an exclusive lease of nearly all the mineral rights of Nova Scotia. The significance of the coal industry to Nova Scotia's economy has been demonstrated both in general histories of 19th century Nova Scotia and in industry studies.[4] In addition, the GMA was examined in 1945 by J.S. Martell who demonstrated the dramatic expansion of the coal industry which occurred after the firm was established, and a number of local studies have documented the scope and the impact of the GMA.[5] More recently, D.A. Muise has given a detailed study of the events resulting in the GMA gaining and subsequently losing exclusive control of Nova Scotian mineral rights.[6] Ian McKay has critically evaluated Association, based on an analysis of the mercantilist biases of the GMA and an interpretation of dependent "enclave" development.[7]

---

for their important contribution as research assistants. This paper was supported by a St. Francis Xavier University, University Council for Research grant.

4   Studies of the early industry by contemporaries are found in Abraham Gesner, *The Industrial Resources of Nova Scotia* (Halifax, 1849); Richard Brown, *Coal Fields and Coal Trade of the Island of Cape Breton* (London, 1871); and C. Campbell, *Nova Scotia in its Historical, Mercantile and Industrial Relations* (Montreal, 1873). Discussions of the early industry are found in C. Ochiltree MacDonald, *The Coal and Iron Industries of Nova Scotia* (Halifax 1909), W.J. Donald, *The Canadian Iron and Steel Industry* (Boston, 1915), W.A. Bell, *The Pictou Coalfield, Nova Scotia* [Geological Survey memoir 225, Department of Mines and Resources of Canada] (Ottawa, 1940).

5   J.S. Martell, "Early Coal Mining in Nova Scotia", *The Dalhousie Review*, 25 (1945), pp. 156-72. A number of other studies have made important contributions. James Cameron, *The Pictonian Colliers* (Halifax, 1974) gives a very thorough overview of the industry in that county. S.J. Hornsby discusses the impact of the coal industry on Cape Breton in his "An Historical Geography of Cape Breton Island in the Nineteenth Century", Ph.D. thesis, University of British Columbia, 1986. The early history is also touched upon in Hugh Millward, "The Development, Decline, and Revival of Mining on the Sydney Coalfield", *The Canadian Geographer*, 28 (1984), pp. 180-5, and his "Mine Locations and the Sequence of Coal Exploitation on the Sydney Coalfield, 1720-1980", in Kenneth Donovan, ed. *Cape Breton at 200: Historical Essays in Honour of the Island's Bicentennial 1785-1985* (Sydney, 1985), pp. 183-202. Hope Harrison, "The Life and Death of the Cumberland Coal Mines", *Nova Scotia Historical Review*, 5 (1985), pp. 73-83 dispenses with little praise in her brief discussion of the Association. David Frank, "Richard Smith" *Dictionary of Canadian Biography*, Vol. IX, (Toronto, 1976), pp. 730-2 provides information on the early days of the GMA.

6   D.A. Muise, "The General Mining Association and Nova Scotia's Coal", *Bulletin of Canadian Studies*, 6/7 (1983), pp. 71-87.

7   "The Crisis of Dependent Development: Class Conflict in the Nova Scotia Coalfields, 1872-1876", *Canadian Journal of Sociology*, 13 (1988), pp. 9-48. The same author in "Industry, Work and Community in the Cumberland Coalfields, 1848-

The lease obtained by the GMA established a property rights regime in which all coal production in the province was controlled by a single firm based in London. This allocation of property rights to metropolitan interests reduced the potential for economic development and diversification in the hinterland of Nova Scotia in several ways: by limiting investment in coal mining, by allowing price discrimination against Nova Scotians and by causing mismanagement of capital, labour and natural resources in mining which increased the cost of coal. The privileges of the GMA did their greatest damage by excluding local entrepreneurs from accumulating capital in a potentially profitable industry and by raising the price and reducing the availability of coal to local consumers.[8] Alternative property rights regimes of granting ownership of subsurface mineral rights with the grant of land or of granting a lease of the right to mine to anyone who applied were likely to have provided a greater stimulus to industrialization.[9] In the later 19th century, concentrated control of coal deposits became common throughout North America, often as vertically integrated firms secured a reliable raw material supply. In the early 19th century that pattern had not yet appeared and is not considered as an alternative to the property rights regime which did prevail.

The argument presented here supports the view that Nova Scotia had a potential for industrialization which it failed to realize because of the negative influence of policies made by distant governments. However, the impact of the government policies was only one factor among the many determining the development of Nova Scotia, and this should not be interpreted as unqualified

1927", Ph.D. thesis, Dalhousie University, 1984, has good reason to note that the early mining activity of the firm was quite limited in Cumberland County.

8   The assumption made here is that a region with a diversified and industrialized economy is likely to generate higher rates of growth in income in the long-run than regions which are narrowly specialized in primary product production. While not everyone agrees that high incomes and satisfactory long-run rates of growth in income are incompatible with an economy dominated by primary product production, the considerable controversies about the role of primary products in economic development cannot be discussed here. An alternative approach to this study would be to attempt to measure changes in per capita income caused by different property rights regimes before the middle of the 19th century. Aside from the practical difficulties of making such a measurement, I believe such a narrow approach misses the more important issues of changes in economic structure which would have influenced the potential for future growth in income in the economy as a whole.

9   These two alternatives would have had very different impacts on Crown revenues from the coal resources. Contemporary objections to the privileges of the GMA were often based on the reduction in the royalties to the Crown from coal believed to have resulted from the grant to the GMA. The impact of the level of royalties on coal on economic development is a separate issue which is not addressed in this paper.

support for the view that a different policy would have ensured the extensive and lasting industrialization of Nova Scotia. The argument that early industrialization benefited from local coal deposits does not imply that all regions with coal were well-suited to industrialization. After all, much of the coal-rich American Appalachia now suffers from economic difficulties similar to those of Cape Breton. While Nova Scotia possessed considerable coal and some iron ore, the lack of abundant good agricultural land might in itself have prevented industrial development by reducing population density and raising the real cost of labour. Geography was kinder to Southern Ontario, for although it lacked the important industrial resources, coal and iron, it did have water power and a cheap supply of food and agricultural raw materials. Access to superior iron and coal was secured through the Great Lakes and allowed continued industrialization when water power became an inadequate energy source. Western Pennsylvania was still more fortunate; it possessed good agricultural land, abundant coal of superior quality, access to iron ore and a location which allowed exports to be floated down the Ohio river at low cost while imports had to be steamed up river or brought overland at greater cost.

Nevertheless by securing exclusive rights to the minerals of the province on far more favourable terms than in previous leases, the firm greatly restricted the early development of the coal industry in the first half of the 19th century and doubtless slowed the growth of local industries dependent on coal. When the GMA gained its exclusive mineral rights in the late 1820s both the demand and supply of coal were limited, but both had the potential to expand greatly. Supplies of British coal to North America were limited by high shipping costs and an export duty of 11 shillings a ton until the early 1830s. The duty was quite substantial, since that coal generally sold for approximately seven shillings six pence at the point of export.[10] British coal became important in some regions, particularly after the export duty was removed in the early 1830s, but only where excess capacity allowed coal to be shipped at a nominal rate. The vast soft coal resources of the United States are west of the Appalachians and were inaccessible to east coast cities in the 1820s. The anthracite of Eastern Pennsylvania suffered from high transportation costs as well as from technical difficulties in its use.[11] Only two regions possessed bituminous coal which could be marketed economically on the eastern seaboard: Nova Scotia and Virginia. The latter area had small deposits of mediocre coal, but their location along the James River made them the major American supplier of bituminous coal until transportation improvements allowed more westerly areas to compete.

---

10   Martell, "Early Coal Mining", p. 168; Roy Church, *The History of the British Coal Industry Volume Three: 1830-1913: Victorian Pre-eminence* (Oxford, 1986), pp. 52, 65.

11   Chandler, "Anthracite Coal", pp. 151-3.

Markets for coal were also limited in the 1820s. In North America wood or charcoal were usually preferred to coal in manufacturing processes using heat, since they lacked the impurities which reduced quality or raised the cost of producing goods with coal. The demand for coal as a source of motive power through the steam engine was restricted by the relative abundance of water power, which made the water wheel an effective competitor with the steam engine until well into the 19th century. For example, although a total of 100 steam engines were in use in the United States by 1832, most of these machines were small and auxiliary to other sources of power.[12] Only four of the 249 American firms outside of the Pittsburgh area with more than $50,000 in capital used steam as their major source of power in 1832.[13]

Coal has advantages over wood that assured its eventual dominance as a fuel; it contains more energy per ton and it is concentrated in one location, not scattered across the landscape, and the potential for a market to develop is demonstrated by the use of coal in regions where it was relatively abundant. While the steam engine was rare elsewhere in 1832, almost all factories in the Pittsburgh area, with its rich bituminous coal deposits, used steam engines.[14] As cities grew and depleted the wood supplies in their hinterlands for domestic heating and for industrial processes requiring heat, the cost of importing firewood rose, and coal could be sold in urban markets. Halifax, Saint John, St. John's, Boston, New York, Philadelphia, Baltimore, Washington and Richmond all had markets for coal by the 1820s.

In spite of the small market for coal, limited alternative supplies meant that investment in Nova Scotia coal had distinct advantages even in the first quarter of the 19th century. That coal was located nearer to ocean shipping than any other North American deposit. Ocean shipping was so much cheaper than inland shipping (even after the construction of canals and early railroads) that the advantage of location near the sea offset the disadvantage of distance from American markets for some time. As a result, Nova Scotia coal had the opportunity to become a significant part of the North American market for bituminous coal and had for a time a degree of potential monopoly power in northeastern Atlantic markets.[15]

Despite these opportunities coal mining was conducted on a very small scale with little investment of capital before the creation of the General Min-

---

12 Temin, "Steam and Waterpower", pp. 196-200.

13 Chandler, "Anthracite Coal", pp. 144-5.

14 *Ibid.*

15 Economic theory indicates that concentrated ownership of mineral rights might have increased provincial income generated by coal production as long as Nova Scotia coal had some monopoly power in the American market. I thank Alasdair Sinclair for this suggestion. Such monopoly power was highly vulnerable to changes in the export market, and in fact was shortlived.

ing Association. Only after the company began operations did output expand significantly. However, the absence of significant investment in coal before 1828 was at least in part the result of a restrictive policy with respect to mineral rights which ultimately allowed that firm to control all the mineral rights of the province. At least some of the expansion which took place after 1828 might have been achieved earlier if a different property rights regime had been in place.

A policy which restricted access to mineral rights was adopted by the Crown in the later 18th century. In grants made earlier in that century, the Crown generally did not reserve mineral rights for itself in colonial land grants, except for silver, gold and precious stones. However, when significant quantities of land were being granted in Nova Scotia towards the end of the 18th century, the Crown widened the range of mineral rights it reserved. Although the specific reserved minerals varied from time to time, rights to coal were excluded in most land grants after 1788 and in all grants made after 1808.[16] Those lands granted in Nova Scotia before coal was reserved seem to have possessed no significant coal deposits.[17]

The Crown's decision to retain control of the mineral resources doubtless stemmed from an increased appreciation of the potential value of a wide variety of minerals to an industrializing region. Controlling deposits of coal and other minerals in Nova Scotia allowed the Crown to collect royalties if the minerals were exploited. However, control of mineral rights could alternatively be used to prevent their exploitation in order to inhibit colonial industrialization. In the late 18th century, British economic policy was still influenced by mercantilist principles; the substantial export duty on British coal helped to ensure that coal would be used at home and would not encourage foreign industrialization.[18] While granting leases to mine coal would have provided revenues, the Crown was not eager to see development of raw materials which could stimulate industries competitive with the mother country.[19]

The Crown had another and more personal motive for retaining control of Nova Scotian mineral rights. In 1788 King George III drafted a lease of the mineral rights (excluding coal) of Nova Scotia in favour of his son, the Duke

---

16   Martell, "Early Coal Mining", p. 157; and *Journals of the House of Assembly of Nova Scotia [JHA]* (1846), Appendix 22; *JHA* (1849), Appendix 21.

17   Iron ore was reserved only after 1808, and deposits near Londonderry and near Nictaux Falls were worked by others in spite of the GMA control over most minerals: Donald, *The Canadian Iron and Steel Industry*, pp. 55, 57-8.

18   The duty also had the attraction of yielding revenues to the government to the extent that it failed to prevent exports, an ambiguity of purpose common in many mercantilist policies.

19   D.A. Muise, "The General Mining Association", pp. 72-6 discusses the internal debate over gaining revenue from the coal resources or avoiding a source of competition.

of York, but the document was not executed, apparently because of the un-promising nature of the resources.[20] In spite of the draft lease in favour of the Duke, some leases of coal were granted to Nova Scotians early in the 19th century, but on far more onerous terms than those subsequently offered the GMA. The lack of free port status for Sydney and Pictou made access to the American market extremely difficult. The terms of these leases greatly hindered significant investment in fixed capital, and the rents and royalties demanded reduced the potential for profitable expansion of output.[21] For ex-ample, George William Bown, Thomas Samuel Bown and William Richard Bown of Sydney received a five-year lease of the coal mines at Sydney in 1822 which specified a maximum price of 23 shillings per Winchester chaldron. The royalty on the coal was seven shillings six pence per Winchester chaldron, 30 per cent of the maximum allowed price. The term of the lease was hardly long enough to justify investment in the steam engines and local railroads the GMA later installed. The Bowns were protected in their lease from other mines which might open in Cape Breton to their disadvantage. A lease of Pictou County coal deposits with the more reasonable term of 21 years was granted in 1818 to Edward Mortimer and George Smith of Pictou and William Liddell, a Nova Scotian resident with business ties to Scot-land.[22] The lease required payment of the arrears of the former tenant of £1,100, a rent of £370 and a royalty of three shillings per Winchester chaldron when production exceeded a few thousand chaldrons.[23]

Not all requests for leases were granted. The important Halifax merchant Samuel Cunard wrote to James Kempt, lieutenant-governor of Nova Scotia, requesting a lease of the Sydney coal mines in 1826 when the Bowns' lease was nearing expiration and the GMA had not yet established a secure claim to

---

20 Martell "Early Coal Mining", pp. 164-5 argues that the granting of leases in the province and the delay in the Duke taking possession of the mineral rights stemmed from the document being mislaid. He discusses the leases granted be-tween 1788 and 1826 in some detail. Muise "The General Mining Association", p. 75 suggests that the document was neglected because the minerals of the province did not seem worth developing.

21 Brown, *Coal Fields and Coal Trade*, pp. 66-67.

22 The firm of Liddell engaged in commerce between Nova Scotia and Glasgow from the late 18th century, and John and William Liddell resided in Nova Scotia. Edward Mortimer maintained business connections with this firm throughout his years in Nova Scotia and formed a partnership with William Liddell and George Smith, another Pictou merchant, in order to export timber and other goods, import general merchandise and build ships. Mortimer died in 1819 and the lease was retained by his partners. Susan Buggey, "Edward Mortimer" *Dictionary of Canadian Biography*, Vol. V (Toronto, 1983), pp. 611-2.

23 Evidence provided by George Smith in *JHA* (1845), Appendix 49. The precise quantity which could be raised before the royalty was due is unclear, although it was no more than 3,500 Winchester chaldrons.

the minerals of Cape Breton. Cunard requested a 30-year lease and stipulated that a free port be named near the mines so that American ships might load there. He offered to pay a yearly rent of £3,000 Halifax currency for the first three years and £6,000 Halifax currency (£5,405 sterling) for the remaining 27 years of the lease, as well as to pay two shillings per chaldron per year on exports exceeding 60,000 chaldrons per year. In light of the request for a free port and with the precedence of heavy rents and royalties in earlier leases, the lieutenant-governor considered his offer too low, and rejected it.[24]

Although leases had been granted to Mortimer, Smith and Liddell and to the Bowns, the draft lease reflecting King George III's intention to grant the mineral resources of the province to his son was still in existence. By 1825 the Duke of York had acquired a significant debt with his jeweller, the firm of Rundell, Bridge, Bigge, and Rundell. The firm, in seeking to collect this debt, perceived an opportunity in the draft lease in favour of the Duke and sent a Cornish mining engineer to determine the value of provincial minerals. To their disappointment, copper was not found, but the value of the coal in the province was duly noted. The Duke's brother, King George IV, authorized the signing and execution of a final lease, with coal added to what was already a considerable list of minerals.[25] The firm's initiatives had resulted in the Duke possessing a 60-year lease of all

> gold and silver, coal, iron, stone, lime-stone, slate-stone, slate-rock, tin, copper, lead and all other mines, minerals and ores and all beds and seams of gold, silver, coal, iron, stone, lime-stone, slate-stone, slate-rock, tin, clay, copper, lead and ores of every kind and description belonging to his Majesty within the Province of Nova Scotia...[26]

Mineral rights previously transferred with land grants did not belong to the King and were not included. The document also included a clause explicitly excluding mines currently leased and in operation. The grant was subject to payment of a nominal rent of one pound sterling and a royalty of one shilling

---

24 Letter from Samuel Cunard to James Kempt, 9 January 1826, MG 1, vol. 3011, no. 20, Public Archives of Nova Scotia [PANS]. The GMA employed Samuel Cunard as their agent, thus compensating him for his lost opportunity in coal mining and transforming a potential enemy into a strong ally. This action could be interpreted as a case of metropolitan interests co-opting a member of the elite in the hinterland.

25 Muise, "The General Mining Association", p. 75 provides an excellent discussion of the granting of the lease to the Duke. The Charter of the GMA of 1846 indicates that the Duke of York struck an agreement with John Bridge, Edmond Waller Rundell, Thomas Bigge, and John Gawler Bridge, directors of the Association, in 1826. However, correspondence of 1828 was written over the names Rundell, Bridge and Rundell. See *JHA* (1847) Appendix 28.

26 "Copy of Lease of Mines of Nova Scotia to the Duke of York, 1826", RG1, vol. 460, no. 9, PANS. Printed in *JHA* (1844), Appendix 58.

sterling per ton of coal raised and sold. The Duke immediately sublet the lease to Rundell, Bridge, Bigge and Bridge in return for 25 per cent of all profits earned from the lease, and they formed the General Mining Association in order to undertake exploitation of this resource.

In spite of the extensive rights granted in the lease to the Duke of York, the document did not transfer the rights to all coal deposits in Nova Scotia, and the GMA quickly acted to secure complete and exclusive control of the resource. Cape Breton was not part of Nova Scotia when King George III had expressed his intention to grant these mineral rights to his son, and therefore its extensive coal deposits were excluded from the lease. In addition, the mines opened under lease to the Bowns and to Liddell and Smith were also excluded from the lease. However, these lessees recognized the impossibility of competing with the new firm and reluctantly surrendered their leases. The General Mining Association then negotiated a new agreement with the Crown which gave it control of all Cape Breton coal as well as the previously opened mines. Under the terms of this new agreement, the GMA agreed to pay a yearly rent of £3,000 sterling and a royalty of two shillings in Halifax currency for each Newcastle chaldron raised and sold, beyond 20,000 such chaldrons per year. In addition, both Pictou and Sydney were granted free port status.[27]

Comparison of the various leases granted in Nova Scotia requires discussion of the different units of measure employed in the leases. The use of a single standardized unit of measure had not become the norm in the early 19th century.[28] The earlier leases used the common unit of measure of coal in both Britain and Nova Scotia, the Winchester chaldron, a measure of volume of 36 bushels. As a measure of volume, the weight of the coal it contained varied with the specific gravity of the coal, the size of the pieces of coal, and the heaping up of the chaldron, so that conversion of chaldrons to tons cannot be exact. GMA agents testifying to a legislative committee stated that a chaldron of Sydney coal weighed about 28 hundred weight and a chaldron of Pictou coal weighed about 31 hundred weight or about 3,136 and 3,472 pounds per chaldron respectively.[29] A conversion factor of 3,136 pounds per Winchester

---

27 "Copy of the Charter of the General Mining Association, 1846", RG1, vol. 460, no. 14, PANS. Printed in *JHA* (1847), Appendix 28. £111 in Halifax currency equalled £100 sterling, at the official exchange rate. The rent in fact paid was £3,333 in Halifax currency.

28 The chaldron was also used in American cities, and generally appears to have been somewhat smaller than the Winchester chaldron. Coal dealers seemed to have been little troubled by lack of standardization in units of measure. Bills of lading for Pictou coal indicate the number of wagon loads put aboard the ship while the same document calculates the freight rate according to a chaldron of 'Custom House Measure'. Phillips Family Papers, Box 10, Essex Institute, Salem, Massachusetts.

29 *JHA* (1854), Appendix 74.

chaldron is implicit in the table of output Richard Brown presents in his study of the Cape Breton coal industry.[30] Contemporary estimates of the weight of the Winchester chaldrons gave results varying from 3,456 to 3,605 pounds.[31] Thirty hundred weight or 3,360 pounds per chaldron seems a reasonable approximation of the weight of a Winchester chaldron of coal on average in Nova Scotia. The Newcastle chaldron specified in the GMA's agreement with the Crown was twice as large as the much more commonly used Winchester chaldron. The Duke's lease specified that the ton on which a royalty of one shilling was to be paid should equal 2640 pounds.[32]

The GMA clearly secured better terms than had been granted to previous lessees. The royalty specified in the Bowns' lease of seven shillings six pence per Winchester chaldron was more than seven times as great as the two shilling royalty for each Newcastle chaldron owed by the GMA. Although the Bowns were not obligated to pay a fixed rent, the royalty owed would equal the rent paid by the GMA when 8,888 Winchester chaldrons had been sold, while the GMA could raise 40,000 Winchester chaldrons for that rent. The lease held by Liddell and Smith was more generous to them, but still required a royalty three times as great as that owed by the GMA. Cunard offered the Crown less in royalties than received from either of the earlier Pictou or Cape Breton leases, but nonetheless he suggested terms far more favourable to the Crown than the GMA lease. The royalty was twice as large as that paid by the Association, and while his terms allowed him to raise 50 per cent more coal free of royalty than the GMA, the rent owed after three years of operations was almost twice as great as that owed by the GMA. Moreover, leasing Cape Breton coal to Cunard would not have prevented the Crown from gaining additional revenues from other coal leases.[33]   When public opinion turned against the GMA, the substantial rent offered by a "principal merchant of Halifax", the large royalties paid by Smith and the Bowns, and the success of the latter operations in spite of these royalties were contrasted with the comparatively small royalties paid by the GMA.[34]

---

30   See his *Coal Fields and Coal Trade*, p. 98-9.

31   McKay, "Industry Work and Community", pp. 870-1. These weights may refer to Pictou coal only.

32   "Copy of Lease of Mines of Nova Scotia to the Duke of York, 1826".

33   He may in fact have offered to pay a rent of £7,000 in subsequent negotiations — at least that sum is referred to as offered by a principal merchant of Halifax in a report of a committee of the House of Assembly in 1845. *JHA* (1845), Appendix 49.

34   *JHA* (1854), Appendix 49. That same report calculates the rents and royalties the Crown would have collected under the earlier leases in 1841, 1842 and 1843 if the former lessees had sold the same amount of coal as the GMA sold in those year. Of course, higher royalties might well have resulted in diminished sales, and the revenues implied by these calculations may have been unattainable.

Not only were the terms of the agreement with the GMA more favourable than those paid by previous lessees, but the son and brother of the kings who controlled the minerals may have secured less favourable terms than those subsequently negotiated by the GMA, although differences in the nature of the leases make the comparison ambiguous. Given the assumption made above about the weight of the chaldron, the royalty specified in the GMA's lease was about 70 per cent of the royalty specified in the Duke's grant; with respect to that payment, the GMA clearly had the less onerous obligation. However, the Duke's lease specified a nominal rent of one pound while the GMA paid an annual rent of £3,000 sterling. The rent was doubtless intended to encourage the GMA to develop the resources as quickly as possible, since the rent had to be paid whether or not any coal was mined.[35] As a result, the revenue owed the Crown by the GMA was more than the obligations specified in the Duke's lease until output reached 23,500 Newcastle chaldrons. The GMA began producing at that level in 1836, when output shifted from an average of less than 20,000 to more than 35,000 Newcastle chaldrons a year. From that time, the GMA's obligations were less than those of the Duke for the same quantity of coal. For example, in 1850 the GMA paid £6,577 rent and royalty for 54,267 Newcastle chaldrons of coal mined. The Duke would have paid £7,666 for the same quantity, or 17 per cent more.[36] Receiving money now is always more advantageous than receiving money later, and the early large rent compensated at least to some extent for the lower royalty and consequently lower total revenues received later. Perhaps the larger rent paid from the beginning of operations was sufficient compensation for the lower royalty, even though clearly more onerous terms would seem to have been reasonable since the GMA lease added all the mineral rights of Cape Breton to the Duke's grant, and, more importantly, eliminated the possibility of regional competition.

The GMA secured an additional benefit to itself at the expense of the Duke when it negotiated the right to work previously opened mines. The Duke had been granted only the unopened mines in Nova Scotia, but the GMA concentrated its production at the previously opened mines, so that the firm was not in fact working the minerals specified in the Duke's grant which they had subleased. As a result, the GMA felt no obligation to pay the share of profits to the Duke of York or his heirs as specified in their sublease.[37] Of course, holding the sublease of the Duke's grant of unopened mines still explicitly prohibited competition from any new mines.

35 See Muise, "The General Mining Association", p. 76 where he refers to concern in the colony that the firm would not develop the resources.

36 *JHA* (1854), Appendix 38; *JHA* (1845); Appendix 49.

37 "Copy of the Charter of the General Mining Association, 1846". The Duke died soon after the GMA was founded and, after legal battles, his heirs did eventually gain some recognition of their rights.

Although the revenues from the mines were paid to the province, the agreement with the GMA was negotiated in London with the Secretary of State for the Colonies, William Huskisson, and the lieutenant-governor of the province of Nova Scotia played little role in the determination of the rents and royalties. The rejection of Samuel Cunard's offer by James Kempt indicates that he certainly expected the mines to yield a greater revenue than that specified in the agreement with the GMA. Huskisson might not have realized the significance of the unit of measure employed and have inadvertently agreed to too low a royalty.[38] Then again, he might have been fully aware of the implications of the agreement and not have considered the terms of the new lease unduly advantageous. In either case, the governor of the province does not seem to have been correctly apprised of the terms of the agreement, due to confusion over the use of the Newcastle chaldron. In late 1829 the new Lieutenant-Governor, Peregrine Maitland, wrote George Murray, then Secretary of State for the colonies, inquiring about the level of the royalty and was told that the rate was two shillings per chaldron, without mention of the type of chaldron. Since the Winchester chaldron was commonly used in both the British and Nova Scotian coal industry, Maitland would naturally assume that the smaller measure was the unit implied. Confusion arose in Nova Scotia about the royalty after output exceeded 20,000 Winchester chaldrons and the GMA indicated that output still had to double before any royalty was due and that the royalty was two shillings per Newcastle, not Winchester, chaldron.[39]

There is no evidence that the GMA used any deceit in having the rent and royalty calculated according to Newcastle chaldrons. In the correspondence of 1828 with William Huskisson and Undersecretary of State for the Colonies R.W. Hay, in which the GMA requested an agreement with the Crown permitting it to work the Cape Breton coal deposits, the firm explicitly referred to the Newcastle chaldron as the unit of measure to be employed.[40] However, the use the GMA made of the two units of measure did nothing to dispel confusion regarding them, since the Winchester chaldron was used in all its business, except in the coal returns prepared for the purpose of calculating the royalty owed. In preparing the coal returns, the number of Winchester chaldrons was halved to give the appropriate measure in Newcastle chaldrons.[41] Nonetheless,

---

38   In 1845 a committee of the House of Assembly of Nova Scotia believed the determination of the unit of measure to have been the result of an error. *JHA* (1845), Appendix 49.

39   *JHA* (1844), Appendix 58 prints the relevant correspondence. Martell, "Early Coal Mining", pp. 166-7 and Muise, "The General Mining Association", pp. 77-8 discuss the confusion over the calculation of the royalty owed.

40   *JHA* (1844), Appendix 58.

41   The records of the GMA's operations at Sydney have been extensively, though not completely, preserved in MG 1419 at the Beaton Institute, University College of

this use of the units of measure was neither illegal nor unethical, and indeed was quite natural, since the Winchester chaldron was commonly used in the coal trade and at the same time the GMA's agreement explicitly specified that the royalty was to be calculated according to the Newcastle chaldron. The GMA were certainly skilled negotiators, and could be justifiably accused of sharp dealing if Huskisson did not understand the significance of a Newcastle chaldron.

By 1828 the GMA had a 60-year lease covering all the coal in Nova Scotia and requiring relatively low rents and royalties. It invested large sums in coal mines, developing them according to the principles of British mining. GMA investments included imported steam engines, railroads and an iron foundry, and the Association supported the immigration of skilled workers and provided housing for them.[42] Output expanded, exports to American markets grew, and in a decade Nova Scotia production surpassed Virginia. (See Figures 1 and 2). By granting a long term lease with rents and royalties which encouraged investment in the industry the crown had significantly improved its earlier policy with respect to the coal resources of Nova Scotia.

Nonetheless, excluding local entrepreneurs so that one firm based in the metropolis could control almost all the mineral resources of the province was far from the best policy attainable, and the restrictive leases of the 1820s had more than likely already held growth below its potential. Wider access to coal deposits on more favourable terms would very likely have promoted more extensive development of the industry than occurred. In the 1820s coal prices were high relative to other goods and to their values later in the century, but in the 1830s, as Pennsylvanian anthracite entered the market, prices fell sharply.[43] Capital invested in coal mines in the 1820s would very likely have provided a greater return than capital invested later. In spite of the onerous

---

Cape Breton, Sydney, Nova Scotia. Shipping lists, MG 1419 D5, demonstrate the procedure used to calculate the royalty. Ian McKay discusses difficulties presented by the units of measure in the appendix of his thesis, "Industry, Work and Community", pp. 869-71. In general, when the chaldron of coal is mentioned without specification of the type of measure, the Winchester chaldron should be assumed; it would be most unusual for any other unit to be used in the ordinary business of the coal industry. In the *Journals of the House of Assembly of Nova Scotia* more caution must be exercised since quantities were reported to them in Newcastle chaldrons. Since the original coal returns are generally printed for the year reported, and are always in Newcastle chaldrons, summary figures given later can be compared with these when in doubt about the unit of measure.

42 Martell, "Early Coal Mining", pp. 167-8.

43 George F. Warren and Frank A. Pearson, *Wholesale Prices in the United States for 135 Years, 1720 to 1932,* Cornell University Agricultural Experiment Station, Memoir 142 (Ithaca, 1932). The price indices for "all goods" and for fuel and light permit this comparison.

Figure One
Total Nova Scotia Coal Output,
1827 - 1850

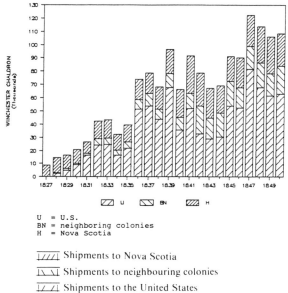

U = U.S.
BN = neighboring colonies
H = Nova Scotia

|////| Shipments to Nova Scotia
|\\\| Shipments to neighbouring colonies
|/ /| Shipments to the United States

SOURCE: *JHA* (1854), Appendix 38.

Figure Two
Ratio of Nova Scotia Coal Output to Virginia Output,
1827 - 1850

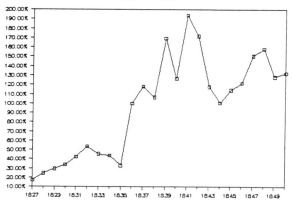

SOURCE: *JHA* (1854), Appendix 38; Howard N. Eavenson, *The First Century and a Quarter of American Coal Industry* (Pittsburgh, 1942), p. 443.

terms of their leases, both the Bowns and Smith and Liddell found their operations in the 1820s profitable and left the industry with great reluctance.[44] If, during the 1820s, they and other local entrepreneurs had obtained access to coal deposits at rents and royalties as low as those paid by the GMA and for a term as long, they might have been quite capable of generating a substantial expansion in the industry during that decade. Thus while the rapid and dramatic growth of the industry immediately after the entry of the GMA is impressive, the likely impact of British policy with respect to Nova Scotia's coal resources was to diminish rather than encourage growth in the early 19th century.

By the time the GMA was given a lease which encouraged substantial investment in coal mines, Nova Scotia's unique place in the North American market was being undermined. Between 1825 and 1832 improvements in transportation and in techniques of burning anthracite led to the rapid expansion of the market for this superior coal.[45] Both Nova Scotia and Virginia output of bituminous coal were overwhelmed by the huge increases in output of Pennsylvanian anthracite in the 1830s and 1840s. In 1825 Virginia produced 66,720 net tons of bituminous coal, and Nova Scotia produced about 5,490 Newcastle chaldrons or 18,446 net tons while Pennsylvania produced 43,119 tons of anthracite. In 1845 Pennsylvanian production had risen to 2,625,757 net tons while Nova Scotian production had reached 150,921 tons and Virginian production along the James River was 134,603 tons.[46] However, a place remained for bituminous coal in American markets because it was burned with anthracite to help regulate the fire and was used for the production of gas. The cost of transporting western deposits of bituminous coal to tidewater markets fell more slowly than the cost of transporting anthracite. The first attempts at connections by canal in the 1830s failed to reduce transportation costs substantially; the natural advantages of transport by water tended to disappear when goods had to be carried uphill across the Appalachians.[47] However, by the early 1850s railroads had been built across the Appalachians and bituminous coal could be brought to tidewater by rail.[48] As a result, any monopoly power Nova Scotian coal might have had in American markets was gone, except to some extent in New England.

---

44 *JHA* (1845), Appendix 49.

45 Chandler, "Anthracite Coal", pp. 155-6.

46 Howard N. Eavenson, *The First Century and a Quarter of American Coal Industry* (Pittsburgh, 1942), pp. 443, 498; *JHA* (1845), Appendix 49; *JHA* (1854), Appendix 38. All figures are net tons.

47 Chandler, "Anthracite Coal", p. 150.

48 Eavenson, *The First Century and a Quarter of American Coal Industry*, pp. 406-11.

Although Nova Scotia's potential share of the American coal market was beginning its inevitable decline by 1828, the GMA had a virtual monopoly in Nova Scotia. The only competition of significance in local markets was imports of British coal in returning ships. The differences in the amount of competition in the two markets would have allowed the GMA to increase its profits through price discrimination, that is by charging more for coal in Nova Scotia than in the United States, even after making allowance for transportation costs. A relatively high price could be charged in Nova Scotia because the limited competition meant that only a small reduction in sales would result. However, a high price which was profitable in Nova Scotia could not be applied in the American market where competition from other suppliers was intense. Indeed because Nova Scotian coal was closed out of more distant American markets by rising freight costs, a policy of spatial price discrimination, charging a higher price in local markets where freight costs add little to the cost to the purchaser and reducing the price of coal in more distant markets where increasing freight costs reduce the product's competitiveness, could also potentially increase sales and profits.[49]

Implementing price discrimination required the separation of markets, so that coal sold cheaply in one market could not be reshipped to the market where it would be sold at a higher price. However, the GMA usually sold its coal at the loading wharves in Sydney and Pictou and had no control over the final destination of the coal. Ships' masters not infrequently bought coal on their own account, making payment in cash, in order to sell the coal on speculation when the ship reached its destination. If a lower price had been charged at the loading wharf for coal destined for the United States than for coal destined for more local markets, the ships' masters could easily have profited by claiming the coal would be delivered in the United States while, in fact, delivering it to local markets. The GMA did occasionally ship coal to agents in American cities to be sold there on its own account. If all coal had been sold in that way, price discrimination would have been much easier, but the GMA would have had to bear the risk of shipping and marketing the coal itself. Selling at the wharf distributed the risk among the customers and ships' masters.

The evidence surviving in the GMA shipping lists gives only limited evidence of price discrimination at the point of sale. The ledgers giving the coal shipments of the GMA in Sydney indicate that the firm normally charged all purchasers the same administered price for coal regardless of its destination. Samuel Cunard was an exception to the uniformity of price at point of sale and received a discount at the loading wharf. This privilege resulted from his special relationship with the GMA, since the firm had hired him as an agent responsible for marketing the coal and managing accounts. There is no

---

49   M.L. Greenhut, and H. Ohta, *Theory of Spatial Price Discrimination* (Durham, 1975), *passim*.

reason to assume that he passed the discount on to his own customers in Halifax.[50]

While price discrimination did not occur at the wharf, there is substantial evidence that the GMA discriminated through discounts on accounts. Customers who regularly purchased large quantities of coal normally gave a ship's master an order to buy coal on their behalf in Nova Scotia. The cost of the coal was charged to the customer's account with the Halifax Agency, managed by Samuel Cunard. Terms for credit and acceptance of bills of exchange, the usual means of payment, were determined on an individual basis, and as a result provided the opportunity for price discrimination. In late 1839 Samuel Cunard noted that at the end of the shipping season the accounts of customers purchasing more than 3,000 Winchester chaldrons were credited with a discount on their purchases of two shillings per chaldron from the 18 shilling price. Others, who took less, received a one shilling discount.[51] Cunard made no mention of when the practice began, or whether the discount was applied only to coal delivered to American markets. However, as the Select Committee on the subject of the coal mines pointed out in 1845 "this arrangement [of offering volume discounts] operates prejudicially upon the coasters supplying the Halifax and other markets, because as they have been in the habit of acting independently, and purchasing coals by the single cargo, they are compelled to pay the higher or retail price".[52] The members of this committee were quite concerned about differences between the domestic and American price of coal. Although they believed that discounts were not dependent on the destination of the coal, they were aware of price differences in local and American markets. They reported that "single cargoes of coal have often been bought from the Agents in the United States, at a less price than they could have been bought for at the pits".[53]

Evidence of price discrimination clearly favouring Americans appears in a letter Cunard wrote to Colonial Secretary Earl Grey in 1848 stating that the GMA offered lower prices to Americans. Complaining of the small profits of the GMA, Samuel Cunard stated: "from these rates [for coal] we have also to make deductions to Manufacturers, resident out of the Province, to induce

---

50 See Sydney Mines Shipping lists, 1747-55, MG 1419 D5 I-J, Beaton Institute, for documentation of the reduced price at which coal was sold to Cunard. A letter from Richard Brown to his son Richard H. Brown dated 11 December 1877 complains that the discount is still received by the agent who sells no more cheaply than others and 'pockets the difference': "Brown Family Papers", MG1, vol. 151, no. 301, PANS.

51 Samuel Cunard to Henry Poole, 25 September 1839, MG 1419, D9B, Beaton Institute.

52 *JHA* (1845), Appendix 49.

53 *JHA* (1845), Appendix 49.

them to use the Coal...". He also complained of the American duty on coal, although in 1846 that had been reduced from the very high rates of 1842 to 30 per cent *ad valorem* or five shillings six pence to six shillings per chaldron. Cunard implied that the firm also absorbed at least a part of that sum.[54]

The practice of offering discounts was continued on a discriminatory basis as late as 1854. In response to questions from a committee of the legislative assembly, agents for the GMA stated that discounts were offered to anyone buying more than 1000 chaldrons of coal and exporting them to the United States. They claimed the largest discount ever made was one shilling nine pence in 1853.[55] This claim is contradicted by the letter mentioned above, and it is quite unlikely that in the improved conditions of the 1850s larger discounts were offered than in the depths of the earlier depression. None of this evidence indicates when the offering of discounts exclusively to Americans began, other than sometime before the late 1840s.

After the late 1830s the temptation to maintain the price of coal to Nova Scotians and offer discounts to Americans would have become very great indeed. At that time economic circumstances became quite difficult, as an inflationary boom ended and the American economy entered a severe recession. The price of coal fell and American demand contracted sharply, reducing coal exports to the United States[56] (see Figure 3). In addition, in 1842 the Americans greatly increased the duty on coal to 13 to 14 shillings for the Winchester chaldron that sold for 18 shillings at the loading wharf. In competitive markets the increase in the American tariff would be expected to sharply increase the difference between the American and the Nova Scotia prices.

Prices charged by the GMA in Nova Scotia failed to reflect either the decrease in American prices from 1840 to 1845 or the increase in the American tariff (See Figures 4 and 5). The price of coal at the loading wharf in Sydney remained unchanged while the difference between the price of coal in Halifax and in New York fell sharply after 1840. Indeed from 1839 into the 1850s the loading wharf price remained unchanged in spite of falling American prices and the firm's commitment to selling coal in that market. This behaviour of prices creates the strong suspicion that the loading wharf price was intended for the Nova Scotia market and that adjustments were made in other ways in response to changes in the American market. The assumption that discriminatory discounts were offered in the depths of the depression of the early 1840s is not unreasonable. The price data do not contradict such a conclusion. There is evidence that in 1839 volume discounts were offered which may well have favoured American customers. In 1845

---

54   JHA (1849), Appendix 21.

55   JHA (1854), Appendix 74.

56   George F. Warren and Frank A. Pearson, *Prices* (New York, 1933), p. 25.

Figure Three

Nova Scotia Exports to the United States,
1827 - 1850

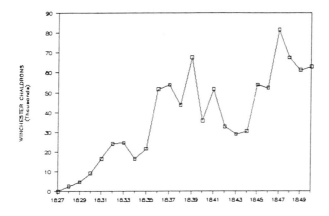

SOURCE: *JHA* (1854), Appendix 38.

members of the legislature believed Nova Scotia coal was available at lower prices in the United States than in Nova Scotia. Finally Cunard admitted in 1848 that discounts were made which explicitly favoured coal to be delivered to the United States, and it seems unlikely that such a policy would have been implemented only after market conditions had improved.

Free entry into the industry would not have completely eliminated price discrimination, but would have reduced it to minor significance.[57] The circumstances of perfect competition, which would tend to establish a price of coal within the province equal to the price in the main American markets, less transportation costs and duties, could occur only when there were no locational differences between firms. Whenever the realities of distance are allowed for, each firm has some degree of monopoly power and can raise the price in a region to that charged by the nearest competitor, plus transportation costs from that competitor. However, free entry would have resulted in near competitors being only a few hundred miles distant from each other and would have greatly reduced the degree of control over price. The more firms operating in Nova Scotia, the more we might expect the domestic price to have fallen with the American price. Lower coal prices in turn could have enabled domestic manufactures to compete more easily in both domestic and export markets.

---

57 Greenhut and Ohta, *Spatial Price Discrimination, passim.*

Figure Four
Coal Prices
(New York, Halifax, Sydney)

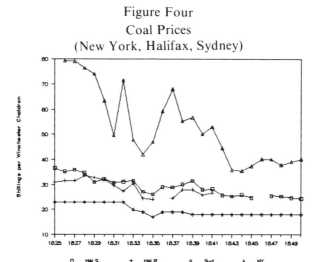

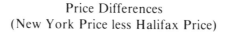

HALS: Price of Sydney coal in Halifax
HALP: Price of Pictou coal in Halifax
SYD: Price of Sydney coal at the loading wharf
NY: Price of anthracite in New York

Prices are converted from shillings to dollars at the standard exchange rate of 5 shillings per dollar.

SOURCES: *The Nova Scotian* (Halifax), 1824-1845; *The British Colonial* (Halifax) 1845-1850; MG 1419, Beaton Institute, Arthur H. Cole, *Working Papers Price Committee*, GA 13.11, Baker Library, Harvard University provided information on coal prices. I also thank Julian Gwyn for generously sharing his own price data with me.

Figure Five

Price Differences
(New York Price less Halifax Price)

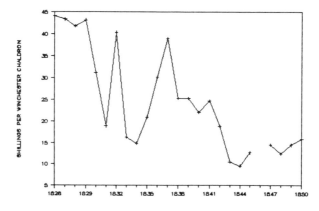

Even if there had been no discrimination on the basis of distance, the firm's ability to block entry into the industry increased the price of coal by raising transportation costs to many Nova Scotians. Coal is not so much produced as moved about, first underground and then above it. Transport of coal overland was far more expensive than sea transport. Although the GMA could for a time supply coal competitively many hundreds of miles down the east coast of the United States, the price of moving coal 50 miles overland within Nova Scotia was prohibitive.

Reservation of mineral rights by the Crown and their subsequent lease to the Duke of York made even the use of coal outcrops in property owners' backyards illegal. While casual use of coal outcrops could hardly have been controlled, the GMA vigorously enforced its property rights and prosecuted anyone who attempted to mine illegally on a significant scale. Few would risk investing even moderate amounts of capital when their business could easily be closed down. John Archibald, writing from Salmon River, Colchester County in 1845 describes the situation well:

> for a number of years I have had reason to believe that there was a good coal field on my property, but I never did anything towards opening the mine till the Winter of 1843... I then sunk a shaft about 30 feet deep, which pierced a seam of coal 2 1/2 feet thick, 30 feet from the surface... At the time I sunk this shaft I thought the Mines contained within this land had not been reserved by the Crown at the time of granting the land, but in the Spring of 1843 the Hon. S. Cunard in passing left word at my house for me to take no further steps or he would prosecute me for so doing...
>
> Farmers must send to the Albion Mines for coal, but as the cost of them when they reach Truro is greater than 40s per chaldron, this operates as a prohibition upon their use, the same chaldron bought at the same price at Salmon River would not cost the consumer over 22s 6d, the result therefore of opening the Mine would be a large increase in the consumption of coal by persons that now do not use it at all. It would also supersede the use of charcoal by blacksmiths, and by supplying at a moderate price what now costs much to them, would enable this class of tradesmen to supply to farmers their blacksmith's work at a cheaper rate, a boon which would be immediately felt now that the low price of Farming produce makes the payment of tradesmen's bills a serious bar to the improvement of the country.[58]

A seam of coal only two and one-half feet thick was not rich by Nova Scotia standards where seams commonly ranged from eight to twelve feet and reached 27 feet at the Foord seam in Pictou County.[59] Thirty feet is not deep

---

58 *JHA* (1845), Appendix 49.

59 Bell, *Pictou Coalfields*, p. 95.

for a mine either, and Archibald himself confessed that the coal was not of the best quality. His mine was unlikely to have become a great enterprise. Yet opening the mine cost him only £100, and so modest an investment might well have earned him a profit, allowing him to accumulate capital for additional investment in this or other enterprises, while also supplying the local population with a cheaper source of fuel than was otherwise available.

Technically, the grant to the Duke allowed for the opening of mines in competition with the GMA under certain circumstances. If the GMA were informed of a coal deposit and given a year in which to decide to open the mine, but declined to do so, the government was allowed to lease the deposit to a rival. In fact, attempts to open mines were unsuccessful. The province was not required to grant any additional leases and as long as the House of Assembly was favourably disposed towards the GMA, it refused to allow rivals to enter the industry, even though coal reserves were left idle. In 1839 Alexander Fraser of New Glasgow petitioned to open a coal mine in his own land outside New Glasgow to serve that market at a small saving to local consumers. His petition was denied on the grounds that the gains to himself and the savings to the people of New Glasgow were too small to justify intruding on the monopoly of a company which had invested so heavily in the region.[60]

In the 1840s the GMA had lost favour with the Assembly, and petitioners were treated differently. In 1844 Abraham Gesner, who developed a process to manufacture kerosene from coal oil, also petitioned to open a mine at Joggins. He noted the increasing shortage of firewood in Cumberland County and argued that:

> The opening of the coal mines of the County of Cumberland alone, would not only supply the lack of fuel above mentioned, but would also immediately open an extensive export trade with the United States and yearly increase the public revenue. ... However creditably and extensively mining may have been carried on in one part of the Province, it does not seem to your memorialist that it should remain inactive in another.[61]

In this case, the House argued that the mine should be opened, but the GMA exercised its prerogative and worked the coal itself through short-term subleases issued to a local resident. Output at that mine remained quite low and GMA investment was minimal. Only after the ending of the GMA control of mineral rights in 1858 did a large number of new mines open in the province.[62]

---

60   *JHA* (1839), Appendix 50.

61   *JHA* (1845), Appendix 50.

62   *JHA* (1854), Appendix 38. See McKay "Industry, Work and Community", pp. 16-21 for a discussion of the limited development of coal mines by the GMA in Colchester County. MacDonald, *Industries of Nova Scotia*, pp. 21-7, and the report of the mines inspector, *JHA* (1863), Appendix 15, show the development of new mines.

If independent entrepreneurs expected a profit from developing these deposits, we might expect the GMA also to have found their exploitation profitable. By subleasing to local entrepreneurs the firm could have garnered a portion of the profits to itself with little risk and little increase in administrative complexity and costs. The neglect of deposits which interested others needs more explanation. Possibly the GMA simply decided that the scale of the operations at these local deposits were too small to warrant attention. What was a significant opportunity to a private person may have been of trivial concern to an export-oriented international corporation. In addition, it is likely that the net gain anticipated by the GMA was less than that anticipated by local entrepreneurs. The firm had considerable excess capacity in Cape Breton and at the Albion mine in Pictou County. Since that capital was already sunk and could not easily be liquidated, its real opportunity cost was very low. As a result, the cost of raising another chaldron of coal at the existing mines was far less than the cost of raising coal at a new mine, where the required investment in new capital had a high opportunity cost. The GMA may also have anticipated that losses in revenue from small reductions in sales of coal at established mines could easily offset the net gains, even if larger quantities were sold at new mines.

For example, the mine proposed by Fraser to serve New Glasgow would have had a direct impact on sales from the GMA's Albion mine. While that new mine might have earned a normal profit, the losses from reduced sales at the Albion mine could have exceeded the gains from the new operation. If so, a profitable opportunity for Fraser would not have been profitable for the GMA. The GMA did ship some coal into the Bay of Fundy, although competition from British coal brought to Saint John as ballast in timber ships was great, and any small gains from its sublease at Joggins may have been offset by reduced sales from Sydney or Pictou. Even at Salmon River a mine might have served enough customers previously purchasing coal from the existing mines to make a new mine unattractive to the GMA, particularly if coal could be shipped along that river.

The GMA's privileges thus prevented small deposits of coal from being developed in places where they could provide cheap supplies of fuel to local customers. In addition, local entrepreneurs found themselves excluded from the coal mining industry. Many of them had specific knowledge of the local resources, economic conditions or potential for local use of coal, but they were denied the opportunity to employ their capital profitably and the industry was denied their capital and management skills. Gesner and other colonial entrepreneurs may have effectively employed their resources in other industries, but restricting avenues for entrepreneurship hardly seems a commendable strategy for economic development.

While the privileges granted to the GMA may have increased the difficulty of economic development in Nova Scotia, there is also evidence that the GMA was inefficient in managing and exploiting the resource. If the GMA chose combinations of natural resources, labour and capital to produce a ton of mined coal which were poorly suited to the local economic environment, the result would have been an increase in the cost of mining coal. Either the price of coal would have increased or the profitability of coal mining would have fallen. While the loss of profits which would have been paid to British shareholders causes little concern here, both an increase in the price of coal and a reluctance to undertake additional investment created by poor returns on earlier endeavours was not beneficial to the province. In general, inefficient use of resources seems a poor way to stimulate development, but this may well be the result when outside interests unfamiliar with the local environment control investment.

In assessing the mining practices of the GMA, it is useful to examine the issue of resource use and appropriate technology in the 19th century. Britain had been a world leader in developing new technology since the 17th century, but their innovations were designed to suit that nation's endowment of resources. Compared to North America, natural resources were scarce in Britain relative to the supplies of capital and labour, especially skilled labour. As a result the "best" technology of the early to mid-19th century used capital and labour relatively freely in order to economize on natural resources. In addition, in Britain generous use of capital to enhance the quality of railroads, canals and other construction projects was justified because reduced maintenance costs offset the relatively low interest payments on the increased capital invested. North Americans were frequently castigated for failing to use the "best" British technology. Indeed North Americans often ignored advanced British techniques, because they were ill-suited to a world where natural resources were abundant and capital and labour, especially skilled labour, were scarce. Railroads or canals were cheaply built, because a reduction in maintenance costs could not compensate for the high interest charges on the increased capital expenditures required to generate the savings. The techniques which were superior in the North American environment economized on the scarce factors of production, capital and labour, and made generous use of abundant natural resources.[63]

Faith in the universal superiority of the most advanced technology is difficult to shake; developed nations today can still be surprised when their highly capital-intensive production methods not only fail to improve Third

---

63 See W.T. Easterbrook and Hugh G.J. Aitken, *Canadian Economic History* (Toronto, 1956), pp. 262, 278-9, 411-13 for discussions of excessive use of capital in various undertakings as a result of British influence. Robert C. Puth, *American Economic History* (Chicago, 1988) pp. 193-4 summarizes the literature on the influence of factor costs on production techniques in the United States. While there has been considerable discussion of the extent to which capital was substituted for labour in the American economy, there is agreement that North American production techniques readily substituted natural resources for both capital and labour.

World conditions, but actually increase suffering by displacing the abundant factor in those conditions, namely labour. The London-based board of directors of the GMA and their British managers may have been similarly slow to realize that the most sophisticated methods of mining coal were not necessarily the best in Nova Scotia. Of course, determining the appropriate mix of capital, labour and natural resources in the Nova Scotia coal industry would require complex and exhaustive calculations based on complete knowledge of all the costs and all the benefits of different combinations of factors of production, information that is not readily available. However, considerable information about resource use can be obtained from the testimony of contemporaries. Also, several insights can be gained by a comparison of resource use in Nova Scotia with that in Pennsylvania, and comparison of steam power use by the GMA with steam power employed in coal mines opened in Nova Scotia after 1858. None of this permits unequivocal conclusions, but the evidence available strongly suggests that the GMA employed resources inappropriately

In 1842 George Wightman, a Halifax engineer, investigated the reasons for losses at the Albion Mine, and his report gives an assessment of the quality of management by the GMA.[64] The investigation on behalf of the lieutenant-governor was undertaken in response to a plea by the GMA for a reduction in royalties because of its difficulty avoiding losses during a period of severe economic depression. By the 1840s, the GMA could no longer gain the support of the legislature, and the government certainly had no desire to lose revenues as a result of reductions in coal royalties, so there can be no assurance that Wightman's report was entirely unbiased. His conclusion, however, indicates quite clearly that proper management would have resulted in higher profits and that the GMA was to blame for the difficulties it suffered.

> On the supposition of coal maintaining its present price at the mines, I have no doubt that were they in the hands of an individual who paid no more for the pits than fair valuation for the labour bestowed upon them, who took no more of the real estate than is really necessary for the working of them, and who paid for the railroad only so much as would bring the carriage by that channel equivalent in expense to what it would be by the old road and the river, he would realise a very ample profit upon his investment.[65]

This observer may have been predisposed to criticize the Association, but it is still most informative to see what he chose to criticize. He did not complain about the quality of the operation of the mines, stating that "the workings are in as perfect a state as I suppose to be possible. There is ample provision for

---

64 Muise, "The General Mining Association", p. 85 identifies Wightman; "Copy of Report No. 37 Book No 463, 1842", RG 21A, vol. 3, PANS.

65 This and the following quotations are from "Copy of Report No. 37 Book No 463, 1842".

drainage, for ventilation, and for clearing off the gas..." The point of vulnerability he detected was not the sophistication of techniques used in the workings of the mines or stinginess in expenditure of capital to provide for drainage and ventilation, but excessive and unwise expenditure of capital. In particular Wightman questioned the wisdom of expenditures on a railroad to move coal from the pithead to the loading wharves:

> Of the class of works unnecessarily expensive, the first in magnitude is the railroad. It was constructed upon a much more expensive plan than the occasion fairly warranted; and besides the work was forced forward at a rate that raised prices far above the usual rates of the country. The cost of construction was £54,754, the average cost of railroads in the United States does not exceed £4000 per mile, which for five miles and a quarter, the length of the road in question, is £21,000, leaving for unnecessary expenditure at least £30,000.

He also questioned the decision to construct housing for immigrant workers before the industry required their labour:

> The policy of the directors seems to have been to provide for a great expansion of the trade, and to this end built a village and imported a colony of miners to inhabit it. The propriety of this policy is very questionable, it would have probably been better to have waited till the contingency had arisen... The amount of building not absolutely necessary may be placed at not less than £8,000.

Wightman gives the clear impression that the GMA had fallen into the trap common to the British of underestimating the value of capital in the new world. Criticizing the GMA for investing too much capital in the coal industry may seem strange, and if the capital invested would otherwise have been unavailable we need not fret at its misuse — the failure to earn a return was the stockholders' concern. Nonetheless, when a region is short of capital it is folly to use it to construct housing which sits empty or to build railways where water transportation can be more cheaply improved. The benefit of the capital to Nova Scotia would have been much greater if it had been controlled by investors who directed it to where it would have been most useful.

In addition to his criticism of the GMA's use of capital, Wightman also attacked the company for hiring too much skilled labour:

> On the mode of carrying on the work I beg leave to state that as far as I could learn the colliers are considered as tradesmen, and as such paid high wages. They fix their prices and will not consent to admit any other persons into the works. Two thirds of their work can be done by common labourers and yet they insist upon doing the whole themselves...

Wightman offers his own explanation for the GMA labour policy:

> The mistake by which this state of things [the high price of labour] was brought about, probably arose from applying the maxims and practice of England to a country under different circumstances. There, from the multitude of labourers every man is forced into a particular calling, and from which he cannot, if he wished it, easily escape. The facility with which men can turn to different employments of the same class is scarcely known, and hence it was thought necessary to import a class of regularly instructed miners. The plaster quarriers follow a business similar to mining, and they are as numerous in Hants as the miners in Pictou; but the idea of forming a separate class never enters their minds, neither is there any apprehension on the part of the employers of not finding a sufficient number of workmen.

If higher wages and greater safety resulted from the employment of skilled workers, then Wightman was no friend of the worker when he criticized these practices. While the GMA may have adopted its labour policy in part out of a humane concern for its workers, it seems likely that Wightman is correct in his assessment that the Association misunderstood the best way to earn a profit, and that the better treatment of labour was an inadvertent result of the misunderstanding. If so, we have further evidence that the GMA applied British production techniques to Nova Scotia without adapting them to local conditions. In the case of labour, however, GMA policy may have been more beneficial to Nova Scotia than a competitive industry would have been, particularly if the use of skilled labour increased the safety of workers, a factor notoriously neglected by capitalist markets. However, we still might worry that unskilled resident Nova Scotians were left idle while skilled British colliers were brought in and given the best paying jobs. And while lower labour costs which produced greater profits to be removed to Britain would have done nothing to benefit Nova Scotia, we can also consider that if lower labour costs resulted in cheaper coal, additional investment in coal-using industries might have occurred.

Wightman's view that excessive capital was invested at the Albion mine is supported by evidence about the capital employed in Pennsylvania mines. Coal production began to expand significantly in the anthracite fields at about the same time that the GMA was establishing production in Nova Scotia. In the United States when land was granted the mineral rights were alienated with the surface land rights, although the landowner could sell the two separately. Mining was conducted on different scales in different regions, depending on ownership of mineral rights and local policy. In Lehigh County, the Lehigh Company purchased 6,000 acres of coal land long before the coal was marketable and was able to control production and the transportation facilities in that county.[66] Schuylkill County, in contrast, was characterized by a large number of independent operators who strongly resisted the granting of charters of incorporation to mine coal in order to keep the scale of operation small. In both counties far smaller sums were invested in individual mines, or even in the mines of an entire county, than the GMA invested. Although the Lehigh Company invested $500,000 in land, capital equipment and transportation improvements, the average capitalization of Schuylkill County mines was $4,000, and $10,000 sufficed to construct a first-class coal mine.[67]

While the amount of capital invested in mining varied greatly and for proper analysis must be compared to the extent of the coal reserve being developed, the GMA clearly used far more capital than firms in Pennsylvania. Its total capitalization in 1826 of £400,000 sterling or about $20 million dwarfs the sums invested in similar areas in Pennsylvania.[68] Some of that capital appears to have been a reserve, not immediately put to use in the coal industry. However, in 1839 a legislative committee estimated that the GMA had invested £109,982 in fixed capital and real estate at the Albion mine alone.[69]

The ratio of total capital invested to output at American mines is difficult to ascertain, but scattered evidence indicates that the ratio of output per horse power in steam engines was much higher in Pennsylvania than in the GMA mines, again indicating less use of capital in the American mines. In 1833 when total coal production was 147,952 net tons "at least" five engines were reported installed in Schuylkill County mines, while in 1844 output had risen to 839,934 net tons and 28 engines were operating with a total of 1,100 horsepower.[70] In contrast seven steam engines with a total of 129 horse power were working at the Albion mine in 1839 to produce 33,871 Winchester chaldrons of coal, or 53,110 net tons of coal.[71] These rough figures imply that in Schuylkill County about 764 tons of coal were raised per unit of horse power while at the Albion mine only 412 tons of coal were raised per horse power in steam engines. The significance and accuracy of these calculations must not

66 Samuel H. Daddow and Benjamin Bannan, *Coal Iron and Oil; or the Practical American Miner*, (Pottsville, Pa. 1866), pp. 114, 123.

67 C.K. Yearly, Jr. *Enterprise and Anthracite: Economics and Democracy in Schuylkill County, 1820-1875*, (Baltimore, 1961), p. 74.

68 McKay, "Dependent Development", p. 19. See also RG1, vol. 460, no. 14, PANS. The pound in Halifax currency was worth about $4.00 at that time and sterling was valued at 11 per cent more than Halifax currency.

69 *JHA* (1839), Appendix 50. Presumably this information had been provided to them by the Association.

70 Yearly, *Enterprise and Anthracite*, p. 112.

71 *JHA* (1839), Appendix 50. The output is the average over the previous three years to reduce distortion caused by the variability of annual output.

Table One
Output per Horsepower in Steam Engines, 1866

	Output	Horsepower	Output per Horsepower
Total Including GMA	684,740	1,555	440
Total Excluding GMA	269,608	428	629
GMA Mines			
Albion	222,437	612	364
Sydney	132,915	440	302
Lingan	59,780	75	797
Joggins	8,478	9	943
Larger Non-GMA Mines			
Acadia	14,662	43	341
Gowrie	35,704	32	1,116
Glace Bay	61,902	65	952
Block House	107,642	90	1,196
International	13,364	7	1,909

SOURCE: *JHA, Nova Scotia* (1866), Appendix 12.

be exaggerated, but in conjunction with other evidence it supports the argument that production in Nova Scotia was more capital-intensive than in Pennsylvania.

The better data on the ratio of output to steam power which one available for mining companies opened in Nova Scotia after 1858 confirm the observation of more intensive use of capital by the GMA. Table One presents information regarding the output of various mines and the horsepower in steam engines of each mine in 1866. This information must be used cautiously, because it is greatly influenced by the level of trade and conditions at each mine, and comparing a long-established mining company with newer mines may distort the results. However, the figures do support the position that the GMA used more capital-intensive methods than even the large, well-capitalized mines such as the Acadia and the International.[72]

---

72 By 1869 output per unit of horsepower at the Acadia mine had risen to 790 tons of coal, in spite of severely depressed conditions throughout the industry. The gap between GMA and non-GMA output per horsepower grew as GMA output fell sharply during the contraction while newer firms experienced either less of a decline or even a rise in production. See *JHA* (1869), Appendix 15.

GMA operations at Lingan and The Joggins are significant exceptions to the pattern of GMA capital intensity. The limited use of steam power at The Joggins may reflect the reluctance of the GMA to open that mine at all. However, the GMA opened the mine at Lingan in 1855 on its own initiative, to exploit a profitable market for gas coal in the United States.[73] Since investment in that mine began only after the firm had gained long experience in Nova Scotia, it is tempting to assume that the GMA established its new mine on principles more suited to Nova Scotian conditions.

The tendency of the GMA to use mining methods which preserved coal resources more than other Nova Scotian coal companies can also be seen in the comments made in 1862 by W.A. Hendry the assistant to the Inspector of Mines:

> Their underground works, so far as I was able to judge from the very limited time at my disposal, are conducted with great regularity and scientific skill. My endeavour was while inspecting the other collieries, to urge upon the proprietors the advantages — as far as circumstances would permit — of adopting the same system as that pursued by Mr. Brown, viz.: to leave a regular and fair distribution of pillarage to support the roof or upper strata until the coal has been worked out from the extreme deep, when the pillars might be removed, and the roof allowed to come down. In some of the new mines, the parties in their first operations removed so much of the coal that the roof or upper strata has come down and prevented the getting out a portion of the coal, which of course is a loss both to the proprietors and the province.[74]

Whether the use of labour and capital in careful mining urged by Hendry to prevent loss of coal reserves was appropriate or excessive cannot be objectively determined now. It may well be the case that he was urging an appropriate level of preservation of coal resources on inexperienced firms who through ignorance had miscalculated the amount of pillarage necessary and created a regrettable loss of coal reserves. Alternatively, taking as much coal as could be easily reached, even though the pillars left failed to support the roof, saved the expense of digging deeply and installing expensive ventilation and drainage equipment, so that while coal was lost, scarce capital was saved.

In summary, the General Mining Association appears to have used more capital and wasted less coal than was usual in North American coal mining. If the excessive capital the GMA invested would otherwise not have been available to Nova Scotia, the loss to the province from excess investment would have been restricted to the impact of any increase in price that resulted from

---

73 Brown, *The Coal Fields and Coal Trade*, p. 86.

74 *JHA* (1863), Appendix, p. 15.

the increased cost of coal mining. However, there is no reason to assume that in the absence of investment by the GMA no foreign capital would have been attracted to the Nova Scotian coal industry. Since Nova Scotia was a small part of the total market for British funds available for foreign investment, the supply of capital to the province should have been quite elastic, although only at a significant premium over the cost of capital in Britain. Moreover, other investors with capital were interested in the coal resources of Nova Scotia, most notably Samuel Cunard who had access to considerable capital, not just from his own wealth, but also through the network of credit typically extended to merchants. Indeed, it is quite possible that if access to the mineral resources of Nova Scotia had been available to all investors, far more capital than the GMA provided might have been attracted to the province, particularly since the company's privileges prevented others from exploiting almost all minerals.

In the absence of the GMA's privileges, the high price paid for capital would have encouraged the use of less capital- intensive techniques and would likely have resulted in more depletion of the coal resources. However, capital would have been saved in the early days of mining when it was expensive, and while additional capital would have been required to open deeper mines to replace the lost coal, the need for that capital would have been pushed into the future, when it became much less expensive. The increased costs of these deeper mines would have been borne by a richer economy which could better afford the expenditure. Capital freed from coal mining in the early 19th century could have been invested elsewhere in Nova Scotia, where it would have been more productive. The inheritors of the coal reserves might then have found that the fruits of alternative investments amply compensated for the coal that had been lost.

Perhaps the only activity more foolish than predicting the future is predicting what might have been in the past. Nonetheless, it seems reasonable to conclude that the allocation of property rights in Nova Scotia coal was made in a distant metropolis in a manner which reduced the potential for industrial development in the hinterland. Widely distributed local control of the resources would have likely increased the degree of industrialization in the province. The distantly owned firm made extensive use of capital and skilled labour so as to conserve natural resources inappropriately. Blocking entry to scattered coal deposits denied local entrepreneurs both an investment opportunity and a cheap source of energy for their businesses.

The gains in economic development which would have resulted from a more competitive coal industry are uncertain. American experience indicates that the pace of industrialization was greatly influenced by the availability of coal, so that when first anthracite and later western bituminous coal became available, the pace of industrialization greatly increased.[75] In Nova Scotia the

---

75 Chandler, "Anthracite Coal", pp. 150-1.

local market was much smaller and other key resources may have been lacking; cheap coal might have been insufficient to cause the sustainable expansion of industry. The events of history have denied us the opportunity of knowing with certainty whether Nova Scotia had the potential to become more highly industrialized. The distribution of property rights in coal in the first half of the 19th century did little to help fulfill what potential was there.

Canadian Regional Commodity Income Differences at Confederation

Kris Inwood and James R. Irwin

Like most medium- and large-sized countries, Canada is marked by significant regional inequality in the material standard of living.[1] The Atlantic Provinces have had Canada's highest unemployment rates and lowest personal income for most of this century.[2] Since the Second World War relative poverty in Atlantic Canada has become a symbol of regional distress and the failure of government policy.[3] Any explanation of relative regional poverty must take account of its historical roots although, admittedly, different analytical perspectives imply different conceptions of the relationship between original

Earlier versions of this paper were presented at the 17th Conference on the Use of Quantitative Methods in Canadian Economic History, Queen's University, November 1990 and at the Workshop on Atlantic Canadian Economic History, Saint Mary's University, September 1990. We are grateful to participants in each conference for helpful comments and suggestions; Lou Cain, Elizabeth Ewan and Jamie Snell made helpful comments on the final draft of the paper. We are especially grateful to Marvin McInnis for correspondence and conversations in which he explained the basis of his national agricultural income calculations. Brian Morber designed the maps reproduced in the paper. The research would not have been possible without financial support from the Social Sciences and Humanities Research Council, which we gratefully acknowledge.

1   Jeffrey Williamson, "Regional Inequality and the Process of National Development", *Economic Development and Cultural Change*, 13 (1965), pp. 1-84.

2   Statistics Canada, *National Income and Expenditure Accounts* and *Provincial Economic Accounts*; Alan Green, *Regional Aspects of Canada's Economic Growth* (Toronto, 1971), appendices A and C. The enormity of regional difference makes it unlikely that they would disappear in any refinement of the estimates. On various measurement issues see Alan Abouchar, "Regional Welfare and Measured Income Differentials in Canada", *Review of Income and Wealth*, 17 (1971), pp. 363-9, and L. Copithorne, *Natural Resources and Regional Disparities* (Ottawa, 1979). During the 1930s the Prairie Provinces, in particular Saskatchewan, experienced a rise in unemployment and decline in income that equalled, and perhaps exceeded, levels in Atlantic Canada.

3   James P. Bickerton, Nova Scotia, *Ottawa and the Politics of Regional Development* (Toronto, 1990); Donald Savoie, ed., *The Canadian Economy: A Regional Perspective* (Toronto, 1986).

appearance and long-term persistence.[4] In this paper we address the extent of a per capita commodity income differential between the Central Canadian provinces of Ontario and Quebec and the Maritime Provinces of Nova Scotia and New Brunswick in 1870.[5]

The historical literature provides two broadly different perspectives on the origin of regional underdevelopment in Canada.[6] One view is that the Maritimes' economic difficulties began with their decision to join the Canadian Confederation because the new national government adopted tax, spending and regulatory policies with a regional bias.[7] David Alexander identifies the tendency to see Confederation as "a critical turning point" and "a disaster" for the Maritime Provinces.[8] A second view is that economic difficulties preceded the union and resulted from some combination of social and political structures inherited from the colonial era and resource/technological developments originating in international markets.[9] One point of divergence between these two broadly different perspectives is the interpretation of Confederation itself, which should include some assessment of regional wealth and poverty around the time of Confederation. If the Maritime Provinces were

---

4   Most analytical perspectives explain first appearance and long-term persistence as being part of the same process; the framework of labour market adjustment allows for an important exception.

5   We refer to Nova Scotia and New Brunswick in this paper as the Maritime Provinces; they were the only Atlantic provinces in Confederation during 1870.

6   Phillip Buckner surveys the historiography of regional grievance in his paper "Rewriting the Past: The Economic History of the Maritimes in the Confederation Era" (unpublished, 1990). A more limited survey of the issues as they relate to industrial activity is Kris E. Inwood, "Maritime Industrialization from 1870 to 1910: A Review of the Evidence and Its Interpretation", *Acadiensis*, XXI, 1 (Autumn 1991), pp. 132-55 and reprinted in this volume.

7   The causes of Confederation are reviewed in Ged Martin, ed., *The Causes of Confederation* (Fredericton, 1990).

8   David Alexander, "Canadian Regionalism: A Central Problem", pp. 44-50 in his *Atlantic Canada and Confederation* (Toronto, 1983) and "Economic Growth in the Atlantic Region, 1880 to 1940", *Acadiensis*, VIII, 1 (Autumn 1978), pp. 47-76.

9   Resource and technology themes are reviewed by Inwood, "Maritime Industrialization". Social and political structures are considered by Ian McKay, "The Crisis of Dependent Development: Class Conflict in the Nova Scotia Coalfields, 1872-1876", in Greg Kealey, ed., *Class, Gender and Region: Essays in Canadian Historical Sociology* (St. John's, 1988), pp. 9-47; Eric Sager and Gerry Panting, *Maritime Capital* (Kingston and Montreal, 1990); Phillip Wood, "Barriers to Capitalist Development in Maritime Canada, 1870-1930: A Comparative Perspective", *Canadian Papers in Business History*, 1 (1989), pp. 33-58 and "Marxism and the Maritimes: On the Determinants of Regional Capitalist Development", *Studies in Political Economy*, 29 (Summer 1989), pp. 123-53.

relatively prosperous at Confederation, then the case for the political union as an economic turning point is strengthened.

The contribution of this paper is to assess regional disparities in 1870, the census year closest to Confederation. The earliest regional income estimate currently available is for 1890.[10] We extend the quantitative record of Canadian regional disparities with estimates of provincial and regional incomes in 1870. Our methodology parallels that of comparable research on the United States in which an estimate of national commodity income is decomposed with indices derived from appropriate regional data.[11] We begin with the national income estimate produced by M.C. Urquhart and a team of associates and reported during the mid-1980s.[12] The indices used to decompose Urquhart's income estimates are constructed from census reports of production in individual census districts; a detailed desription of our methods is given in Appendix A. In Appendix B we consider briefly several potential sources of bias in our procedures. It is useful to acknowledge the possible biases even though they are unlikely to undermine our main findings.

Table One summarizes our regional income estimates, which point to a pattern similar to that experienced today.[13] Ontario's per capita income was some 20 per cent above the national average, Quebec was below average and the Maritime Provinces (together) even further below average. Comparisons with modern data are problematic because of changes in the definition of income, but the pattern at Confederation is similar to that of today except that Nova Scotia and New Brunswick have reversed positions.[14] It is quite clear that Canada began its national existence with strong regional inequalities. The

10　Green, *Regional Aspects*. The appearance of new national income estimates to replace those underlying Alan Green's seminal study reinforces the importance of a new regional decomposition.

11　Richard Easterlin, "Interregional Differences in Per Capita Income, Population, and Total Income, 1840-1950", in *Trends in the American Economy in the Nineteenth Century*, vol. 24 (Princeton, N.J., 1960), pp. 73-170.

12　M.C. Urquhart, "New Estimates of Gross National Product, Canada, 1870-1926: Some Implications for Canadian Development", in Stanley Engerman and Robert Gallman, eds., *Long-Term Factors in American Economic Growth* (Chicago, 1986), pp. 9-94.

13　For convenience we use per capita income as an abbreviation for per capita commodity income, and we freely interchange the concepts of output and income derived from output.

14　Personal and earned income per capita in Nova Scotia were five to 10 per cent above that in New Brunswick from the 1960s through the 1980s, but our commodity income per capita in Nova Scotia is 10 per cent lower than New Brunswick's in 1870. See Statistics Canada, *National Income and Expenditure Accounts* and *Provincial Economic Accounts*.

Table One
Population Density and Commodity Income Per Capita
Relative to National Average, 1870

Region	Income per Capita	Population per Inhabited Square Mile
Canada	100	100
Nova Scotia	75	65
New Brunswick	86	47
Quebec	86	104
Ontario	119	143
Eastern Nova Scotia	65	57
Central Nova Scotia	84	71
Western Nova Scotia	71	68
Southern New Brunswick	93	59
Northern New Brunswick	65	29
Gulf of St. Lawrence	68	42
Lower St. Lawrence	73	114
Northern Quebec	82	42
Southeastern Quebec	101	270
Montreal area	91	211
Eastern Ontario	100	116
Huronia	117	145
Golden Horseshoe	144	343
Western Ontario	133	172
Northern Ontario	97	42

Source: see Appendix A. Population per inhabited square mile is reported for only those census sub-districts with a population density greater than two people per square mile (see Appendix C).

phenomenon of regional disparities was a challenge inherited by the first national government rather than a consequence of its actions.

There was considerable variation within provinces. For ease of presentation we organize the data in 15 regions described in Map 1; each region is an aggregation of several census districts whose boundaries are reconstructed in Appendix D. The data reported in Table One and Map 2 reveal a pronounced east-west gradient. Per capita income was relatively low in eastern Quebec and the Maritimes; on a regional basis the lowest regions (eastern Nova Scotia, northern New Brunswick and Quebec's Gulf region) averaged only two-thirds of the national average. By contrast per capita income was one-third above the national average in western Ontario and even higher in the Golden Horseshoe region. Income levels in the middle regions of western Quebec and eastern Ontario approximated the national average.

Diversity within the Atlantic Region is illustrated in Map 3. Central Nova Scotia and southern New Brunswick approached the national average in contrast to certain counties in eastern and western Nova Scotia which registered less than half of that level.[15] The eastern-most regions of Quebec along the lower St. Lawrence River and the Gulf of St. Lawrence resembled the less affluent parts of Nova Scotia and New Brunswick to a striking extent.

It is also worth noting that the lower-income regions tended to be those with a low population density. The Maritimes and eastern Quebec outside of Quebec City were settled with a spatial density of population roughly one-half of the Canadian average, in contrast to southern Ontario which was significantly above average (Table One). A slightly different point is that one-half of all Maritimers (57 per cent in New Brunswick and 42 per cent in Nova Scotia) lived in census subdistricts with a population density under 25 people per square mile, in contrast to 19 per cent in Quebec and only eight per cent in Ontario.[16] The correlation between density of settlement and commodity income was by no means complete but the cross-sectional evidence in Table One challenges a simple Malthusian idea that per capita income was driven down by high population density. Perhaps the most important implication of these data is that Canada in 1870 was a remarkably diverse country in terms of the spatial density of settlement and material standard of living, both of which tended to increase from east to west.

Diversity is evident as well in the sectoral composition of income reported in Table Two. Manufacturing contributed one-third of all commodity income in Canada, although the proportion varied from only 27 per cent in Nova Scotia to 39 per cent in New Brunswick. There was considerable variation

15 Bellechasse Sud in the lower St. Lawrence region and parts of northern Ontario also registered commodity income less than one-half of the national average on a per capita basis.

16 See Appendix C.

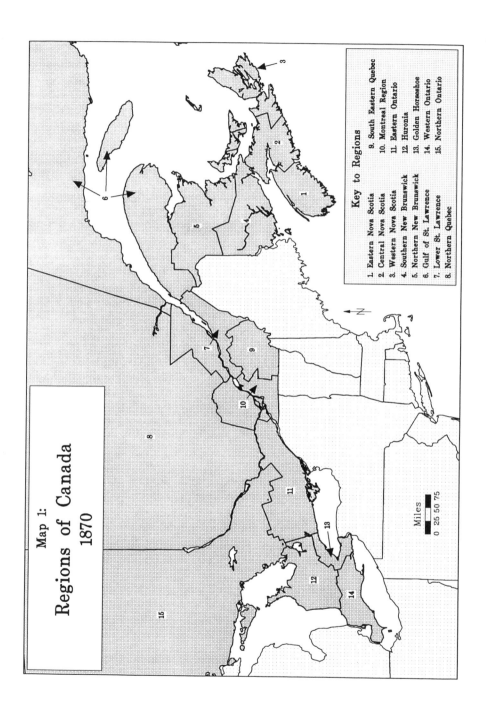

Map 1:

Regions of Canada
1870

Key to Regions

1. Eastern Nova Scotia
2. Central Nova Scotia
3. Western Nova Scotia
4. Southern New Brunswick
5. Northern New Brunswick
6. Gulf of St. Lawrence
7. Lower St. Lawrence
8. Northern Quebec
9. South Eastern Quebec
10. Montreal Region
11. Eastern Ontario
12. Huronia
13. Golden Horseshoe
14. Western Ontario
15. Northern Ontario

Miles

0 25 50 75

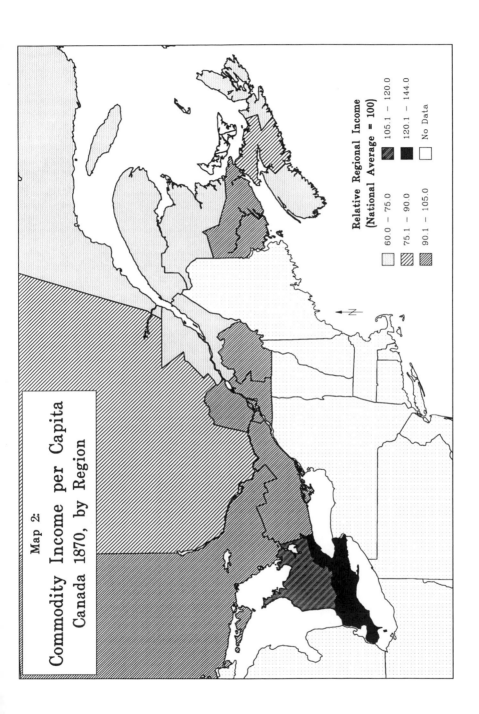

Map 2:

Commodity Income per Capita
Canada 1870, by Region

Relative Regional Income
(National Average = 100)

60.0 – 75.0
75.1 – 90.0
90.1 – 105.0
105.1 – 120.0
120.1 – 144.0
No Data

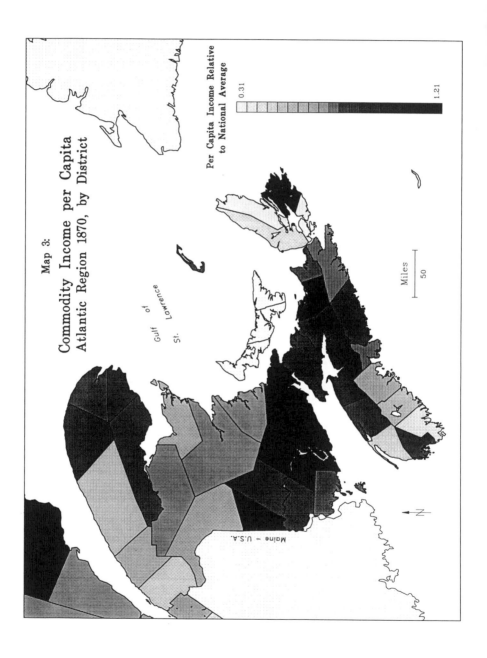

Map 3:

Commodity Income per Capita
Atlantic Region 1870, by District

Per Capita Income Relative
to National Average

0.31

1.21

Gulf of St. Lawrence

Maine — U.S.A.

Miles
50

N

within provinces as well. Manufacturing accounted for 52 per cent of income in the Golden Horseshoe but only 22 per cent in Huronia and northern Ontario. Maritime regions ranged from nine per cent in eastern Nova Scotia to 44 per cent in southern New Brunswick. We have not presented the data but diversity was even greater at the level of individual districts.

The diversity of sectoral structure within individual provinces carries one important implication for the assessment of government policy. At the end of the 1870s the Canadian government began to favour the manufacturing sector through an elaborate set of tariffs and subsidies. There has been considerable concern about possible provincial bias in the impact of these tariffs.[17] However, the analysis of tariff impact is complicated by the existence of relatively industrialized and non-industrialized areas within each province. If there were winners and losers as a result of the tariff, the industrial areas of the Maritimes may have been among the winners, just as the agricultural areas of Quebec and Ontario may be counted among the losers.[18]

It is sometimes suggested that manufacturing was a leading sector whose expansion was crucial to modern economic growth.[19] The evidence reported in Tables One and Two is ambiguous on this point. The richest province (Ontario) had the second smallest manufacturing share of income. Indeed, Ontario stands out most of all for having the largest share of income devoted to agriculture. Another way of expressing the ambiguity is to observe that Ontario led in manufacturing output per capita, but its lead in agricultural output per capita was even greater. On a regional level, the Golden Horseshoe region had the highest manufacturing share of income and the highest overall income per capita. On the other hand, industry in this region clearly served a market area encompassing the affluent but non-industrial regions of Huronia and western Ontario. Moreover, comparing Tables One and Two, all other regions

17 T.W. Acheson, "The National Policy and the Industrialization of the Maritimes", *Acadiensis*, I, 2 (Spring 1972), pp. 3-28 and "The Maritimes and 'Empire Canada'", in David Bercuson, ed. *Canada and the Burden of Unity* (Toronto, 1977), pp. 87-114; Inwood, "Maritime Industrialization"; B. Lesser, "The Maritimes and Confederation: A View of the Regional Impact of the National Tariff Policy of 1879", Paper presented at the University of New Brunswick, April 1977; Robin Neill, "National Policy and Regional Development", *Journal of Canadian Studies*, 9 (1974), pp. 12-18; S.A.Saunders, *The Economic History of the Maritime Provinces* (Fredericton, 1984 [1939]); Hugh Pinchin, *The Regional Impact of the Canadian Tariff* (Ottawa, 1979).

18 The analysis of tariff impact is complicated since the mix of industry varied across districts, some industries were protected and some were not, input tariffs in some cases reduced effective protection, and industries serving export and strictly local markets were not in a position to benefit from protection.

19 This view is implied by some of the structuralist literature surveyed in Inwood, "Maritime Industrialization".

Table Two
The Sectoral Distribution of Income

Region	Farm	Factory	Forestry	Mines	Fish	Income per capita
Canada	.54	.33	.10	.02	.01	100
Nova Scotia	.46	.27	.07	.12	.07	75
New Brunswick	.47	.39	.11	.01	.03	83
Quebec	.49	.37	.12	.01	.01	86
Ontario	.59	.32	.09 .	.01	.00	120
E. Nova Scotia*	.46	.09	.08	.27	.10	65
C. Nova Scotia	.40	.39	.05	.12	.03	85
W. Nova Scotia	.54	.25	.08	.01	.12	71
S. New Brunswick	.48	.44	.09	.01	.02	89
N. New Brunswick	.50	.23	.19	.02	.06	65
G. of St. Lawrence	.49	.13	.16	.02	.18	68
L. St. Lawrence	.49	.37	.11	.01	.01	74
N. Quebec	.43	.23	.30	.02	.00	82
S.E. Quebec	.61	.19	.16	.04	.00	102
Montreal area	.45	.46	.08	.00	.00	91
E. Ontario	.58	.30	.10	.00	.00	100
Huronia	.70	.22	.08	.00	.00	117
G. Horseshoe	.43	.52	.04	.00	.00	145
W. Ontario	.61	.27	.09	.02	.00	133
N. Ontario	.41	.22	.29	.06	.01	97

Source: see Appendix A
*See Table One for full titles of regions

with per capita income above the national average had manufacturing shares below the national average.

These data provide little support for the idea that industrialization was essential for high per capita income. Indeed, following the staple thesis, one might argue that the primary sector rather than manufacturing functioned as a kind of leading sector in 19th-century North America. Even those averse to the staple thesis will recognize that the primary sector mattered a great deal simply because it was large.

The largest component of primary income was earned in agriculture. Indeed, agriculture was by far the largest single sector in all parts of the country, ranging from 40 per cent in central Nova Scotia to 70 per cent in Huronia. Other sectors assumed considerable significance in particular areas. Forestry contributed 20 per cent of commodity income in northern New Brunswick and 30 per cent in the northern portions of Ontario and Quebec. In eastern Nova Scotia a combination of coal and gold mining accounted for 27 per cent of income. In both eastern and western Nova Scotia fishing contributed one-tenth of income and nearly double that level in Quebec's Gulf region.

Although the various non-agricultural primary sectors assumed considerable local importance, they were nowhere large enough to substitute for agriculture. Wherever agriculture contributed a large share of primary sector incomes, total income per capita was high. Conversely, total income was low wherever fishing, mining or forestry loomed large. We are not yet in a position to say if this was a coincidence or the result of some systematic influence. Nevertheless, it is worth noting that in a descriptive sense eastern and northern Canada was poor because fishing, mining and forestry were unable to compensate for the relatively low levels of agricultural income.

These observations naturally direct attention at the agricultural sector. We cannot hope to document fully, much less explain, the regional differences in agriculture or their importance. Nevertheless, a first glance at the agricultural data in Table Three is suggestive. Income per farm follows the familiar east-west gradient with low levels in eastern Quebec and the Maritimes, intermediate levels in eastern Ontario and western Quebec, and high levels in western Ontario.[20] This ranking is similar to that of per capita income except that the variation is greater. For example, the average Ontario income per farm was more than twice that in Nova Scotia.

---

20 It is worth noting that income per farm is not the same as income per farm family, since many people living in farm-based households earned at least some of their income from other kinds of activities. On this point see Larry McCann, "'Living a Double Life': Town and Country in the Industrialization of the Maritimes", and Robert McKinnon and Graeme Wynn, "Nova Scotian Agriculture in the 'Golden Age': A New Look", in Douglas Day, ed., *Geographical Perspectives on the Maritimes* (Halifax, 1988).

The level of income per farm was the product of two influences: improved acres per farm and income per improved acre. The former is a measure of the size of farm and the latter a partial measure of productivity. The relative importance of these two factors in determining the pattern of income per farm varied considerably. Farm size in much of Quebec approached the national average but land productivity was relatively low. By contrast, New Brunswick's productivity was larger and farm size smaller than in Quebec. Nova Scotia farms were small and their land was relatively unproductive. Ontario, on the other hand, was above average in both farm size and productivity; two-thirds of its lead in income per farm originated with income per acre and one-third with acres per farm.

As always, individual regions show considerable heterogeneity. Income per acre in southern New Brunswick, for example, was the highest of any region in the eastern three provinces; only the Montreal region shows a higher income per farm. Elsewhere in the Maritimes income per farm was much lower; eastern Nova Scotia and northern New Brunswick registered only one-quarter of the level visible in the Golden Horseshoe region of Ontario.

Ontario farmers devoted much more of their land to wheat than did farmers in the other three provinces, but this explains surprisingly little of Ontario's lead in income per acre. Even if we exclude wheat income and acreage, Nova Scotia income per acre rises only from 62 per cent to 67 per cent of the Ontario level, New Brunswick from 76 per cent to 82 per cent and Quebec from 68 per cent to 72 per cent. The modest impact of this recalculation indicates that wheat explains little of the variation in income per acre (which itself explains only two-thirds of Ontario's lead in income per farm). To some extent this may reflect the relative decline of wheat in Ontario, whose farmers were already shifting away from arable production in favour of husbandry.[21]

The degree of commitment to husbandry is demonstrated by the share of all improved acreage devoted to hay and pasture, the principal sources of fodder (Table Three). Even in a prime wheat region such as the western half of Ontario, two-fifths of all land was given to hay and pasture. At the other extreme, three-quarters of all improved farmland was devoted to hay and pasture throughout Nova Scotia, where the moist, short growing season was particularly well-suited to hay and pastures and ill-suited to the most valuable cereals.

---

21   Robert Ankli and Wendy Millar, "Ontario Agriculture in Transition: The Shift from Wheat to Cheese", *Journal of Economic History*, 42, 1 (March 1982), pp. 207-15; Bill Marr, "The Wheat Economy in Reverse: Ontario's Wheat Production, 1887-1917", *Canadian Journal of Economics*, XIV, 1 (February 1981), pp. 136-45; Marvin McInnis, "The Changing Structure of Canadian Agriculture, 1867-1897", *Journal of Economic History*, 42, 1 (March 1982), pp. 191-8 and "Perspectives on Ontario Agriculture, 1815-1930", in Donald H. Akenson, ed., *Canadian Papers in Rural History*, vol. VIII (Gananoque, Ont., 1992), pp. 17-128.

Table Three

Agricultural Income per Improved Acre and per Farm,
and the Share of Improved Acreage Devoted to Pasture and Hay

Region	Income per Farm	Imp. Acres per Farm	Income per Imp. Acre	Imp. Acres in Pasture and Hay
Canada	1.00	1.00	1.00	0.51
Nova Scotia	0.58	0.78	0.74	0.76
New Brunswick	0.70	0.78	0.91	0.61
Quebec	0.81	1.00	0.81	0.55
Ontario	1.30	1.10	1.19	0.43
E. Nova Scotia*	0.45	0.66	0.69	0.78
C. Nova Scotia	0.67	0.87	0.77	0.75
W. Nova Scotia	0.61	0.82	0.74	0.75
S. New Brunswick	0.80	0.88	0.90	0.66
N. New Brunswick	0.49	0.53	0.92	0.43
G. of St. Lawrence	0.52	0.71	0.74	0.53
L. St. Lawrence	0.78	0.98	0.80	0.54
N. Quebec	0.81	0.91	0.88	0.69
S.E. Quebec	0.94	1.19	0.79	0.51
Montreal area	0.56	0.73	0.77	0.52
E. Ontario	0.63	0.82	0.77	0.56
Huronia	1.07	1.13	0.95	0.47
G. Horseshoe	1.33	1.06	1.26	0.37
W. Ontario	1.95	1.37	1.42	0.41
N. Ontario	1.41	1.04	1.36	0.44

Source: see Appendix A

* See Table One for full titles of regions

Our brief overview of agriculture indicates a commitment to husbandry that was strong in all parts of the country and strongest in the east. Agricultural income per farm and per improved acre also followed the familiar east-west gradient although, again, there were important exceptions. The most interesting exception appears to be southern New Brunswick, where farm size and land productivity approached the national average. We also observe that Ontario's lead was not simply the result of its suitability for wheat production.

The regional income estimate describes the diversity of the Canadian economy about the time of Confederation. Income per capita and population density were lowest in the Maritimes and eastern Quebec and highest in the western-most regions of Ontario. The image of an east-west gradient correctly characterizes the spatial distribution of population and income, although there was considerable diversity within individual provinces. The sectoral structure of economic activity does not reflect a clear east-west pattern. Indeed, it is difficult to discern any correlation between sectoral structure and per capita income, except that total income per capita was high wherever agriculture contributed a large share of primary sector activity. There is no evidence that income earned in manufacturing was somehow more important than other kinds of income.

Probably the most important implication of our estimates is that the regional pattern visible in 1870 is broadly similar to that of today. This weakens the argument that Confederation was an important cause of regional underdevelopment. On the other hand, the persistence of this pattern for more than one hundred and twenty years implies that the political union has been a failure to the extent that it was intended to raise the Maritime standard of living closer to the level in Central Canada.[22]

It is possible, of course, that per capita income in New Brunswick and Nova Scotia was even lower relative to Ontario in 1850 or 1860, and that the political union had the effect of stopping what would otherwise have been a process of catching up. There is no evidence to this effect, but it is possible. Unfortunately, our understanding of the pre-Confederation era is incomplete in a variety of dimensions. Brookes observes that out-migration began during the mid-1840s, abated during the 1850s and 1860s, and then increased again in subsequent decades. According to Brookes, increasing out-migration was a natural aspect of the settlement process throughout North America during the 19th century.[23] Gwyn and Siddiq take the more pessimistic view that Nova

---

22 Of course, enthusiastic boosters of the political union might argue that it prevented Nova Scotia and New Brunswick from sinking even lower relative to Central Canada.

23 Alan Brookes, "The Golden Age and the Exodus: The Case of Canning, King's County", *Acadiensis*, XI, 1 (Autumn 1981), pp. 57-82. The diminishing availability of land during the maturation of an agricultural community underlies an important line of research about 19th century North America. See Richard Easterlin, "Population Change and Farm Settlement in the Northern United States", *Journal of*

Scotia agriculture experienced a neo-Malthusian crisis during the 1850s and 1860s.[24] However, other research on Nova Scotia[25] and New Brunswick[26] tends to present a different picture. Inwood and Chamard report that manufacturing expanded more slowly in the Maritimes than in Central Canada during the pre-Confederation era.[27] Sager and Panting caution that the considerable

Economic History, XXXVI, 1 (March 1976), pp. 45-75; David Gagan, *Hopeful Travellers: Families, Land and Social Change in Mid-Victorian Peel County, Canada West* (Toronto, 1981); Bill Marr, "Family Size Limitation in Canada West, 1851: Some Historical Evidence", *Canadian Papers in Rural History*, VII (1989), pp. 273-93; Marvin McInnis, "Marketable Surpluses in Ontario Farming, 1860", *Social Science History*, VIII, 4 (Fall 1984), pp. 395-424 and "Childbearing and Land Availability: Some Evidence from Individual Household Data", in Ronald D. Lee, ed., *Population Patterns in the Past* (New York, 1977).

24   Julian Gwyn, "Golden Age or Bronze Moment? Wealth and Poverty in Nova Scotia: The 1850s and 1860s", *Canadian Papers in Rural History*, VIII (1992), pp. 195-230; Julian Gwyn and Fazley Siddiq, "Wealth Distribution in Nova Scotia during the Confederation Era, 1851 and 1871", *Canadian Historical Review*, vol. LXXIII, no. 4 (December 1992), pp. 435-452; Lars Osberg and Fazley Siddiq, "The Acquisition of Wealth in Nova Scotia in the Late Nineteenth Century", in E.N. Wolff, ed., *Research in Economic Inequality*, vol. 4., Festschrifte to Nancy Ruggles (forthcoming).

25   Rusty Bittermann, "Middle River: The Social Structure of Agriculture in a Nineteenth Century Cape Breton Community", M.A. thesis, University of New Brunswick, 1987, and "The Hierarchy of the Soil: Land and Labour in a 19th Century Cape Breton Community", *Acadiensis*, XVIII, 1 (Autumn 1988), pp. 33-55; Rusty Bitterman, Robert McKinnon and Graeme Wynn, "Of Equality and Interdependence in the Nova Scotian Countryside, 1850-1879", *Canadian Historical Review* (forthcoming); Kris Inwood and Phyllis Wagg, "Wealth and Prosperity in Nova Scotian Agriculture, 1850-1870", Paper presented to the Canadian Historical Association, June 1992; McKinnon and Wynn, "Nova Scotian Agriculture"; Alan McNeil, "Cultural Stereotypes and Highland Farming in Eastern Nova Scotia, 1827-1851", *Histoire sociale/Social History*, XIX, 37 (May 1986), pp. 39-56, and "Society and Economy in Rural Nova Scotia, 1761-1861", Ph.D. thesis, Queen's University, 1991, chs. 4, 5; Graeme Wynn, "'Exciting a Spirit of Reform Among the Plodholes': Agricultural Reform in Pre-Confederation Nova Scotia", *Acadiensis*, XX, 1 (Autumn 1991), pp. 5-51.

26   In this volume see T.W. Acheson, "New Brunswick Agriculture at the End of the Colonial Era" and Béatrice Craig, "Agriculture in a Pioneer Region: The Upper St. John River Valley in the first half of the Nineteenth Century". The latter accompanies Craig's "Marketable Surpluses in Northeastern New Brunswick and Northern Maine", Paper presented to the Canadian Historical Association, June 1992. Even Peter McClelland reports considerable real growth in farm output during the 1850s and 1860s; see his "The New Brunswick Economy in the Nineteenth Century", Ph.D. thesis, Harvard University, 1966, pp. 50, 53.

27   Kris Inwood and John Chamard, "Regional Industrial Growth in the 1890s: The Case of the Missing Artisans", *Acadiensis*, XVI, 1 (Autumn 1986), pp. 101-17.

growth of Maritime-registered shipping was accompanied and to some extent caused by a decline in the British purchase of Canadian ships, increased longevity of the vessels and a weakening of linkages with the local economy.[28] There is much discussion of a timber crisis in New Brunswick, but even McClelland reports a fivefold increase in the value of timber exports from 1848-52 to 1868-1872.[29] Overall, the evidence does not yet support a definitive judgement about economic change in the Maritimes during the 1850s and 1860s.

Clearly, more research is needed to determine whether and in what sense the political union was an economic turning point. Resolution of this issue is complicated by the problem of distinguishing the impact of Confederation from the closing of raw material reciprocity with the United States, the rise of American-manufactured tariffs, the end of the American Civil War, the fast expansion of a continental rail network or other developments coincident with political union in Canada. And it is entirely possible — indeed likely — that some Maritime sectors and subregions suffered while others benefited from the changes wrought by political union.[30]

The research presented in this paper does not resolve any of these issues, nor does it identify alternative causes of relative regional poverty. Nevertheless, the existence in 1870 of something like the modern pattern of regional disparities clearly encourages further research about the pre-Confederation era. Our evidence also points to the importance of the agricultural sector; its large size everywhere in 19th century Canada gave it an importance impossible to omit from any explanatory perspective.[31]

---

28 Sager and Panting, *Maritime Capital*, ch. 5.

29 McClelland, "The New Brunswick Economy", Table XV. The export data miss some of the harvesting of wood for local consumption, which undoubtedly expanded with the general growth of the farm economy. McNeil points to the importance of farm-based wood harvesting in this period; see his "Society and Economy", ch. 6.

30 It would appear that manufacturing output increased faster in Nova Scotia than in New Brunswick, although some parts of Nova Scotia performed weakly in the immediate post-Confederation era; see Inwood, "Maritime Industrialization," and Inwood and Chamard, "Regional Industrial Growth".

31 This is not to say that a complete explanation can be based solely in natural resources and the physical environment to the exclusion of political factors and social structure.

Appendix A: The Estimation of Commodity Income by Census District

1. Agriculture

Agriculture accounts for more than half of all commodity income reported by Urquhart.[32] In this sector income is the difference between gross farm income (net of seed and feed) and operating costs (inputs purchased from outside of agriculture). We differ with Urquhart in designating the farmers' production of forest products as forestry rather than agriculture. Urquhart's estimates for 1870 include Prince Edward Island (P.E.I.) and Canada. As described in Table A1, we deduct an estimate for P.E.I. from the Urquhart totals to arrive at an 1870 national total, which is allocated among 206 districts in the four 1870 provinces.

We allocate national (i.e., excludingP.E.I.) totals of gross farm income from each of wheat, potatoes, hops, flax, flaxseed, tobacco, and grass/clover seed in proportion to census reports of physical production. The seed requirement is the same proportion of production everywhere except for wheat, which following Lewis and McInnis is proportional to acreage.[33]

Gross income from cattle and calves, hogs, and sheep and lambs is allocated in proportion to each district's share of animals killed or sold. Gross income from horses is allocated in proportion to the census report of horses under three years and our estimate of "other horses" (below). Income from wool, apples, grapes, honey, maple sugar and syrup, cheese and butter is allocated in proportion to the census report of production. Milk income is allocated in proportion to milch cow inventories. Income from poultry and eggs is assumed to be constant per farm, and is allocated in proportion to the total number of farms in each district. Vegetable and small fruit income is allocated in proportion to acres in gardens and orchards.

We allocate net income from feed grains (hay, oats, barley, and rye taken together) in proportion to the difference between feed availability and feed requirement in each district. Both are calculated in oat-equivalent units. Feed availability is derived from census reports of hay, oats, rye, barley, corn, buckwheat, turnips, other roots, peas and beans.[34] Feed requirement is calculated in three steps. (i) We calculate an index of national total feed

---

32 Urquhart, "New Estimates", p. 11 (GDP by sector), p. 43 (agricultural gross income by commodity) and p. 50 (farm operating cost by component).

33 Frank Lewis and Marvin McInnis, "Agricultural Output and Efficiency in Lower Canada, 1851", *Research in Economic History*, 9 (1984), pp. 45-87. The seed ratio is 1.75 bushels per acre of wheat, which nationally averages slightly more than 12 per cent of production, p. 76.

34 Thirty bushels of oats are equivalent to one ton of hay; other oat-equivalences are taken from L.H. Bailey, *Cyclopedia of American Horticulture, vol. III* (New York, 1906), p. 67. The concentrated feeds are converted to oats based on their "dry matter" content per pound and Canadian bushel weights; see Bailey, *American Horticulture, vol. III*, p. 100 and L.H. Bailey, ed., *Cyclopedia of Farm Crops* (New York, 1922), p. 152. It is necessary to allow for seed requirements. Lewis and McInnis, "Agricultural Output", p. 76, supply a seed ratio for oats and barley; for other crops we estimate seed requirements as a percentage of production from Lewis and McInnis' seed requirements per acre and yields per acre reported by Bailey, *Cyclopedia of Farm Crops*, pp. 135-6, 153-5, 207, 212, 511.

requirements for each animal using the rations assumed by Lewis and McInnis.[35] (ii) We estimate the actual national total requirements by scaling the index for consistency with the total feed income reported by Urquhart.[36] (iii) We allocate national total feed requirements to districts in proportion to the income produced by the corresponding livestock and, in the case of draft animals, according to estimated inventories.[37] For example, the feeding needs of milch cows is allocated according to dairy income.

We distribute farm operating costs for blacksmithing according to the district's complement of draft horses; all other expenses are allocated in proportion to gross agricultural output.

2. Forestry

Forestry accounted for about 10 per cent of all commodity income in 1870 according to Urquhart, who divides forestry into non-agricultural (just under six million) and agricultural components (around 16 million).[38] The latter is allocated in proportion to district shares of firewood recorded in the census and the former according to the value of remaining forest products. The census report of quantities is valued using 1880 prices, most of which are calculated from data in the census of 1881. Table A2 summarizes sources and methods, estimated prices and the share of each item in the forestry total.

3. Fisheries

According to Urquhart, fisheries income was slightly more than one per cent of all commodity income. We allocate Urquhart's total ($2,921,000) less $131,790 for P.E.I. in proportion to an index of the value of district-level fish quantities reported in the 1870-71 census. The index, when combined with reported census values, generates the unit values reported in Table A3.

4. Mining

Urquhart's total ($4,431,000) less $638,000 for P.E.I. is allocated in proportion to an index of the value of mining products calculated from census reports of mining items. The index uses prices reported in Table A4, which also summarizes the relative contributions of different minerals and mining products. Mining accounted for about two per cent of all commodity income.

---

35   The animals are draft horses, other horses, oxen, other oxen, milch cows, other cattle, sheep and swine.

36   Urquhart's gross income from feed is converted to oat-equivalent units using an oat price of 40 cents per bushel; see M.C. Urquhart and K.A.H. Buckley, *Historical Statistics of Canada*, 2nd ed., series M229 (Ottawa, 1983).

37   We assume one oxen for every 25 acres of cropland; remaining oxen are designated "other". If there are insufficient oxen, horses make up the difference (if available); remaining horses are designated "other".

38   The two components are the "Forestry excluding agriculture" component of GNP and the "Forest Products" component of gross farm income; see Urquhart, *Historical Statistics of Canada*, Table 2.1 and 2.14. P.E.I. accounts for $239,040 of the $22,192,000 income in 1870, assuming that New Brunswick and P.E.I. produced in the same proportions during 1870 and 1880.

5. *Hunting and Trapping*

Hunting and trapping generated .001 of Canadian commodity income in 1870. Urquhart's total ($211,000) less $870 for P.E.I. is allocated in proportion to the value of fur items in the 1870-1 census.

6. *Manufacturing*

The regional index underlying our manufacturing estimate is based on a tabulation of the enumerators' manuscripts of industrial establishments.[39] One difficulty is the loss of enumerators' manuscripts for King's Ward of Saint John and parts of District 89 in northern Ontario. We interpolate the latter on the assumption that per capita industrial income in the missing subdistricts was similar to that in adjacent subdistricts. For industries located in Saint John (district 174) we use the official summary of manufacturing published in 1873.[40] Our calculation ignores establishments such as quarries, dentistry, painters and glaziers, and gas works which clearly were not manufacturing or were excluded from Urquhart's tabulation. We also ignore inactive establishments[41] and those producing less than $50 of output.[42] We subtract the total value of raw materials from value of production for each firm and then aggregate to district totals. A 10 per cent deduction is made for heat, light and other miscellaneous costs. The ratio of P.E.I. to Canadian income in 1870 is assumed to be the same as it was in 1880.

---

39 The manuscripts have been made machine-readable by a team at the University of Guelph consisting of Kris Inwood, Gerald Bloomfield and Elizabeth Bloomfield. Three distinct versions of this database are available. *IBB* (February 1990) is a version for internal use consisting of the manuscript data as they were entered by research assistants with modest error-checking and coding. *Canind71* (December 1990) is produced and marketed by the Bloomfields, and is virtually identical to *IBB*. *1870-71 Canadian Industrial Database* (October 1992) is an extensively revised and recoded version prepared by Inwood and used in this paper.

40 *Census of Canada, 1870-1*, Vol. III. This imputation incorporates adjustments for the ratio of value added to gross value of production (34 per cent) and the ratio of recompiled total to the originally published tabulation (1.05). These ratios are the average for New Brunswick outside of Saint John (districts 175 to 187).

41 If a firm records no variable inputs (labour quantities, wages and raw material values) or months of activity it is treated as inactive.

42 The published industrial tabulations of the 19th century census apparently excluded very small firms; see Canada, *Special Bulletin on the Mechanical and Manufacturing Industries*, Appendix to the Report of the Minister of Agriculture for 1894, Sessional Paper 8D, 1895. We are grateful to Gordon Holmes for this reference.

Table A1
Removal of P.E.I. Agriculture from Urquhart's 1870 GDP Estimate

Component	Urquhart	Canada	P.E.I.
Total	143406	139731	3675
Wheat	22160	21809	351
Potatoes	7463	6966	497
Seed, grass & clover	351	339	12
Flax fibre	112	111	1
Cheese	2271	1897	374
Butter	12853	12826	27
Cattle & calves	32561	31798	763
Hogs	16153	15557	598
Sheep & lambs	4202	4015	187
Horses	2586	2488	98
Milk	8700	8497	203
Wool	2272	2171	101
Oats	3275	3275	0
Barley	3688	3688	0
Rye	174	174	0
Hay	3125	3125	0
Flaxseed	161	159	2
Hops	149	148	1
Maple sugar	1649	1647	2
Honey	351	348	3
Tobacco	63	63	0
Apples	2480	2475	5
Small fruit	1730	1723	7
Grapes	102	102	0
Orchard fruit	241	240	1
Vegetables	8558	8298	260
Poultry	1383	1341	42
Eggs	4579	4440	139

Source: Urquhart, *Historical Statistics of Canada*, table 2.14 (Canada plus P.E.I.). Wheat, potatoes, flax fibre, butter, cheese, cattle, sheep, hogs and horses are allocated in proportion to 1870-1 census totals of each in Canada and PEI. Milk is allocated in proportion to cattle, wool in proportion to sheep, flaxseed in proportion to flax. We assume P.E.I. self-sufficiency in feedstuffs; hence all oats, barley, rye and hay remain with Canada. We assume that P.E.I. had the same share of Maritime output in 1870 as in 1880 of hops, tobacco, maple sugar, honey, apples, grapes and other fruit. The distribution of vegetables, poultry and eggs assumes equal production per farm across the country. The proportion of operating costs in gross farm output is assumed to be the same in P.E.I. and Canada.

Table A2
Prices for Forest Items, Census 1871-1

Census Item	Unit	Price/Unit (1881$)	Share of Item in National total
Square pine, white	cubic feet	0.204	16.1 %
Square pine, red	"	0.164	1.1 %
Square oak	"	0.345	3.7 %
Tamarac	"	0.120	2.2 %
Birch/maple	"	0.137	1.0 %
Elm	"	0.230	1.4 %
Walnut, black	"	0.913	0.3 %
Walnut, soft	"	0.345	0.2 %
Hickory	"	0.469	0.3 %
Other timber	"	0.239	20.9 %
Pine logs	number	0.830	33.5 %
Other logs	"	0.500	15.3 %
Masts and spars	"	0.900	0.3 %
Staves	thousands	7.170	0.8 %
Lathwood	cords	5.000	0.5 %
Tanbark	"	4.500	2.4 %

Sources: Unless otherwise noted, prices are calculated from the quantities and values of forest products of Canada in the census of 1881 reported in James Elliott Defebaugh, *History of the Lumber Industry of America, Volume 1* (Chicago, 1906), pp. 78-9. Black walnut and hickory are based on prices relative to oak for the U.S. in 1899; Defebaugh, *History of Lumber Industry*, p. 520. Soft walnut is assumed equal in price to oak based on prices in 1909 and 1915, as reported in Henry B. Steer, *Lumber Production in the United States, 1799-1946*, United States Department of Agriculture (USDA), Misc. Publication No. 669, (Washington, D.C., 1948), Tables 5, 84; and on prices in Chicago in 1896, as reported in the USDA, *Annual Report for 1896*, p. 415. Other timber: Defebaugh reports other timber together with walnut and hickory; see *History of Lumber Industry*, p. 78. We subtract walnut and hickory quantities and values (using the prices in the table) from his totals to get an average "other timber" price that excludes those woods. "Other logs" is "Spruce and Other Logs" in the 1881 census.

Table A3
Unit Values of the Fisheries Items, 1870-1 Census

Census Item	Unit	Price ($)	Percentage of value of National total
Cod	quintals	4.21	41.80
Haddock, hake, pollock	"	2.50	4.30
Sounds and tongues	barrels	7.00	0.10
Herring	"	3.00	18.10
Gaspareaux	"	4.03	1.70
Mackerel	"	10.00	11.20
Sardines	"	5.00	0.50
Halibut	"	5.00	0.30
Salmon	"	16.00	3.70
Shad	"	9.00	1.60
Eels	"	8.00	0.90
Whitefish	"	7.38	2.50
Trout	"	10.00	2.80
Other fish	"	4.05	4.70
Cured roe	"	6.00	0.30
Oysters	"	3.04	0.60
Cod liver oil	gallons	1.01	0.04
Other fish oil	"	0.50	4.90

Sources: Unit values are for 1870, calculated from the fisheries output in 1870 in Urquhart, *Historical Statistics of Canada*, and our index of the value of the fisheries items reported in the *Census of Canada, 1870-1*. The index is based on "yields" and "values" for 1885 as reported in Canada, *Statistical Abstract and Record for the Year 1886*, pp. 323-4 for all items except sardines, halibut, salmon, trout, whitefish and roe. The value of these items was based on their values relative to cod in 1870, as reported in Canada, "The Report of the Commissioner of Marine and Fisheries for 1870-71", Sessional Paper No. 5, Appendix F.

Table A4
The Value of Mining Products, 1870-1 Census

Census Item	Unit	Price per Unit (1890$)	Share in National Total
Gold	ounces	20.67	12.1 %
Silver	"	1.05	1.9 %
Copper ore	tons	21.05	7.2 %
Iron ore	"	2.03	6.7 %
Pyrites	"	2.50	0.2 %
Manganese	"	24.51	0.4 %
Other ores	"	2.95	1.1 %
Coal	"	2.08	40.1 %
Peat	"	2.56	1.0 %
Plumbago	"	29.71	0.2 %
Gypsum	"	0.86	2.5 %
Phosphate of lime	"	11.37	0.6 %
Mica	pounds	0.09	0.0 %
Crude petroleum	gallons	0.0337	11.2 %
Marble	cubic feet	0.273	0.1 %
Building stone	"	0.0934	12.4 %
Roofing slate	squares	4.23	2.4 %

Sources: Items are as reported in the *Census of Canada, 1870-1*. Except as noted below, prices were calculated from the quantities and values of mineral products in Canada in 1890; see Canada, Department of Agriculture, *The Statistical Year-Book of Canada for 1891* (Ottawa, 1892), pp. 305-06. Gold and silver prices are calculated from the 1890 value and quantity reported in Dominion Bureau of Statistics, *Chronological Record, 1604-1947, Historical Production Tables, 1886-1946* (Ottawa, 1949), p. 28. Copper is based on its price relative to iron ore calculated from national total quantities and values in the census of 1901 (p. 403), and the iron ore price reported here. Other ore is assumed to have been coke; over 90 per cent of this item was recorded in Nova Scotia, the rest in New Brunswick. Peat is based on the price relative to coal in the census of 1901 (p. 403), and the coal price reported here. Marble is based on the price relative to slate in the census of 1911 (p. 138), and the slate price reported here. Slate is based on the price relative to brick in the census of 1901 (p. 404), and the brick price in the 1891 *Statistical Year-Book*.

Appendix B: Potential Sources of Bias in Regional Decomposition

We rely almost exclusively on census data to make a geographic decomposition of national income. If the census undercounts production in one district relative to another, then our estimate is biased. Fortunately, the 1870-1 census was a reasonably comprehensive attempt to document many aspects of Canadian society; we are aware of no evidence indicating that enumeration was less accurate in one part of the country than in others.

A more subtle potential for bias is hidden in the size of different sectors. If Urquhart's national income estimate undercounts one sector relative to another, then we will understate relative income in districts relying heavily upon that sector. For example, enumerators made little effort to enquire about commodities produced and consumed within households. Some evidence suggests that household production was relatively more important in the Maritimes, which implies that an exclusive reliance on census data will overstate somewhat the size of provincial income differentials.[43] Fortunately, the degree of bias was small relative to the size of overall income differential.[44] There is also some concern that census enumeration was less complete for fishing than for other sectors.[45] Again the potential bias is small, since a doubling of all fishing income would raise Nova Scotia from 76 per cent to only 79 per cent of the national average.

A third possible bias is that our estimate encompasses income derived from the production of commodities but not services, which accounted for about one-third of all income according to Urquhart. As in the case of household production, census information about services is quite limited. Fortunately, there is no clear reason to think that service activity was distributed differently than commodity income.[46] The inclusion of shipping would improve the relative position of Saint John and the Nova Scotia coastal communities, but this would be offset by the inclusion of railways and other forms of transportation in Central Canada. A recognition of financial and commercial income would raise the position of Toronto and Montreal relative to Maritime towns.

A fourth concern is income remitted across geographic boundaries. For example, Nova Scotia income is actually less than it appears to the extent that profits were remitted to the British and American owners of provincial coal mines. Of course, foreigners also owned

---

43 Inwood, "Maritime Industrialization", Tables One and Nine.

44 In the Nova Scotia of 1870, unlike Ontario, more butter, cheese and cloth was produced on farms than in factories. Across the entire manufacturing sector, however, the inclusion of farm-based activity raises per capita output in Nova Scotia relative to Ontario from 53 per cent (factory only) to only 57 per cent (factory plus farm).

45 Carman Bickerton and Phyllis Wagg (personal communications) warn about the difficulties of enumerating income generated in fishing by Maritime residents; under-enumeration of fishermen as an occupational group is recognized by McClelland, "The New Brunswick Economy", p. 55.

46 The oft-mentioned observation that services tend to increase their share of all income as per capita income rises suggests that the ratio of service to commodity income may have been higher in high-income Ontario than in the low-income Maritimes. If so, the true extent of regional disparities is understated by the use of commodity income.

some of the enterprise in Central Canada. Income also flowed in the opposite direction; Canadians working in the United States remitted to their families at home considerable income which offset the profit outflow. There is no evidence that these intra-family transfers were more important for one region than for another.

One final question is the difference in prices of various commodities between and even within provinces. Unfortunately, the lack of regional price indices continues to obstruct the evaluation of price effects. Although it would be useful to have some estimate of regional price differences, they are unlikely to be of a magnitude that would alter the most important regional patterns identified below.

In principle, each of the above measurement issues has the potential to alter estimates such as those reported in this paper. For these and other reasons the estimates are more approximate than is suggested by the crisp precision of quantitative evidence. Nevertheless, the broad outlines of regional disparities are unlikely to be influenced by any corrections along the lines suggested above.

Appendix C: The Measurement of Population and Economic Density

The 1870-1 Canadian census reports population and area at the level of the subdistrict used for census administration, which tended to be townships or parishes in rural areas and city wards in urban areas.[47] The average subdistrict encompassed 370 families and was small enough to be canvassed by one or two enumerators. Data reported at this level permit us to calculate the average density of population and income for the entire subdistrict. Unfortunately, in 1870 as today, Canada encompassed vast expanses of largely unpopulated territory. One distinctive feature of the unsettled territory is that measures of average population density systematically understate the densities at which people lived.

The problem may be visualized by thinking of a large northern region in which there is a single community built on employment in a mine or lumber mill. The people within the town live in proximity to each other with a density of settlement comparable to that of many other small towns. But the average population density of these people can only be calculated using the area of the entire region. The vast territory in which nobody lived introduces a downward bias to the measure of population density. Given the availability of data, the only remedy for this measurement problem is to ignore subdistricts reporting a very low density of population, on the grounds that density cannot be measured meaningfully at extremely low levels.

In Table C1 we report the effect of excluding districts which fall below the thresholds of two persons per square mile (psm) and 10 psm. The data indicate that one per cent of the population lived in subdistricts accounting for two-thirds of the land surface with a density less than two psm, while eight per cent of the population lived on four-fifths of the area at less than 10 psm. Ignoring the latter would eliminate almost all of the three northernmost regions (northern Ontario, northern Quebec and the Gulf of St. Lawrence), two-fifths of Nova Scotia's land surface and one-tenth of its population, and three-quarters of New Brunswick's land surface and one-quarter of its population. The less drastic two psm rule excludes two-thirds of the Canadian land surface, mostly in the three northern regions. No other region outside of northern New Brunswick loses more than one per cent of its population. We conclude that the exclusion of subdistricts with fewer than two psm will eliminate the most serious problems of density measurement while retaining a study area that roughly corresponds to the inhabited portions of all four provinces.

---

47 *Census of Canada, 1870-71*, Vol. I, Table 1.

Table C1
Area, Population and Population per Square Mile

	Den	Den2	Den10	Pop2	Pop10	Area2	Area10
Canada	10.3	30.3	44.8	0.99	0.92	0.34	0.21
Nova Scotia	18.5	19.8	27.5	1.00	0.89	0.93	0.60
New Brunswick	10.5	14.1	29.1	0.98	0.72	0.73	0.26
Quebec	6.4	31.6	50.9	0.98	0.92	0.20	0.11
Ontario	15.9	43.3	51.3	0.99	0.97	0.37	0.30
E. Nova Scotia	16.5	17.2	24.6	1.00	0.85	0.96	0.57
C. Nova Scotia	21.5	21.6	28.6	1.00	0.90	1.00	0.68
W. Nova Scotia	17.3	20.5	29.1	0.99	0.91	0.83	0.54
S. New Brunswick	16.7	17.8	31.5	0.99	0.79	0.93	0.42
N. New Brunswick	5.2	8.8	21.9	0.94	0.53	0.55	0.13
G. of St Lawrence	1.2	12:8	27.0	0.86	0.69	0.08	0.03
L. St. Lawrence	25.6	34.4	56.3	0.99	0.93	0.74	0.42
S.E. Quebec	20.5	21.1	29.0	1.00	0.92	0.97	0.65
Montreal area	62.0	63.8	78.9	1.00	0.98	0.97	0.77
N. Quebec	1.0	12.6	26.6	0.89	0.67	0.07	0.02
N. Ontario	0.9	12.7	24.5	0.82	0.60	0.06	0.02
E. Ontario	31.2	35.2	46.5	0.99	0.96	0.88	0.64
Huronia	42.8	44.0	45.5	1.00	0.99	0.97	0.93
G. Horseshoe	103.8	103.8	103.8	1.00	1.00	1.00	1.00
W. Ontario	52.2	52.2	52.3	1.00	1.00	1.00	1.00

Den = people per square mile (psm)

Den2 = psm in subdistricts exceeding two psm

Den10 = psm in subdistricts exceeding 10 psm

Pop2 = the share of all people in subdistricts exceeding two psm

Pop10 = the share of all people in subdistricts exceeding 10 psm

Area2 = the share of all area in subdistricts exceeding two psm

Area10 = the share of all area in subdistricts exceeding 10 psm

Appendix D: The Boundaries of Canadian Census Districts

The maps are computer-generated using digitized census district boundaries.[48] We began with the basic landform depicted on a modern topographical map that provides an accurate cartographic framework within which local level detail from 19th century sources may be situated.[49] The staff of the *Historical Atlas of Canada* provided the map, on which was indicated their understanding of census district boundaries in 1891. We confirmed and in several cases modified these boundaries with a district-by-district examination of the 1894 *Electoral Atlas*.[50]

In effect, our starting point was the 1894 Electoral Atlas represented in a modern cartographic framework. Later maps are undesirable as a starting point because the greater number of boundary changes between 1850 and the date of publication complicate the task of recreating 1850 boundaries. Earlier maps are likely to suffer unacceptable distortion because the mathematics of cartographic projection were not yet well understood by contemporaries.

The 1895 electoral map was then modified to reflect successive changes in electoral boundaries between 1867 and 1895; these changes were introduced backwards through time.[51] For example the 1895 map was modified to "undo" the effects of an 1893 district change; the map resulting from this procedure was modified to "undo" the effects of an 1892 change, and so on. It was necessary as well to adjust for differences between electoral and census districts. This followed information reported by the Bureau of the Census which explicitly identifies the extent to which census and electoral boundaries were coincident.[52]

---

48 We are grateful for advice on mapping from David Frost and Patricia Thornton of Concordia University, Jan Mersey at the University of Guelph, Byron Muldofsky and Ron Walder of the Historical Atlas of Canada Project, and the staff of the National Map Library. Cory Sanders and Brian Morber digitized the district boundaries; the latter designed the maps used in this paper. The digitized boundary files are available from Kris Inwood at the University of Guelph.

49 The Canadian Department of Energy, Mines and Resources produces the base map at a scale of 1:4 million which was enlarged to 1:2 million. This map uses a Lambert Conformal Conic projection with a northern parallel 77 degrees, southern parallel 49 degrees, and an origin 96 degrees longitude and 45 degree latitude. We are grateful to Brian Muldofsky and Ron Walder of the Historical Atlas of Canada Project for selecting and supplying a copy of this map.

50 *Electoral Atlas of the Dominion of Canada as Divided for the Revision of the Voters' Lists in 1894* (Ottawa, 1895).

51 The relevant source is the Representation Act and its amendments. See 30-1 Victoria, ch. 3, "The British North America Act" (1867); 31 Victoria, ch. 78 (1868); 32-3 V., ch. 45 (1869); 32-3 V., ch. 46 (1869); 35 V., ch. 13 (1872); 36 V., ch. 29 (1873); 37 V., ch. 12 (1874); 39 V., ch. 11 (1876); 45 V., ch. 3 (1882); 49 V., ch. 6 (1886); 55-6 V., ch. 11 (1892); 56 V., ch. 9 (1893).

52 Canadian census publications that we consulted include 1851-2 township lists; *1870-1 Census*, Vol. I, pp. xiv-vi and pp. 435-47; *1870-1 Census*, Vol. V, pp. 388-434; *1880-1 Census*, Vol. I, Tables V & S; *1890-1 Census*, Tables II & VI; 1891 *Census Bulletin #2*. Also helpful were *Map Showing the Electoral Divisions of the Dominion of Canada*, 1875, National Map Collection 79301, and *New Railway and Postal Map of the Dominion of Canada*, 1875, National Map Collection 80230.

The Industrial Context of Inequality: Female Participation in Nova Scotia's Paid Labour Force: 1871-1921

D.A. Muise

Eighteen year old Marie LeBlanc was typical of the largest category of working women of her generation in Nova Scotia.[1] In April 1901 she was employed as a servant in the household of Amherst merchant Samuel Geddes. Like most servants (77 per cent in 1901) Marie came from the countryside. Though a Roman Catholic, she worked in a Methodist household; here, too, her experience proved typical in an era when the middle classes were predominantly Anglo-Protestant and servants often Catholic. Marie reported earnings of $140 the previous year, which did not include board and was based on twelve months employment. The Geddes' household comprised 43 year old Samuel, his wife Alice, who did not work outside the home, two sons of six and two years and Marie. It was a comparatively small household in 1901, especially in "Busy Amherst" where boarders and working children more than equalled the numbers of householders in the workforce.

In contrast to Marie, yet like numerous other working women in the province, 22 year old Georgina Willard taught grade school in the bustling coal town of Sydney Mines. She lived at home with her parents, three teen-

ACKNOWLEDGEMENTS: This study has been assisted by grants from the Social Sciences and Humanities Research Council for the project: "COMMUNITIES IN TRANSITION: MARITIME TOWNS AND THE NATIONAL POLICY, 1870-1921". Students in my research seminars at Carleton between 1986 and 1989 helped its early conceptual development as did my colleague Carman Bickerton. Bob MacIntosh created some of the Sydney Mines data bases as part of his Ph.D. thesis on child labour in the coal fields. Carleton and SSHRCC funded research assistants to code and re-code census manuscripts: Kerry Badgley, Barbara Clow, Daniel Yee, Sue Jenkins, Sean Purdy, Mike Bernards, Keith Hodgins, Tom Matheson, Sheila Day, Fulton Rhymes and Dorothy McGrath. Data assembly and initial analysis was assisted by Carleton's Computer and Communications Service Group — Bruce Winer, Greg Morrison, Jane Wilson and Jane Miller. An early version of this paper was presented to the Atlantic Canada Workshop at Saint Mary's University in Halifax in September, 1989. This version has benefited from the reading and comments of Carman Bickerton, Alison Prentice, Gillian Cleese, Suzanne Morton and by *Acadiensis'* ever vigilant anonymous readers. This article is reprinted from *Acadiensis*, XX, 2 (Spring 1991), pp. 3-31.

1   Pseudonyms are used for all these individuals, who are drawn from the 1901 manuscript census. This census is available to researchers under the provisions of the Access to Information Act.

aged sisters and a younger brother, in a large frame house on Oxford Street, in the mine town's fashionable "Upper Town". No servants lived in the Willards' house; however, teen-aged girls were expected to assist with normal housework and the family may have employed help that did not live in, for many servants and cleaning ladies lived at home. As Baptists, the Willards were a minority in the predominantly Presbyterian, Anglican and, increasingly, Catholic town. But they would not have felt out of place among the town's almost exclusively Anglo-Protestant professional and managerial elite. While Georgina's annual earnings of just under $200 totalled less than half the mean salary reported by the town's male teachers, her modest income was almost double the average reported by servants, by far the largest group of employed women in Sydney Mines, where there were very few other opportunities for paid employment for women.

Thomas Willard, her father, was a clerk at the offices of the General Mining Association. Fifty-one years old in 1901, he reported an income of $600, which, while not a management-level salary, was well above the mean income of $455 reported by miners heading their own households that year in Sydney Mines. Still, the combined family income of father and daughter did not match that of many miners with one or two sons working underground.[2] Enjoyment of a family income for at least parts of a family's life-course was becoming common, as Nova Scotia's bustling urban economy provided a variety of new opportunities for employment.

Surplus rural workers, such as Daisy Miller, also took advantage of these new opportunities. Daisy, who came from the nearby rural community of Hebron, lived in a boarding house on Gardiner Street in north-end Yarmouth and worked in the massive spinning room of the nearby Yarmouth Duck and Yarn Cotton mill. Her experience typified that of yet another large group of young working women whose employment in factories and lives as boarders in households, to which they were not connected by family, marked a new departure for the provincial society. Half of the 150 workers employed in the mill in 1900 were female. Daisy's move to Yarmouth was part of a massive demographic shift occurring throughout rural Nova Scotia. All five of her fellow lodgers were young country-born women who, like 17 year old Daisy, worked as spinners for Yarmouth Duck and Yarn. The six cotton girls shared two large rooms and, in 1901, reported suspiciously identical annual earnings of $167. While it is unlikely that, given the very high turn-over rate at the mill, all six would have worked the entire previous 12 months, a time-pay book for the previous decade shows that, for six full 10 hour days, spinners and doffers

---

2   Robert McIntosh, "'Grotesque Faces and Figures': Child Labour in the Canadian Coalfields, 1820-1930", Ph.D. thesis, Carleton University, 1990, ch. 4.

3   Cosmos Cotton Collection, Paybooks, 1887-1897, Yarmouth County Historical Society.

earned wages of $3.00-$3.25 per week.[3] Room and board was advertised in Yarmouth that year for between $2.00 and $2.50 per week. After paying board, Daisy and her fellow cotton workers may have had little left over. But, as elsewhere, young women were prepared to endure low wages and difficult working conditions to escape the drudgery of household labour.[4]

Lizzie Williams, the 51 year old widow who owned and operated Daisy's boarding house, had yet another earning experience typical of women during that period of transition. She had no children living at home, but cared for her 70 year old mother. From the $700 she reported as her earnings from rentals that year, Lizzie provided the food and other services that went with maintaining a boarding house, including $90 paid in wages to her young servant girl.

Though much has been written about the nature, structure and significance of the industrialization of the Maritime provinces, women's participation in the new workforces created in the course of industrialization remains little understood.[5] Scholars dealing with the history of women during the period have

---

4   Many such women migrated from rural to urban areas. See Alan Brookes, "Out-Migration from the Maritime Provinces, 1860-1900: Some Preliminary Considerations", *Acadiensis*, V, 2 (Spring 1976), pp. 26-55. Patricia Thornton, working from the demographic evidence of those who remained behind, has argued that women were among the most mobile in the migration from the countryside. See "The Problem of Out-Migration from Atlantic Canada, 1871-1921: A New Look", *Acadiensis*, XV, 1 (Autumn 1985), pp. 3-30.

5   Useful surveys of recent trends in women's history are Bettina Bradbury, "Women's History and Working-Class History", *Labour/Le travail*, 19 (Spring 1987), pp. 23-43; and Gail Campbell, "Canadian Women's History: A View from Atlantic Canada", *Acadiensis*, XX, 1 (Autumn 1990), pp. 184-99. Most studies deal with the experience of women in larger centres and focus on systemic inequalities faced on entry into the labour force. All focus on increases in participation by women and increased diversity, a process characterized by Marjorie Griffin Cohen as "the modernization of inequality", which failed to change relative positions of men and women in a patriarchal system reinforced under capitalism. See *Women's Work: Markets and Economic Development in Nineteenth Century Ontario* (Toronto, 1988), p. 152. Notable as well are B. Bradbury, "Women and Wage Labour in a Period of Transition: Montreal, 1861-1881", *Histoire sociale-Social History*, XVII (May 1984), pp. 115-31; Joy Parr, *The Gender of Breadwinners: Women, Men and Change in Two Industrial Towns, 1880-1950* (Toronto, 1990). Five recent studies centred in the Maritimes are Sheva Medjuck, "Women's Response to Economic and Social Change in the Nineteenth Century: Moncton Parish, 1851 to 1871", *Atlantis*, XI (Fall, 1984), pp. 5-19; Ginnette Lafleur, "L'industrialization et le travail remunéré des femmes, Moncton, 1881-1891", in Peta Tancred-Sheriff, ed., *Feminist Research: Prospect and Retrospect* (Kingston, 1988), pp. 127-40; Margaret McCallum, "Separate Spheres: The Organization of Work in a Confectionary Factory, Ganong Bros., Saint Stephen, New Brunswick", *Labour/Le travail*, 24 (Autumn 1989), pp. 69-90; and Shirley Tillotson, "The Operators Along the Coast:

highlighted the twin drives for suffrage and educational equality by middle class women, both of which aimed to expand women's sphere of activity in the public realm.[6] While "Working Girls" became objects of enquiries into urban life's potentially unwholesome consequences, their working and living experiences remain largely unexplored in the scholarship dealing with the regional transition.[7] Knowledge of the changing patterns of female participation in paid labour remains limited as well.[8] This paper explains the changing nature of women's paid work during Nova Scotia's industrial transition. It contributes to a literature on the gendered dimensions of class formation in the context of the specific realities of given communities. A primarily quantitative probe, this article describes the major trends during the transition, locating

A Case Study of the Link Between Gender, Skilled Labour and Social Power, 1900-1930", *Acadiensis*, XX, 1 (Autumn 1990), pp. 72-88, and "'We Will all soon be "first-class men"': Gender and Skill in Canada's early twentieth century urban telegraph industry", *Labour/Le travail*, 27 (Spring 1991), pp. 97-126.

6   Judith Fingard, "College, Career and Community: Dalhousie Coeds, 1881-1921", in Paul Axelrod and John G. Reid, eds., *Youth, University and Canadian Society: Essays in the Social History of Higher Education* (Montreal, 1989), pp. 26-50; E.R. Forbes, "Battles in Another War: Edith Archibald and the Halifax Feminist Movement", in *Challenging the Regional Stereotype: Essays on the 20th Century Maritimes* (Fredericton, 1989), pp. 67-89; and John Reid, "The Education of Women at Mount Allison, 1854-1914", *Acadiensis*, XII, 2 (Spring 1983), pp. 3-33.

7   Margaret McCallum, "Keeping Women in their Place: The Minimum Wage in Canada, 1910-25", *Labour/Le travail*, 17 (Spring 1986), pp. 29-58; Janet Guildford "Coping with De-industrialization: The Nova Scotia Department of Technical Education, 1907-1930", *Acadiensis*, XVI, 2 (Spring 1987), pp. 69-84; Christina Simmons, "Helping the Poorer Sisters: The Women of the Jost Mission, Halifax, 1905-1945", *Acadiensis*, XII, 1 (Autumn 1984), pp. 3-28. An example of women coping in an industrial setting is offered in David Frank, ed., "The Miner's Financier: Women in the Cape Breton Coal Towns, 1917", *Atlantis*, VII (Spring 1983), pp. 137-43.

8   Although this study will not focus on participation rates, preliminary evidence seems to confirm hypotheses presented by the more general literature. Prior to the 1920s at least, the general trend was for women to leave the labour force by their mid-20s: dropping from a maximum participation rate of about 40 per cent between the ages of 17 and 25 to less than 15 per cent for those over 25. The basic study of female participation rates in Canada remains Sylvia Ostry, *The Female Worker in Canada* (Ottawa, 1968); more contemporary is Patricia Connelly, *Last Hired, First Fired: Women and the Canadian Workforce* (Toronto, 1978). American women's experience is treated in Lynn Y. Weiner, *From Working Girl to Working Mother* (Chapel Hill, 1985). Some analysis is found in Canada, *Sixth Census of Canada, 1921*, Volume IV (Ottawa, 1929), Table 5, which depicts high rates at younger age levels and a decline after the mid-20s. Participation rates rose steadily over the past century.

women workers within the new workforces in three selected towns: Yarmouth, Amherst and Sydney Mines.

Nova Scotia's urban population grew from under 20 per cent of the provincial total in 1871 to just under 50 per cent by 1921.[9] Yet the province's over-all population hardly increased at all. In fact, Nova Scotia's share of Canada's population declined sharply during this period, exacerbating a political crisis that was reducing the Maritime region's political clout in Ottawa.[10] At the same time, the unprecedented growth of the Canadian economy involved Maritime towns increasingly in nation-forming exchanges, as the resource enclaves which had characterized the pre-industrial period were replaced by a set of interlocking dependencies tying the provincial economy to the steam-based technologies that were coming to dominate North American life.[11]

Located at Nova Scotia's southern, northern and eastern extremities, Yarmouth, Amherst and Sydney Mines responded to the challenges of an integrated national economy with intensive capitalization and extensive physical growth. New railroad construction linked the three towns to each other and to the rest of the province. Public construction brought the trappings of a modern state, with the establishment of new institutional structures, ranging from post offices and fire halls to a variety of churches and educational institutions. In a spirit of "Boosterism" common to the age, the local governments acquired the technological means to service their rapidly increasing populations. Publicly and privately funded electricity and street railways, telephone exchanges, sewerage and water works proliferated, adding a new dynamic to town growth. To carry out such projects the towns sought incorporation under

9   L.D. McCann, "Staples and the New Industrialism in the Growth of Post-Confederation Halifax", *Acadiensis*, VII, 2 (Spring, 1979), pp. 47-79. Definitions of "urban" vary somewhat, but by the end of World War I, a population shift favoured Pictou, Cumberland and Cape Breton where the heavier industrial towns absorbed more and more of the population, at the expense of the rural parts of the province. On intra-regional population shifts see Thornton, "The Problem of Out-Migration from Atlantic Canada"; and Brookes, "Out-Migration from the Maritime Provinces".

10 E.R. Forbes, "'Never the Twain Did Meet': Prairie-Maritime Relations, 1910-1927", *Canadian Historical Review*, LXI,1 (March 1978), pp. 18-37.

11 The seminal discussion of the economic transition is T.W. Acheson, "The National Policy and the Industrialization of the Maritimes, 1880-1910", in P.A. Buckner and David Frank, eds., *Atlantic Canada After Confederation* (Fredericton, 1985), pp. 176-201. An assessment of recent writing is provided in Eric Sager, "Dependency, Underdevelopment, and the Economic History of the Atlantic Region", *Acadiensis*, XVII, 1 (Autumn 1987), pp. 117-36. See also Ian Mckay, "The Crisis of Dependent Development: class conflict in the Nova Scotia coal fields, 1872-1876", in Gregory S. Kealey, ed., *Class, Gender, and Region: Essays in Canadian Historical Sociology* (St. John's, 1988), pp. 9-49.

Nova Scotia's new municipal legislation: Amherst and Sydney Mines incorporated in 1889, Yarmouth in 1890. The established elites controlling these new local governments, sought, through the provision of local services, to attract more industry to their communities.[12]

At the beginning of the period, in 1871, Yarmouth, Amherst and Sydney Mines ranked as Nova Scotia's second, third and fourth urban centres. By 1921, their populations, which ranged in size from 2,000 to 3,000 in 1871, had climbed to between 7,000 and 10,000. Reflecting various dimensions of the province's social and ethnic construction, each offers a distinctive window into community responses to the challenges of this period of unprecedented growth. Yarmouth's population surge coincided with the massive redeployment of mercantile capital towards manufacturing in the 1880s. Amherst's growth surge occurred in the 1890s and early 1900s; in Sydney Mines, the establishment of a primary steel-making complex in 1902-3 initiated a surge in population growth (see Figure 1). In the three towns taken together, the number of women in the workforce rose from just over 300 (10 per cent) in 1871 to almost 2000 (22 per cent) by 1921, a rate of increase half again as fast as that of the male workforce. But that growth was unevenly distributed, reflecting significant differences in patterns of development among the three towns (see Table One).[13]

Yarmouth, metropolitan centre of the southwestern counties for the previous century, had been Nova Scotia's most dynamic "Wood, Wind and Sail" community. Because of its very active mercantile sector, it was often referred to as the province's most "American" town, a view reinforced by the fact that it was made up almost entirely of descendants of pre-Loyalist American migrants to the area.[14] Its merchants, along with those of the Pictou area,[15] were among the province's most astute in responding to opportunities

---

12 D.A. Muise, "The Great Transformation: Changing the Urban Face of Nova Scotia, 1871-1921", *Nova Scotia Historical Review* (Autumn 1991) (forthcoming); and L. Anders Sandberg, "Dependent Development, Labour and the Trenton Steel Works, Nova Scotia, c.1900-1943", *Labour/Le travail*, 27 (Spring 1991), pp. 127-62.

13 Figure 1, Table One and all subsequent Figures and Tables are based on data bases created for the "Maritime Communities in Transition" project. They include all census attributes for the entire workforce as recorded in the manuscript census returns for the towns of Yarmouth, Amherst and Sydney Mines for each of the six national censuses between 1871 and 1921. Together, all the data files comprise upwards of 40,000 cases. All data for this paper has been analysed using SPSS PC+ and Microsoft Chart.

14 Robert Aitken, "Loyalism and National Identity in Yarmouth, Nova Scotia, 1830-1870", M.A. thesis, Trent University, 1975, ch. 3.

15 L.D. McCann, "The Mercantile-Industrial Transition in the Metal Towns of Pictou County, 1857-1931", *Acadiensis*, VIII, 2 (Spring 1979), pp. 47-79.

Figure 1
Population Growth in Three Nova Scotia Towns, 1871-1931

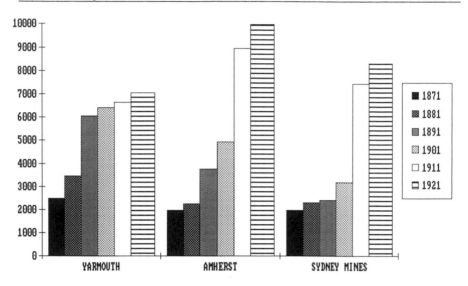

Figure 2
Workforce Growth (by gender); Yarmouth, Amherst and Sydney Mines

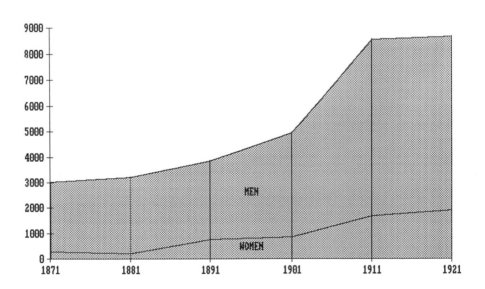

Table One
Workforces in Transition: Female/Male Ratios

		1871 F/M	1881 F/M	1891 F/M	1901 F/M	1911 F/M	1921 F/M
Yarmouth							
	number	136/1447	93/1200	421/1291	500/1650	709/1752	863/1907
	per cent	9/91	6/94	25/75	23/77	28/72	31/69
Amherst							
	number	112/709	144/659	355/1078	322/1516	732/2733	707/2620
	per cent	13/87	18/82	25/75	18/82	22/78	22/78
Sydney Mines							
	number	54/581	14/720	14/702	50/950	265/2417	370/2254
	per cent	9/91	2/98	6/94	5/95	10/90	14/86
Total							
	number	302/2737	251/2579	793/3073	872/4116	1706/6902	1940/7681
	per cent	10/90	9/91	21/79	17/83	20/80	22/78

presented by the 1878 National Policy. Two major community-based in-dustries emerged there in the 1880s. Both were connected to the "Wood, Wind and Sail" era and controlled, initially at least, by local entrepreneurs. The expanded and diversified Burrill-Johnson Foundry, which had originated in the 1850s as a supplier of iron knees and fastenings for Yarmouth's large ship-building and outfitting industry, built stoves and other housewares, as well as watermain piping, steam engines and pumps, which were sold regionally, na-tionally and internationally. In the 1880s the company added a boat-building yard where small steam powered vessels were constructed. At full production, the expanded foundry employed over 150 workers, none of them women. The second industry, Yarmouth Duck and Yarn, was formed following a meeting in 1883 of a few of Yarmouth's most prominent merchants. Importing the neces-sary technology and managerial skills from neighbouring New England, it quickly developed into a major sailcloth factory. The number of employees grew steadily to over 200 by 1900 and to more than 300 by 1921, almost half of them women. These two factories, along with a woollen mill and a shoe factory on the northern outskirts at Milton, gave Yarmouth the province's most concentrated industrial workforce south of Halifax. Because of the nature of its expansion, Yarmouth offered women the greatest variety of opportunities for paid work. And women responded: the proportion of women in the workforce rose from a low of six per cent in 1881 to a high of 31 per cent by 1921 (see Table One).

Amherst, located on the edge of the pasturelands of the Tantramar Marsh, also has a rich lumbering and agricultural hinterland in Cumberland County. Although disadvantaged by its lack of immediate access to tide water, the town performed most of the usual local metropolitan functions. When the Intercolonial Railway passed through in the 1870s, possibilities for industrial development emerged, especially after Saint John and Amherst based investors succeeded in having a spur line constructed to tap the rich coal resources of nearby Springhill.[16] With a supply of coal assured, Amherst entrepreneurs set out to expand their town's industrial base.[17] Rhodes-Curry began as a construction and manufacturing firm taking advantage of opportunities in public construction and railway expansion. Eventually it successfully contracted to build everything from wooden railway rolling stock and mine cars, supplied in the thousands to both regional and national markets, to housing developments and public buildings. After 1909, however, as steel cars replaced wooden-bodied ones, the massive car plant was gradually shut down. The construction end of the firm's business collapsed with the recession in the region's building boom after 1911, and the firm shut down altogether early in the 1920s. Robb Engineering, the town's second major industry, began when the son of a small local foundry operator returned from New England to expand the family's operations. By the 1890s Robb's manufactured its own line of steam engines and boilers which sold throughout Canada and internationally. Eventually, the firm would assemble railway locomotives as well.[18] Clearly, women would find no opportunities for paid employment in the town's major industries. But Amherst was also home to Hewson's, one of the province's largest woollen mills, and to the huge Amherst Boot and Shoe factory, both of which employed large numbers of women. Women had, in any case, always represented a significant proportion of Amherst's paid workforce, comprising 13 per cent as early as 1871. By 1911, when the town's workforce reached its peak for the period, the proportion of women stood at 22 per cent (see Table One). Although Amherst's factories collapsed after World War I, for a time

16 Ian McKay, "The Realm of Uncertainty: The Experience of Work in the Cumberland Coal Mines, 1873-1927", *Acadiensis*, XVI, 1 (Autumn 1986), pp. 3-58

17 The major study of Amherst's emergence as an industrial community is Nolan Reilly, "The Emergence of Class Consciousness in Industrial Nova Scotia: A Study of Amherst, 1891-1925", Ph.D. thesis, Dalhousie University, 1982, chs. 1 and 2; and "The General Strike in Amherst, Nova Scotia, 1919", *Acadiensis*, IX, 2 (Spring 1980), pp. 56-77. See also MacKay, "The Realm of Uncertainty".

18 A survey of the *Amherst Daily News* (1900-1911) revealed the link between the town's rise and the expansion of other Maritime industrial communities. Almost daily its reports included announcements of contracts or orders awarded Rhodes-Curry or Robb Engineering for public construction, railroad rolling stock, or the supply of equipment to industries and communities throughout the region.

they made "Busy Amherst" the region's most intensely developed industrial town of its size, with an integrated capitalist class which coordinated community development.

Following the arrival of the General Mining Association [GMA] in the 1820s, Sydney Mines had come to occupy a central place in Nova Scotia's coal mining industry. In 1901 it was probably Nova Scotia's most "British" town, primarily due to its continuing domination by paternalistic Richard H. Brown, whose father had run the GMA's operations in Cape Breton for its first 40 years. The Browns' preference for Scots and English miners helped maintain the dominance of British mining systems, along with the social organization of the community that it implied. The takeover of the GMA, in 1901, by the Pictou and Halifax based Nova Scotia Steel and Coal Company, was followed by massive new investment in a primary steel plant.[19] The new owners turned to the United States for their technology, as well as for coal mining machinery and many of the key steel-makers. The bulk of the workers remained local, however, and continued to live in company owned housing and to buy their goods at the company store. With its occupational base narrowly confined to mining and related trades prior to 1902 and commercial opportunities limited by company control over trade, the town lacked the leadership and capital that drove Yarmouth and Amherst to diversify their economic bases. Its expansion was troubled by the uncertain corporate history of the Nova Scotia Steel Company and ended abruptly with the absorption of the company by Dominion Steel and Coal in 1921. Within weeks, the Sydney Mines plant was dismantled and Sydney Mines reverted to its role as a coal town.[20] None of its industries ever employed women, save for a few clerks in the post-1900 period. As a result, women's participation in the paid workforce remained limited: just two per cent of the workforce in 1881, they had risen to 14 per cent by 1921 (see Table One).

Generally speaking, Nova Scotia's industrial moment was brief. Yarmouth, Amherst and Sydney Mines all ceased to grow by 1911 and would contract thereafter. Yet the transformation wrought by the industrial process remained,

---

19   McCann, "The Mercantile Industrial Transition"; and Kris Inwood, "Local Control, Resources and the Nova Scotia Steel and Coal Company", Canadian Historical Association, *Historical Papers* (1986), pp. 254-82.

20   D.A. Muise, "The General Mining Association and Nova Scotia's Coal, 1827-1857", *Bulletin of Canadian Studies*, X (1983), pp. 23-40; "The Making of an Industrial Community: Cape Breton Coal Towns, 1867-1900", in Brian Tennyson and Don MacGillivray, eds., *Cape Breton Historical Essays* (Sydney, 1980), pp. 76-95; McCann, "The Mercantile-Industrial Transition"; Craig Heron, *Working in Steel* (Toronto, 1988), chs. I-II; and "The Great War and Nova Scotia Steelworkers", *Acadiensis*, XVI, 2 (Spring 1987), pp. 3-34; and W.J.A. Donald, *The Canadian Iron and Steel Industry: A Study in the Economic History of a Protected Industry* (Boston, 1915).

both in the physical structures put in place to enable towns to deal with their dramatically increased populations and, even more significantly, in the experience and memories of the people who flocked to and through the towns. As Yarmouth, Amherst and Sydney Mines responded to their varied industrial opportunities, the size, the sex and the structure of their workforces were transformed. Their new industries depended on thousands of new workers, including hundreds of women, whose arrival dramatically affected the household and social structures of the three communities.

While all three attracted new workers from outside the region and country, they depended on their immediate hinterlands for most of their new recruits.[21] In Amherst a rise in the numbers of New Brunswick born, at least half of whom were Acadian, changed forever the ethnic composition of the town. Yarmouth remained the most uniformly Nova Scotian in terms of its residents' birthplaces, but, like Amherst, it acquired a large Acadian minority, most from surrounding rural communities. Sydney Mines remained relatively homogeneous as well, though a small cadre of British born miners and a larger throng of young Newfoundland labourers, clustered at opposite ends of the occupational ladder, helped define the more central place occupied by the Cape Breton majority.[22] All in all, foreigners remained a very small portion of the workforce in all three towns, though some Italians and Poles were recruited to Sydney Mines. Few immigrant women entered the paid workforce during the pre-1920s period, probably because few women accompanied men on the initial voyage to Canada. Large numbers of country-born women did, however, find their way to the jobs becoming available in the towns.

The experiences of Marie, Georgina, Daisy and Lizzie represent aspects of the impact of the industrial transition on women's opportunities for paid work. Although Nova Scotian women had long participated in the household economies of fishing and farming, their contributions were subsumed within the male dominated family unit and characterized as supplementary or in-

---

21 In 1901 census takers asked respondents if they had been born in an urban or rural location. While Yarmouth workers and householders were almost even in terms of rural/urban birth, the other two towns were quite different. Immediately prior to the major expansion of the steel industry, 71 per cent of the workers in Sydney Mines were urban born; in contrast, just 32 per cent of Amherst's workers reported urban origin.

22 On the migration of Newfoundlanders to industrial Nova Scotia see Peter Neary, "Canadian Immigration Policy and Newfoundlanders, 1912-1939", *Acadiensis*, XI, 2 (Spring 1982), pp. 69-83; Ron Crawley, "Off to Sydney: Newfoundlanders Emigrate to Industrial Cape Breton, 1890-1914", *Acadiensis*, XVII, 2 (Spring 1988), pp. 27-51; Mary-Jane Lipkin, "Reluctant Recruitment: Nova Scotia Immigration Policy, 1867-1917", M.A. thesis, Carleton, 1982.

cidental to the production of staples.[23] Most women working for remuneration had been concentrated in jobs associated with home-making and child rearing, chiefly as servants in middle and upper class households, or as producers of goods or services for other women, as milliners or dressmakers. As teachers of very young children in the emerging educational institutions of the pre-Confederation period, numerically they were coming, by the 1870s, to dominate a profession notorious for discriminating against them.[24] Even so, women had been largely absent from waged work before the arrival of cotton and woollen mills and shoe factories. And though they had previously figured hardly at all in clerical occupations, women would also come to dominate this sector after 1900, as towns acquired more complex social and economic structures. By 1900, as never before, women's labour was becoming a factor in the province's economic development. And the number of women in the workforce continued to grow until, by 1921, in Yarmouth, Amherst and Sydney Mines at least, women comprised over 20 per cent of paid workers (see Figure 2).

The first striking increase in the numbers and occupational range of women in the paid workforce under review occurred between 1881 and 1891, with the establishment of Yarmouth's cotton mill; then, between 1900 and 1911, the number of women in the workforce almost doubled again, increasing from 872 to 1706 as job opportunities further increased and diversified (see Table One). But this over-all trend must be understood in the context of the zones of women's employment, for there were sharp contrasts. In the coal and steel centred economy of Sydney Mines, women's participation remained confined to the service sector, while in Yarmouth upwards of 20 per cent of the female labour force worked in factories by the turn of the century, and close to a third by the end of World War I. The sharp decline in the number of women factory workers in Amherst following closure of the woollen mill and shoe factory there offers mute testimony to the narrow range of industrial occupations open to women. There, as elsewhere, many women who worked in factories during the war lost their jobs soon afterward. After 1901, stenographic, clerical and secretarial occupations, along with such new trades

---

23   See Cohen, *Women's Work* for a discussion of the main contours of the role of rural women in staples producing economies. For the Atlantic region, a broad range of scholarship deals with women as part of a family economic strategy in resource zones like the fishery. See, for example, Marilyn Porter, "She Was Skipper of the Shore Crew: Notes on the History of the Sexual Division of Labour in Newfoundland", *Labour/Le travail*, 15 (Spring 1985), pp. 105-23.

24   Janet Guildford, "'Separate Spheres' and the Feminization of Public School Teaching in Nova Scotia, 1838-1880", Paper presented to the Atlantic Canada Studies Conference, Orono, Me., May, 1990.

as telephone and telegraph operators, brought larger numbers of women into new areas of the workforce.[25]

Even as the occupational profile of women workers became more complex, the most prominent feature of their participation in paid work continued to be their concentrations in the personal service sector (see Figure 3).[26] Only in Amherst, and then not until 1921, were household servants ever eclipsed in numbers, in that case by the increasingly diversified group of clerical workers. Yet, the places where women did housework for pay changed over the 50 year period. In 1871, servants were employed mostly in middle class households; after industrialization, servants and those in related occupations, such as washerwomen, became more involved in reproducing the labour power of their fellow workers in a wide variety of boarding houses and hotels. At various times, over half of all male and female workers boarded or lived as dependent relatives in houses headed by others. Such a volatile young workforce, as well as contributing to the malleability of households, demanded expansion of boarding-house keeping, an occupation dominated by widows.

Yarmouth and Amherst's middle classes had supported large numbers of seamstresses, dressmakers and milliners through the turn of the century; Sydney Mines had always lagged behind in providing opportunities for waged work in traditional women's artisanal areas, a consequence of the absence of many middle class spenders, as well as its proximity to the more developed service and commercial sector in nearby North Sydney, where most of the

---

25 Graham S. Lowe, "Women, Work and the Office: The Feminization of Clerical Occupations in Canada", *Canadian Journal of Sociology*, 5 (1980), pp. 361-81; "Class, Job and Gender in the Canadian Office", *Labour/Le travail*, 10 (Autumn 1982), pp. 11-37; and "Mechanization, Feminization and Managerial Control in the Early Twentieth-Century Canadian Office", in Craig Heron and Robert Story, eds., *On the Job: Confronting the Labour Process in Canada* (Kingston/Montreal, 1986), pp. 177-209.

26 To assist analysis women's occupations have been divided into five categories: PROFESSIONS (teachers, nurses, etc.); CLERICAL (clerks, stenographers, secretaries and telephone/telegraphic operators); ARTISANS (milliners, dressmakers, seamstresses, etc); FACTORY (spinners, weavers, factory hands etc.); and SERVICE (servants, washerwomen, maids etc). The scale implied by this structuring of workers includes independent producers who may have been a part of the service area and the denigration of women who controlled their own economic destiny, such as the small number of female boarding-house keepers, who were in fact petty-proprietors who often employed servants. It also excludes those involved in various types of household production that may not have been included in the census categories. On the problems inherent in any attempt to build occupational scales see Michael B. Katz, Michael J. Doucet, and Mark J. Stern, *The Social Organization of Early Industrial Capitalism* (Cambridge, 1982).

Figure 3
Female Workers (by sector), 1901-1921; Yarmouth, Amherst and Sydney Mines

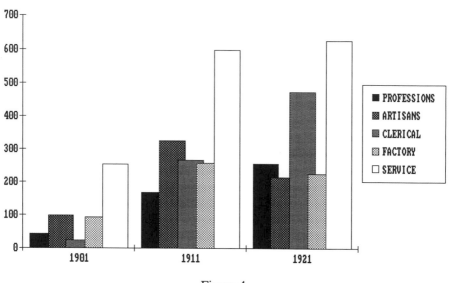

Figure 4
Age Distribution of Workers (by gender), 1921

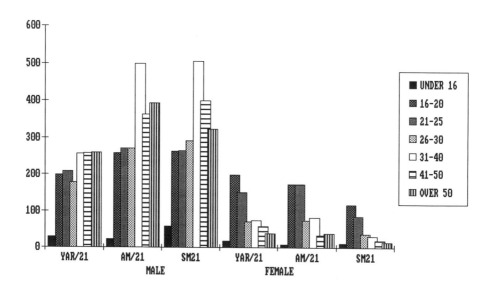

needs of the tiny group of middle class women could be met. But integration with an emerging consumer-oriented economy and rapid urban development brought dramatic increases in the availability of ready-made clothing, a corollary of which was a decline in artisanal production. As more of the local market was absorbed by the expansion of regionally and nationally organized retail outlets, more women came to work as clerks selling clothing and other consumer goods than were ever employed producing those sorts of items in artisanal shops.[27]

Studies of the demographic attributes of female workers during the early stages of industrialization focus on their comparative youth and fractional earnings relative to their male counterparts. Relative earnings of male and female workers reflect the basic disparities faced by women, although any comparison of individual earnings or occupational mobility is problematic unless individuals can be linked over time through successive censuses or in some other fashion.[28] Some limited observations are made possible by considering the relationship between age and earnings at 10 year intervals and subjecting the findings to a gendered analysis. Figure 4 provides age profiles for male and female workers in 1921. The downward trend of women in the workforce beyond the age of 21 contrasts significantly with the comparative stability and upward trend among male workers after the age of 30. The relatively short time women spent in the work force reinforced wage differentials, further inhibiting the achievement of wage parity.[29]

---

27 Mercedes Steedman, "Skill and Gender in the Canadian Clothing Industry, 1890-1940", in Heron and Story, eds., *On the Job*, pp. 152-76. An enduring theme in both Amherst and Yarmouth newspapers following the turn of the century was the complaint that workers and others were buying goods produced outside their community, particularly from central Canadian chains or mail order houses being established during the period. Maritimers, it was argued, should spend their money where they had earned it so that it could recirculate to prompt more employment. On the extension of Canadian businesses, including some discussion of retail chains, to the region see L.D. McCann, "Metropolitanism and Branch Businesses in the Maritimes, 1881-1931", *Acadiensis*, XIII, 1 (Autumn 1983), pp. 112-25.

28 Linkages have not yet been attempted with this data, though such a strategy is likely to be more useful when focussing on male workers, who tended to stay in the workforce for more extended periods. Women were seldom in the workforce for a 10 year period, so are difficult to trace in successive censuses.

29 Fluctuations in the age structure of the workforce occurred for a variety of reasons. For example, in 1901 a large in-migration of younger men, many of them day-labourers employed in construction trades, drove the average age of male workers to all-time lows, though their mean age rose gradually to a high of 38.5 by 1921. The mean age of working women tended to be under rather than over 25, but also rose to a new high of 29 by 1921.

Figure 5
Mean Earnings By Age and Gender, 1921

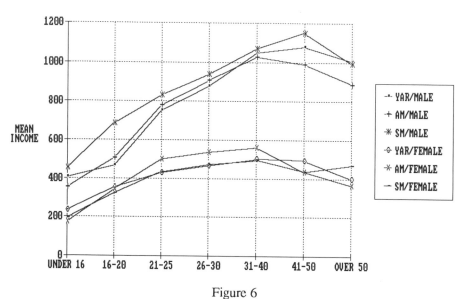

Figure 6
Women's Occupations By Ethnic Origin, Yarmouth and Amherst, 1911

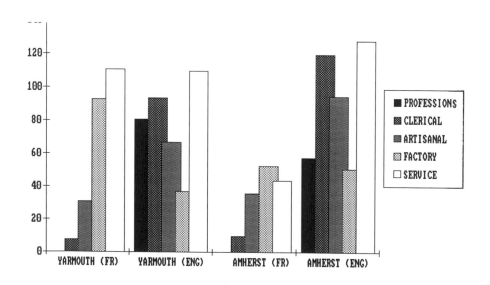

A comparison limited to single workers provides further insight into the changing nature and structure of the workforce. In post-1900 Yarmouth, for instance, single female workers outnumbered single male workers. On average, these women were one to two years older than their male counterparts. Obviously, the presence of a cotton mill with its specific requirements for both male and female youth could have a decisive impact on the demographic composition of the workforce. In Amherst and Sydney Mines, where the proportion of single women *vis à vis* single men was never as large, this relationship was reversed, although the mean ages of single male and female workers remained quite close.[30] Marriage, of course, changed matters significantly, for males were expected to retain their jobs after marriage while women were socially and culturally barred from doing so.

Cultural norms limiting women's participation in paid work to the years between childhood and marriage prevented them from progressing to more responsible, and therefore more lucrative, positions within those sectors they occupied. In the main, earnings were a function of age, which is a rough surrogate for years in the workforce no matter what the area of the economy or the gender of workers (see Figure 5). But most industrial jobs, virtually all skilled trades not specific to women, such as seamstress or milliner, and all management positions, were controlled by males throughout the period. Male earnings rose sharply after 20, peaked between 31 and 40 and, in most instances, declined somewhat after 50. Women's earnings, as well as being far below those of men at all ages, rose more gradually, peaking by about age 30 and generally declining thereafter. Though primary earning years differed somewhat across communities and for different occupations, the earning curves were remarkably similar in all three towns.[31]

---

30 In both cases the number of single men employed declined by a third, while the number of single working women remained stable or actually increased. With so many young miners in its workforce, Sydney Mines had a much different profile than the other communities. In 1911 and 1921, single males averaged just over 25 years while females averaged 24.5. In Amherst, men and women both averaged 24.5 years in 1911; the average age of single women had risen to 26 ten years later while that of their male counterparts remained unchanged. Though these increases may not seem dramatic, they reflected the fact that women were remaining spinsters for longer periods and were also remaining in the workforce.

31 Similar curves drawn for 1901 and 1911 reveal identical relationships, with the slightly higher earnings of Amherst women and Sydney Mines men equally apparent. The reason for the former lies with the more diverse nature of its female workers, particularly in the artisanal and later in the clerical areas. Higher earnings for workers in Sydney Mines reflect the concentration of mining and industrial jobs and the general absence of common labourers, whose earnings tended to lower the averages for younger men.

But while the general patterns proved similar, women's actual earnings fluctuated widely from town to town and across occupations. Table Two captures some of that variation through a comparison of Amherst and Yarmouth in 1911 and 1921.[32] The experience of Sydney Mines was similar, although the numbers and varieties of occupations were much smaller. While professional and new white collar workers generally out-earned their working class sisters, there was significant variation from town to town. In Amherst, rapid expansion in the clerical sector contributed to the comparatively higher average earnings there by 1921, though the strong male labour movement in the town may also have influenced the women's wages. Yarmouth's cotton workers were hierarchically structured, with weavers among the highest paid blue collar workers. The relatively poor performance of artisanal workers, such as tailors, may have reflected a more intermittent involvement in the workforce. But who were the tailors and weavers as opposed to the clerks or teachers?

Religion and ethnicity have held a certain primacy in analyses of factors in the formation of Nova Scotia's communities, though their intersection with class formation in the industrial period is less developed in the literature.[33] Yet the convergence of religion, ethnicity and class in shaping both individual and community experience can readily be illustrated through a comparison of British and Acadian workers in Amherst and Yarmouth. Recent arrivals on the urban scene, Acadian workers were the least prepared, either socially or educationally, to compete for those professional or clerical sector jobs where English literacy or higher levels of educational achievement were a precondition of employment. In 1891, for instance, 38 per cent of Yarmouth's Acadian female workers reported that they were unable to read, while only five per cent of non-Acadians were so disadvantaged. Reduced language and literacy skills helped restrict women's employment options in cases where contact with the public or literacy was required. Acadian women, as demonstrated in the 1911 census, were all but excluded from clerical and professional positions

---

32   The figures in Table Two include only those who reported earnings of at least $100, thereby eliminating casual workers. Occupations that were not represented across both censuses were also excluded, as were occupational categories which included fewer than five individuals.

33   The Scots experience in eastern Nova Scotia is assessed in R.A. MacLean and D. Campbell, *Beyond the Atlantic Roar: A Study of the Nova Scotia Scots* (Toronto, 1974). An example dealing with urban formations is Elizabeth Beaton, "Religious Affiliations and Ethnic Identity of West Indians in Whitney Pier", *Canadian Ethnic Studies*, XX, 3 (1988), pp. 25-45; For a more contemporary analysis asserting a basic equality in French/British attainments see E. Hugh Lautard and Donald J. Loree, "Occupational Differentiation Between British and French in the Atlantic Provinces, 1951-1971", in *Labour in Atlantic Canada: Social Science Monographic Series*, vol. IV (Saint John, 1981), pp. 32-41.

in Yarmouth and Amherst. In both towns, over two thirds of Acadian women were employed either as servants or as hands in the shoe or woollen factories (see Figure 6).[34]

Most of these Acadian women were migrants from the countryside, and their experience typified that of other rural migrants. Recruitment of surplus labour from rural communities was a strategy for filling less attractive jobs for women as well as men. In Amherst and Yarmouth, upwards of 80 per cent of all servants were country-born; and in Yarmouth 90 per cent of female cotton mill workers described themselves as rural-born. Clerical workers and teachers, on the other hand, were much more likely to be urban-born and included no appreciable number of Acadians or Catholics in their ranks. Educational opportunities in town were undoubtedly greater than those in the countryside, though probably as important were the contacts established while growing up within the social and cultural milieus that conditioned the transformation of communities.[35]

Cross-gender case studies of Yarmouth's cotton workers and of teachers in all three towns further illustrate the relative importance of gender, age, ethnicity and birthplace in understanding women's experience of waged work. From the moment it entered production in 1884, Yarmouth's cotton mill needed a workforce to tend and feed its giant machines; and, in an industry in which success was dependent on exploiting the willingness of younger workers to endure harsh conditions and low wages, the workforce required constant replenishment.[36] While the more technical jobs were filled by experienced New England workers, most production jobs at the new mill could be performed by relatively inexperienced young men and women.[37] By 1901, 20 per cent of Yarmouth's working women were employed at the mill. Unlike

---

34   The only group lower on the occupational ladder was the smaller contingent of black women, who were invariably servants.

35   Sydney Mines' small number of female workers were mainly from urban backgrounds (77 per cent), though there, as elsewhere, women workers were almost universally daughters of the working class.

36   A brief qualitative analysis of cotton company time/pay books for the 1880s-1890s period reveals a dramatic turn-over in employees in the basic spinning and weaving jobs, particularly among female employees and among young Acadian workers of both sexes. Cosmos Cotton Collection, Paybooks, vol. I, Yarmouth County Historical Society.

37   For a comparative perspective on the employment of young women in cotton mills, see Peter deLottinville, "Trouble in the Hives of Industry: The Cotton Industry Comes to Milltown, N.B., 1879-1892", *Historical Papers* (1980), pp. 100-15; Gail Cuthbert-Brandt, "Weaving it Together: Life Cycle and the Industrial Experience of Female Cotton Workers in Quebec, 1910-1950", *Labour/Le travail*, 7 (Spring 1981), pp. 113-26. The more family centred practices of some American

Milltown and Marysville in New Brunswick, or the much larger mills of Quebec or New England, neither corporate owned housing nor company sponsored boarding houses were provided in Yarmouth. Most recruits were drawn either from surrounding communities or from within the town itself, and appear to have found accommodation within existing housing stock close by the waterfront location of the plant or in expanding working class districts in the town's burgeoning south end. A small hand-drawn sample of those mill girls who lived at home indicates that they were members of working class families; most were daughters of men who worked either in the cotton mill or at the nearby iron foundry.[38] Obviously, the need for a family wage was an element in the decision taken by numerous young women to go to work in the mill. But the large numbers of boarders among women mill workers indicates that country girls were also attracted on an individual basis by the chance for waged employment and limited 'independence'.

Cotton mill workers can be readily identified in the 1911 and 1921 censuses, since individuals were required to report their places of employment. In 1911, 108 men (47 per cent) and 124 women (53 per cent), from the manager down to the lowest ranking operative, identified the cotton mill as their place of employment. The vast majority of women employees were under 25, with over half concentrated in the 16-20 age cohort. Male workers, more evenly spread across the age spectrum, were also older on average (28), more likely to be of British origin (65 per cent) and more highly paid ($449 per annum). Women were younger (20 on average), more likely to be Acadian (70 per cent) and less well paid ($267 per annum). Though comprising just 23 per cent of Yarmouth's population, Acadians made up 54 per cent of all cotton mill employees in 1911. Acadian women earned marginally less than English women ($256 vs. $275), but they were also younger on average (19 vs. 25). Like their sisters, Acadian males, the third largest group after Acadian females and English males, tended to be younger than male anglophone workers (23 on average vs. 30) and were more likely to be single. They reported mean earnings of $343 as compared to an average of $509 for their anglophone counterparts. Most single Acadian males at the mill worked alongside their sisters in production areas. The more skilled and higher paying loom-fixing or

---

mill towns does not seem to have been the norm in Yarmouth. See Tamara Hareven, *Family Time and Industrial Time: The Relationship Between Family and Work in a New England Industrial Community* (Cambridge, Mass., 1982).

38   One of the strategies of capitalists during this period was to blend the industrial formations within communities to provide employment for a variety of different types of workers in order to encourage development of a family wage among the numbers of operatives within the town and thereby ensure a wider series of opportunities for workers of either sex and at various stages of their working lives.

Table Two
Mean Annual Wages for Women in Selected Occupations

| | 1911 | | 1921 | |
	Yarmouth	Amherst	Yarmouth	Amherst
Teachers	$412 (31)	$320 (21)	$697 (32)	$656 (48)
Nurses	$344 (7)	$345 (10)	$576 (18)	$745 (12)
Stenos.	$304 (32)	$374 (34)	$503 (38)	$604 (85)
Clerks	$166 (14)	$286 (43)	$430 (23)	$642 (42)
Tel. Operstors	$192 (5)	$377 (7)	$510 (9)	$450 (14)
Tailors	$272 (19)	$250 (23)	$394 (9)	$446 (30)
Weavers	$357 (29)	$354 (11)	$565 (57)	$447 (14)
Servants	$168 (100)	$235 (136)	$224 (154)	$238 (152)

supervisory roles were invariably occupied by married English males. Multivariate analysis of declared earnings suggests the link between gender, age and ethnicity in determining wage rates. Those reporting yearly earnings above $300 were concentrated in the over-20 group confined mostly to males (see Figure 7). There was little gendered distinction in earnings between workers under the age of 20 doing the same jobs.

The mill's workforce grew by 40 per cent between 1911 and 1921 (from 232 to 372 workers). The male-female ratio reversed: 221 (60 per cent) males to 151 (40 per cent) females; the proportion of single workers fell to 56 per cent of all workers as compared to 72 per cent in 1911. The number of Acadian women remained virtually the same as in 1911 (88); English women increased from 29 to 51. The mean age of single women workers was a full two years higher than that of single males (22 vs. 20). Overall, males averaged 32 years in 1921, females 23, a significant increase in both cases. Although women's mean earnings had risen to $539 by 1921, mean earnings for men had risen to $859. Married males averaged $1995, single men $573, and single women $532; single Acadian men averaged $569 and single Acadian women $525. As in 1911, Acadian males proved much more likely to be single and, like Acadian women, continued to be ghettoized in weaving, spinning, spooling and carding jobs on the shop floor. British males, who tended, on average, to be older, continued to hold down the most lucrative and responsible jobs. Age, gender and ethnicity continued to play a significant role in determining earnings and job hierarchy. The gap in earnings between women and men, Acadians and British, and married and single workers had not narrowed ap-

Figure 7

Mean Earnings of Yarmouth Cotton Workers By Age and Gender, 1911, 1921

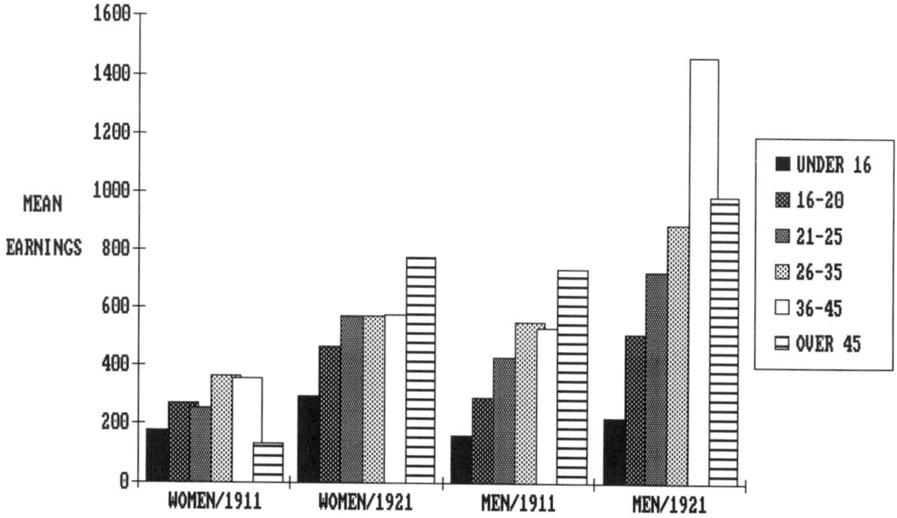

preciably, even though men were now performing many jobs previously done by women. Discrepancies are most clearly illustrated in the earning curves for men and women workers. By 1921 women had caught up with the earning levels of men in 1911. But by 1921, men above the age of 25 were earning far more than any woman (see Figure 7).

Throughout the period, Yarmouth Duck and Yarn recruited a high proportion of its workers from among rural youth displaced by the over-population of subsistence farms. In earlier periods such surplus workers might have left the province in search of employment. But now, given an opportunity to remain in Nova Scotia, some, at least, chose to accept work closer to home, despite harsh conditions and low wages. For young single women, the promise of a pay packet almost as large as that earned by their unmarried brothers (93 per cent of male counterparts' in the 16-25 age cohorts in 1921) may have made mill employment especially attractive. These young recruits contributed to the formation of a broad new urban proletariat, regularly replenished from the countryside in a situation that saw a constant turnover among operational staff, while management and those highly skilled workers who maintained or repaired the machines remained relatively stable.

The case of the Yarmouth cotton mill provides a concrete illustration of the significant intersection of gender, class and culture; the relatively low status of women and Acadians was critical to the restructuring of the town's workforce. The cotton industry initiated into waged labour young women and men who might not otherwise have had the opportunity for waged work locally. But significant disparities between women's and men's earnings persisted and were reflected in job ghettoization based on gender, ethnicity and age. If female workers sometimes reported earnings as high as those achieved by male workers performing the same or similar tasks, the men in question were often young Acadians, who, like their female counterparts, found fewer opportunities for advancement within the industry. Like Acadian males, women were denied the prospects for upward mobility accorded to non-Acadian males. Resistance to the inequities imposed by the industry did occur and, during the war, when the demand for labour was high and rich war contracts resulted in increased production, workers' committees succeeded in negotiating a number of wage increases.

Not all women workers were as immediately affected by the process of urbanization and industrialization as the new class of factory girls. But the changes brought by urbanization revolutionized community life and no worker could completely escape their impact. To some extent, each town's approach to the provision of public education was a function of its socio-cultural profile. Yarmouth and Amherst had very active local middle classes committed to the commercial and industrial advancement of their communities. They took pride in providing their children with extensive educational opportunities at public expense and borrowed heavily to construct new school buildings, which were discussed in glowing terms in the local press. Sydney Mines' less notable educational accomplishments reflected the coal industry's failure to value universal literacy for its workforce. But the coal town, which sent its sons into the workforce at earlier ages than was common elsewhere, had almost no resident middle class to push for the implementation of educational reforms.[39] And because the coal company owned the majority of homes, the proportion of privately owned property was too small to provide a tax base to support the school system. Hence, town incorporation in 1889 brought little change.

Whatever different attitudes toward provision of educational facilities may have prevailed within each community, gender balances among teachers proved remarkably similar as feminization rose from just under 70 per cent in 1871, to over 90 per cent by 1921.[40] School boards composed of middle aged,

---

39 Robert McIntosh, "The Boys in the Nova Scotia Coal Mines, 1873-1923", *Acadiensis*, XVI, 2 (Spring 1987), pp. 35-50; Kate and John Currie, "A History of Education in Sydney Mines, 1828-1900", unpublished Paper, Beaton Institute, University College of Cape Breton, 1980.

40 Central Canada as well as New Brunswick underwent a similar shift during this period. Alison Prentice, "The Feminization of Teaching in British North America and Canada, 1845-1875", *Social History/ Histoire Sociale*, 8 (1975), pp. 5-20; Marta Danylewycz, Beth Light and Alison Prentice, "The Evolution of the Sexual Division of Labour in Teaching: A Nineteenth Century Ontario and Quebec Case

largely middle class men hired young women as teachers because they were readily available. In the process, women experienced a type of ghettoization similar to that of their sisters in the cotton mill, even though their ethnic and religious traits differed sharply. A tendency to British Protestant dominance and under-representation of Catholics reflected a bias against full access to education for minority groups and the lack of higher Academies in rural areas where most Catholics had lived prior to industrial transformation. Daughters of the middle and lower middle classes for the most part, these young women worked for much lower wages than their male colleagues, or even than their female counterparts in factories or offices. They did so because they could afford to and because they shared a missionary attitude towards their profession that permitted them to accept low wages, even while remaining in the workforce for longer and longer periods.

Women teachers were older, on average, than other groups of female workers but they were still significantly younger than their male colleagues. In 1901 the mean age for women teachers was less than 23, while the mean age for men and women taken together was 25. In 1911, only three of the 19 male teachers, as compared to 51 of the 77 female teachers, were under 25. In 1921, all 10 male teachers were over 25, but the largest number of women (47) were over 30 and less than half were under 25. By that time, the overall mean age had risen to 33 (44 for males and 31 for females). As in the cotton mill, age variance reflected a bias against employing married women. But the rise in the mean age of women teachers between 1901 and 1921 indicates that women were remaining spinsters and in the workforce for longer periods.

Jarring discrepancies typified earnings of male and female teachers. In 1921, for example, male teachers averaged over $1200 per annum, compared to women's mean earnings of $667. Moreover, the earning curve for female teachers remained flat, while that for males rose sharply with age (see Figure 8). Gendered bias in teachers' salaries reflected the notion that married male teachers with families to support required higher salaries than did single women living at home. To some extent, this perception was accurate. Virtually all male teachers headed their own households, while over 90 per cent of female teachers were single, living at home or as boarders in households headed by others. Even so, the few widowed women who headed their own households were unable, either by virtue of their status as family heads or their longer experience, to earn what might have been considered a 'family wage'

Study", *Social History/Histoire Sociale*, 16 (1983), pp. 81-109; and Marta Danylewycz and Alison Prentice, "Teacher's Work: Changing Patterns and Perceptions in the Emerging School Systems of Nineteenth and Early Twentieth Century Central Canada", *Labour/Le travail*, 17 (Spring 1986), pp. 59-82. For the Nova Scotia experience see Janet Guildford, "'Separate Spheres'".

Figure 8
Teacher's Mean Earnings By Age and Gender, 1911, 1921

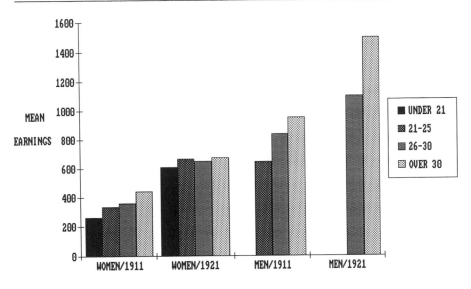

of the sort that male teachers were able to command. Gender based licensing systems reinforced these inequalities.

Although the number of teachers rose dramatically as local school boards expanded their services, the increase, from just 50 in 1871 to 133 by 1921, did not match the rate of population growth in the towns. Student/teacher ratios increased over the period as the schools adopted a strict grade system and increased the numbers in each classroom. With the division of students into age specific grades, female teachers became ghettoized in the lower grade levels. In classrooms, the introduction of industrial-like modes of organization led to a division of labour similar to that of the factory. As in factories, males dominated all supervisory positions, which were thought to require higher qualifications and the male qualities of leadership and discipline. Prior to World War I, the jobs available in the new high schools, except for a few home economics teachers, were invariably staffed by men. There, men commanded higher salaries while instructing fewer students, a system that would not change very much over the following half century.

Until further investigation into women's direct experience of paid work in Nova Scotia has been completed, any conclusions concerning the impact of industrialization or women's part in the transformation of communities must remain tentative. However, this analysis of their involvement in paid work provides the basis for a number of observations. Women workers tended to be younger, almost invariably unmarried, and to stay in the workforce for shorter periods than their male counterparts. While this general pattern persisted throughout the period, significant changes did occur between 1911 and 1921, probably as a consequence of the war. Though the most common field of employment for women continued to be the service sector, the places where servants worked came to vary considerably over time. And, like their male counterparts, women faced discrimination based on their ethnic and religious backgrounds. Thus, servants were often Catholics and factory workers often Acadian. And both groups were drawn largely from the countryside. In contrast, jobs requiring literacy or communication skills, such as teaching and clerking, went mainly to British-stock Protestant women emerging from the lower middle classes within the towns.

While men and women may have experienced migration somewhat differently, new women workers, either by themselves or in the company of kin, participated actively in labour force expansion. Paralleling the diversification of work opportunities was a change in the ethnic composition of urban Nova Scotia, the result of large scale migrations of Acadians, rural Scots and Newfoundlanders from the countryside into towns. In Yarmouth, Amherst and Sydney Mines, Roman Catholics who came to dominate the lower rungs of the occupational ladder transformed predominantly Protestant towns. At this stage we can only speculate on the cultural impact of this major shift in institutions and social structure.

Everywhere, the most striking characteristic of women workers was their youth relative both to male workmates and to the remainder of the adult female community. Women's participation in the workforce was effectively limited to the years between childhood and marriage. Culturally determined responsibility for child rearing and household maintenance precluded continuing participation in the labour force by married women. Those widows not dependent on earnings of kin were generally confined to menial occupations, although those who owned property could convert their homes into boarding houses. Those with skills, such as teachers, could occasionally re-enter the workforce, but not usually at a level appropriate to their age or experience. It is quite likely that many married women participated in hidden economies of production not recorded by the census taker and it is evident that artisanal production specifically directed towards serving the needs of other women continued for some time and was probably dominated by women in the older age ranges.

Wherever they worked and whatever their backgrounds, women earned less than their male counterparts, though in some cases that may have been as much a function of the relatively short time they spent in the workforce as of their gender. The more diverse a town's economic base, the wider the choices for prospective women workers. After 1891, Yarmouth and Amherst provided many new opportunities in industrial and commercial sectors, including clerical jobs in stores and businesses, which Sydney Mines only began to match by 1921. Disappearance of the female equivalent of the honest artisan, who might have controlled some of her own means of production and regulated work processes in her own home, was as pronounced for women as it was for men during the same period. Indeed, in many ways, Nova Scotia women's experience of work degradation mirrored that of their male counterparts.

Although conclusions remain speculative, understanding how women experienced capitalism can also shed light on community economic development through these years when manufacturing and urban development reoriented the regional economy. Women in the forefront of that transition were subject to all the frustrations of working in factories controlled by machines and processes foreign to any of their prior experiences. Yarmouth and Amherst, which attracted the largest and most diverse group of women workers, were exposed to the vicissitudes of the new competitive system into which the region had been thrust following Confederation. When deindustrialization replaced the expansiveness of the 1880-1910 period, women, as well as men, faced enormous dislocations as consolidation of production resulted in over-production. The only way to make machines pay for themselves was to eliminate interruptions. The cut-throat competition, in which Maritime producers were disadvantaged by distance and concentrations of capital, made the region particularly vulnerable to the inroads of central Canadian companies determined to eliminate them. Such competition not only suppressed earnings but also threatened the very existence of the region's industrial base and the urban structures dependent upon it.

In the end, women became as marginalized as men by the new dependence on capitalist consumer-oriented economies; deindustrialization threatened their new jobs as much as it did those of male workers. Those unskilled and semi-skilled women who remained in the workforce, finding their job options reduced or eliminated, were trapped in dependent relationships, often as servants of those middle class groups who were managing this latest process of transformation. Teachers and nurses remained ghettoized at the bottom of systems unable or unwilling to meet their expectations, and continued to receive very low pay despite their demonstrably higher educational attainments. Ironically, a dramatic rise in opportunities for women in clerical work, where they were often employed by some of the same central Canadian businesses that were engineering the consumer-oriented revolution overtaking the region, reflected a broader social submission to a central Canada dominated economy. Nova Scotia's passage from colonial dependence on staple exports, through capitalist transformation, industrialization and urbanization to dependence and deindustrialization was as much a female as a male experience. Women's place in the process can begin to be understood now that we are coming to know more about who they were, where they worked and some dimensions of their labour and their lives.

Maritime Industrialization from 1870 to 1910: A Review of the Evidence and its Interpretation

Kris E. Inwood

Regional differences in Canadian manufacturing have attracted a good deal of attention in a literature dominated by two conceptual perspectives. The "staple" theory popular during the middle decades of this century recognizes the influence of location, resource and technology on the growth of manufacturing. "Structuralism", which became influential during the 1970s and 1980s, associates Maritime development with a loss of local control over political and economic decision-making. Still missing from the discussion is a careful documentation of the nature and extent of provincial manufacturing differences before the First World War.

This paper presents census data describing early industrial progress in Eastern Canada. A brief consideration of this information sharpens our understanding of the terrain contested by staple and structuralist interpretations. It is clear that important differences existed between Central Canadian and Maritime industry, between New Brunswick and Nova Scotia, and among the various industries. The degree of heterogeneity suggests that no single explanation is likely to account for all facets of the regional industrial experience. The second part of the paper argues that the data do not inspire confidence in the new orthodoxy of structuralism and that themes broadly consistent with a staple approach invite further consideration. Elements from both analytic traditions are likely to figure in an improved explanation for arrested industrialization in Canada's eastern periphery.[1]

It is useful to begin with a recognition that industrial production in any society inevitably reflects the local pattern of settlement. In the 19th century New Brunswick and Nova Scotia were thinly settled even by Canadian standards. Only 8 per cent of Maritimers lived in census districts with a population density exceeding 25 persons per square mile in 1851, against 53 per cent in

---

1   In this paper I consider Canada's original four provinces; data are unavailable for other provinces during the early part of the period under consideration. I use "industrialization" in the sense of a rise in manufacturing share of all commodity production. I thank the many people who have influenced the writing of this paper. The most recent draft has benefited from the constructive criticism of Morris Altman, Phyllis Wagg, participants in the Economic History Workshop at the University of Toronto and the editors and referees of this journal. The Social Sciences and Humanities Research Council of Canada funded much of the research on which this paper is based.

Quebec and 75 per cent in Ontario.[2] In 1881 the population density of settled areas in the Maritimes was one-third that in Quebec and Ontario.[3] By 1891, only 20 per cent of the Maritime population lived in urban areas against 29 per cent in Quebec and 35 per cent in Ontario.[4]

The rural nature of society undoubtedly contributed to the less centralized pattern of production in the Maritimes. The available evidence for cloth and dairy products reported in Table One confirms that on-farm processing was more important in the Maritime provinces than in Ontario. Although farm households everywhere gradually abandoned manufacturing in order to specialize in agricultural production, this change came more slowly in New Brunswick and Nova Scotia.[5]

A belated arrival of the factory system in the Maritimes parallels important provincial differences within the factory system. The typical industrial establishment in 1870 was smaller in Nova Scotia and New Brunswick than in Ontario (Table Two). Moreover, the size difference increased during the first four decades of Confederation. In Nova Scotia, for example, the average factory was only two-thirds that of one in Ontario in 1870 and one-half in 1910. The average New Brunswick factory was ten per cent smaller in 1870 and 60 per cent smaller in 1910. There were exceptions; several industry groups in 1870 New Brunswick exceeded their Ontario counterparts in size. On average, however, Maritime factories were relatively small in 1870 and even smaller in 1910 particularly in the consumer goods sector.

Maritime mills and shops also tended to be less efficient. New Brunswick and Nova Scotia labour productivity averaged only three-quarters of the Ontario level in 1870 (Table Three). By 1910 relative labour productivity in Nova Scotia had changed little while in New Brunswick it had declined dramatically. Capital productivity in Nova Scotia was four-fifths of the Ontario level in 1870 and even lower in 1900 (Table Four). Capital productivity in New Brunswick, by contrast, was comparable to that in Ontario throughout the period. The productivity gap tended to be smaller for capital because Maritime firms were more efficient in using capital than labour. Maritime productivity was weakest in the consumer goods industries which in 1910 experienced capital and labour productivity less than half that in Ontario.

---

2   Canada, *Census, 1931*, vol. 1, Table 6.

3   O. Sitwell and N. Seifried, *The Regional Structure of the Canadian Economy* (Toronto, 1984), p. 46.

4   Bill Marr and Don Paterson, *Canada: An Economic History* (Toronto, 1980), p. 429.

5   Further discussion of regional differences in domestic textile production is provided by Janine Grant and Kris Inwood, "Gender and Organization in the Canadian Cloth Industry", *Canadian Papers in Business and Economic History*, 1 (1989), pp. 17-32.

Table One
The Farm Share (%) of all Processing

	Butter and Cheese				Woolens and Linens			
	NS	NB	PQ	ONT	NS	NB	PQ	ONT
1870	100	99	98	84	98	98	69	60
1890	62	49	47	17	28	19	27	5

SOURCES: Sources are Canada, *Census, 1870*, volume 3, Tables XXIV, XXXIV and XXXVI and 1891, Tables III and IV; J. Snell, "The Cost of Living in Canada in 1870", *Histoire sociale/Social History* 12 (1979), pp. 186-9; R.H. Coats, *Wholesale Prices in Canada* (Ottawa, 1910), pp. 84-5, 132-4, 136, 290 and 146-7. In 1870 the price of ticking is used for linen, and the price of tweed for woolens. For 1890 Coats supplies the butter and cheese prices; the linen price is obtained by scaling the 1870 price with the DBS textile index J38; and the woollen price is obtained by scaling an 1897 price with Coats' textile index.

NOTE: Unless otherwise noted all data are derived from volume III of the Canadian censuses of 1870-71, 1890-91 and 1910-11. The industry groups are those of the 1948 Standard Industrial Classification used to organize Canada's early national accounts. I have ignored certain industries such as dentistry and painting which were not manufacturing activities in any sense. The consumer, durable and intermediate goods sectors are my own constructions. Output is calculated as value of production less raw materials. All values are in nominal terms; available price indices do not permit satisfactory adjustment for regional price differentials or price change over time. Note that these data do not support a measure of productivity change from 1870 to 1910 because (i) there is no adjustment for price change, (ii) the 1910 data exclude firms with fewer than five employees which were included in 1870, and (iii) capital in 1870 is restricted to fixed capital whereas 1910 encompasses both fixed and working capital. The 1910 data at the level of individual industries reflect the suppression of information about some production by census authorities concerned to preserve confidentiality in districts where fewer than three firms comprised the entire industry.

Because regions differed in their capital/labour ratio, a comparison of efficiency requires the combination of labour and capital in an index of total factor productivity (TFP) reported in Table Five. In 1870 Nova Scotia industry appears to have been seriously inefficient while the productivity handicap of Quebec and New Brunswick was modest. Indeed, certain industry groups in New Brunswick rivalled or bettered Ontario efficiency; these tended to be the same industry groups in which the average size of establishment exceeded that in Ontario (chemicals, clothing, non-ferric metals, paper and transportation equipment).

The relative position of efficiency among the various provinces changed during the following decades. By 1910 Quebec had caught up with Ontario in terms of relative provincial efficiency. Maritime chemicals, coal, transportation equipment (New Brunswick) and non-ferric metals (Nova Scotia) were relatively efficient in 1910 although production was small. On the other hand, inefficiency in the large wood and food processing sectors contributed to an overall level of total factor productivity only three-quarters of the level in Ontario and Quebec. The first 40 years of Confederation apparently produced the unhappy result that New Brunswick factories fell to a level of relative inefficiency experienced by Nova Scotia in 1870, and that Nova Scotia unlike Quebec failed to improve its relative position.

Low labour productivity typically brings with it low wages. For this reason we are not surprised to learn that the average factory worker in 1870 earned 14 per cent and 17 per cent less in New Brunswick and Nova Scotia than in Ontario. By 1910 these differences had jumped to 32 per cent and 25 per cent.[6] There are obvious difficulties with these data because of possible variation in the cost of living, payments in kind, composition of workforce, length of working week and occupational pluralism. Nevertheless, the general pattern is confirmed by information about mill hands and general labourers gathered by immigration agents in 1890 and by Department of Labour information on carpenters, electricians, plumbers and labourers (1901), female cotton spinners (1911) and pulp grinders (1913).[7]

It appears that Maritime workers worked for relatively low wages before the First World War and perhaps as early as 1870.[8] But what about their employers? Did investments in manufacturing pay as well in the Maritimes as they did in Ontario? The estimates of profitability reported in Table Six indicate a steady decline in the rate of profit in New Brunswick from 1870 to 1910, absolutely and relative to Ontario and Quebec. Manufacturing in Nova Scotia follows a more interesting pattern; profitability was low in 1870 but it had largely recovered by 1890 after a decade of National Policy expansion. Between 1890 and 1910, however, the rate of profit in Nova Scotia as in New Brunswick fell absolutely and relative to both Central Canadian provinces.

The data describing factory size, efficiency and profitability suggest a pattern in which *intra*-regional differences diminished while *inter*-regional differences became more pronounced between 1870 and 1910. The indicators for New Brunswick in 1870 are not unlike those for Central Canada while Nova Scotia industry was noticeable less robust. Nevertheless, Nova Scotia did relatively well during the following 40 years in contrast to the disastrous

---

6   Canada, *Census, 1870-71*, vol. 3, Table LIV and *Census, 1911*, vol. 3, Table I. Here I divide the total wage bill by the number of workers to obtain a measure of average labour earnings.

7   M.C. Urquhart and K.A.H. Buckley, Historical Statistics of Canada (Toronto, 1965), D40-43, D48-51, D90, D96, D117, D127, D204-205 and D206-207. Here the information is a wage per worker per unit of time.

8   Phillip Wood reads the evidence differently; see his "Barriers to Capitalist Development in Maritime Canada, 1870-1930: A Comparative Perspective", *Canadian Papers in Business History*, 1 (1989), pp. 33-58 and "Marxism and the Maritimes: On the Determinants of Regional Capitalist Development", *Studies in Political Economy*, 29 (Summer 1989), pp. 123-53.

Table Two
Average Output of Industrial Establishments (relative to Ontario)

	1870			1910		
	NS	NB	PQ	NS	NB	PQ
all firms	0.65	0.90	0.94	0.51	0.41	0.72
consumer goods	0.71	0.75	1.19	0.26	0.21	0.54
durable goods	0.65	0.78	0.81	0.34	0.56	1.21
intermediate goods	0.66	1.07	0.84	0.80	0.65	0.96
chemical products	0.47	2.30	1.61	0.52	0.20	1.32
clothing	0.88	1.54	1.51	0.41	0.27	1.22
coal & petroleum products	0.97	0.29	0.91	0.65	0.91	0.69
electrical goods	na	na	na	na	na	1.79
food & beverages	0.51	0.43	1.08	0.25	0.19	0.19
iron & steel products	0.48	0.80	0.71	0.74	0.58	0.80
leather & fur products	0.92	0.99	1.95	0.63	0.72	1.09
nonferric metal products	0.92	1.20	2.38	0.29	0.15	1.14
nonmetallic mineral products	2.19	1.59	1.51	0.54	0.52	1.17
printing	1.16	0.72	1.32	0.36	0.48	1.02
paper products	0.23	0.98	1.74	na	0.21	3.11
rubber goods	na	na	10.49	0.01	na	0.20
transport equipment	1.14	1.17	1.38	0.22	0.72	2.13
tobacco products	4.94	0.51	4.78	0.16	na	2.06
textiles	0.23	0.41	0.35	1.05	2.31	3.36
wood products	0.47	0.95	0.62	0.35	0.72	0.67

experience of New Brunswick industry. By 1910 the two provinces have converged toward the pattern of industrial weakness familiar in the 20th century.

Provincial differences in the level and growth of output reported in Tables Seven, Eight and Nine follow a similar pattern.[9] New Brunswick's level of manufacturing activity was within ten per cent of Ontario's in 1870 (Table Nine) but it fell increasingly behind in both subsequent sub-periods (Tables Seven and Eight). By contrast, the Nova Scotia manufacturing sector started out remarkably small but it grew quickly from 1870 to 1890 in the consumer and intermediate goods industries. Even in Nova Scotia, however, consumer goods production decelerated at a tremendous rate after 1890 while durable goods production declined absolutely.

9   Growth is examined from 1870 to 1890 and from 1890 to 1910 because the Canadian census changed its basis of enumeration after 1890; see Kris Inwood and John Chamard, "Regional Industrial Growth in the 1890s: the Case of the Missing Artisans", *Acadiensis*, XVI, 1 (Autumn 1986), pp. 101-17.

One point of similarity between New Brunswick and Nova Scotia was the slow growth of durable goods production. Over the entire four decades durable goods output eked out an increase of 25 per cent in Nova Scotia and 50 per cent in New Brunswick, in contrast durable goods output quadrupled in Quebec and Ontario. Overall, Ontario increased its strength in consumer goods and durable goods while the Maritimes tended to specialize in intermediate goods industries. These tendencies were so pronounced that by 1910 Maritime output per capita of consumer and durable goods was less than one-quarter that in Ontario.

Perhaps the most important regional contrast is that Maritime manufacturing expanded with equal vigour in the two sub-periods (1870-1890 and 1890-1910) whereas Ontario and Quebec manufacturing expanded much more quickly in the second interval. Most scholars attribute the acceleration in Canadian economic growth to the effect of the wheat boom, a dramatic quickening in the pace of Prairie settlement during the 1890s.[10] One popular view is that the wheat boom influenced the pace of extensive growth but did not bring structural change in the sense of an industrial recomposition.[11] Nevertheless, the inability of Maritime factories to benefit from the wheat boom created structural change of a different kind involving a locational shift of production within Eastern Canada.

The importance of the wheat boom depends somewhat upon one's choice of conceptual framework. Scholars influenced by the staple perspective view the wheat boom as a prime example of the importance of natural resources and location. Structuralists, on the other hand, have tended to ignore the direct impact of the wheat boom on the Canadian market for manufactures.[12] The structuralist literature combines the tradition of regional economic grievance with the social science ideology of dependency to argue that political and

---

10 M.C. Urquhart, "New Estimates of Gross National Product, Canada, 1870 to 1926", in S. Engerman and R. Gallman, eds., *Long-Term Factors in American Economic Growth* (Chicago, 1986), p. 9-88; M. Altman, "A Revision of Canadian Economic Growth: 1870-1910 (a challenge to the gradualist interpretation)", *Canadian Journal of Economics*, XX, 1 (February 1987), pp. 86-113; Kris Inwood and Thanasis Stengos, "Discontinuities in Canadian Economic Growth, 1870-1985", *Explorations in Economic History*, vol. 28, no. 3 (July 1991), pp. 274-86.

11 Alan Green and M.C. Urquhart, "New Estimates of Output Growth in Canada: Measurement and Interpretation", in Douglas McCalla, ed., *Perspectives on Canadian Economic History* (Toronto, 1987), pp. 182-99; Gordon Bertram, "Economic Growth and Canadian Industry, 1870-1915: The Staple Model and the Takeoff Hypothesis", *Canadian Journal of Economics and Political Science*, XXIX (1963), pp. 159-84. Morris Altman has argued that adjustments for price change provide greater evidence of structural change; see his "A Revision of Canadian Economic Growth". Useful perspective is brought to bear on the debate by Ken Norrie and Doug Owram, *A History of the Canadian Economy* (Toronto, 1991), pp. 293-8, 329-33 and 359-68.

12 Influential contributions by historians include T.W. Acheson, "The National Policy

Table Three
Labour Productivity ($value added/worker), 1870 and 1910

| | 1870 | | | | 1910 | | | |
	NS	NB	PQ	ONT	NS	NB	PQ	ONT
all firms	419	432	487	574	925	683	1053	1182
consumer goods	490	408	503	572	570	535	1014	1292
durable goods	437	468	463	558	831	908	1063	1056
intermediate goods	363	424	487	591	1102	700	1087	1182
chemical products	569	1496	1403	986	654	765	1437	1739
clothing	368	333	430	350	644	597	809	779
coal & petroleum products	2196	1018	1472	3226	3662	2279	3789	2962
electrical goods	na	na	na	na	na	na	1704	1156
food & beverages	589	479	1092	1443	498	441	1110	1980
iron & steel products	447	561	504	598	1039	1011	1230	1177
leather & fur products	513	488	523	497	981	1119	985	1427
nonferric metal products	550	769	524	631	946	492	842	1112
nonmetallic mineral products	397	307	407	326	662	555	1127	1153
printing	755	591	553	641	878	862	1001	1073
paper products	609	774	646	730	na	474	1178	1017
rubber goods	na	na	285	2250	237	na	1512	2125
transport equipment	462	487	403	559	859	988	876	983
tobacco products	727	205	647	380	1024	na	1351	1523
textiles	371	434	487	486	611	670	938	812
wood products	274	373	368	429	629	590	730	932

and the Industrialization of the Maritimes", *Acadiensis*, I, 2 (Spring 1972), pp. 1-28 and "The Maritimes and 'Empire Canada'" in David Bercuson, ed., *Canada and the Burden of Unity* (Toronto, 1977), pp. 87-114; E.R. Forbes, *The Maritimes Rights Movement* (Toronto, 1977) and "Misguided Symmetry: The Destruction of Regional Transportation Policy for the Maritimes", pp. 60-86 in Bercuson, ed., *Canada and the Burden*; David Frank, "The Cape Breton Coal Industry and the Rise and Fall of the British Empire Steel Corporation", *Acadiensis*, VII, 1 (Autumn 1977), pp. 3-34; James Frost, "The 'Nationalization' of The Bank of Nova Scotia", *Acadiensis*, XII, 1 (Autumn 1982), pp. 3-38; Greg Kealey, Ian McKay and Nolan Reilly, "Canada's 'Eastern Question': A Reader's Guide to Regional Under-development", *Canadian Dimension*, Vol. 13, No. 2 (1978), pp. 37-40. Contributions from social science include R. J. Brym and J. Sacouman, eds., *Underdevelopment and Social Movements in Atlantic Canada* (Toronto, 1979); Michael Clow "Politics and Uneven Development: The Maritime Challenge to the Study of Canadian Political Economy", *Studies in Political Economy*, 14 (Fall 1984), pp. 117-40 and his "Situating a Classic: Saunders Revisited", *Acadiensis*, XV, 1 (Autumn 1985), pp. 145-52; Ralph Matthews, *The Creation of Regional Dependency* (Toronto, 1983).

financial control by outsiders undermined regional interests.[13] Although diverse, the literature tends to focus on the loss of local control over public policy and private enterprise following Confederation, which is viewed as a "critical turning point" for the region.[14]

Evidence supporting or contradicting the 'turning point' hypothesis is elusive since the first good census in British North America was not undertaken until three years after the alleged turning point. Nevertheless, there is some evidence that the manufacturing lag antedates Confederation; Inwood and Chamard have reported that Maritime industrial employment lagged in six large industries during the 1850s and 1860s even after adjusting for differing provincial rates of population growth.[15]

Confidence in the turning point hypothesis is further undermined by evidence reported above that as early as 1870 Maritime factories were small, unproductive in their use of capital and labour, paid low wages and, at least in Nova Scotia, relatively unprofitable. New Brunswick manufacturing was more robust in 1870 but even its per capita output was noticeably less than that in Ontario.

Obviously, the political union cannot be blamed for something which preceded it. It remains possible, however, that the policies of the new Canadian government may have made matters worse than they otherwise would have been. According to this line of argument, an inward-looking or

---

13   Keith Griffin and John Gurley, "Radical Analyses of Imperialism, the Third World and the Transition to Socialism", *Journal of Economic Literature*, XXIII, 3 (September 1988), pp. 1089-143; Cristobal Kay, *Latin American Theories of Development and Underdevelopment* (New York, 1989); S. Lall, "Is Dependency a Useful Concept in Analyzing Underdevelopment?" *World Development*, 3, nos. 11-12 (1975), pp. 799-810; Patrick O'Brien, "A Critique of Latin American Theories of Dependency", in I. Oxaal, *et al*, eds., *Beyond the Sociology of Development* (London, 1975), pp. 7-27; Alec Nove, "On Reading Andre Gunder Frank", *Journal of Development Studies*, 10, nos. 3-4 (April-July 1974), pp. 445-55 and Eric Sager, "Dependency, Underdevelopment and the Economic History of the Atlantic Provinces", *Acadiensis*, XVII, 1 (Autumn 1987), pp. 117-37. I borrow the term 'structuralism' from the Latin American literature; see Joseph Love, "The Origins of Dependency Analysis", *Journal of Latin American Studies*, 22, no. 1 (February 1990), pp. 143-68.

14   David Alexander, "Economic Growth in the Atlantic Region, 1880-1940", *Acadiensis*, VIII, 1 (Autumn 1978), p. 47. See also Canada, *House of Commons Debates*, 1879, pp. 1306-8 and Phillip Buckner, P. B. Waite and William Baker, "The Maritimes and Confederation: A Reassessment", *Canadian Historical Review*, LXXI, 1 (March 1990), pp. 1-45.

15   Inwood and Chamard, "Regional Growth during the 1890s", Table Four. The industries are tanning, foundries and machine shops, brewing and various mills (carding, fulling, weaving, saw, flour and grist). Regrettably, shipbuilding is not represented.

Table Four

Capital Productivity ($value added/$capital), 1870 and 1910

	1870				1910			
	NS	NB	PQ	ONT	NS	NB	PQ	ONT
all firms	1.08	1.32	1.15	1.31	0.33	0.47	0.51	0.47
consumer goods	1.56	2.55	1.48	1.65	0.50	0.73	0.52	0.67
durable goods	1.67	2.34	1.37	1.66	0.42	1.06	0.78	0.46
intermediate goods	0.67	0.95	0.88	0.96	0.30	0.37	0.41	0.36
chemical products	0.71	1.25	0.91	1.07	1.01	1.11	0.51	0.46
clothing	1.69	5.00	1.41	2.18	0.44	1.50	1.06	0.89
coal & petroleum products	0.24	0.14	0.25	1.18	0.20	0.27	0.11	0.15
electrical goods	na	na	na	na	na	na	0.71	0.39
food & beverage	0.79	0.87	0.77	1.15	0.53	0.65	0.45	0.67
iron & steel	1.07	1.66	1.34	1.66	0.55	0.55	0.57	0.38
leather & fur	1.61	1.85	2.07	2.00	0.60	0.63	0.57	0.58
nonferric metal products	1.13	2.35	0.92	1.54	1.32	0.59	0.45	0.50
nonmetallic mineral products	0.55	1.22	2.00	2.42	0.30	0.73	0.59	0.65
printing	1.09	1.37	0.77	1.24	0.47	0.67	0.43	0.59
paper products	0.70	1.46	1.06	0.70	na	0.49	0.34	0.45
rubber goods	na	na	0.31	7.50	0.99	na	1.23	0.65
transport equipment	2.39	3.35	1.24	1.64	0.29	4.16	1.17	0.61
tobacco products	3.58	4.76	1.95	2.15	2.16	na	0.48	1.14
textiles	0.61	0.71	0.78	0.75	0.23	0.29	0.39	0.35
wood products	0.88	1.07	1.09	1.04	0.56	0.37	0.39	0.46

continentalist Central Canada dominated the political union and established policies unsuitable for an outward-looking Maritime region. But what policies? During the first few years of Confederation the national government spent heavily in the Maritimes in order to construct the Intercolonial Railway. It is difficult to discern a spending bias against the Maritimes in this period, although a careful regional accounting of expenditures by various government departments might alter this judgement.

A more persistent controversy surrounds changes in the tax or tariff on manufactured imports. Such a tariff acts as a subsidy to manufacturing and hence to any region in which manufacturing predominates or has the potential to grow. The first effect of political union in 1867 was to abolish tariffs on trade between the Maritimes and the Canadas. Although it is at least possible that Maritime factories suffered through a Confederation-related change in protection, any effect along these lines cannot have been large since tariffs were relatively low before and immediately after 1867.[16]

Much has been made of the 1879 shift in Canadian government policy which systematically increased the Canadian tariff on manufactured imports as part of a new "National Policy". Canadian historians commonly assume that tariff changes allowed the domestic price of manufactured goods to rise and that in response domestic firms substituted their output for imported goods. This view credits the National Policy with responsibility for a manufacturing boom during the early 1880s and perhaps a permanently faster rate of industrial growth. Maritime firms contributed some of the extra output in the short term. It would not be surprising that Maritime interests benefitted from the tariff since powerful Maritime politicians dominated the finance ministry during the 1880s and 1890s and gave regional interests a voice in the delicate negotiations over tariff structure. In the longer run, however, increases in domestic production came disproportionately from Central Canada.

Why did Ontario manufacturing come to dominate the tariff-bound Canadian market? One answer might be that Ontario was more industrialized and hence enjoyed the advantages of a more developed industrial infrastructure. Support for this answer is undermined, however, by the evidence of Table Ten that Ontario was no more industrialized than the Maritimes in 1870. Another answer suggested by the structuralist literature is that Canadian manufacturing over-expanded as a short term response to the National Policy tariffs. Subsequent rationalization of capacity provided an opportunity for ownership to concentrate. As part of this process Central Canadians acquired control of Maritime plants and shut them down. The regional economy suffered unfairly in the rationalization because central Canadian owners trimmed their excess capacity with a regional bias.[17]

This argument comes in two parts — that tariffs were responsible for output growth and that ownership changes caused industry to re-locate. The first part suffers from a difficulty that characterizes almost all discussion of the 19th century tariff. Economic historians have been remarkably unsuccessful in identifying Canadian industries which were significantly affected by the tariff.[18] The fundamental problem is a lack of evidence indicating that the tariff

---

16 S.A. Saunders, *The Economic History of the Maritime Provinces* (Fredericton, 1984, [1939]), p. 25.

17 Acheson, "The Maritimes and 'Empire Canada'" and Henry Veltmeyer, "The Capitalist Underdevelopment of Atlantic Canada", in Brym and Sacouman, eds., *Underdevelopment and Social Movements in Atlantic Canada*, pp. 37-58.

18 John Dales, *The Protective Tariff in Canada's Economic Development* (Toronto, 1966) and "'National Policy' Myths, Past and Present", *Journal of Canadian Studies*, 14 (Fall 1979), pp. 39-50; Ian Drummond, *Progress without Planning* (Toronto 1987), pp. 112-14; Kris Inwood, *The Canadian Charcoal Iron Industry* (New York, 1986), pp. 46-51.

Table Five

Total Factor Productivity Relative to Ontario, 1870 and 1910

	Relative NS	TPF NB	1870 PQ	Relative NS	TPF NB	1910 PQ
all firms	0.78	0.88	0.86	0.74	0.77	0.99
consumer goods	0.90	1.09	0.89	0.59	0.71	0.78
durable goods	0.87	1.05	0.83	0.83	1.27	1.23
intermediate goods	0.66	0.86	0.88	0.88	0.77	1.02
chemical products	0.61	1.35	1.13	1.14	1.28	0.99
clothing	0.90	1.50	0.88	0.68	1.04	1.09
coal & petroleum products	0.25	0.14	0.24	1.30	1.41	0.86
electrical goods	na	na	na	na	na	1.55
food & beverage	0.61	0.62	0.69	0.57	0.64	0.64
iron & steel	0.70	0.97	0.83	1.09	1.09	1.03
leather & fur	0.91	0.95	1.04	0.86	0.94	0.84
nonferric metal products	0.81	1.35	0.72	1.61	0.77	0.83
nonmetallic mineral products	0.56	0.70	1.03	0.51	0.77	0.94
printing	1.04	0.99	0.75	0.81	0.91	0.86
paper products	0.92	1.55	1.19	na	0.71	0.94
rubber goods	na	na	0.07	0.67	na	1.39
transport equipment	1.06	1.26	0.74	0.71	1.93	1.16
tobacco products	1.86	0.70	1.52	0.88	na	0.73
textiles	0.79	0.92	1.02	0.70	0.83	1.13
wood products	0.73	0.94	0.95	0.88	0.71	0.81

NOTE: Total factor productivity (TFP) is a weighted average of labour and capital productivity. I define relative TFP as labour productivity in one province relative to that in Ontario and raised to the power of the labour share of factor costs, multiplied by capital productivity in one province relative to that in Ontario and raised to the power of the capital share of factor costs; see W.E. Diewert, "Exact and Superlative Index Numbers", *Journal of Econometrics*, 4 (May 1976), pp. 115-45. Factor costs are computed as total value of production less raw material costs and imputed miscellaneous costs. The latter are assumed to be the same ratio to total product for each industry group in 1870 and 1910 as they were in 1900, in which year the census report on manufacturing was particularly detailed. Shares are calculated by industry group. The labour share derives from reported wage and salaries; the capital share is a residual derived from total factor costs less labour. The residual capital share may be overestimated because miscellaneous costs are likely to be underestimated. This would imply a bias to portray Maritime factories as being more efficient than they actually were, since Maritime factories tended to make more productive use of capital than labour. I follow the published census in using fixed capital in 1870 and both fixed and working capital in 1910.

really mattered. Maritime manufacturing provides a useful example here. We might be tempted to credit the tariff with Nova Scotia's fast manufacturing growth from 1870 to 1890. It is equally plausible, however, that Nova Scotia was experiencing a kind of "catch-up" from a low level of activity in 1870 because of improved railway services, because the coal trade was growing so quickly or because 1870 was an unusually bad year for Nova Scotia business. Without a careful study of individual industries, it is difficult to make firm conclusions about the impact of the tariff.[19]

Another line of argument might draw upon the economics of international trade for an analysis of regional welfare effects.[20] Unfortunately, these techniques are of doubtful relevance to our problem since capital and labour were mobile among sectors and regions, factor endowment in 1870 does not appear to have differed markedly between Ontario and the Maritimes, and there is no evidence of sectoral differences in factor proportions. Use of traditional trade analysis is further limited by the common structure shared by Ontario and the Maritimes; both regions exported primary products, imported manufactures and shortly after Confederation had a manufacturing sector accounting for approximately one-third of all commodity production (Table Ten).

The second part of the argument suggests that there may be some connection between ownership change and industrial relocation. This is difficult to sustain in part because we know so little about ownership. No systematic evidence is available to support the presumption of an ownership shift at the end of the 19th century. Indeed, evidence of capital outflow and the career patterns of Maritime promoters suggest that local capital may have increased its influence over firms outside the region during the late 19th century, rather than the reverse.[20] The presumed shift in ownership might have been linked to an apparent decline in Maritime output during the 1890s, but the linkage would be spurious since the appearance of output decline (relative and absolute) during the 1890s is an artifact created by enumeration changes which introduced a regional bias into census data.[22]

The argument is flawed more fundamentally by its implied portrait of capitalists and capital markets. The pursuit of profit led Canadians in this period to invest in a wide variety of enterprise throughout Canada, in Latin

---

19   Lou Cain, "Ontario's Industrial Revolution", *Canadian Historical Review*, LXIX, 3 (1988), pp. 300-7.

20   James Markusen and James Melvin, *The Theory of International Trade and its Canadian Applications* (Toronto, 1984), pp. 384-90.

21   Chris Armstrong, "Making a Market: Selling Securities in Atlantic Canada before World War I", *Canadian Journal of Economics*, XIII, 3 (August 1980), pp. 438-54; Neil Quigley, "Bank Credit and the Structure of the Canadian Space Economy, 1890-1935", Ph.D. thesis, University of Toronto, 1986.

22   Inwood and Chamard, "Regional Industrial Growth". I circumvent this problem in the present paper by reporting data for 1870-1890 and 1890-1910.

Table Six
Estimated Profitability in Manufacturing

	NS	NB	PQ	ONT
1870				
production	12338	17368	77205	114707
return to capital	1881	2589	14153	18735
capital	11159	9439	56813	81725
profitability	0.17	0.27	0.25	0.23
1890				
production	30968	23850	147460	239242
return to capital	4569	3018	17111	40002
capital	19823	15823	118292	175972
profitability	0.23	0.19	0.14	0.23
1910				
production	52706	35422	350902	579810
return to capital	9020	5179	57709	109784
production	79596	36125	326947	595395
profitability	0.11	0.14	0.18	0.18

NOTE: Profitability is estimated as the ratio of profit (the value of production less labour, material, depreciation and miscellaneous costs) to capital invested. All values are reported by the census except depreciation which is calculated at 10 per cent of physical capital, miscellaneous costs which are taken to be same share of product value in 1870 and 1910 as they had been in 1900, 1870 working capital which is taken to be the same share of total capital as in 1890 and salaries are imputed in 1870 and 1890 in the same proportion to wages as they were reported in 1910. This method of estimating profitability is described in more detail elsewhere; see F. Bateman and T. Weiss, *A Deplorable Scarcity: The Failure of Industrialization in the Slave Economy* (Chapel Hill, 1981), Appendix C.

America and Europe.[23] There seems little reason to think that they would have avoided investment in Maritime factories if there had been some reasonable anticipation of profit. But how profitable were these factories? Evidence reported in Table Four suggests that Nova Scotia factories were less profitable in 1870, and that throughout the region relative profitability deteriorated after 1890. It is difficult to resist the conclusion that poor profitability undermined the willingness of Maritime business to borrow at interest rates paid by Ontario business and thereby directed Maritime saving into extra-regional investments.[24] If this is correct, then the well-documented capital outflow simply reflects a dearth of good investment opportunities within the region.

23 Armstrong, "Making a Market"; Greg Marchildon, "Promotion, Finance and Merger in the Canadian Manufacturing Industry, 1885-1918", Ph.D. thesis, The London School of Economics and Political Science, 1990.

24 Armstrong, "Making a Market"; Quigley, "Bank Credit".

Of course, we might seek to explain the poor profitability in the Maritimes in other ways. Structuralists suggest that the Canadian government increased freight rates on the Intercolonial Railway in 1912 and 1917, and in so doing hurt Maritime manufacturing.[25] Unfortunately, little is known about Intercolonial costs and pricing. By 19th century standards the Intercolonial carried relatively few passengers and less freight. The low density of traffic possibly made it difficult to implement technological advances enjoyed by other North American railways, in which case shipping from Maritime factories to the Ontario market would have been costly.[26] But a dearth of relevant evidence makes it difficult to evaluate the contribution of other influences such as pricing by competing carriers (water and rail) and government policy. Although further research is needed, one point already is clear. The changes alleged to have handicapped Maritime manufacturers came too late to explain a regional lag that originated in the 19th century. The 1912 and 1917 policy decisions may have aggravated an already difficult situation for local manufacturing, but they could not have been the sole cause.

The influence of transportation, tariff and other factors is easier to discern for individual industries than for the manufacturing sector as a whole. Advocates of the structuralist perspective have pioneered consideration of an important case study, the steel and coal industry. In this industry Nova Scotia companies participated in a tariff-assisted expansion of Canadian capacity between 1890 and 1910. In the latter year the local owners of a profitable regional firm successfully thwarted a hostile takeover bid by Central Canadian promoters. Ten years later a second takeover bid by British interests was successful. Almost immediately the Nova Scotia steel industry plunged into a disastrous period of contraction and wage reduction. The drain of capital out of the region allegedly was facilitated by the watering of stock during the early 1920s.[27]

The story of Maritime steel and coal has been interpreted as an example of de-industrialization on the periphery resulting from the loss of local control. From this perspective, the regional industry was a casualty in the international concentration and centralization of capital. However, an alternate interpretation of the industry is available. In this view corporate re-organization in the Nova Scotia steel industry was a belated and largely unsuccessful effort to salvage firms already facing bankruptcy.[28] A small scale of operations,

---

25 Forbes, *Maritime Rights* and "Misguided Symmetry".

26 Ken Cruikshank, "The Transportation Revolution and its Consequences", *Communications historiques/Historical Papers* (1987), pp. 112-37.

27 Acheson, "The National Policy"; Frank, "The Cape Breton Coal Industry".

28 Kris Inwood, "Local Control, Resources and the Nova Scotia Steel and Coal Company", *Communications historiques/ Historical Papers* (1986), pp. 254-82.

Table Seven
Percentage Change in Manufacturing Output, 1870-1890

	NS	NB	PQ	ONT
all factories	128	42	104	116
farm production	60	67	50	34
all manufacturing	120	44	101	113
consumer goods	160	95	100	119
durable goods	30	-10	83	61
intermediate goods	214	50	120	162
chemical products	210	3	149	410
clothing	224	49	125	277
coal & petroleum products	164	321	365	-5
electrical goods	na	na	na	na
food & beverages	361	292	122	82
iron & steel products	142	21	92	90
leather & fur products	-1	-12	50	41
nonferric metal products	348	204	191	854
nonmetallic mineral products	114	121	186	215
printing	54	111	86	177
paper products	48	-52	313	254
rubber goods	na	na	202	4311
transport equipment	3	-38	154	26
tobacco products	-78	64	162	265
textiles	505	443	406	150
wood products	213	21	64	143

NOTE: Farm output includes butter, cheese and cloth only. I have adjusted the 1870 data for missing data on railway workshops; see P. Craven and T. Traves, "Canadian Railways as Manufacturers, 1850-1880", *Communications historiques/Historical Papers*, 1983, pp. 254-81. In order to make the adjustment I assume that the capital/labour ratio was the same for unreported as for reported firms and that labour productivity in the Great Western's Hamilton shop was identical with that of the Grand Trunk in its Brantford shop.

diminishing resources and distance to market undermined profits and contributed to a declining share of national output long before the first takeover bid. Capital drain via stock-watering was impossible since there was seldom sufficient profit to pay dividends. The Nova Scotia firms faced much more fundamental problems as mining costs rose in a time of excess capacity worldwide and decreased domestic demand.[29]

29 Barry Supple, "The Political Economy of Demoralization: the State and the Coal-mining Industry in America and Britain between the Wars", *Economic History Review*, XLI, 4 (November 1988), pp. 566-91.

International market conditions and a rising cost of extraction would have brought hard times to the Nova Scotia coal fields regardless of ownership and organizational arrangements. It is possible of course that the industry would have adapted more effectively to its difficult circumstances under local ownership. However, this conjecture has not yet been investigated. Careful examination of other industries one day may provide more support for the structuralist perspective than does the example of steel and coal, but the case will have to be made.

The structuralist failure to account for many aspects of Maritime manufacturing before the First World War redirects attention to the staple theory, an older explanatory tradition emphasizing the adverse effect of resource characteristics and technological developments.[30] Several key developments figure in most staple accounts of Maritime development.[31] Thin soil, a short growing season and lack of a nearby urban market hampered agricultural adjustment in the Maritimes during the 19th century.[32] Technological change in ocean shipping undermined local wooden shipbuilding and shipping industries.[33] The eclipse of cane by beet sugar doomed the West Indies trade.[34] Limited water-power and hydroelectric potential impeded the diffusion of new industrial

---

30 Douglas North, "Location Theory and Regional Economic Growth", *Journal of Political Economy* LXIII (February-December 1955), pp. 243-58 and *The Economic Growth of the United States, 1790-1860* (New York, 1966); A.D. Scott, "Policy for Declining Regions: A Theoretical Approach", in W.D. Wood and R.S. Thoman, eds., *Areas of Economic Stress in Canada* (Kingston, 1965), pp. 73-93; R. Caves and R. Holton, *The Canadian Economy: Prospect and Retrospect* (Cambridge, 1961), pp. 141-95; Boris Schedvin, "Staples and Regions of Pax Britannica", *Economic History Review*, XLIII, 4 (November 1990), pp. 533-59.

31 A. Blackbourn and R. Putnam, *The Industrial Geography of Canada* (London, 1984), Chapter 7; Caves and Holton, *The Canadian Economy*, p. 145; A.W. Currie, *Canadian Economic Development*, (Toronto, 1942), p. 131; C.R. Fay and H.A. Innis, "The Economic Development of Canada 1867-1921: The Maritime Provinces", in *The Cambridge History of the British Empire*, Volume VI (Cambridge, 1929), pp. 657-71; Harold Innis, *Essays in Canadian Economic History* (Toronto, 1956), pp. 148, 226 and 349; R.C. Harris and J. Warkentin, *Canada Before Confederation* (New York, 1974), pp. 208-10; L.D. McCann, "Staples and the New Industrialism", *Acadiensis*, VIII, 2 (Spring 1979), pp. 47-79; S.A. Saunders, *The Economic History* and *The Economic Welfare of the Maritime Provinces* (Wolfville, 1932).

32 Currie, *Canadian Economic Development* p. 123.

33 Eric Sager and Lewis R. Fischer, "Atlantic Canada and the Age of Sail Revisited", *Canadian Historical Review*, LXIII, 2 (June 1982), pp. 126-150; Eric Sager and Gerald Panting, *Maritime Capital: The Shipping Industry in Atlantic Canada, 1820-1914* (Kingston and Montreal, 1990).

34 W.A. Mackintosh, *The Economic Background to Dominion-Provincial Relations* (Ottawa, 1939), p. 34.

Table Eight
Percentage Change in Output of Factories
Employing Five or More Workers, 1890-1910

	NS	NB	PQ	ONT
factories with more than 5 employees	129	78	187	214
consumer goods	26	48	184	277
durable goods	-4	68	214	260
intermediate goods	248	92	171	142
chemical products	-11	-71	227	319
clothing	-45	26	237	165
coal & petroleum products	224	377	139	615
electrical goods	-100	na	2435	1288
food & beverages	16	39	64	228
iron & steel products	101	65	132	279
leather & fur products	47	86	103	315
nonferric metal products	6	-65	173	373
nonmetallic mineral products	-56	-19	33	196
printing	99	73	163	193
paper products	-100	150	478	309
rubber goods	na	na	18	1332
transport equipment	-33	172	162	340
tobacco products	-7	-100	315	351
textiles	-2	29	202	30
wood products	38	72	134	93

SOURCE: K. Inwood and J. Chamard, "Regional Industrial Growth in the 1890s: the Case of the Missing Artisans", *Acadiensis*, XVI, 1 (Autumn 1986), pp. 101-17.

technologies,[35] as did the small size of local market. The decline of the fishing industry during the early 20th century in spite of increased prices suggests either a reduction in accessible stocks or the withdrawal of labour for some other reason.[36] Diminishing returns and rising costs undermined the region's coal and steel industries.[37] The Maritimes had no natural hinterland; a location south of the St. Lawrence River and north of the great east-west rail routes brought little stimulus from the booming trade between the North American

---

35 Peter Wylie, "When Markets Fail: Electrification and Maritime Industrial Decline", *Acadiensis*, XVII, 1 (Autumn 1987), pp. 74-96.

36 Canada, Dominion Bureau of Statistics, *The Maritime Provinces since Confederation* (Ottawa, 1929), p. 56.

37 Inwood, "Local Control".

interior and Europe.[38] Finally, it is argued that the major primary products in the Maritimes did not sustain as much processing as in Central Canada, either because of the intrinsic characteristics of a product or because it could not be produced locally at a competitive cost.[39]

A systematic evaluation of these arguments is not possible with summary information of the sort available in this paper. Nevertheless, the impact of resource availability is visible in the data reported in Table Nine. New Brunswick's per capita output among wood-using industries was very high in 1870 because of local timber availability, just as Ontario's strength in food and beverage manufacturing reflected that province's excellent supply of farm products. Maritime industrial growth after 1870 was strongest in the Nova Scotia coal belt in part because of a strong demand for coal originating in the substitution of coal and steel in a wide variety of industrial applications.[40] Another development reflected in these data was the replacement of Great Britain by the United States as the source of fuel, machinery or semi-finished iron used by Canadian industries. Manufacturers in Montreal and the Maritimes were favoured as long as these imports originated in Britain. When American supplies displaced the British late in the century south-western Ontario acquired the locational advantage.[41]

A full evaluation of these suggestions will require precise information about regional price differentials that is not yet available. It is also suggested that resource availability limited the size and population density of the region, which in turn prevented Maritime factories from adopting new technologies requiring a large scale of production. Research using American data permit a preliminary consideration of this point. Jeremy Atack has used census data to identify the scale of production needed to minimize production cost in 1870 American factories.[42] In a wide range of industries the minimum efficient size identified by Atack was considerably larger than the average Maritime fac-

---

38   Saunders, *The Economic History*, p. 24.

39   Caves and Holton, *Canada*, p. 180.

40   Inwood and Chamard, "Regional Industrial Growth".

41   Kris Inwood, "Transportation, Tariffs and the Canadian Iron Industry", University of Guelph Economics Working Paper 89-3 (1989). The point is more often made in the literature on Quebec; see A. Faucher and M. Lamontagne, "History of Industrial Development", in C. Falardeau, ed., *Essays on Contemporary Quebec* (Quebec, 1953), p. 23-37 and Morris Altman, "Resource Endowments and Location Theory: A Case Study of Quebec and Ontario at the Turn of the Twentieth Century", *Journal of Economic History*, XLVI, 4 (December 1986), pp. 999-1009.

42   Jeremy Atack, "Returns to Scale in Antebellum United States Manufacturing", *Explorations in Economic History*, 14, 4 (October, 1977), pp. 337-59.

Table Nine
Per Capita Manufacturing Output ($), 1870 and 1910

	1870				1910			
	NS	NB	PQ	ONT	NS	NB	PQ	ONT
all factories	16.76	27.66	27.48	31.41	54.13	48.04	83.02	111.67
farm production	2.01	2.00	1.93	1.33				
total	18.77	29.66	29.41	32.74				
consumer goods	4.25	5.27	10.31	9.76	9.18	9.67	31.51	43.67
durable goods	6.61	7.56	6.31	10.11	5.40	7.82	19.55	31.30
intermediate goods	5.90	14.83	10.85	11.54	39.54	30.55	31.96	36.69
chemical products	0.19	0.63	0.57	0.22	0.30	0.10	2.30	2.45
clothing	0.83	1.62	2.08	1.98	0.82	1.57	7.41	9.31
coal & petroleum products	0.23	0.12	0.21	1.09	1.52	1.98	1.39	4.24
electrical goods	0.00	0.00	0.00	0.00	0.00	0.00	2.23	1.66
food & beverages	1.34	1.38	3.47	6.32	5.88	5.44	6.58	21.03
iron & steel products	2.37	3.90	3.63	5.72	6.52	4.64	7.46	20.90
leather & fur products	2.65	2.88	5.37	2.99	1.29	1.94	8.20	6.06
nonferric metal products	0.12	0.31	0.44	0.19	0.17	0.17	1.52	2.79
nonmetallic mineral products	0.87	0.64	0.85	0.83	0.59	0.89	1.85	4.53
printing	0.51	0.50	0.72	0.89	0.94	1.45	2.01	4.19
paper products	0.01	0.14	0.24	0.16	0.00	0.13	3.46	1.43
rubber goods	0.00	0.00	0.12	0.00	0.04	0.00	0.25	1.06
transport equipment	3.28	3.41	1.80	2.52	1.50	3.93	6.42	6.44
tobacco products	0.49	0.05	0.64	0.17	0.08	0.00	4.12	1.66
textiles	0.36	0.66	0.58	1.40	1.37	3.55	4.87	2.71
wood products	3.41	11.35	6.31	6.79	9.78	18.09	12.77	18.19

tory.[43] This comparison recommends further consideration of the possibility that Maritime factories were inefficient *because* they were small.

Smallness may have handicapped regional transportation systems as well. With the possible exception of coal, regional commodities were not shipped in sufficient volume to support bulk transportation technology of the kind used on the Great Lakes.[44] The geography of the continent made it difficult for

43 Using Atack's Table 2, the industries are meat packing, distilleries, cotton textiles woolen goods, men's clothing, millinery, furniture, tanneries, boots and shoes, sheet metal, agricultural implements, wagons and carriages. The exceptions appear to be bakeries, flour milling, saw milling, tobacco manufacture and engine building.

44 J. Laurent, "Trade, Transportation and Technology: The American Great Lakes, 1866-1910", *Journal of Transport History*, 4 (March 1983), pp. 1-24; Sam H. Williamson, "The Growth of the Great Lakes as a Major Transportation Resource", *Research in Economic History*, 2 (1977), pp. 103-83.

Halifax and Saint John to attract the large volume of freight needed to justify the modern material handling equipment or to become a home base for ocean liners.[45] A similar point might be made about land transportation. Railways such as the Intercolonial carried surprisingly small volumes of freight, and this must have made it difficult to reduce costs using the new railway technology of large cars and long trains.[46]

Another hypothesis entertained by staple theorists is that the small size and slow growth of primary sector income undermined the local demand for manufactures and hence the growth of industry. Census-based estimates confirm that farm family income was lower in the Maritimes; this affected the demand for manufactures in a variety of ways.[47] Limited income-earning opportunities in the primary sector undoubtedly spurred out-migration by young Maritime men and women. The local demand for durable goods would have been stronger if the level of primary production had supported greater capital formation in primary production and transportation. Moreover, income earned by rural families was an important potential market for factory-made consumer goods.[48]

The various links between the primary sector and industrial demand complement input price and scale considerations in the analysis of slow Maritime industrial beginning in the pre-Confederation era. By 1870 New Brunswick was relatively industrialized but, as we have seen, its manufacturing grew slowly in subsequent decades. On the other hand, Nova Scotia industry was quite anaemic in 1870 and expanded quickly during the following 20 years. Neither Maritime province was able to match the dramatic acceleration experienced elsewhere in Canada after 1890. The pattern of growth presumably reflected the distinctive characteristics of Maritime industry. By and large factories were smaller and operated at a lower capital-labour ratio in the Maritimes. Household production survived much later. Factor productivity and wages were lower. Relative profitability also declined in New Brunswick between 1870 and 1910 and in Nova Scotia between 1890 and 1910.

These distinctive characteristics of Maritime manufacturing became more pronounced between 1870 and 1910. Their early visibility in 1870, however,

---

45   Saunders, *The Economic History*, pp. 21, 27.

46   Cruikshank, "The Transportation Revolution".

47   Kris Inwood and Jim Irwin, "Inter-regional Differences in Canadian Commodity Output in 1870: Preliminary Estimates", Paper presented to the 17th Conference on the Use of Quantitative Methods in Canadian Economic History, October 1990.

48   Higher primary sector incomes also would have made available greater savings for investment in manufacturing. I do not dwell on this mechanism because capital, like entrepreneurship, was relatively mobile between regions. There is no evidence of a failure to undertake sound business opportunities within the region because of scarce capital or entrepreneurship.

Table Ten
The Manufacturing Share of Commodity Production

	Inwood — Irwin		Green	
	1870	1890	1890	1910
Nova Scotia	.27	.39	.36	.34
New Brunswick	.39	.46	.35	.42
Quebec	.37	.52	.47	.55
Ontario	.32	.45	.40	.49

SOURCE: Inwood and Irwin, "Inter-regional Differences", and Alan Green, *Regional Aspects of Canada's Economic Growth* (Toronto, 1971), Appendix B. The Inwood-Irwin estimates are based on a regional decomposition of M.C. Urquhart's new national income estimates for Canada; see M.C. Urquhart, "New Estimates of Gross National Product, Canada, 1870 to 1926", in S. Engerman and R. Gallman, eds., *Long-Term Factors in American Economic Growth* (Chicago, 1986), pp. 9-88. Green follows an earlier estimating methodology used by O.J. Firestone, *Canada's Economic Development, 1867-1953* (London, 1958).

adds to the evidence of slow pre-Confederation growth and undermines the idea that Confederation marked a major turning point in regional development. Indeed, a more significant turning point may have been the onset of the wheat boom during the late 1890s. Maritime manufacturing continued to grow at a steady pace during this period but in so doing it missed out on the biggest boom in Canadian history.

The staple theory provides a simple locational explanation for the Maritime failure to capture linkages from western settlement. Among other factors, transportation costs to the west were lower from southern Ontario than from the Maritimes. Structuralists, on the other hand, might cite the influence of Central Canadian control over capital markets, tariffs and transportation. A comprehensive explanation for the salient characteristics of Maritime industrial development is likely to require some consideration of hypotheses drawn from the staple tradition as well as influences associated with political and financial control.

It may be helpful to view Maritime industry in the context of American and British industrialization. European industrial success in the 19th century involved the intensive use of craft labour. This model was difficult to adopt in the high-wage North American environment, and especially so in a corner of the continent relatively remote from the larger centres of innovation and fashion. The literature on North American growth, on the other hand, has tended to emphasize the effect of abundant natural resources and an expanding frontier; Gavin Wright argues that natural resources were the key to success even in the manufacturing sector.[49] The American model was difficult to adopt in regions such as the Maritimes with a weak resource endowment. Was there a third alternative, a distinctive Maritime strategy for industrial success? It would seem not, or at any rate if some alternative existed, history has not revealed it to us.

One final question concerns the relative importance of manufacturing within the wider economy. Manufacturing largely was ignored by an earlier generation of Maritime historians working in the staple theory tradition. One important contribution of the structuralist literature has been to correct this imbalance and draw attention to the phenomenon of arrested industrialization east of Montreal. We are now aware that manufacturing evolved along distinctive lines in Canada's thinly-settled eastern periphery. Nevertheless, the modern fascination with industrial growth should not lead us to equate industrialization with economic development, or at least not without careful thought. It is not obvious that manufacturing growth is essential for satisfactory social and economic development.[50] Some economies manage to support a growing population at higher and higher incomes through the judicious exploitation of natural resources and the efficient supply of services. Recent discussions of the 19th century rural household have reminded us that regional development ultimately depends upon individual and family struggles for survival and betterment.[51] For an individual household, the nearby presence of factory employment provided a useful alternative, but it was not the only option. Income earned in primary production or the service sector was, for many families, as helpful as the same level of income earned in manufacturing. The manifest ability of Maritime families to survive and prosper in the absence of industrialization provides a useful caution to the modern scholarly passion for smokestacks.

---

49 Gavin Wright, "The Origins of American Industrial Success, 1879-1940", *American Economic Review*, LXXX, 4 (September 1990), pp. 651-68.

50 Indeed, some would argue that fast industrialization breeds increased income inequality and poverty. For an introduction to this literature see Cynthia Taft Morris and Irma Adelman, *Comparative Patterns of Economic Development, 1850-1914* (Baltimore, 1988) and Ben Polak and Jeffrey G. Williamson, "Poverty, Policy and Industrialization: Lessons from the Distant Past", World Bank Working Paper, WPS 645, April 1991.

51 Rusty Bittermann, "The Hierarchy of the Soil: Land and Labour in a 19th Century Cape Breton Community", *Acadiensis*, XVIII, 1 (Autumn 1988), pp. 33-55; Rosemary Ommer, "The Truck System in Gaspé, 1822-77", *Acadiensis*, XIX, 1 (Autumn 1989), pp. 91-114.

The Intercolonial Railway, Freight Rates and the Maritime Economy

Ken Cruikshank

The Intercolonial Railway occupies an important place in the new historiography of Maritime economic development. Beginning in the 1970s, T.W. Acheson and Ernest Forbes, among others, sought to counter the fatalistic view of Maritime economic decline that had become current in the scholarly and popular mind.[1] In his pathbreaking work, Acheson demonstrates that the Maritimes did make the transition from the age of wind, wood and water and enjoyed a period of industrial growth under the aegis of the National Policy customs tariffs. Forbes links Maritime industrial growth to another national policy — the freight rates adopted on the government-owned and operated Intercolonial. He contends that the freight rate structure overcame the serious obstacles to growth that other scholars so often cite in explaining the problems of the Maritime economy — the absence of a large local population and the distance of the region from the industrial heartland of North America. The region's geographic situation did become a factor after 1912, Forbes argues, when rate advances effectively cut off many Maritime businesses from their markets in Central Canada. He concludes that as Maritime political influence waned in Ottawa, the government, the regulators on the Board of Railway Commissioners and the new managers of the Intercolonial became less sensitive to the region and "demolished the intricate rate structure developed over the previous forty years" in accordance with the misguided notion that rates should be equal throughout Canada.[2]

---

1   T.W. Acheson, "The National Policy and the Industrialization of the Maritimes, 1880-1910", *Acadiensis*, I, 2 (Spring 1972), pp. 3-28; T.W. Acheson, "The Maritimes and 'Empire Canada'", and E.R. Forbes, "Misguided Symmetry: The Destruction of Regional Transportation Policy for the Maritimes", in David J. Bercuson, ed., *Canada and the Burden of Unity* (Toronto, 1977), pp. 87-114, 60-86; E.R. Forbes, *The Maritime Rights Movement, 1919-1927* (Montreal, 1979). Early versions of this paper were presented to the Workshop on Atlantic Canadian Economic History, 30 September 1990, and to a meeting of the Canadian National Railways History Project in October 1990. I thank all the participants at those meetings, and, in particular, would like to thank Peter George for once again providing an astute commentary of my work. This paper is part of a larger examination of the role of the Canadian Government Railways in the Maritime economy, supported by the Canadian National Railways, whose assistance I gratefully acknowledge.

2   Forbes, "Misguided Symmetry", p. 67.

Forbes' influential article places freight rates and the Intercolonial at the centre of Maritime economic development. Since its publication, other scholars have relied on Forbes' argument in assessing the development of the region. Although the analysis of Maritime business and economic history has relied on more sophisticated models of underdevelopment and dependency since the mid-1970s, it is still possible for L.D. McCann to note the importance of the changes in the rate structure in his contribution to the *Historical Atlas of Canada*. And James Bickerton can similarly assert, following a comprehensive review of the literature on Maritime development, that "The most immediate and readily identifiable factor that triggered the deindustrialization of the Maritimes was the destruction of the ICR (Intercolonial Railway) as an instrument of regional development in Canada".[3]

Oddly enough, given the central role attributed to the Intercolonial in the development of the Maritimes, the railway has been virtually ignored by historians and economists since the publication of Forbes' work. In a recent review of the literature on Maritime development, Kris Inwood, one of the few scholars who has grappled with the subject of transportation costs in the region, concludes that the Intercolonial Railway and its freight rate policies remain something of an enigma.[4] This paper is intended to make the railway less of an enigma, to raise questions about the conclusions reached by Forbes in his pioneering article and to reactivate debate about the role of the Intercolonial in the development of the Maritimes. The starting point for this reassessment is the Intercolonial itself, its position in the Maritime transportation system, its operations and its freight rates.

The Intercolonial, some observers have argued, was an instrument of public policy, whose freight rates and other policies were part of the Confederation bargain between the formerly separate British North American colonies of Nova Scotia, New Brunswick and the Canadas. Section 124 of the British North America Act committed the new government of Canada to the construction of a railway between the St. Lawrence River and Halifax, and undoubtedly was intended to strengthen the political and economic relations between the otherwise diverse colonies. Unable to interest private

---

3   L.D. McCann, "Industrialization and the Maritimes", in Donald Kerr and Deryck Holdsworth, eds., *Historical Atlas of Canada, Volume III: Addressing the Twentieth Century* (Toronto, 1990), Plate 24; James Bickerton, *Nova Scotia, Ottawa and the Politics of Regional Development* (Toronto, 1990), p. 45. For reviews of this and the earlier literature, see James B. Cannon, "Explaining Regional Development in Atlantic Canada: A Review Essay", *Journal of Canadian Studies*, 19 (1984), pp. 65-86; Eric Sager, "Dependency, Underdevelopment and the Economic History of the Atlantic Provinces", *Acadiensis*, XVII, 1 (Autumn 1987), pp. 117-37.

4   Kris Inwood, "Maritime Industrialization from 1870 to 1910: A Review of the Evidence and its Interpretation", *Acadiensis*, XXI, 1 (Autumn 1991), p. 146.

entrepreneurs in the project, the Canadian government constructed and operated the Intercolonial Railway itself. Officials on the public railway reported to the Minister and Deputy Minister of Railways and Canals, provided regular information to the Auditor General of Canada and were directly accountable to Parliament. The Intercolonial's managers did not enjoy the kind of autonomy their successors at Canadian National would enjoy when the railway was incorporated into that system in 1923; instead, they ran a public enterprise highly sensitive to its political masters.

Those political masters sometimes debated the ways in which the railway should be operated so as to promote economic relations between the Maritime Provinces and the rest of Canada. For the most part, however, successive governments shared a common view of the public railway. The Intercolonial's manager after 1879, David Pottinger, summarized what he understood to be the government's position when he told the Deputy Minister of the Department of Railways and Canals that "it seems to be your desire and that of the department to operate the railway in such a way that the carriage will balance the expenses".[5] Governments did not care if the railway paid any return on the capital invested, and could expect to be criticized if net operating earnings were too large. On the other hand, continued operating deficits were a serious political liability to any government, which was bound to be accused of seriously mismanaging the railway. Pottinger and other government officials responsible for the railway remained acutely sensitive to the concerns of their political masters over the Intercolonial's performance, and sought to balance operating expenses and earnings.

The Intercolonial's managers, therefore, did have a potential advantage over their private counterparts — they did not need to worry about paying a return on the capital invested in their enterprise. Many private managers, whose railways were loaded with debt, frequently were driven by the need to meet the next interest payment. Financial pressures tempted private freight officials to cut rates dramatically in an attempt to attract immediate, if only temporary, increases in revenues. They sought to carry as much traffic as they could. Officials at the Intercolonial did not face these same pressures, and therefore were in a position to adopt a more conservative and less expansionary approach to their business. They did not necessarily need to scramble for all the business they could get, but rather could try to find the best mix of freight traffic for meeting their more limited objective of covering operating costs. Even that objective, however, would prove elusive.

---

5   David Pottinger to Collingwood Schreiber, 27 March 1888, vol. 12301, Records of Canadian National Railways System, RG30, National Archives of Canada, Ottawa [NAC]. For a further discussion of the debate over the purpose of the railway, see Ken Cruikshank, "The People's Railway: The Intercolonial Railway and the Canadian Public Enterprise Experience", *Acadiensis*, XVI, 1 (Autumn 1986), pp. 87-91.

Freight officials on the Intercolonial were not free to set rates in any way they wished, of course, but had to learn how to operate in their particular operating environment. The route of the Intercolonial played a crucial role in shaping the kinds of strategic choices they could make. In locating the railway, the Canadian government "danced to a military tune" and kept the railway a maximum distance from the American border.[6] A traveller on the Intercolonial in 1876 journeyed from Halifax, through Truro and Amherst to Moncton, where the train would either travel to Saint John or continue across the North Shore of New Brunswick, through Chatham, Bathurst and via the Matapedia Valley to the terminus at Rivière du Loup. By the mid-1880s the railway had expanded west and east, acquiring direct access to Quebec City and Sydney. In 1897 the Laurier government's railways minister, A.G. Blair, the former premier of New Brunswick, weathered a storm of protest in extending the Intercolonial into Montreal. In spite of these changes, the basic route of the Intercolonial remained unchanged, and it was this route which profoundly influenced the nature of its operations, and its freight rate policies.

The government railway was located, as one observer remarked, "between two devils and the deep blue sea".[7] The two devils, the Grand Trunk and the Canadian Pacific railways, provided the Intercolonial with its main connections to Central Canada, at Quebec and, after 1897, at Montreal. Their co-operation was necessary to the maintenance of a flow of traffic and to the establishment of through rates. And they were not always co-operative. On a number of occasions when the Intercolonial sought to assist local shippers by granting reduced rates on shipments to Ontario, officials at the Grand Trunk refused to participate.[8] "Our experience", complained Pottinger in 1903, "is that the Grand Trunk does nothing to assist the Intercolonial with industry along the line", although the Canadian Pacific was "usually more amenable". The general manager was concerned that neither railway was willing to set rates that would prevent the iron and steel industry in Cape Breton from using steamers rather than the railway. For a time in 1899, Pottinger did convince the Canadian Pacific to participate in a low rate on steel from the Nova Scotia Steel Company to points west of Montreal, but there was one catch: they would only agree to the reduction if the freight were shipped to Saint John and then over its own lines to Central Canada. Such a condition made the special rate a far less attractive proposition to the Intercolonial's traffic officers.[9]

---

6   *Debates of the House of Commons*, 12 August 1891 (L.H. Davies).

7   *Commons Debates*, 10 May 1892 (T. Kenny).

8   Pottinger to Schreiber, 11 January 1889, vol. 12302, RG30, Pottinger to Schreiber, 2 May 1900, vol. 12137, RG30, E. Tiffin to Pottinger, 22 February 1901, file 91167, vol. 867, Records of the Department of Railways and Canals, RG43 A1, NAC.

9   Pottinger to Schreiber, 26 June 1903, vol. 12142, RG30; Pottinger to Andrew G. Blair, 3 November 1899, vol. 12136, RG30, NAC.

Clearly, the dependence of the Intercolonial on other railways for access beyond Montreal circumscribed its activities.

The reluctance of the "two devils" to co-operate arose in part because both companies had their own eastern operations to consider. Both the Canadian Pacific and the Grand Trunk also competed with the government railway for oceanborne and oceanbound freight in the winter, when the port of Montreal was cut off from navigation. The Grand Trunk shipped goods between Montreal and Portland, Maine, and the Canadian Pacific began operating its line between the Montreal area and Saint John via Maine in 1890, making the city its official winter port beginning in 1895. These routes provided formidable competition for the Intercolonial: whereas trains travelling between Montreal and Saint John or Halifax on the government railway had to cover some 740 or 837 miles respectively, trains travelled only 297 miles on the Grand Trunk route between Montreal and Portland or 481 miles between Montreal and Saint John via the Canadian Pacific's "Short Line". Throughout the 19th century, the export rates to North American seaboard ports generally were equalized, so that rates on various goods, from hardware to grain, travelled at the same rate to Saint John, Boston, or Portland, regardless of the distance or route. To attract any export or import traffic, therefore, the Intercolonial had to accept the rates set by competitors with superior routes to the Atlantic.[10]

To develop the port of Halifax and create traffic for the Intercolonial, the government determined in the late 1870s to have its railway carry grain and other produce for export at "cost". After consulting with various officials on the railway, a rate on grain between Rivière du Loup and Halifax was fixed at a maximum of just over three cents a bushel. The rate had no effect on grain rates from the west to the Atlantic seaboard — these were set in relation to the New York to Chicago rates — but simply limited the Intercolonial's share of that overall rate. Little export grain traffic developed, given the shorter routes and more developed ports available to grain merchants. In any event, by the late 1880s, the general manager of the Intercolonial, David Pottinger, discouraged his officials from soliciting this traffic, since it paid the railway so little.[11] The only clear effort by the Canadian government to direct the freight

---

10 Testimony of L.J. Seargeant, Montreal, 16 December 1887, vol. 46, Records of the Privy Council Office, RG2, Series 3, Dormants, Minutes 1074, 25 February 1898, Minutes 1123, 18 February 1899, vol. 10817, Canadian Freight Association Minutebooks, RG30, NAC; Elizabeth McGahan, *The Port of Saint John: From Confederation to Nationalization* (Saint John, 1982), pp. 108-14, 133-40. Rates to Halifax likely would have been the same, except that the Intercolonial agreed to maintain a .01 differential over Saint John as part of its agreement with the Grand Trunk to reach Montreal. The differential became a sore point among the Halifax business community: see correspondence, file 6949, pt.1, vol. 372, RG43, NAC.

11 Correspondence Re Shipment of Grain or other articles by way of Intercolonial Railway, *Sessional Papers* (1879), 21R; Pottinger to Schreiber, 29 December 1888, vol. 12302, RG30, NAC.

rate policies of its railway failed to achieve the desired objective. The policy was frustrated by the inferior route offered by the Intercolonial, and the strength of railway competition for the grain trade.

The Canadian Pacific also competed with the government railway for some traffic originating in, or being shipped to, the Maritimes. It says something about views of the effectiveness of the Intercolonial, and about the faith in railway competition in the 19th century, that some Maritime leaders pressed the Canadian government to encourage the Canadian Pacific to build a more effective stretch of railway between the Maritimes and Central Canada — the Short Line from Saint John via Maine to Montreal. As one inducement, the government generously agreed to allow the Canadian Pacific to solicit traffic bound from Ontario and the west to stations on the Intercolonial and carry it via its Saint John route, a practice which was renegotiated and limited after 1900. Nevertheless, even after 1900, the Canadian Pacific remained in a position to compete for a portion of the traffic from shippers who in other circumstances would have had no choice but to ship their goods over the Intercolonial's entire line. A number of shippers much preferred the Canadian Pacific route, which reduced the time during which freight was in transit. A Nova Scotia firm, the Stanfield Brothers, insisted that it would not use the Intercolonial unless the railway agreed to deliver freight travelling between its firm and the west to the Canadian Pacific at Saint John.[12]

Apart from the "two devils", the "deep blue sea" also shaped the operations of the government railway. The coastal location of the Intercolonial — a product of Maritime geography and the choices made in locating the railway — produced competition, both real and potential, from water carriers. Regular and tramp steamers and other ships active in coastal trade stopped at many of the same ports that the railway served, and generally could offer to carry goods at rates considerably lower than any railway could afford. Water competition kept pace with the technological improvements on the railway; the freight capacity of individual steamers and schooners increased significantly in the final decades of the 19th century, and the facilities of various ports, as well as the St. Lawrence River system, were updated and improved.[13]

Water carriers gave some Maritime shippers alternatives to the Intercolonial in carrying their goods — offering routes directly to other points along the railway and along the St. Lawrence to Montreal, or connecting them to other rail carriers serving major centres on the Atlantic seaboard such as Boston or Portland. Managers of the government railway introduced special

---

12   Tiffin to G.P. Graham (Minister of Railways), 4 December 1911, pp. 34734-39, file 532, E. Tiffin, vol. 62, G.P. Graham Papers, MG27 II D 8, NAC.

13   G.P. de T. Glazebrook, *A History of Transportation in Canada, Volume II* (Toronto, 1964), pp. 220-34; Eric W. Sager with Gerald E. Panting, *Maritime Capital: The Shipping Industry in Atlantic Canada, 1820-1914* (Montreal, 1990), pp. 47-60.

rates to meet some of this competition. For example, the Intercolonial had a special freight tariff on most goods travelling between Saint John and Halifax to compete with steamers travelling between the two ports. Large shippers of coal received rebates at Halifax, Saint John and Moncton, since they were in the best position to resort to water carriers as an alternative. Grain and flour rates from Ontario had to be maintained at lower levels at points such as Halifax, Saint John, Moncton, Sackville and Sydney in order to prevent merchants from importing their goods from Montreal, Boston or Portland by water. Water competition could not always be met. In the late 1880s, the Intercolonial could not establish rates low enough to stop the sugar refinery at Halifax from shipping a portion of its business to Ontario using a combination of steamers to Boston and American railway connections. When the Intercolonial Coal Company of Pictou agreed in 1900 to cancel one of its steamers to Montreal in exchange for reductions in its rail freight rates, the arrangement was short-lived. Officials at the railway decided the traffic was not worth having at the low rate they had to offer.[14]

Steamers also gave shippers from outside the region various points of access to the Maritime market; to sustain traffic for the railway, Intercolonial managers fixed rates to protect the market position of local producers. For example, the rates on nails and other hardware from Saint John and Halifax to New Glasgow, as well as the rates on a number of commodities from Halifax to Sydney, were fixed to meet the competition from freight brought in by steamers from Montreal. The dramatic reduction in ocean freight rates in the late 19th century produced overseas competition for local manufacturers as well; managers of the railway were pressured to ensure that their freight rates allowed iron, steel and coal producers to compete in local markets that their English competitors were able to penetrate.[15]

Not all policy choices of Intercolonial freight officials were shaped entirely by competitive forces. Like most railways, the public railway sought to encourage the development of central distribution points, by granting lower rates to merchants operating out of larger centres. And, as with most railways, more and more towns and cities were able to acquire these special lower rates while few towns lost them, so that by the early 20th century, merchants in Halifax, Stellarton, Truro, New Glasgow, Trenton, Ferrona Junction, Westville, Amherst, Moncton, Saint John, Chatham, Fredericton, Gibson, Marysville, Levis

---

14 Pottinger to Schreiber, 7 June 1881, vol. 12201, Pottinger to Schreiber, 10 November 1894, vol. 12132, Pottinger to Blair, 24 February 1897, vol. 12134, Pottinger to Schreiber, 25 January 1889, vol. 12303, RG30, NAC.

15 Pottinger to Schreiber, 22 May 1888, vol. 12303, Pottinger to Schreiber, 10 May 1900, vol. 12137, Pottinger to Schreiber, 9 July 1903, vol. 12142, Pottinger to Schreiber, 10 November 1894, vol. 12132, RG30, NAC. For complaints re ocean rates, see Testimony to Tariff Commission, Londonderry, 27 January 1906, pp. 62, 112-3, 118, vol. 8, Tariff Commission 1906, RG 36/17, NAC.

and Quebec, all could distribute goods in their local area at rates lower than those listed in the general tariff.[16]

Managers of the Intercolonial also decided to follow the practice of many North American railways in granting lower westbound than eastbound rates. Other railway officials had found that traffic towards the Atlantic ports was generally heavier than incoming traffic, and made rate concessions to try to increase the loading of westbound trains. This policy did not make as much sense on the Intercolonial, because a strong export trade did not develop through the port of Halifax. During the 1880s, the railway carried more import than export freight at Halifax, by a margin of about two to one. Exports did exceed imports at Halifax by the opening decade of the 20th century, but railway officials still contended that, overall, more of the Intercolonial's traffic moved west rather than east. They were convinced that there was no benefit to the railway in maintaining lower rates on westbound traffic.[17]

Those small, casual shippers who sent goods between stations on the Intercolonial and who did not benefit from any of the myriad of special rates, relied on the freight classification rules and the general tariff to determine their rates. Under this tariff, they paid less in freight charges than their counterparts elsewhere, even within the Maritimes. When it began operating in the region, the Canadian Pacific introduced the tariff used in Central Canada. The origins of the Intercolonial's local tariff are obscure. Generally, new railways simply used the merchandise tariff in effect on similarly located lines, and worked revisions from there. For example, the government of Nova Scotia's railway,

---

16 Pottinger to Blair, 24 January 1900, vol. 12136, RG30, NAC; Freight Tariffs: C.A. 1 (Saint John), 1 March 1898, C.B. 1 (Moncton), 1 March 1898, E.A. 1 (Halifax), 1 March 1898, W.B. 1 (Quebec), 1 March 1898, E.C. 1 (New Glasgow, Stellarton, Ferrona Junction, Trenton and Westville), 18 April 1898, C.C. 2 (Amherst), 24 July 1900, C.D. 1 (Fredericton, Gibson and Marysville), 1 September 1904, C.E. 1 (Chatham), 1 September 1904, vol. 7983, RG30, NAC.

17 Traffic at Halifax calculated from Annual Reports of the Department of Railways and Canals, *Sessional Papers*, and from Dominion Bureau of Statistics, *Trade of Canada, 1867-1928* (Ottawa, 1929), Table 25A. Although it is not clear how they made their calculations, in 1908 the Intercolonial's experienced general manager, David Pottinger, estimated that just under 40 per cent of the railway's freight traffic was eastbound, and one year later Deputy Minister Butler claimed that eastbound freight had exceeded westbound freight prior to 1905: Pottinger to M.J. Butler (Deputy Minister), 3 February 1908, vol. 12153, RG 30; NAC; Butler to Graham, 24 March 1909, 5722-3, file 97 M.J. Butler, vol. 12, MG 27 II D 8, NAC. There is some contradictory evidence: Howard Darling cites a remark in the House of Commons to claim that in 1906 three-quarters of the Intercolonial's traffic was eastbound, Howard Darling, *The Politics of Freight Rates* (Toronto, 1980), p. 87. With the exception of traffic at Halifax, I have been unable to find any other useful figures, but am inclined to accept Pottinger and Butler's statements, since they are consistent with one another.

which was incorporated into the Intercolonial system, had charged rates the same as elsewhere in Canada.[18]

The initial scale of rates established on the Intercolonial in 1874 was slightly lower than elsewhere, but significant reductions were made in 1876. A small Maritime merchant shipping merchandise 100 miles in 1877 could expect to pay from $60 to $24 for a 20,000 pound carload, whereas a similar shipment made in Ontario would cost from $72 to $34. The Maritime tariff may have been lower than that of Ontario because water competition was more pervasive, or freight officials may have estimated that the lower scale of rates represented figures equal to those of other railways, less the profit. Whatever the reasons, officials on the government railway did not use subsequent adjustments in the tariff to increase the scale of rates. In 1889, when officials adopted the freight classification and general rules used on other eastern Canadian railways, they sought to limit the disruption created by these changes by actually reducing the tariff. A further adjustment in 1898 brought consistency in the construction of the tariff between the Intercolonial and other railways, and did advance some rates. Nevertheless, in 1899 a local shipper in the Maritimes would pay $56 to $28 to ship 20,000 pounds of freight 100 miles, whereas the same shipment would cost $72 to $36 in Ontario.[19]

The general merchandise tariff did not apply to a large proportion of traffic carried on any railway. The amount of freight carried under this tariff and under the special distributing rates out of particular towns and cities probably never amounted to more than 15 per cent of the Intercolonial's traffic. It therefore does not provide the best measure for comparing the overall rate structure of the Intercolonial with other railways. The best available measure is the average earning on every ton of freight carried one mile, a measure which is unfortunately only available for the Intercolonial prior to 1887 and after 1908.[20] Earnings per ton mile followed a similar pattern on the Intercolonial as they did on three other eastern North American railways — the Grand Trunk, New York Central and Erie railways — declining sharply in the 1870s and 1880s and thereafter becoming more stable. The median average rate on the

---

18 E.G. Carty, *Maritime Freight Rates, 1867-1931: Comparison with Freight Rates in Ontario and Quebec,* 30 May 1931, file 372, vol. file 6949 #162, vol. 372, RG43, NAC.

19 P.C. 1476, 12 December 1874, Freight Tariff, 2 October 1876, P.C. 314, 25 February 1889, file 5360, pt. 1, vol. 340, RG43, NAC; J.A. Argo, "Historical Review of Canadian Railway Freight Rate Structure, 1876-1938", in R.A.C. Henry and Associates, *Railway Freight Rates in Canada* (Ottawa, 1939), Schedule 23. My figures follow the tariffs cited and not Argo; he does not include the 1874 tariff and uses a different and somewhat higher 1876 tariff introduced in June of that year.

20 For a discussion of this statistic, see Kris Inwood, "Freight Rates and the Canadian Primary Iron and Steel Industry", Paper delivered to Fourth Atlantic Conference, Halifax, 8-10 October 1981, pp. 11-12.

Intercolonial was 73 cents in the decade 1878-87, compared with 71 on the Grand Trunk, 74 on the Erie and 80 on the New York Central, although there was considerable annual variation on all of these railways. Earnings per ton mile were much more consistent between 1908 and 1914.[21] By that time, earnings per ton mile on the Intercolonial were down to 58 cents, compared with 69 cents on the Grand Trunk, 63 on the New York Central and 59 on the Erie. For every dollar the Intercolonial earned moving freight a given distance, therefore, the Grand Trunk earned $1.18, the New York Central took in $1.08, and the Erie collected $1.01. The Intercolonial's figure most closely resembles earnings per ton mile on the northeastern American railways, which carried substantially larger quantities of freight.[22]

A comparison can also be made between the earnings per ton mile on the Intercolonial and the two eastern Canadian Pacific divisions, serving similar territory — Quebec and the Maritimes. In the four years 1908 to 1911, for which the Canadian Pacific figures are available, the two Canadian Pacific divisions carried similar quantities of goods as the Intercolonial in terms of freight tons carried per mile. The earnings per ton mile, however, were quite different, with those on the two Canadian Pacific divisions ranging from 70 to 74 cents, compared with a range of 55 to 60 cents on the Intercolonial. For every dollar in freight revenue collected by the Intercolonial in this four-year period, the Canadian Pacific collected between $1.17 and $1.32. The Canadian Pacific, with a somewhat different rate structure and a different mix of low- and high-paying traffic than the Intercolonial, was able to earn more money on the freight it carried in the region.[23]

Beyond the fact that the managers of the Intercolonial did not have to worry about paying a return on the capital invested in the railway, there is little evidence of conscious public policy decisions shaping the rate structure on the

---

21   The coefficient of variation on the ICR was 9.5 per cent, compared with about 3 per cent on the Grand Trunk and 6 per cent on the American railways in the 1878-87 period. Between 1908 and 1914, the coefficient of variation remained highest on the Intercolonial, at 4.7 per cent, compared with 1.3 per cent on the Grand Trunk, 1.7 per cent on the Erie, and 2.3 per cent on the New York Central.

22   The statistics contained in this and subsequent paragraphs are calculated from information contained in: *Poor's Manual of Railroads, 1878-1916*, also known as *Poor's Railroad Manual of the United States* (the Erie, New York and Grand Trunk); "History of the Grand Trunk Railway", vol. 10934, RG30, NAC; Annual Reports of the Department of Railways and Canals, Railway Statistics, *Sessional Papers*, 1879-1923 (Intercolonial and Grand Trunk); "Evidence, Royal Commission on Railways", vol. 46, RG 2, Series 3, NAC (Intercolonial and Grand Trunk).

23   Canadian Pacific figures calculated from Western Freight Rates Enquiry, Productions of the Canadian Pacific Railway, file 18755 (#32-41), volume 579, RG 46, NAC. The Intercolonial carried a significantly larger proportion of coal and lumber; the Canadian Pacific more grain.

Intercolonial. Most through rates and many local rates were fixed in an effort to attract freight away from competing carriers, or to ensure that locally produced freight could compete in various markets with similar freight. Given the distance of its route, its proximity to water and rail carriers with distinct competitive advantages, and its dependence on "two devils" for access to the North American railway network, the Intercolonial was not in a strong position to serve as a rate setter or to be used as an instrument of public policy. As the Confederation-inspired link between the Maritimes and the rest of the North American continent, the Intercolonial was seriously flawed.[24]

The rate structure of the Intercolonial created problems for the public railway's managers. Rates might have been sustainable if, as Forbes suggests they did, those rates generated more traffic and greater earnings for the railway. Unfortunately, although the Intercolonial's freight traffic did grow steadily in the early 20th century, a successful balancing of expenses and earnings remained elusive. Cost pressures in turn forced the managers of the railway to conclude that changes in the rate structure were necessary, and to focus on those rate policies over which they had some control.

Although Forbes has suggested that the flexible approach to rate-making that he associated with the period of the 1890s and 1900s produced greater prosperity for the railway, the evidence is not clear.[25] Freight traffic did grow, and the railway's managers were able to put an end to the constantly growing deficits of the Intercolonial in the 1880s. Nevertheless, the early 20th century proved quite volatile, witnessing both the best and worst years in the history of the railway. Overall, the Intercolonial lost $2.5 million between 1898 and 1914. In one nightmarish year, 1904-05, expenses outstripped earnings by $1.7 million.

Why did the railway have so much trouble breaking even? As Forbes rightly suggests, the traditional argument that political patronage produced excessive costs on the railway has to be taken with a grain of salt.[26] Indeed, the claim seems to be undercut by the fact that the expenses associated with moving freight trains, which was one way of assessing efficiency, were comparatively low on the Intercolonial. Based on the median for the decade 1878-87, for every dollar it cost the Intercolonial to move a freight train, it cost the Grand Trunk $1.78, the New York Central $1.87, and the Erie $1.92. As the Intercolonial matured as a business, expenditures more nearly approximated those of the Grand Trunk. For every dollar expended to move an

---

24 In some instances, managers of private railways in such a weak position might engage in rate wars, but only so as to force a merger with more powerful lines, and enhance the value of their road in any such merger. This strategy obviously made no sense for the Intercolonial.

25 Forbes, "Misguided Symmetry", p. 64.

26 Cruikshank, "The People's Railway", pp. 86-7.

Intercolonial train in 1908-12, the Grand Trunk spent $1.01, and the New York Central and Erie railways spent $1.39.

Unfortunately, the real business of the railway was carrying freight, not running trains. Estimates of the median cost of moving a ton of freight one mile produce quite different results, and show decidedly against the Intercolonial. In the decade after 1878, for every dollar expended by the Intercolonial to move freight a given distance, the Grand Trunk and Erie railways spent 69 cents and the New York Central spent only 64 cents. As the Intercolonial became a more developed line, it was able to reduce the gap, but expenditures were still considerably greater than those on other railways. In the seven years before the outbreak of the First World War, the Grand Trunk, New York Central and Erie railways expended only 86, 79 and 70 cents for every dollar it cost the Intercolonial to move freight. On the other hand, in operating in the same region, the Canadian Pacific spent more than the public railway, $1.03 for every $1.00 of Intercolonial expenditure.[27]

These high costs per ton-mile suggest that, although they were able to control the cost of moving trains, the managers of the Intercolonial had trouble capturing some of the potential cost savings made possible by changes in railway technology. With the development of more powerful locomotives, the cargo capacity of individual freight cars could be enlarged. In 1891 the Intercolonial began strengthening its freight cars so as to increase their capacity from 24,000 to 34,000 pounds; within a decade it had begun to introduce box cars that could carry 60,000 pounds of freight, and by 1911 platform cars had a carrying capacity of 80,000 pounds.[28] As a result, on the Intercolonial and other railways the amount of freight carried by each train grew dramatically in the 19th and into the 20th centuries. In the years before the war, an Intercolonial train carried some 275 tons of freight, a considerable increase from 79 tons in the 1880s. A Grand Trunk freight train carried about 20 per cent more than its Intercolonial counterpart. The New York Central and Erie railways carried considerably more freight on each train, loads 60-90 per cent greater than those on the Intercolonial.[29]

While inferior trainloading may be a sign that railway officials were scheduling too many trains given the freight available, it may also indicate that the Intercolonial simply could not attract and carry enough traffic to fill the new larger trains in which it was investing. Freight traffic density — the quan-

---

27   For freight expenses I use the estimate commonly used by railway officials, the total expenses multiplied by the proportion of freight earnings to total earnings.

28   Annual Reports of the Department of Railways and Canals, *Sessional Papers*, 1892, 1902, 1912. For a discussion of technological changes on other railways, see Thomas Shaugnessy to Lord Strathcona, 16 November 1901, pp. 59-65, Shaugnessy Letterbooks #76, MG 28 II 20, NAC; Albro Martin, *Enterprise Denied* (New York, 1971), pp. 55-71

29   Trainload = Ton-miles/Freight Trainmiles.

tity of freight carried one mile for every mile of line — provides some indication of the traffic on the railway.[30] Despite considerable improvement between the 1880s and the years before the First World War, the Intercolonial remained a relatively small operation. The freight traffic density on the Grand Trunk was not that much greater, about 30 per cent larger than that of the Maritime railway. On the other hand, the freight traffic density on the two northeastern American railways was three to four times that of the Intercolonial. The public railway was not alone in facing traffic problems — the Canadian Pacific divisions serving Quebec and the Maritimes had an even lighter density than the Intercolonial in the period 1908-11. Operating lightly travelled routes, officials on the Intercolonial and on the Canadian Pacific's easternmost divisions were not in a position to capture some of the economies associated with traffic density.

In the case of both the Intercolonial and the Canadian Pacific's operations in the Maritimes and Quebec, light traffic resulted in relatively high costs for moving freight. The earnings per ton-mile on the Intercolonial, however, were significantly lower than those on the Canadian Pacific. The combination of high costs and low earnings placed considerable pressure on the Intercolonial's officials to maintain and even advance existing rates. While continuing to monitor costs, the managers and freight traffic officials at the Intercolonial looked for ways of increasing rates. They saw an opportunity to defend such advances beginning in 1905, following two years of the worst deficits ever recorded on the Intercolonial. In those two years, the railway spent $2.6 million more than it earned. Such politically embarrassing and treasury-draining losses could not be ignored, not even by the Maritimes' H.R. Emmerson, the Minister of Railways, who appeared more committed than any of his predecessors or successors to the idea that the Intercolonial should be run in the interests of Maritime development.

In 1905 officials at the Intercolonial advanced a number of the special distributing rates offered merchants in selected communities. Originally intended to encourage the centralization of mercantile activity, the rates no longer seemed to serve that or any other purpose, and produced endless complaints and demands for equality from those towns which were excluded. The advances in these distributing rates made in 1905 were quite limited: only the summer rates to points from Quebec City to the region between the city and Matapedia were changed, and the reduced rates still applied to the most heavily populated territory served by businesses in Halifax, Truro, New Glasgow, Amherst, Moncton and Saint John. Beginning in 1910, the Intercolonial's traffic officer pressed his superiors to eliminate the distributing rates altogether. Following the appointment of F.P. Gutelius as manager of the Intercolonial by the government of Robert Borden, freight officials appear to have achieved much of their objective: the rates were not eliminated, but they were increased

---

30   Freight Traffic Density = Ton-miles/Mileage of Railway

in 1912 and in 1913. The 1912 and 1913 changes in the special distributing rates resulted in some quite dramatic rate advances on traffic carried between Maritime communities and stations on the Intercolonial from Quebec City to Montreal.[31]

In 1913 Intercolonial managers also advanced the general tariff on their railway. This general tariff prescribed mileage rates, which were applied on goods shipped between smaller communities, and which were not covered by some other special distributing or commodity tariff. The federal cabinet had approved a new higher general tariff back in 1906, but railway officials chose not to introduce it. The new tariff, when finally implemented in April 1913, increased the cost of shipping a carload of fifth class merchandise 100 miles by $6. Additional advances in 1915 resulted in a further $6 being added to shippers' costs, so that the cost of shipping a carload of freight 100 miles rose from $42.00 in 1912 to $54 in 1916. Maritime shippers using the general tariff paid, for the most part, the same rate for a local shipment that shippers on Ontario railways, on the Canadian Pacific railway lines in the Maritimes, or for that matter on the Intercolonial lines west of Quebec City had been paying since 1907.[32]

Distributing rates and the general merchandise tariff applied to a small proportion of the Intercolonial's traffic, but they provided some of the only manoeuvring room that the railway's managers had — they were among the only rates that were fixed in the absence of competitive pressures. Even special commodity rates applying on local traffic escaped the full brunt of the advances between 1913 and 1915. The special local Maritime rates on coal, from Springhill Junction, Stellarton and Sydney to various centres, were readjusted several times, in 1913, 1916 and 1917, but generally produced only a slight advance.[33] In another case, it was late in 1916 before railway officials advanced a special tariff offered to stove manufacturers shipping their goods

---

31   Tiffin to W.A. Campbell, 30 August 1910, pp. 34704-15, file 532, vol. 62, MG27 II D8, NAC; Tiffin to Managing Board of Intercolonial, 3 February 1912, file 5360, pt. 2, vol. 341, RG43, NAC; Freight Tariffs, 17 July 1905: C.A.3 (Saint John), C.B. 3, (Moncton), C.C. 3 (Amherst), E.A. 3 (Halifax); Freight Tariffs, 15 May 1912: C.A.3 supplement 7 (Saint John), C.B. 3 supplement 7, (Moncton), C.C. 3 supplement 4 (Amherst), E.A. 3 supplements 6 and 7 (Halifax), vol. 7983, Freight Tariffs, 28 May 1913: J.5 (Saint John), vol. 8007, H. 2 (Halifax), vol. 8002, RG30, NAC; Argo, "Canadian Railway Freight Rate Structure", Schedule 25.

32   P.C. 23 February 1906, 29 May 1906, file 5360, pt. 1, vol. 340, RG 43, NAC; Freight Tariffs, Z 2, 21 April 1913, Z 8, 27 July 1915, Z 9, 1 November 1915, vol. 7999, RG30, NAC; Tiffin to Campbell, 5 July 1910, Memorandum [for Minister?] from Campbell, 2 June 1913, file 5360, pt. 2, vol. 341, RG43, NAC; Argo, "Canadian Railway Freight Rate Structure", Schedule 23.

33   Freight Tariffs: C.C. 3, 18 March 1909, C.C. 10, 1 February 1913, C.C. 15, 25 June 1913, C.C. 19, 1 June 1916, C.C. 19 supplement 16, 28 June 1917, vol. 7984, C.C. 22, 15 August 1917, vol. 7984, RG 30, NAC.

locally by about 10 per cent, an increase similar to that approved in the same year by the railway commission for Ontario.[34] In general, therefore, between 1905 and 1917, Maritime businesses engaged in local trade faced a series of advances. Because special distributing rates and the general merchandise tariff bore the brunt of these advances, merchants, farmers and small manufacturers, as well as other casual users of the Intercolonial, would have been most affected by the changes.

While officials at the Intercolonial were altering the freight tariffs enjoyed by some local shippers for several years, important changes were being made in the rates paid on freight shipped between the Maritimes and Central Canada. Intercolonial officials did not initiate these changes, but appear either to have approved them, or at least felt that they were not in a position to counteract them. The changes began in 1908, when the Board of Railway Commissioners negotiated a substantial revision of Central Canadian rates. To understand why and how these changes affected the Maritimes, it is necessary to understand how rates between the two regions were formulated.

In constructing through rates between the Maritimes and Central Canada, there were three pivotal points: Saint John, Montreal and Toronto. The freight tariff between Toronto and Saint John was composed of the regular winter rate between Toronto and Montreal plus an "arbitrary" between Montreal and Saint John, an artificial rate which was considerably lower than the actual rate paid on Saint John shipments to Montreal.[35] (Although Maritime Rights advocates would later claim that this "arbitrary" had been fixed at 20 cents per 100 pounds on first-class freight since the 1880s, Table One demonstrates that it had varied a good deal during the 19th century.) Rates to or from other parts of the industrial heartland of southwestern Ontario were fixed at various proportions above the Toronto rate; rates to or from the Maritimes were fixed at levels above the Saint John rate. Thus, the tariff on fifth class merchandise from Halifax to Windsor in 1900 would have been 40 cents per 100 pounds, composed of a one cent differential from Halifax over Saint John, a 10 cent "arbitrary" from Saint John to Montreal, a 22 cent winter rate from Montreal to Toronto, and a seven cent differential to Windsor over Toronto.

The construction of rates between Saint John and Toronto involved a second issue. Throughout much of the period before 1908 the eastbound rates to Saint John were higher than the westbound rates from the same port. For the most part, as Table One shows, this was not determined by the "arbitrary", which was the same on freight bound in either direction, but by the freight tariff from Montreal to Toronto, which had been from an early date lower than that on traffic moving from Toronto to Montreal. Such a difference in the rates

---

34 Freight Tariffs: C.I. 6, 15 April 1909, vol. 7977, C.I. 89, 20 December 1916, vol. 7976, RG 30, NAC.

35 Rates to or from points east of Toronto would have been calculated using the winter tariff rate between those stations and Montreal, plus the Montreal to Saint John 'arbitrary'.

Table One

Construction of Through Rates Between Saint John and Toronto
Eastbound (E) versus Westbound (W)
First Class Freight, Cents Per 100 Pounds

	Toronto and Montreal		+	Montreal and Saint John ('Arbitrary')		=	Toronto and Saint John	
	E	W		E	W		E	W
1882	50	60		40	20		90	80
1885	50	34		40	38		90	72
1886	50	36		40	36		90	72
1890	50	38		34	34		84	72
1891	50	42		30	30		80	72
1896	50	42		30	28		80	70
1898	50	42		20	28		70	70
1900	50	44		20	20		70	64
1908	44	44		20	20			

Source: E.G. Carty, *Maritime Freight Rates, 1867-1931: Comparison with Freight Rates in Ontario and Quebec*, 30 May 1931, Appendix 1, file 6949 #162, vol. 372, RG43, NAC.

ostensibly, and to a certain extent in fact, corresponded to water competition between the two points. The low rates seem to also have been influenced by traditionally powerful Montreal business interests.[36]

The difference in the westbound and eastbound rates between Montreal and Toronto occasioned considerable complaint throughout the late 19th century. Manufacturers in Toronto and southwestern Ontario complained that higher eastbound rates made it more difficult for them to penetrate markets anywhere east of Montreal. The railways' private association, the Canadian Freight Association, to which the Intercolonial belonged, undertook a number of studies of the question, but concluded that no changes were necessary.[37] In 1908, as part of a much larger response to a variety of complaints about the rate structure of Ontario and Quebec, the Board of Railway Commissioners ordered that, except during the season of navigation when water competition had some impact, rates to and from Montreal and Ontario had to be equal. This winter rate was one of the main components of the through rate between the Maritimes and Ontario, and the component which had resulted in differen-

36 See *Dominion Sugar Co. v. Grand Trunk, Canadian Pacific, Chatham Wallaceburg and Lake Erie and Pere Marquette Railway Cos.* (1913), 17 *Canadian Railway Cases*, Commissioner Drayton, p. 245.

37 Minute 562, 5 June 1902, Minute 634, 4 September 1902, vol. 10818, Canadian Freight Association Minutebooks, RG30, NAC.

ces between eastbound and westbound rates. By 1908, therefore, Maritime-Ontario trade was governed by what Forbes terms a "misguided symmetry".[38]

Officials at the Intercolonial do not appear to have taken any steps to change the formula so as to make westbound rates lower than those eastbound. In fact, they gradually equalized westbound and eastbound rates on traffic carried locally. Although the "arbitrary" used in the construction of through rates between the Maritimes and Montreal had been unaffected by the direction of the traffic since 1900, the actual rate on goods destined for Montreal from the Maritimes had been lower than that on goods shipped from Montreal to the region. This preference on westbound freight to Montreal continued after 1908, since it applied to local traffic on the Intercolonial, and did not have to be set in agreement with other railways or in accordance with the standards of the railway commission. Nevertheless, railway officials gradually equalized the eastbound and westbound rates as other modifications were made in the rate structure. For example, when advances were made in the special distributing rates from centres such as Amherst, Saint John and Halifax to Montreal in 1912 and 1913, the new rates applied "to and from Montreal" instead of "to Montreal".[39] In 1914 the special commodity rate on bar iron and steel applied for the first time to traffic carried "to and from Montreal", phasing out yet another important preference on westbound traffic.[40]

By 1917, therefore, on the eve of a series of horizontal rate advances, the Maritime rate structure had already been transformed. Officials at the Intercolonial had used the discretion they enjoyed with respect to local rates to advance a number of tariffs, and, following the equalization of westbound and eastbound rates between the Maritimes and Ontario, to effect a similar equalization on their own road. Between 1918 and 1920, officials on the government railway followed three rate advances approved by the Board of Railway Commissioners to assist Canada's private lines in meeting the spiralling costs of labour and supplies associated with the war.[41] The impact of the horizontal advances on the earlier changes can be seen in Tables Two, Three and Four. By 1916, a merchant in Amherst paid 38 per cent more to import a carload of merchandise from Saint John than in 1900.[42] This rate then was

---

38 Report of the Chief Traffic Officer re International and Toronto Board of Trade Rate Cases, 27 June 1907, *Annual Report of the Board of Railway Commissioners* (1908), pp. 5-23; E.G. Carty, *Maritime Freight Rates, 1867-1931: Comparison with Freight Rates in Ontario and Quebec*, 30 May 1931, file 6949 #162, vol. 372, RG43, NAC.

39 Freight Tariffs, 15 July 1912: H. 1 (Halifax), J. 3 (Saint John), vol. 8007, RG30, NAC.

40 Freight Tariff C.I. 40, 22 April 1914, vol. 7977, RG30, NAC.

41 On the horizontal advances, see Ken Cruikshank, *Close Ties: Government, Railways and the Board of Railway Commissioners, 1851-1933* (Montreal, 1991), ch. 8.

multiplied by a 15 per cent and 25 per cent advance in 1918, and a 40 per cent increase in 1920. Although the 40 per cent advance was short-lived, even after two reductions at the beginning and the end of 1921, the carload of merchandise still cost 77 per cent more to transport from Saint John than it had in 1916, and 146 per cent more than in 1900. Even considering that inflation would have increased the value of that carload of merchandise, in constant 1900 dollars the advance between 1900 and 1922 still amounted to about 35 per cent. A similar shipment from Toronto cost 80 per cent more in 1922 than in 1900 which amounted to a very slight reduction of under one per cent in constant dollars.

What was the impact of these apparently dramatic changes on the competitive situation of merchants and manufacturers in the Maritimes? Merchants generally paid the freight charges on the goods they ordered, but manufacturers sometimes absorbed part of the freight cost in order to compete. Tables Two, Three and Four attempt to assess the potential impact of the rate changes on competition in the Maritimes, in southwestern Ontario and in Montreal. It is clear from Table Two that in 1922, a Toronto manufacturer shipping goods to Amherst might have to absorb even more of the freight rate costs than at the turn of the century in order to compete with a Saint John business. A similar situation would face an Amherst manufacturer competing with a firm in Montreal for business in Toronto, as Table Three demonstrates. The change between 1900 and 1922 is not identical, however: the Toronto manufacturer would need to absorb only 43 per cent more in freight rate costs to compete in Amherst, while the cost of absorbing freight rate costs would have doubled for the Amherst manufacturer competing in Toronto. Nevertheless, both Tables indicate that the horizontal advances had one main impact — to increase the freight rate advantage of shippers serving their own region.

In Montreal, as Table Four illustrates, the prewar changes in Intercolonial rates increasingly gave the edge to Toronto against the Maritimes, a competitive edge then sharpened by the horizontal advances. An Amherst manufacturer might have to absorb $39 more in freight charges in 1922 than in 1900. While Toronto manufacturers probably paid the 1908 official rate as early as 1900, the relative changes in the rate structure still appear most dramatic in terms of shipments to Montreal.[43] Given that Montreal was one of the largest markets close to the Maritimes, Table Four may indicate why some later Maritime observers recalled the year 1912 as a turning point, rather than 1908, 1913 or 1915.

---

42 These figures are based on changes in the special distributing rates enjoyed by Amherst merchants.

43 Minute 337, 1 November 1896, vol. 10820, Canadian Freight Association Minutebooks, RG30, NAC.

Table Two
Interaction of Rate Changes: Competition in Maritimes
Fifth Class Merchandise, Carload of 30,000 Pounds

	Saint John to Amherst	Toronto to Amherst	Difference in favour of Saint John
1900	$39.00	$108.00	$69.00
1905	45.00	108.00	63.00
(1900$)	42.41	101.80	59.39
1908	45.00	99.00	54.00
(1900$)	38.69	85.12	46.43
1913	48.00	99.00	51.00
(1900$)	37.12	76.57	39.45
1915	54.00	99.00	45.00
(1900$)	37.96	69.57	31.62
1916	54.00	108.00	54.00
(1900$)	30.58	61.16	30.58
March 1918	61.50	124.50	63.00
(1900$)	23.98	48.54	24.56
August 1918	76.50	156.00	79.50
(1900$)	29.82	60.82	31.00
September 1920	106.50	219.00	112.50
(1900$)	37.04	76.17	39.13
January 1921	103.50	210.00	106.50
(1900$)	52.35	106.20	53.85
December 1921	96.00	195.00	99.00
(1900$)*	52.66	107.00	54.34

*1922 Price Index

Source: Freight Tariffs, C.A. 1, 1 March 1898, C.A. 3, 17 July 1905, vol. 7983, J. 5, 28 May 1913, vol. 8007, RG30; E.G. Carty, *Maritime Freight Rates, 1867-1931: Comparison with Freight Rates in Ontario and Quebec*, 30 May 1931, file 6949 #162, vol. 372, RG43; Exhibit 35, pp. 177-92, vol. 337, Exhibits — Board of Railway Commissioners, RG46, NAC.

Table Three
Interaction of Rate Changes: Competition in Central Canada
Fifth Class Merchandise, Carload of 30,000 pounds

	Amherst to Toronto	Montreal to Toronto	Difference in Favour of Montreal
1900	$99.00	$66.00	$33.00
1908	99.00	66.00	$33.00
(1900$)	85.12	56.75	28.37
1916	108.00	69.00	39.00
(1900$)	61.16	39.07	22.09
March 1918	124.50	79.50	45.00
(1900$)	48.54	30.99	17.55
August 1918	156.00	99.00	57.00
(1900$)	60.82	38.60	22.22
September 1920	219.00	138.00	81.00
(1900$)	76.17	48.00	28.17
January 1921	210.00	135.00	75.00
(1900$)	106.20	68.29	37.91
December 1921	195.00	123.00	72.00
(1900$)*	107.00	67.47	39.53

*1922 Price Index

Source: E.G. Carty, *Maritime Freight Rates, 1867-1931: Comparison with Freight Rates in Ontario and Quebec*, 30 May 1931, file 6949 #162, vol. 372, RG43; Exhibit 35, pp. 177-92, vol. 337, Exhibits — Board of Railway Commissioners, RG46, NAC.

Table Four
Interaction of Rate Changes: Competition in Montreal
Fifth Class Merchandise, Carload of 30,000 Pounds

	Amherst to Montreal	Toronto to Montreal	Difference in favour of Toronto
1900	$72.00	$75.00	-$3.00
1905	75.00	75.00	0.00
(1900$)	70.69	70.69	0.00
1908	75.00	66.00	9.00
(1900$)	64.49	56.75	7.74
1912	84.00	66.00	18.00
(1900$)	64.17	50.42	13.75
1916	90.00	69.00	21.00
(1900$)	50.96	39.07	11.89
March 1918	103.50	79.50	24.00
(1900$)	40.35	30.99	9.36
August 1918	129.00	99.00	30.00
(1900$)	50.29	38.60	11.69
September 1920	180.00	138.00	42.00
(1900$)	62.61	48.00	14.61
January 1921	174.00	135.00	39.00
(1900$)	88.01	68.29	19.72
December 1921	159.00	123.00	36.00
(1900$)*	87.22	67.47	19.75

* 1922 Price Index

Source: Freight Tariffs, C.C. 2, 24 July 1900, C.C. 3, 17 July 1905, C.C. 3 supplement 4, 15 May 1912, vol. 7983, RG30; E.G. Carty, *Maritime Freight Rates, 1867-1931: Comparison with Freight Rates in Ontario and Quebec*, 30 May 1931, file 6949 #162, vol. 372, RG43; Exhibit 35, pp. 177-92, vol. 337, Exhibits — Board of Railway Commissioners, RG46, NAC.

The traditional rate structure of the Maritimes, it has been argued, provided a measure of protection for shippers within the region, while at the same time allowing them to penetrate the larger markets of Central Canada. This analysis appears to confirm the argument, and shows that while Maritime shippers still enjoyed a competitive advantage in their own region in 1922, they faced increased barriers to penetrating markets in Montreal and Central Canada. Maritime manufacturers whose product had no other competitive advantage might have to absorb a larger portion of the freight costs in 1922 than they had in the early 20th century. Just how significant those barriers would actually be, of course, would depend on the significance of the freight rate in the overall value of the commodity, and the degree of competitiveness within a particular type of business.

How much did these changes in the rate structure affect Maritime trade? This is, of course, the real crux of the matter, and the most difficult to assess. The most compelling approach to this problem would be made by a comparison of specific manufacturers in different regions, which would integrate changing transport advantages into a larger analysis of changing labour and other production cost advantages and disadvantages. For the purposes of this paper, however, an alternative approach is adopted, one which examines the ways the rate changes affected the quantity or nature of the freight carried on the Intercolonial. The sources for even so modest a project are limited, but they do offer some insights that demand further attention.

One of the assumptions upon which much of the literature on the Intercolonial rests is that the rate structure allowed Maritime shippers to penetrate markets in Ontario and Western Canada. What is most striking about Figure 1, however, is the dominance of local traffic and trade throughout much of the railway's history. From the turn of the century until the First World War, freight destined for points on the railway, regardless of origin, accounted for at least 75 per cent of the Intercolonial's business. The amount of freight that the Intercolonial delivered to other carriers for shipment beyond its line began to decline in the early 1890s, perhaps not surprisingly at the same time as the Canadian Pacific began to compete for Maritime business over its Short Line. Between the extension of the railway into Montreal in 1897 and the equalization of westbound rates in 1908, the average through freight traffic amounted to just over 500,000 tons annually, reaching a high of 900,000 tons in 1908. It would be 1911 before the railway carried more than 1,000,000 tons of freight for delivery for points beyond the line. Just as a point of comparison, in 1911 water carriers handled more than twice as much freight tonnage through the St. Lawrence canal system in and immediately west of Montreal. Little wonder that when David Pottinger was asked in 1913 to assess the possible impact of the opening of the Panama Canal on the railway's operations, he

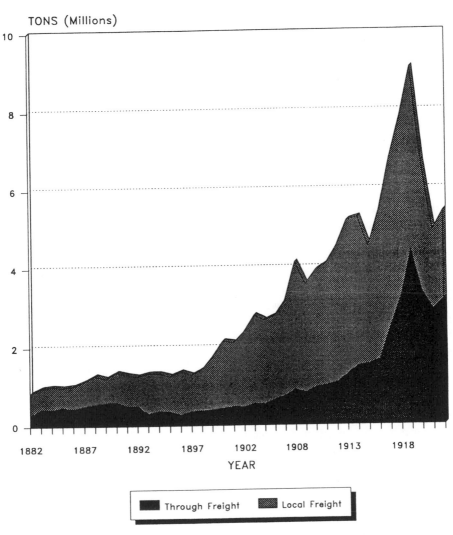

FIGURE 1
INTERCOLONIAL RAILWAY, 1882-1922
LOCAL AND THROUGH FREIGHT TRAFFIC

Annual Reports, Department of Railways
and Canals, 1917–1923

responded that the impact would be minimal. The Intercolonial, he noted, was involved in the carriage of local traffic.[44]

It is perhaps not surprising that during the First World War, when the Intercolonial became a favoured all-Canadian transportation route while the United States remained officially neutral, and when all lines to Atlantic ports were congested, through traffic grew quite dramatically. What is somewhat more surprising is that this trend continued into 1922, just before the Intercolonial was incorporated into the Canadian National Railways system. This is quite the opposite of what one might predict given the changes in freight rates. The change in eastbound and westbound rates after 1908 and the horizontal freight advances appear to have made interregional trade more difficult, yet deliveries beyond the railway remained almost twice as high as their prewar levels. At the same time, deliveries to local points, which were given a measure of protection from the horizontal advances, declined well below prewar levels.

Prior to 1916, the Intercolonial kept track of the contribution of a few types of traffic — coal, grain, European goods, fish and sugar — to the development of through and local traffic. The decision to select these goods reflects the kind of trade that supporters of the Intercolonial hoped it would create. With the exception of coal, however, these goods never amounted to more than 15 per cent of the total local and through traffic. In all but one of the categories, local traffic dominated. Only refined sugar appears to have been a major item in interregional trade by rail, with about half of the tonnage carried by the Intercolonial being delivered west of Montreal. Coal accounted for 25-30 per cent of all through traffic in the 1880s and early 1890s, but ceased to be a factor in shipments beyond the railway after 1900. Both before and after 1900, coal provided the Intercolonial with the largest amount of freight for delivery in the Maritimes, representing 35-40 per cent of this local tonnage. Related figures on originating and local traffic indicate that much of this coal originated from regions served by the public railway.[45]

The iron and steel sector is often identified as key to Maritime industrial growth. Between 1908 and 1920, it accounted for 10-15 per cent of the total traffic of the Intercolonial. Although no record appears to have been kept of through and local traffic, there is a record of the source of the traffic; that is, whether the freight originated on the railway or had been delivered to the Intercolonial from another carrier. Changes in these categories may at least suggest whether the transformation of the rate structure produced increased competition for local producers in their own markets. Between 1908 and 1914, there does appear to have been a slight increase in the quantity of iron and steel products received by the Intercolonial from other carriers, although more

---

44   Pottinger to A.W. Campbell, 26 October 1912, vol. 12165, RG30, NAC.

45   Annual Report of Department of Railways and Canals, *Sessional Papers* (1880-1917).

than 85 per cent of all such products did originate on the railway. In 1920 this figure had declined to 75 per cent, although the horizontal advances would seem to have provided local manufacturers with more, not less, protection within their own markets.

Most of the changes noted above, moreover, can be attributed to changes in one particular category of iron and steel commodities. A very high percentage of the pig and bloom iron, bar and sheet metal, and iron and steel rails carried by the Intercolonial throughout the period originated on the railway. The category of freight the railways called "other castings and machinery" showed the most dramatic change. Between 1908 and 1912, the proportion of this type of freight, which originated on the Intercolonial line, declined from over 80 to 60 per cent. By 1920, over 50 per cent of this commodity was received from other lines. The fact that the most dramatic change is isolated to one particular group of secondary iron and steel commodities, and that even the change that can be measured occurred before there were any major changes in rates on this type of freight, suggests that freight rate changes alone cannot account for this new traffic pattern.[46]

This analysis of the Intercolonial's freight traffic raises some questions about the standard interpretation of the railway in the development of the Maritimes. The major focus of the railway on local traffic, while perhaps not really that surprising given the disadvantages of its through route and connections, does tend to weaken the assumption that it played a major role in interregional trade. Moreover, observers such as Forbes always confidently link freight rate changes to trading difficulties. Some caution is obviously needed in making such assumptions: the growth of through traffic and the decline of local business after the war is quite the opposite of what one would predict on the basis of the degree of transportation protection within regions that the wartime rate changes would have produced. The Intercolonial became more, not less, active in delivering goods outside the region.

The role of the Intercolonial in the development of the Maritime economy is in need of careful reassessment. The route of the Intercolonial severely hampered its ability to provide an effective transportation link between the Maritimes and the rest of Canada, or to be used as an instrument of public policy. With the longest rail route between the interior and the Atlantic seaboard, dependent on the co-operation of other railways for access to points west of Montreal, and competing with steamers for traffic at many points along the line, the Intercolonial was hardly in a position to be the "undisputed rate-maker between the Maritimes and Central Canada".[47]

---

46 Railway Statistics, *Sessional Papers* (1909-23).

47 Forbes, "Misguided Symmetry", p. 63.

Nor is there a great deal of evidence to suggest that the railway's freight rates were implemented as part of a government regional development policy. Most of the special rates on the railway resulted from the competition of other railways and from water carriers, and the concern that local businesses be able to compete in certain markets, all factors which shaped rate-making decisions on private railways. While not concerned with its mounting capital account, the managers of the railway believed they had a mandate to carry goods so as to meet their operating expenses. No government suggested otherwise. As costs rose, they were more than willing to abandon what they believed was money-losing traffic and to attempt to raise those rates they were in a position to change.

There is little doubt that changes in the rate structure after 1905 could have altered the competitive position of some shippers on the railway, and that the changes facing these shippers were somewhat more dramatic than in other regions. It is not clear, however, whether those changes actually had any impact on trade. Between the mid-1890s and the First World War, the Intercolonial largely delivered goods to local stations, and delivered only a small amount of freight for carriage to points beyond its own lines. During and after the war, it was local business which declined most sharply, in spite of the fact that freight rate changes would have provided more protection for interregional trade.

Throughout Canada, railways represented one of the most visible symbols of the emerging industrial nation, and were apt to be the target of criticism among those who were dissatisfied with those changes. Such criticism was not always misguided, and should not be dismissed out of hand. Nevertheless, in the case of the Intercolonial, there appears to be some reason for being more cautious and critical of the claims of the advocates of Maritime Rights in the 1920s, upon which scholars have relied. It may be time to adopt a more modest image of the Intercolonial, not as the critical transportation link between the Maritimes and Central Canada and the developmental key to Maritime industrialization, but rather as a relatively small regional railway oriented towards serving local markets.

John F. Stairs, Max Aitken and the Scotia Group: Finance Capitalism and Industrial Decline in the Maritimes, 1890-1914

Gregory P. Marchildon

The contours of the aggregate social, economic and demographic changes that occurred in the Maritime Provinces from Confederation until the First World War are reasonably distinct. Except for Nova Scotia, which enjoyed a notable industrial expansion between 1870 and 1890, post-Confederation Maritime economic growth did not keep pace with that of Central Canada. After 1890, even Nova Scotia's growth slowed relative to that of Central Canada, and in the decades that followed, Maritimers increasingly felt the brunt of plant closures, unemployment and population outflow as the regional economy began its precipitous decline.[1] Although there are many possible explanations, the nature of financial intermediation in the Maritimes has often been isolated as a causal factor in the region's industrial decline. In particular,

The author would like to thank A. Posluns, M. Whitcomb and three anonymous referees for their comments. The author is particularly indebted to J.B. Cahill and K. Inwood for their very constructive criticism.

1 T.W. Acheson, "The National Policy and the Industrialization of the Maritimes, 1880-1910", *Acadiensis*, I,2 (Spring 1972), pp. 3-27; David Alexander, "Economic Growth in the Atlantic Region, 1880 to 1940", *Acadiensis*, VIII, 1 (Autumn 1978), pp. 47-76; Kris Inwood and John Chamard, "Regional Industrial Growth During the 1890s: The Case of the Missing Artisans", *Acadiensis*, XVI, 1 (Autumn 1986), pp. 106-17; and Kris Inwood, "Maritime Industrialization from 1870 to 1910: A Review of the Evidence and its Interpretation", *Acadiensis*, XXI, 1 (Autumn 1991), pp. 132-55. Much has been written concerning the impact of industrial decline. See David Frank, "The Cape Breton Coal Industry and the Rise and Fall of the British Empire Steel Corporation", *Acadiensis*, VII, 1 (Autumn 1977), pp. 3-34; L.D. Mc-Cann, "Staples and the New Industrialism in the Growth of Post-Confederation Halifax", *Acadiensis*, VIII, 2 (Spring 1979), pp. 47-79, "The Mercantile-Industrial Transition in the Metal Towns of Pictou County, 1857-1931", *Acadiensis*, X, 2 (Spring 1981), pp. 29-64, and "Metropolitanism and Branch Businesses in the Maritimes, 1881-1931", *Acadiensis*, XIII, 1 (Autumn 1983), pp. 112-25; Nolan Reilly, "The General Strike in Amherst, Nova Scotia, 1919", *Acadiensis*, IX, 2 (Spring 1980), pp. 56-77; Patricia A. Thornton, "The Problem of Out-Migration from Atlantic Canada, 1871-1921: A New Look", *Acadiensis*, XV, 1 (Autumn 1985), pp. 3-34; and Ernest Forbes, *The Maritimes Rights Movement, 1919-1927: A Study in Canadian Regionalism* (Montreal, 1979).

it has been asserted that Maritime industry suffered from an inadequate supply of capital and financial entrepreneurship.[2]

The purpose of this article is to test this hypothesis by reconstructing the actions of a group of Maritimers that first gathered around the financier John F. Stairs and, later, his protégé, William Maxwell (Max) Aitken (later Lord Beaverbrook). These individuals were heavily involved in long-term industrial finance in the Maritimes, particularly in Nova Scotia, and shall be referred to as the "Scotia group" because of their intimate connection with the New Glasgow steel and coal company of the same name. The group provides a particularly fertile ground for examining a subsidiary notion that continues to have popular currency: that financiers such as Aitken somehow betrayed the Maritimes by facilitating the exodus of financial capital out of the region while other financiers such as Stairs were loyal to, and consistently supported, Maritime industry. In fact, the evidence reveals that Stairs and his associates were steering Maritime capital abroad well before they were joined by Aitken. Moreover, Aitken's later actions were in fact consistent with the pattern he had absorbed from his mentor, John F. Stairs.

In addition to its two most conspicuous members, the Scotia group consisted of George Stairs, Robert E. Harris and Charles H. Cahan, as well as a number of financiers eventually brought in by Aitken as employees of the group, among them Arthur J. Nesbitt and Izaak Walton Killam.[3] The group's constellation of financial institutions included the Union Bank of Halifax, the Eastern Trust Company and the Royal Securities Corporation. The principal attributes of the Scotia group were a strong financial, industrial and political base in Halifax; an outward-looking and cosmopolitan business ethos that encouraged searching for capital and profitable ventures outside the Maritimes; and a financial entrepreneurship that embraced merger promotion as a means of extending the group's influence over the enterprises that it financed. These attributes can be inferred from the manner in which Nova Scotia Steel was financed, from the original strategy behind John F. Stairs' attempted Maritime

---

2   See T.W. Acheson, "The Maritimes and 'Empire Canada'", in David J. Bercuson, ed., *Canada and the Burden of Unity* (Toronto, 1977); James D. Frost, "The 'Nationalization' of the Bank of Nova Scotia, 1880-1910", *Acadiensis*, XII, 1 (Autumn 1982), pp. 3-38; and R.T. Naylor, *The History of Canadian Business, Vol. I* (Toronto, 1975), p. 150. For a critical analysis of this hypothesis, see Kris Inwood, *The Canadian Charcoal Iron Industry, 1870-1914* (New York, 1986), chs. 5-7, and L.T. Evans and N.C. Quigley, "Discrimination in Bank Lending Practice: A Test Using Data from The Bank of Nova Scotia 1900-1937", *Canadian Journal of Economics*, XXIII, 1 (February 1990), pp. 210-25.

3   The Scotia group was first discussed in Gregory P. Marchildon, "International Corporate Law from a Maritime Base: The Halifax Firm of Harris, Henry and Cahan", in Carol Wilton, ed., *Beyond the Law: Lawyers and Business in Canada, 1830 to 1930* (Toronto, 1990).

bank merger, and finally, from the operations of the Royal Securities Corporation.

The scion of a wealthy Halifax merchant family, John F. Stairs was the central figure within the Scotia group.[4] His grandfather, William M. Stairs, had founded the provisioning firm of William Stairs, Son and Morrow, and his father, William J. Stairs, further expanded that firm and diversified into industrial and financial enterprises such as the Dartmouth Ropeworks, the Starr Manufacturing Company, the Halifax Gas Light Company and the Union Bank of Halifax. William J. Stairs eventually became the president of both the Union Bank and the Halifax Chamber of Commerce. As the eldest surviving son, John F. Stairs was groomed to take over these family enterprises. At the age of 21 he became a partner in Stairs, Son and Morrow and, at the same time, was made general manager of the Dartmouth Ropeworks.[5] In 1886, Stairs helped to reorganize the insolvent Nova Scotia Sugar Refinery firm in Halifax and became a director of the company. He also became a director of the Halifax Sugar Refining Company, which had its plant near Dartmouth.[6] Stairs later expanded his industrial operations through mergers. In 1890 he consolidated the Dartmouth Ropeworks with six other Halifax and Saint John rope enterprises to create the Consumers Cordage Company under the managerial control of his younger brother, George Stairs.[7] In 1893, working on behalf of a syndicate of Scottish sugar merchants and brokers that were attempting to consolidate the Canadian sugar refining industry into one firm under their control, John F. Stairs merged the Nova Scotia Sugar Refinery and the Halifax Sugar Refining Company with a third Maritime sugar refining company to form the Acadia Sugar Refining Company, of which he became president.[8]

Despite the significance of these enterprises in the Maritime economy, Stairs would become most closely identified with Nova Scotia Steel. After helping to establish a secondary steel manufacturing enterprise at New

---

4   Much of the biographical information concerning the Stairs family and John Stairs' political career was culled from James D. Frost, "The Business and Political Careers of John F. Stairs of Halifax", B.A. Honours essay, Dalhousie University, 1976, and J.B. Cahill, "John Fitzwilliam Stairs", forthcoming in *Dictionary of Canadian Biography*, vol. XIII.

5   Cahill, "John Fitzwilliam Stairs".

6   Cahill, "John Fitzwilliam Stairs".

7   Acheson, "Industrialization of the Maritimes", p. 19. George Stairs remained managing director of Consumers Cordage until his death in 1908: *Halifax Herald*, 2 April 1908, p. 1.

8   Frost, "Careers of John F. Stairs", pp. 56-8, 68; Cahill, "John Fitzwilliam Stairs", pp. 9-10; *Monetary Times*: 23 January 1891, p. 897; 4 August 1893, p. 131; 7 December 1900, p. 720.

Glasow in 1882, Stairs then raised the necessary capital for a new primary iron company in 1890-1. In 1895, again with Stairs' financial assistance and advice, the primary and secondary steel firms were merged into Nova Scotia Steel and Coal, Canada's first integrated iron and steel company.[9] The new board of directors of Nova Scotia Steel was roughly divided between the New Glasgow industrialists on the one hand and the Halifax financiers — including one Quebec director, James Ross, representing a small amount of Central Canadian investment — on the other. This mixture of New Glasgow management and Halifax finance supplemented by a smaller amount of Central Canadian capital would characterize Nova Scotia Steel until the First World War. Stairs was elected president of the new company in 1897 and Nova Scotia Steel thus became an illustration of the symbiotic, if often difficult, relationship that could potentially exist between regional Maritime industrialists and Halifax financiers.[10]

Although his industrial interests expanded rapidly during the 1890s, John F. Stairs remained essentially a promoter and financier during this time.[11] He was instrumental in the creation of the Eastern Trust Company in 1893, which he then used to finance the Acadia Sugar Refining Company merger and to recapitalize Nova Scotia Steel, of which he was made president in 1897 in recognition of his financial services.[12] A few years later, Stairs became interested in utility ventures in the West Indies mainly as vehicles for issuing and underwriting stock issues. He was joined in all of these enterprises by his brother George Stairs and two Halifax lawyers, Robert E. Harris and Charles

9   I have relied upon McCann, "Metal Towns of Pictou County", Cahill, "John Fitzwilliam Stairs" and "Graham Fraser's Biography by Joseph Dix Fraser", MG 1, vol. 2155, microfilm, Public Archives of Nova Scotia [PANS] in reconstructing Scotia's early history. I am indebted to J.B. Cahill for informing me of the existence of the latter.

10 The New Glasgow interests appeared to have two different, although perhaps not wholly inconsistent, views of the Scotia group. They appreciated their financial services, particularly when the Scotia group was able to raise funds during the financial downturn of 1903 without substantially lowering Scotia's stock prices. But they were also suspicious of the financial methods used by the Scotia group to manipulate stock prices and were particularly angry when they discovered that some "Halifax parties" were making a large profit from short-selling Scotia securities: "Joseph Dix Fraser", MG 1, vol. 2155, microfilm, PANS; letters, T. Cantley to Aitken, 18 January 1904, and T. Cantley to J.C. Mackintosh, 5 August 1904, letterbook, Thomas Cantley Papers, MG 1, vol. 169, PANS.

11 The Halifax *Morning Herald*, 2 April 1908, p. 1, described John F. Stairs as "essentially a promoter, having a genius in this direction surpassed by few", while his younger brother was characterized as both "a great financier" and a successful industrial manager.

12 Cahill, "John Fitzwilliam Stairs", p. 12.

H. Cahan. Cahan acted as the Scotia group's foreign scout, rummaging through dilapidated tramway, lighting and thermal power operations in Latin America and the Caribbean to find those worth modernizing and capable of turning over a good profit.[13] In British Guiana, Cahan helped set up the Demerara Electric Company in 1899.[14] His next stop was Port-of-Spain where the Trinidad Electric Company was established in 1900 — a venture that was synonymous with the Scotia group and its interests from the beginning.[15]

John F. Stairs hired Max Aitken a couple of years after the establishment of the Demerara and Trinidad companies. Travelling across the Maritimes selling insurance and bonds, the 23-year-old Aitken met Stairs on a train from Truro to Halifax in 1902. Aitken was ambitious but frustrated after an abortive law career in New Brunswick and a number of unsuccessful business forays in Western Canada, and he therefore welcomed the opportunity to become Stairs' personal assistant. Aitken's first financial success was his acquisition of the Commercial Bank of Windsor on behalf of John F. Stairs and the Union Bank of Halifax in 1902.[16] This merger appears to have been the first step in Stairs' scheme to consolidate many of the smaller banks of the Maritimes into a large regional bank controlled by the Scotia group. In April of 1903, Stairs and Robert E. Harris took the second step when they purchased a controlling interest in the People's Bank of Halifax in April of 1903.[17] Two months later, while the Halifax Bank Corporation was being purchased by the Toronto-controlled Canadian Bank of Commerce, Stairs unveiled the Alliance Bank of Canada, a federally incorporated shell for his new pan-Maritime banking corporation.[18] In an interview with Canada's largest business weekly, the Toronto-based

---

13 Harris and Cahan are discussed further in Marchildon, "International Corporate Law".

14 The Scotia group was initially overshadowed in this venture by Sir William Van Horne, who became Demerara's first president, and by B.F. Pearson, another Halifax lawyer-promoter who had more experience then Stairs in utility ventures. *Canadian Journal of Commerce*, 17 November 1899, p. 1309.

15 Christopher Armstrong and H.V. Nelles, *Southern Exposure: Canadian Promoters in Latin America and the Caribbean, 1896-1930* (Toronto, 1988), p. 34; Gregory P. Marchildon, "Promotion, Finance and Mergers in Canadian Manufacturing Industry, 1885-1918", unpublished Ph.D. thesis, London School of Economics, 1990, pp. 56-60.

16 Lord Beaverbrook, *My Early Life* (Fredericton, 1965), pp. 116-17.

17 The merger scheme was rumoured to have included the People's Bank of New Brunswick and the Bank of Charlottetown as well as the People's Bank of Halifax. *Monetary Times*, 17 April 1903, p. 1416; 24 April 1903, p. 1449.

18 *Monetary Times*, 26 June 1903, p. 1760.

Monetary Times, Stairs explained the motive behind the Alliance Bank merger scheme:

> I am very strongly in favor of maintaining our own banking institutions instead of allowing them to get into the hands of Western [Central Canadian] corporations. I would like to see our banks continue the policy which has prevailed here for forty or fifty years, that of being controlled by local interests. Having them absorbed by Western institutions creates a likelihood of our interests being sacrificed for those of the West.[19]

Until this time, Stairs had managed his diverse business interests mainly through his, and his father's, joint control of Maritime financial intermediaries such as the Union Bank of Halifax and Eastern Trust. Now, it looked increasingly as if the independent Maritime banks would soon be absorbed by Central Canadian interests, thus taking operative control away from Maritime financiers such as himself. The antidote was thus a consolidation of the remaining profitable Maritime banks. Stairs' defence of the Scotia group's interests (which he portrayed as being synonymous with the Maritimes' interests) did not, however, preclude Central Canadian participation; indeed, consistent with the Scotia group's ethos, Stairs viewed such involvement as extremely valuable, perhaps even essential, as long as he and his Halifax associates controlled the new Alliance Bank.

Stairs spent much of his energy in 1903 trying to bring the Metropolitan Bank of Toronto into his proposed bank merger. The Metropolitan Bank was controlled by A.E. Ames, who was connected by business and marriage to George Cox's powerful financial group in Ontario. Ames and his bank would give the Scotia group access to Central Canadian capital and financial influence.[20] After months of discussion, however, Ames decided against joining forces with the Scotia group, perhaps fearing that the Metropolitan Bank would lose its corporate identity in the new organization.[21] This decision, in addition to John F. Stairs' unexpected death in 1904, scuttled the Alliance

---

19   John F. Stairs quoted in *Monetary Times*, 3 July 1903, p. 19.

20   *Annual Financial Review*, appendix to Vol. II (January 1903), p. 48; 1903 correspondence, A/2/Ross, Beaverbrook Papers, House of Lords Record Office, London [BBK]. On the Cox group and A.E. Ames, see Ian M. Drummond, "Canadian Life Insurance Companies and the Capital Market, 1890-1914", *Canadian Journal of Economics and Political Science*, XXVIII, 2 (May 1962), pp. 211-16; and Michael Bliss, *A Canadian Millionaire: The Life and Times of Sir Joseph Flavelle, Bart. 1859-1939* (Toronto, 1978), *passim*.

21   Letters, Aitken to W.D. Ross, June 1903, 24 July 1903; and newspaper articles, Toronto *World*, 14 November 1903, A/2/Ross, and Moncton *Times*, 29 October 1904, A/3/M, BBK.

Bank scheme. One year later, the Scotia group sold its majority holding in the People's Bank of Halifax, allowing that institution to be taken over by the Bank of Montreal.

The reasons for this ironic outcome can be traced back to the original purchase of the People's Bank by the Scotia group. When John F. Stairs first approached the officers and directors of the People's Bank in 1903 his consolidation plan was welcomed, but not for reasons that the Scotia group could have appreciated at the time. Stairs and Robert E. Harris paid 140 per cent of par for $280,000 par worth of shares, or almost $400,000 in total, for control of a bank whose directors had just discovered a large account backed by fraudulent collateral, fatally weakening the bank's asset base. "The concealment was necessary", the People's Bank managers later claimed, "because the Bank was then at a crisis, and unless Mr. Stairs' prestige and the increase of stock had been secured, the Bank would have failed".[22]

After John F. Stairs' death, George Stairs, Max Aitken and the Royal Securities Corporation purchased his shares from the estate, still not aware of the initial fraud. By this time, the top officials of the People's Bank had uncovered a further $100,000 worth of bogus collateral in the form of non-existent schooners, and they again failed to inform any of the Scotia group. Instead, they confessed their predicament to the Bank of Montreal and asked to be bought out to prevent the imminent collapse of the bank. Edward Clouston, the general manager of the Bank of Montreal, agreed to make the purchase, but only at a price that reflected the real asset value of the People's Bank. When Harris and George Stairs were subsequently approached by the Bank of Montreal for their consent to the sale, they learned for the first time about the People's Bank's fragile financial position. Feeling betrayed by the People's Bank's directors, they refused to sell their shares at the low price agreed upon by the other shareholders. Instead, Harris and George Stairs, with Aitken in tow, travelled to Montreal to demand a higher price from Clouston. When Clouston refused, the Scotia group stormed out of his office. Clouston asked, however, that Aitken return to his office and the two then privately negotiated a settlement.[23] The Scotia group agreed to sell their shares at a price agreed upon by the other shareholders upon Clouston's agreement that their shares could be exchanged for Bank of Montreal shares at a slightly discounted rate. Aitken explained the result shortly after the Montreal meeting:

> Our loss will amount to about $11,000.00 each and the Royal Securities will lose about $11,000.00....Mr. Clouston apparently appreciates the way in which we have acted. I have a personal letter from him this

---

22 Letter, Aitken to W.D. Ross, 14 March 1905, G/1/1, BBK.

23 Letter, Aitken to W.D. Ross, 14 March 1905, G/1/1/, BBK. I am indebted to Peter Waite for first bringing this letter to my attention. This letter bears out Aitken's later account in Beaverbrook, *My Early Life*, pp. 140-1.

morning in which he tells me that he thinks I have done right. At any rate innumerable small shareholders, whose small monies may be as much to them as our large sums, will be saved from the loss which would have resulted to them if we had attempted to set aside the deceiptfull [sic] contract made with Mr. Stairs....

...Mr. Clouston seems to think that we have sacrificed ourselves for the small shareholders. Nobody raised any question about the certainty of our succeeding if we were to bring an action to recover everything.[24]

Putting Aitken's sanctimonious remarks about small shareholders aside, the reality was that the Scotia group held a majority of shares in the People's Bank. The group was more concerned about recovering as much of their investment as possible than it was about keeping the People's Bank of Halifax a regional institution. Selling out on a slightly more advantageous basis than the directors of the People's Bank and its "innumerable small shareholders" was the best solution for the Scotia group under the circumstances.

While the Alliance Bank scheme and the People's Bank of Halifax fiasco were the subject of great attention at the time, John F. Stairs' most successful creation — the Royal Securities Corporation (RSC) — raised nary an eyebrow when incorporated in 1903.[25] This type of investment house, a combination of stockbroking firm and investment bank, was in fact a major financial innovation.[26] The only similar financial intermediary in Canada was the Dominion Securities Corporation, established in Toronto two years earlier.[27] The RSC embodied the Scotia group. All five original shareholders — John F. Stairs, George Stairs, Robert E. Harris, Charles H. Cahan and Max Aitken — were made directors in the corporation. John F. Stairs was voted president, and Aitken became secretary and de facto managing director.[28] The RSC would be the

---

24 Letter, Aitken to W.D. Ross, March 14, 1905, G/1/1, BBK.

25 The RSC was incorporated on 18 April 1903 under Nova Scotia law as a joint stock company with a modest capital of $50,000. *Journals of the Nova Scotia House of Assembly* (Halifax, 1904), pp. 56-9.

26 For a discussion of the difference between investment banks (entrepreneurial entities that act as principals in the market for new securities) and stockbrokers (more passive entities that act as agents in the sale of securities), see Gregory P. Marchildon, "British Investment Banking and Industrial Decline before the Great War: A Case Study of Capital Outflow to Canadian Industry", *Business History*, XXXIII, 3 (July 1991), p. 74.

27 *Monetary Times*, 3 February 1905, p. 1022. A brief history of the origins of the Dominion Securities Corporation can be found in Bliss, *A Canadian Millionaire*, pp. 60-9.

28 Although the evidence is less than clear, John F. Stairs may have paid one-half or more of Aitken's original share subscription in the RSC. Letter, Harris to Aitken,

Scotia group's central selling agency for the bonds and shares of its Maritime industrial enterprises and its new utility enterprises in the Caribbean. The RSC would also serve as a retailer of a variety of securities.[29] As Aitken explained at the time to one curious Maritime investor, the RSC "is to carry on the business of buying and selling high grade investment securities such as Government, Municipal and Corporation Bonds, with special attention to steam and electric railway securities and first class industrial bonds".[30]

In the beginning, the RSC's most important client was Nova Scotia Steel, which had been financially reorganized in 1901 by the Scotia group and the New Glasgow directors. Capitalization was substantially increased in order to construct a fully integrated primary iron and steel making complex at Sydney Mines, Cape Breton, to compliment the secondary steel making facilities at New Glasgow.[31] Three major Scotia security issues were floated between 1901 and 1904 to finance the expansion.[32] The pressure was particularly intense before the final and largest flotation in 1904; Stairs and Aitken travelled together to Toronto on 8 September to negotiate Central Canadian participation in the Scotia flotation.[33] On the morning after their arrival, however, Stairs suddenly collapsed and was taken to hospital. Stairs died 17 days later of heart disease complicated by kidney failure and pneumonia.[34]

A few weeks after John F. Stairs' funeral, Aitken took over the Nova Scotia Steel negotiations with the Toronto financiers and successfully brought them to a conclusion. Aitken agreed to manage the underwriting syndicate for the

27 May 1903, A/1/H; letter, Aitken to I.W. Killam, 25 September 1908, A/23/Killam, BBK.

29 Christopher Armstrong's article "Making a Market: Selling Securities in Atlantic Canada before World War I", *Canadian Journal of Economics*, XIII (August 1980), pp. 438-54, reviews the RSC's early retail stock and bond operation.

30 Letter, Aitken to W.H. Rodgers, 11 September 1903, A/2/Q-R, BBK.

31 McCann, "The Mercantile-Industrial Transition", p. 53.

32 Scotia sold $2.5 million par value of bonds and sold or transferred $3.8 million par value of common stock from 1901 to 1903. See Kris Inwood, "Local Control, Resources and the Nova Scotia Steel and Coal Company", Canadian Historical Association, *Historical Papers* (1986), p. 257.

33 According to Cahill, Stairs was also attempting to raise capital in Toronto for the Alliance Bank scheme: see "John Fitzwilliam Stairs", p. 16.

34 As Aitken later remembered: "We were together in the morning at breakfast at the King Edward Hotel in Toronto. Mr. Stairs was negotiating for the sale of bonds in the Nova Scotia Steel and Coal Co. The blow fell before he had begun to carry out his task. During the month that elapsed between the first attack and his death I remained in constant attendance". Beaverbrook, *My Early Years*, p. 135. See also Cahill, "John Fitzwilliam Stairs", p. 16.

$1.5 million bond issue needed by Scotia to finish its new steel plant. The RSC received $600,000 worth of underwriting. Aitken and the other members of the Scotia group took a further $215,000 underwriting in their personal capacity. The remaining $685,000 was divided among the Toronto interests (including Massey Harris, Osler & Hammond and the Imperial Bank) and the Scotia group's interests (including the Union Bank of Halifax and the People's Bank of Halifax) — all joined for good measure by the New Glasgow directors of Nova Scotia Steel. The issue proved successful, but Aitken was dissatisfied. The RSC had been paid $10,000 for its services, a sum he considered far too small considering the RSC's burden of risk and responsibility.[35]

The Nova Scotia Steel experiences encouraged Aitken to begin concentrating on the more profitable new issue business provided by companies such as Demerara Electric and Trinidad Electric, and he thus plunged deeper into new utility promotions.[36] The RSC's profits swelled with each new utility security issue to the point that in late 1905, the RSC's shareholders (George Stairs, Harris, Cahan and Aitken) were able to vote themselves a 100 per cent stock dividend.[37] The Scotia group and Maritime investors were publicly reproached for engaging in this capital outflow. The author of the Halifax column in the *Monetary Times* complained that it "would be better for Halifax if her monied men would talk less about Cuban or Trinidad railroads, South American enterprises or Mexican plantations and give a little more consideration and money to the establishment of small local manufacturers and other companies that would benefit a wide circle of people".[38]

The criticism would not alter the behaviour of the Scotia group. In 1905 the RSC spun off another promotional holding company, the Dominion Trust Co., in order to raise even more Central Canadian capital for its foreign utility ventures while continuing to prevent the Scotia group's Montreal partners from demanding shares and directorships in the RSC. Dominion Trust's original shareholders included Edward Clouston and Sir William Van Horne, in addition to the Scotia financiers George Stairs, Robert E. Harris and Max Aitken.[39] At the same time, Aitken created the Colombian Securities Corporation to raise money for the projected Barranquilla Tramway Light & Power Company. Colombian Securities' shareholders included the Dominion Trust Company, Aitken, William D. Ross of the Metropolitan Bank of Toronto, and

35   Letter, Aitken to McCuaig Bros. & Co., 5 October 1904, A/3/M, BBK.

36   Letter, Aitken to C. Simpson Garland, 15 October 1904, A/3/D-G, BBK.

37   Letter, Managing Director of RSC (Aitken) to Aitken (as RSC shareholder), 14 November 1905, A/6/R, BBK.

38   *Monetary Times*, 22 April 1904, p. 1417.

39   Letters: Aitken to A.R. Doble, 28 October 1905, A/5/D-E; Aitken to W.D. Ross, 3 June 1905, A/7/Ross, BBK.

two Halifax lawyer-promoters, B.F. Pearson and W.B. Ross.[40] Aitken also sent out scouts to investigate utility possibilities in Ecuador, Guatemala, Panama and Venezuela, although some of the Halifax financiers, in particular Robert E. Harris and W.B. Ross, were wary of making investments beyond the Caribbean. Because of their views, Aitken ultimately limited himself to two new utility ventures in Puerto Rico and Cuba, now perceived as stable regions for investment because of their new status as American "possessions".[41]

The large profits derived from foreign utility promotions allowed the RSC to expand rapidly from 1905 to 1906. More employees were hired; Aitken carefully selected a remarkable stable of bond salesmen that included Arthur J. Nesbitt from Saint John and Izaak Walton Killam from Yarmouth. By 1906 branch offices had been opened in Saint John and Montreal, with further offices planned for Quebec City and London, England. And, in the minds of Canadian investors, the RSC was beginning to become more associated with West Indian utility companies than with Maritime manufacturing companies.

Caught up in the fever of foreign utility promotion, Aitken became increasingly impatient with the lower profits available from reorganizing and floating the securities of Maritime industrial enterprises in general, and with servicing Nova Scotia Steel in particular. Prior to 1905, Aitken had in fact devoted most of his energy to the needs of regional Maritime manufacturers. In Amherst, for example, Aitken had raised capital for Rhodes, Curry & Co., Amherst Boot and Shoe, Amherst Foundry, and Robb Engineering.[42] Aware of his growing passion for foreign utility promotions, some Maritime industrialists, such as D.W. Robb of Robb Engineering, asked for special treatment out of a sense of loyalty:[43]

---

40 Letter, Aitken to W.D. Ross, 3 June 1905, A/7/Ross, BBK.

41 Letter, Aitken to Teele, 6 January 1906, A/10/Teele, BBK. In his letter of 11 January 1906 to W.D. Ross (A/9/R/, BBK), Aitken admits "that Ecuador is a long way off, but I am confident the securities can be underwritten" and urges the older Halifax financiers to entertain the deal, if not on the basis of the underwriting, then on the smaller but less risky profits that can be had on the "stock commission out of the promotion". As Aitken explained to Cahan in 1906, however, both " Mr. Harris and Mr. Ross do not think very much of going so far away from home": A/8/Cahan, BBK.

42 Letter, N. Curry, president of Rhodes Curry & Co. to Aitken, 5 May 1905, and reply, 8 May 1905, A/6/R; 1906 correspondence between Aitken and B.G. Burrill, A/8/Burrill; BBK. These four firms alone employed 2,000 workers out of a population of slightly less than 10,000 in Amherst. *Monetary Times*, 9 November 1907, p. 749.

43 "Memo on Robb Engineering Works Limited", compiled by F.F. Mackenzie, Historical Employees file, Miscellaneous Papers Box, Robb Engineering Company

I am quite well aware that at the present time you can make a great deal more money in other lines and that your Corporation expects you to devote your attention to business that will give you the best results, but, in view of the relations that have existed between yourself and the Robb Engineering Co. you might consider it a fair thing....I feel sure that if I could be relieved of the financial end of it and devote myself to the manufacturing end exclusively it would add several years to my life to say nothing of the advantage of the business.[44]

The appeal succeeded. Temporarily putting aside his earlier complaint that the RSC's profit in selling Robb Engineering securities was "too little", Aitken assigned one of his salesmen to work full-time on the Robb account and urged him to put his best foot forward:[45]

Mr. Robb relies upon our Corporation to carry out his present financial arrangements. His reason in doing so, that our Corporation, and I personally, have carried on all his financial arrangements since the Robb Engineering Co. invited outside capital. I believe he could better his terms sometimes if he dealt with others...but he sticks firmly to us; and for that reason...we shall now use every endeavor to carry out his present financial arrangements in such a way as will bring most good to his companies. In other words, I am willing that the Corporation should forego possible underwriting profits if a decided benefit can be secured to Mr. Robb's companies.[46]

Robb Engineering, however, was the exception that proved the rule. Aitken was generally more apt to turn away Maritime manufacturing enterprises previously financed by the Scotia group, particularly those with a declining profit record. He argued, for example, that the Starr Manufacturing Company, one of the first industrial investments made by William J. Stairs, "is not in a very good position financially and of late years there has been practically no dividend upon the stock". Thus "any reorganization or amalgamation with a view to raising more capital would hardly be successful".[47]

Papers, Dalhousie University Archives. Aitken was first involved with Robb Engineering when it was recapitalized by the Scotia group in 1900 with John F. Stairs being put on the board. In 1902, D.W. Robb called upon the Scotia group to help him set up an American subsidiary, the Robb-Mumford Boiler Company. For their efforts, Aitken and Robert Harris were then put on the board of this new company.

44   Letter, D.W. Robb to Aitken, 6 September 1906, A/9/Robb-Mumford, BBK.

45   Letter, Aitken to D.W. Robb, 11 November 1904, A/4/Robb-Mumford, BBK.

46   Letter, Aitken to G. Farrell, 16 October 1906, A/8/Farrell, BBK.

47   Letter, Aitken to T. Bell, 22 May 1903, A/1/B, BBK.

Aitken's perception of profitability, involving as it did a judgement about the future of a company as well as an assessment of its past performance, could be mercurial. As late as 1905, Aitken decided that he would

> go into...boot and shoe manufacturing....The [Amherst Boot and Shoe Company] has a capital of about $10,000....The men engaged in this business are all young, and pretty bright and active....
>
> I am banking entirely on individuals, and the certainty that the East must manufacture that which it consumes at least...[48]

Just eight months later, however, despite Robert E. Harris' judgement that the RSC should funnel funds to the firm for another year, Aitken refused to facilitate a new share issue for Amherst Boot and Shoe because, in his view, the firm's profits were "entirely too small" to support a successful share flotation.[49]

In other cases, Aitken would demand such a hefty fee for issuing and underwriting the securities of Maritime enterprises that the RSC would lose the business altogether. Whether this meant that the manufacturing firm affected went elsewhere for financial servicing or was forced to forego obtaining new capital is difficult to trace in most instances, but one case is known. When a merger between paint and varnish manufacturers Henderson & Potts Ltd. of Halifax and Brandram Bros. & Co. was proposed in 1906, Aitken's fee was so high that the promoter behind the scheme refused to allow the RSC to act as the principal house of issue and underwriter. This would not be surprising except that the promoter in this case was Robert E. Harris, the vice-president of the RSC! Harris went on to successfully facilitate Brandram-Henderson's issue without the help of the RSC. Aitken knew his decision angered Harris, and he confessed in a confidential letter that he had asked for far too much to do the underwriting, admitting that

> the loss of such hazardous industrial undertakings as Brandram-Henderson.. and other undertakings of that description do not concern me. For myself, I prefer to confine my operations to Public Utilities and undertakings of greater certainty than industrials of the foregoing nature.[50]

There are many other instances of Aitken's growing reluctance to finance Maritime industrial enterprises. For example, while Aitken personally held

---

48 Letter, Aitken to W.D. Ross, 27 December 1905, A/7/Ross, BBK.

49 Letter, A.R. Nesbitt (on behalf of Aitken) to RSC, 19 September 1906, A/10/RSC, BBK. Nesbitt goes on to say that "Mr. Aitken wishes to advise you that he does not care about taking on any more industrial propositions at present".

50 Letter, Aitken to E.G. Kenny, 11 October 1906, A/8/Commercial Trust Company, BBK.

$1,300 worth of shares in the Munro Wire Works of New Glasgow, he refused to purchase a further $100 in 1905, his pro rata share of new stock being issued by the firm to finance the establishment of a Winnipeg branch office.[51] He had similarly negative views of the Stanfield Company and the Nova Scotia Woolen Mills, as revealed in this letter to John F. Stairs' eldest son, James Stairs:[52]

> You will be surprised to know that I have refused for myself and for the Corporation to take any underwriting or participate in the Stanfield Flotation, but I am satisfied that the future will justify my course, however good the Stanfield project may look at the present time.
>
> Now I have a word of advice for you, and that is; do not touch the Nova Scotia Woolen Mills now or in the future no matter how good things look on the outside.
>
> I do not say that these Mills will not make a success, but I think the chances of success are slight. If success does attend their efforts, then the measure of that success will be so small, that you will not be recompensed for the risk you have taken.
>
> In the case of the Stanfield Co., I believe the chickens will come home to roost some day, because capitalization is too large, amounting as it does to about $1,200,000 more than is represented in value of property.[53]

Aitken preferred Caribbean utility ventures in large part because of the average investor's increasing preference for utility shares relative to industrial shares. This was, in turn, the product of the greater stability of utility companies' earnings relative to manufacturing enterprises before the Great War.[54] The issue, however, goes beyond this one fact. Implicitly, Aitken was also making a judgement about the future potential of the companies in question and, more generally, the Maritime economy. Indeed, Aitken felt increasingly pessimistic about the future of Maritime industry, and by 1907 he

---

51   Letters, Munro Wire Works to Aitken, 4 November 1905, and reply, 6 November 1905, A/6/M, BBK.

52   Frost, "Careers of John F. Stairs", appendix A, Stairs family tree.

53   Letter, Aitken to James A. Stairs c/o Nova Scotia Steel & Coal Co., 18 January 1906, A/10/S, BBK.

54   As explained in the *Monetary Times*, 22 July 1911, p. 423: "Public utility issues rank higher generally than industrials, because their earnings fluctuate less". The future would reveal, however, that many of these utility ventures would fare no better, and sometimes much worse, than the industrial issues. See Duncan McDowall, *The Light: Brazilian Traction, Light and Power Company Limited, 1899-1914* (Toronto, 1988); Armstrong and Nelles, *Southern Exposure;* and Marchildon, "Corporate Law from a Maritime Base".

had come to the firm conclusion that the future of Canadian manufacturing lay in Central Canada.[55]

On rare occasions after 1905, Aitken took a more constructive approach to Maritime industrial firms. He went so far as to give advice to some firms on how to improve their profitability, and even offered to arrange long-term financing for the proposed changes. One example involved the Hewson Woolen Mills of Amherst. After discussions with the president, H.L. Hewson, Aitken offered to finance the construction of a new knitting mill factory that would resemble the most progressive factories in Canada, which, according to Aitken, were the Ellis Knitting Mills of Hamilton and the Simpson Knitting Mills of Toronto. Aitken suggested to Hewson that they should first find and hire a manager who was capable of running such a modern operation. After due consideration, however, Hewson rejected Aitken's advice. Instead, Hewson used his own more limited capital to build an extension to his mills and ran the slighter larger operation with existing personnel. Six years later, Hewson sold out to Stanfields, Ltd., of Truro, receiving a mere 20 per cent of par for every share.[56]

Some of Aitken's most damning criticism of the way in which Maritime firms were managed was aimed at Nova Scotia Steel itself. Less than one year after Aitken's campaign to raise $1.5 million for Scotia, Aitken's own confidence in the company was eroded substantially. Upon hearing that two new sizeable Toronto investors were travelling to Nova Scotia to inspect Nova Scotia Steel's new plants and later conduct a bull campaign on the stock market, Aitken disclosed his doubts about the company:

I have not the same feeling towards Scotia that I have towards electric propositions, and moreover, there is really nobody back of Scotia who can avert a calamity....The Company is managed without any system, and there is not at the present time a capable head, therefore, although I believe the market will advance under the manipulation of Ames and Johnson, still I am not satisfied with the ultimate intrinsic value of Scotia stock, and hesitate about loading up with this security when there are so many other good things.[57]

---

55 This conclusion is based on Aitken's numerous but fragmentary statements in many letters during 1907, "A" series, BBK.

56 Letters, Aitken to H.L. Hewson, 3 April 1906, and reply, 25 May 1906, A/9/H, BBK. *Monetary Times*, 18 November 1911, p. 2121.

57 Letter, Aitken to W.D. Ross, 29 August 1905, A/7/Ross, BBK.

Aitken's view, not accepted at first by the Toronto boosters of Scotia, was vindicated months later by Scotia's sudden fall in profitability.[58]

Aitken's criticism of Nova Scotia Steel's management was no doubt directed at Scotia's general manager, Thomas Cantley, but it may also have been levelled at fellow RSC director Robert E. Harris, who had succeeded John F. Stairs as president of Scotia in 1905.[59] At this time, Harris and Aitken entered on a collision course that would soon divide the Scotia group and eventually culminate in Aitken's attempted takeover of Nova Scotia Steel in 1910. The first division between the two concerned Aitken's increasingly close business ties with Harris' sometime ally, sometime rival W. D. Ross. In early 1905 Aitken joined forces with Ross to create the Commercial Trust Co., which Harris perceived (quite accurately) as a threat to Eastern Trust. Ross became president, and Aitken vice-president, of the new company. The plot thickened when H. Almon Lovett joined Commercial Trust and was made second vice-president. Only a few months before, Lovett, a senior Halifax lawyer, had been invited by Harris to join Harris, Henry and Cahan.[60]

It is not hard to imagine Harris' reaction when he discovered that his new law partner had joined Ross and Aitken in the Commercial Trust Co. Harris and Aitken immediately found themselves fighting bitterly over which trust company should act as the transfer agency, trustee for bonds, or provide other trust company services to the RSC's stable of companies. As Aitken explained to W.D. Ross, who only months before had flipped a coin with Harris to decide who would become president of Trinidad Electric,[61] "it would be best if you would allow me to negotiate with you as President of the Trinidad Co. for the transfer job and close it up at once". Aitken was afraid that the Eastern Trust Company would "offer to do this job for nothing" rather than let the Commercial Trust Co. get the work.[62] The same tactics were applied to other firms serviced by the RSC. Within one year, the Commercial Trust Co. had become the transfer agent, registrar or trustee for Porto Rico Railways, Camaguey Company, Demerara Electric, Dartmouth Electric, Robb Engineer-

---

58   Letter, W.D. Ross to Aitken, 9 March 1906, A/10/Ross, BBK: "The course of Scotia shows that your judgment of the situation was correct. The statement showing net earnings of 2 per cent for 1905 was really a revelation to me. I did not anticipate for a moment that it would be so bad".

59   January, February and March 1905 correspondence between Aitken and W.D. Ross, A/7/Ross, BBK.

60   Letters, R.H. Murray to Aitken, March 31, 1905, A/5/C; B.F. Pearson to Aitken, 26 May 1905, A/6/N-P; The Commercial Trust Company Limited, Annual Report 1906, A/13/Commercial Trust Co., BBK. B.F. Pearson appears to have been in partnership with his brother, G. Fred Pearson, and H. Almon Lovett.

61   Letter, Aitken to W.D. Ross, 24 November 1904, A/3/Ross, BBK.

62   Letter, Aitken to W.D. Ross, 29 September 1905, A/6/Ross, BBK.

ing, Amherst Foundry, Victor Wood Works, Maritime Heating Company, Robb-Mumford Boiler Company and the Minards Linament Company.[63]

The rivalry between Aitken and Harris intensified after Aitken shifted the RSC and its associated enterprises to Montreal. When Aitken first established the Montreal branch office at the end of 1905, however, he had done so with the complete support of the Scotia group. Neither Harris nor Aitken thought that this office would eventually become the centre of the RSC's operations.[64] Contrary to both their expectations, however, the Montreal office began to generate an enormous volume of work almost immediately, and Aitken found himself spending more time in Montreal and less in Halifax.[65] Before the end of 1906, the RSC's two most talented bond men, Arthur J. Nesbitt and Izaak Walton Killam, whom Aitken had moved from the Maritimes to Montreal, found themselves barely able keep up with all the securities business produced by Aitken's new utility ventures in Cuba and Puerto Rico. Aitken himself was reluctant to leave Halifax permanently, but two events soon pushed him in this direction. The first was Aitken's bitter disappointment when the other members of the Scotia group, led by Robert E. Harris, refused to give Aitken a salary raise despite his increasing duties as managing director of the RSC. In June of 1906, Aitken finally blew up and shared his frustration in a letter to his closest friend, William D. Ross:

> I leave for New York to-night to discuss there an offer which I have received and which it is my intention to refuse. However, my associates and co-shareholders must immediately waken up to the fact that I can not afford to live without salary any longer, and the time is far past for giving me the consideration for which my efforts have entitled me. I waited a long time for Mr. Stairs and Mr. Harris to voluntarily increase my salary....I gave warning to Mr. George Stairs before I left Halifax, but he kept assuring me of the many reasons why I should stay in Halifax, and utterly failed to see that my one reason for moving was that those chaps were starving me out. Harris gets a very fine salary himself from the Nova Scotia Steel & Coal Company, but cannot possibly understand anybody else wanting any salary....
>
> I am most anxious to make a successful Corporation of the Royal Securities. I mean success in the general sense of the word. It is my intention to follow up the business with great vigour, and I believe all the

---

63 The Commercial Trust Company Limited, Annual Report 1906, A/13/Commercial Trust Co., BBK.

64 Letter, Aitken to H.A. Porter, 11 October 1906, A/10/Royal Securities Corporation, and 1906 correspondence between Aitken and F.W. Teele, A/10/Teele, BBK.

65 Letters, Aitken to W.D. Ross, 27 December 1905, A/7/Ross; Aitken to P.G. Gossler, J.G. White & Co., 11 January 1906, A/9/G, BBK.

necessary qualities for success lie in the staff which I have gathered about me. But while my intention to remain is firm, I cannot help getting most annoyed at the continued indifference with which my connection is apparently due when my salary remains at $4,000. This is the first time I have given real expression to my thoughts....

I feel that if I went on thinking about it much longer, my train of reas[on]ing would eventually lead me to the conclusion that it would be much better for me to accept the biggest salary I could get outside, and begin to feather my own nest a little bit, rather than look after profits for other people all my life.[66]

The second episode was Aitken's decision eight months later that he and his fellow shareholders in the Commercial Trust Co. should purchase the Montreal Trust and Deposit Co. Aitken's plan was to turn the rather small and stagnant trust company into a first-rate national enterprise offering both a broad range of trust services as well as investment banking services. Aitken then (temporarily as it turned out) resigned from the RSC to become general manager of Montreal Trust, and moved to Montreal in April of 1907 to take up his new duties. Weeks later, Aitken continued to assert that he was not yet prepared to "desert" permanently his old residence and explained that he was "very homesick" for Halifax.[67] Nonetheless, one week after this letter, Aitken began to speak of Halifax in the past tense and complained of his mistreatment by his old business associates:

When I look back at my days in Halifax I think I can carefully say I have been most unselfish. Never went back on a friend. Modesty should compel me to wait for others to say these things, but...I feel badly that any of my old associates in Halifax should say their profits have not been big enough and that I got too big a share.[68]

The rest, as they say, is history. Aitken began to run the RSC and the majority of its spin-offs from Montreal. The Commercial Trust Co., which became a subsidiary of Montreal Trust, was managed from Montreal by Aitken until 1909, when he sold it and Montreal Trust to interests associated with the Royal Bank of Canada. Aitken then devoted all of his energies to a refurbished RSC, now purged of Robert E. Harris, which he used to promote huge industrial mergers such as Canada Cement, Canadian Car and Foundry, and the Steel Company of Canada.

---

66 Letter, Aitken to W.D. Ross, 16 June 1906, A/10/Ross, BBK.

67 Letter, Aitken to McCurdy, 22 May 1907, A/15/Mac-Mc, BBK.

68 Letter, Aitken to M.S. Clarke, 30 May 1907, A/13/Clarke, BBK.

Aitken was helped through it all by his old Maritime associates, many of whom were taking up permanent residence in Montreal. In 1907, Charles H. Cahan had dropped his partnership in Harris' law firm and moved to Montreal where he helped service Aitken's growing business empire.[69] W.D. Ross also moved to Montreal that year and, although he returned to Halifax a short time later (presumably more homesick than Aitken), he continued to support Aitken in his strategy of running their operations from Montreal.[70] Finally, after much prodding by Aitken, H. Almon Lovett left Harris' law firm towards the end of 1907 to work with Aitken in Montreal. After Aitken left for London in July of 1910, Cahan and Lovett joined forces, established their own investment bank and continued promoting consolidations from their base in Montreal.[71]

As for Arthur J. Nesbitt and Izaak Walton Killam, the RSC employees who had moved to the Montreal office in 1906, they would remain in Central Canada for the rest of their lives. Nesbitt would leave Aitken in 1908 to become an important merger promoter and financier in his own right during the merger waves of 1909-13 and 1925-9, first as general manager of the Investment Trust Company and later as president of Nesbitt, Thompson & Company. Killam would succeed Aitken as president of the RSC in 1915 and become one of the most powerful "St. James Street" financiers during the decades that followed.[72] All of these moves represented, in fact, an exodus of entrepreneurial capital which, although not the original cause of Maritime industrial decline, may have exacerbated difficulties for generations afterwards.

And what of the Maritime manufacturing enterprises which the Scotia group had financed since the early 1890s? Rhodes Curry & Co. of Amherst became part of the Canadian Car and Foundry merger — masterminded by the president of Rhodes Curry, Nathaniel Curry, and executed by Aitken. Curry then moved from Amherst to Montreal as president of Canadian Car, and carried out his scheme of rationalization, which centralized operations in

---

69   From 1903 until 1909, Cahan's principal residence was in Mexico City, where he was chief counsel and managing director of the Mexican Light and Power Company, but he kept a second residence in Halifax and later in Montreal through these years.

70   1908 correspondence, A/23/Killam, BBK.

71   Cahan and Lovett's subsequent careers are briefly summarized in Gregory P. Marchildon, "The Role of Lawyers in Corporate Promotion and Management: A Canadian Case Study and Theoretical Speculations", *Business and Economic History*, 2nd ser., 19 (1990), pp. 193-202.

72   *Monetary Times*, 25 May 1912, p. 2143; 14 January 1916, p. 7; Beaverbrook, *My Early Years*, p. 126; Douglas How, *Canada's Mystery Man of High Finance: The Story of Izaak Walton Killam and His Glittering Wife Dorothy* (Hantsport, N.S., 1986), p. 36.

Montreal and scaled down the Maritime plants.[73] Robb Engineering found itself with an outstanding debt load of $900,000 by 1912 and was put into
receivership. Its assets were sold to Corporation Agencies, a new investment
house created by Cahan and Lovett, who then created the International Engineering Works, with Cahan as president, to operate Robb Engineering's
Maritime assets. Cahan replaced many of the old Robb Engineering managers
with new blood, and by 1917 International Engineering was earning enough
revenue to be sold off at a profit to the Dominion Bridge Company of
Montreal.[74]

Nova Scotia Steel also came under the covetous eyes of the transplanted
Maritimers. From 1909 until early 1910, Aitken tried to purchase a controlling
interest in the firm on behalf of Nathaniel Curry, himself and some allied
Montreal interests. Aitken and Curry (with legal assistance from Cahan and
Lovett) were defeated in their takeover attempt by Harris and Cantley but the
latter were unable to arrest Scotia's decline. Five years after fighting for what
he claimed was "local control", Harris abandoned Scotia in favour of a provincial supreme court judgeship, thus leaving the presidency to Cantley. Later
that same year, control was transferred to American interests. After the war,
Nova Scotia Steel was folded into the disastrous British Empire Steel Corporation by which time the Maritime steel industry was a mere shadow of its
former self.[75]

To the extent that Stairs and the Scotia group were the most important
facilitators of long-term investment capital in the Maritimes, this case study
does illustrate the supportive role of indigenous finance. Nonetheless, the
energies of the Scotia group were already being pulled out of the Maritimes
before the turn of the century and before Max Aitken had arrived on the scene.
Although continuing their servicing of local industrial enterprises, Stairs and
his circle began to search aggressively for investment opportunities in the
West Indies and Latin America. Aitken furthered this policy, increasingly
avoiding what he perceived as unprofitable Maritime manufacturing companies while enthusiastically pursuing more rewarding enterprises outside the
region. By 1906, the RSC was becoming better known for its utility securities
than for its Maritime industrials.

The Scotia group's interest in, and subsequent preoccupation with, utility
ventures was a reaction to the already declining profitability of Maritime

---

73   Marchildon, "Promotion, Finance and Mergers", pp. 105-16.

74   *Monetary Times*, 20 July 1912, p. 180; 10 August 1912, p. 270; 28 December 1912,
     p. 962; 8 February 1913, p. 324; 26 April 1913, p. 768; 17 April 1914, p. 180; 21
     December 1917, p. 14.

75   The Scotia raid is discussed by Inwood, "Nova Scotia Steel and Coal Company",
     pp. 260-3, and Marchildon, "International Corporate Law", pp. 217-18. See also
     Frank, "The Cape Breton Coal Industry".

enterprises, not the cause of that decline. For example, evidence supports the conclusion that Nova Scotia Steel's deteriorating resource base was the single most important factor in its relatively poor performance after 1900, not the lack of external capital that continued to flow to Scotia despite Aitken's negative view of the firm's prospects.[76] John F. Stairs and his associates were first drawn into financing manufacturing firms, such as Nova Scotia Steel, because of their profitability; high earnings meant rapid growth, large dividends and lucrative security issues. During the early 1900s, when its earnings began to fall, Nova Scotia Steel became a less remunerative investment. Aitken, using the same profitability criterion as other Maritime or Central Canadian financiers, understandably became less willing to funnel long-term investment capital to Nova Scotia Steel.

This pattern was repeated with most of the Maritime manufacturing enterprises serviced by the Scotia group. Aitken's decision to continue financing Robb Engineering in 1906 did little to prevent that firm's ultimate insolvency. Unfortunately, the real cause of Robb Engineering's difficulties, as well as most other Maritime manufacturing enterprises that slid into decline at this time, remains an enigma. In the end, the fact that the RSC's head office had shifted to Montreal by 1907 was less important in terms of its impact on the financing of Maritime industry than John F. Stairs' original decision to begin promoting foreign utility ventures and Aitken's eventual decision to concentrate on this type of business from his base in Halifax.

Personality plays a subsidiary role in the shift described above. Aitken's continual disputes with his Halifax associates, in particular Harris, may have accelerated his decision to move from Halifax, but it did not fundamentally alter the RSC's preference for foreign utility financing, a preference that was shared by all members of the Scotia group. And while Aitken may have had a more pessimistic view of the future of Maritime industry than Harris, in the long (or even the medium) term, Harris was no more inclined to support Maritime enterprises out of a sense of community than was Aitken. All of the members of the Scotia group were, in the final analysis, calculating capitalists. There may have been shades of difference among the individual members of the Scotia group, but they were all dedicated to one main principle — the maximization of profit — and this meant reaching beyond the Maritimes from at least the turn of the century.

Thus, contrary to conventional belief, there was no profound difference in outlook between John F. Stairs, George Stairs and Harris on the one hand, and Aitken, Cahan, Curry, Killam, Lovett and Nesbitt on the other. All these

---

76 Inwood, *The Canadian Charcoal Iron Industry*, pp. 255-6, and "Nova Scotia Steel and Coal Company". For a brief summary of the various competing hypotheses that have been advanced concerning Nova Scotia Steel's decline, see L. Anders Sandberg, "Dependent Development, Labour and the Trenton Steel Works, Nova Scotia, c. 1900-1943", *Labour/Le travail*, 27 (Spring 1991), p. 128.

Maritimers were born or worked their way into the elite of the Canadian business community, and their primary loyalty was not to their region, but to their class. All profited by facilitating capital outflow in the form of promoting, issuing and retailing the securities of non-Maritime enterprises in one form or another. The most controversial figure in the group, Max Aitken, did not so much break with the characteristics that defined John F. Stairs in the late 19th century, as continue his legacy into the 20th century.

Regional Transfers of Funds through the Canadian Banking System and Maritime Economic Development, 1895-1935

Neil C. Quigley, Ian M. Drummond and Lewis T. Evans

A persistent theme of Canadian historiography has been that in the late 19th and early 20th centuries the availability of credit and the pattern of economic development were determined to a large extent by discrimination against borrowers of different types and in different regions. Spatial transfers of funds through the banking system[1] have often been viewed as the mechanism through which the preferences of Canadian bankers distorted patterns of economic development, demonstrating the existence of discriminatory credit allocation policies. Alternatively, it may be argued that in an efficient integrated national credit market the spatial pattern of bank lending will bear no necessary relationship to the distribution of deposits because such lending will be determined solely by the location of the most credit-worthy applicants for loans. From this standpoint, any difference between the pattern of lending and the distribution of deposits in the banking system may simply be the result of efficient transfers of funds to those regions in which the return from their use, and thus the growth of the economy as a whole, will be maximized.

This paper provides an assessment of the magnitude and direction of flows of funds through the branch networks of the Canadian banks and their impact on the relative industrial and commercial decline that occurred in the Maritimes between 1890 and 1935. In the first section we review the available evidence on banking in the Maritimes, examining the relationship between financial structure and economic development and providing a critique of the literature that has attempted to establish a causal link between the policies of Canadian banks and the economic problems of the Maritime Provinces. We suggest that although it will never be possible to definitively test the

We have benefited from the comments of participants in seminars at the University of Western Ontario, Rutgers University and the Maritime Economic History Workshop, Halifax, September 1990, as well as from Kris Inwood and anonymous referees.

1   Because the payments mechanism provided by the banking system is based on the transfer of ownership of bank deposits, for most practical purposes banks do not actually undertake the physical movement of funds through space. However, we use the terminology "transfers of funds" in this paper because any phrase that is more precise will necessarily be much more cumbersome.

hypothesis that the operation of the banking system had a negative effect on the rate of Maritime growth, this hypothesis is not persuasive on theoretical grounds and lacks evidential support. In the second and third sections we utilize data from two banks with strong historical roots in the Maritimes — the Bank of Nova Scotia (BNS), and the Royal Bank of Canada (RBC) — to examine the charge that two large banks "discriminated against the Maritimes". We conclude that the evidence suggests otherwise.

The antecedents of the debate about regional transfers of funds through the Canadian banking system and its implications for the Maritimes must be understood in the context of the development of Canadian banking in the 19th century. During the recession that occurred in the Maritimes in the mid-1880s, all of the banks operating in that region experienced problems because of the concentration of their loan exposure in local industry and commerce. The official history of the RBC[2] describes how "two of Nova Scotia's largest industries, heavily indebted to the Bank, passed into the hands of receivers", at heavy cost to the bank. The BNS experienced similar problems as a number of its most important customers failed and those who were solvent reduced their level of borrowing commensurate with lower levels of output.[3] It was at this time that the Maritime bankers began to first use the terminology "surplus funds" to describe a situation in which their cash reserves were at an unprofitably high level because of their inability to find suitable loan propositions through their own branches.

At least some Maritime bankers considered the lessons of the 1880s to be that they should attempt to reduce the impact of future depressions on their business through a policy of regional diversification. From this time onwards the larger and more entrepreneurial banks in the Maritimes and Central Canada expanded out of the regions in which they had first been established, and began the process of transforming themselves into truly national and international banks. Because of the importance of surplus funds as a stimulus for this expansion, diversification often involved in the first instance the establishment of branches in major commercial centres where they concentrated on making large commercial loans. By the late 1890s the BNS was established in Minneapolis/Chicago, Kingston (Jamaica), Toronto and Montreal, and the

---

2   Until 1900 the Royal Bank of Canada was registered under the name Merchants' Bank of Halifax, but to avoid confusion we use the former title throughout this paper.

3   *Anniversary of the Royal Bank of Canada* (Montreal, 1919), p. 17; Joseph Schull and J. Douglas Gibson, *The Scotiabank Story* (Toronto, 1982), pp. 67-70. In the mid-1880s the losses of the Bank of Nova Scotia due to bad debts were higher than at any other time in its history when expressed as a proportion of total lending. See N.C. Quigley, "Bank Credit and the Structure of the Canadian Space Economy", Ph.D. thesis, University of Toronto, 1986, ch 7.

RBC had agencies in Havana and New York as well as Toronto and Montreal.[4] For both the RBC and the BNS this transition was both symbolized and affected by the decision to move their head offices out of Halifax. The RBC moved its head office to Montreal in 1901, while the BNS moved its general manager's office to Toronto in 1900, three years after the opening of its first branch in that city.

The success of these diversification strategies was closely linked to the development of retail deposit banking. For the first time the banks began to establish branches in a variety of small centres where the prospects for making commercial loans were very poor, but where a large volume of deposits could be collected by providing banking facilities for the general public. Retail deposit banking was in fact a necessary complement to the development of wholesale lending branches, and only after the successful establishment of these branches did the large-scale collection of retail deposits have utility for the banks.

Alternatively, many Maritime banks followed a strategy of continuing to focus their business in the Maritimes (see Table One). In 1890, 11 of the 13 banks with head offices in the Maritimes had no branches outside the region. Indeed, seven of them — the Bank of New Brunswick, the People's Bank of New Brunswick, the St. Stephens Bank, the Summerside Bank, the Bank of Yarmouth, the Commercial Bank of Windsor and the Exchange Bank of Yarmouth — had no branches at all. Two of these banks reacted to excess liquidity in a way that is antithetical to the notion of unexploited opportunities for successful lending in the Maritimes: they repaid capital to their shareholders!

By December 1900 the result of the expansion and diversification of the RBC and the BNS was the accretion of a sophisticated asset portfolio and an overall balance sheet position which clearly distinguished them from the other Maritime banks shown in Table Two. The financial markets in larger centres offered instruments that differed from those available in the Maritimes in terms of their liquidity and the collateral against which they were secured. By 1900 both the BNS and the RBC were making extensive use of the call loan markets in Montreal, Toronto and New York/Boston, while the BNS continued to utilize funds in short-dated loans secured by commercial paper and grain in Chicago. Offices in New York, Boston, Montreal and Toronto also offered the opportunity for the largest Maritime banks to begin the process of accumulating and actively managing a diversified securities portfolio,[5] while the

---

4   N.C. Quigley, "The Bank of Nova Scotia in the Caribbean 1890-1940", *Business History Review*, 63 (1989), pp. 797-838.

5   Because the Bank of Nova Scotia disclosed the details of its securities holdings in the annual reports of the first decade of the 20th century, we know that it was not totally neglecting the long-term capital needs of its home region. At the end of 1906 the bank reported "investments" — all bonds — which totalled $5.5 million.

Table One
Banks with Branches in the Maritime Provinces, 1900 and 1925

| Bank | Branches in 1890[a] | | Branches in 1925[a] | |
	Maritimes	Total	Maritimes	Total
Banque Provinciale du Canada			18	133
Bank of British North America	3	16		
Bank of Montreal	4	35	29	584
Bank of New Brunswick	1	1		
Bank of Nova Scotia	27	30	83	299
Bank of Yarmouth	1	1		
Canadian Bank of Commerce			33	526
Commercial Bank	1	1		
Dominion Bank			1	118
Exchange Bank	1	1		
Halifax Banking Company	15	15		
Merchants Bank, P.E.I.	2	2		
People's Bank, Halifax	6	6		
People's Bank, N.B.	1	1		
Royal Bank of Canada	22	24	94	899
St. Stephens Bank, N.B.	1	1		
Standard Bank			1	210
Summerside Bank	1	1		
Union Bank, Halifax	3	3		

a = does not include sub-agencies

Sources: N.S. Garland, ed., *Garland's Banks, Bankers and Banking in Canada* (Ottawa, 1890); *Canada Year Book* (Ottawa, 1926).

remoteness of the small Maritime banks from the major financial centres meant that even where they held securities they were constrained in their attempts to manage and diversify their portfolio.

The balance sheets of the BNS and the RBC at the end of 1900 demonstrate a level of liquidity and diversification that, with the benefit of hindsight, we may take as implicitly defining the requirements for success in Canadian banking in this period: expansion of the notes issued and the deposits obtained (which pushed the ratio of capital to other liabilities below 25 per cent), a cash ratio in excess of ten per cent, access to the call loan markets in the U.S., and a liquid assets ratio in excess of 45 per cent. While other banks had strengths in one or two of these areas, none could provide depositors and shareholders with the combination of liquidity and diversification of investments offered by these two institutions. For example, the Bank of New Brunswick apparently lacked the ability to expand its deposit base and note circulation so as to reduce its capital ratio to the competitive level, and held few assets in securities or foreign call loans. The Union Bank of Halifax had a (relatively) large holding of securities, but had required a loan of $1 million from the Bank of Toronto[6] to purchase these, and overall had a very inferior cash and net liquid asset position (see Table Two).

For the Maritimes, the assimilation into a national and international banking system portrayed by Tables One and Two was just one part of a more general economic and cultural integration associated with the post-Confederation period. A significant body of opinion in the Maritimes in the 1860s had opposed entry into the Canadian confederation on the grounds that it would be "a recipe for economic disaster". Despite the prosperity of the Maritimes from the late 1880s until the First World War, this sentiment was revived in the 1920s, when the industrial economy of the region collapsed, and historians began to write as if entry into Confederation represented a major turning point in the economic prosperity of the region.[7] Among recent scholars, Acheson has most clearly continued this tradition by arguing that national integration was responsible for the collapse of the industrial base of the Maritimes and

---

Of this total 20.1 per cent were in Maritime securities, $109,000 in the bonds of Nova Scotia industries, and $997,000 in the bonds of Maritime provincial and municipal governments.

6   This loan was almost equal in size to the value of the paid-up capital and reserve fund of the Union Bank of Halifax.

7   P.A. Buckner, "Rewriting the Past: The Economic History of the Maritimes in the Confederation Era", unpublished manuscript, University of New Brunswick, 1990. On the prosperity of the Maritimes see David Alexander, "Economic Growth in the Atlantic Region, 1880 to 1940", *Acadiensis*, VIII, 1 (Autumn 1978), pp. 47-76.

Table Two
The Balance Sheets of the Banks Based in the Maritime Provinces
(as at 31 December 1900)

Bank	Capital [a]	Cash [b]	Securities [c]	Call Loans	Net Assets [d]	Liquid Assets [e]
Bank of New Brunswick	43.3	10.2	1.1	18.9	8.6	38.8
Bank of Nova Scotia	23.6	11.8	13.0	12.3	8.3	47.4
Bank of Yarmouth	53.5	6.3	4.0	0.0	13.9	24.2
Commercial Bank of Windsor	37.2	3.9	0.0	0.4	7.4	11.7
Exchange Bank of Yarmouth	120.7	6.2	17.4	0.0	16.8	40.4
Halifax Banking Co.	25.7	9.2	12.5	3.8	2.6	28.1
Merchants Bank of P.E.I.	28.1	3.0	0.7	0.0	5.8	9.5
Peoples Bank, Halifax	34.1	6.4	2.9	4.6	4.5	18.4
Peoples Bank, N.B.	75.9	3.4	5.6	0.0	10.4	19.4
Royal Bank of Canada	26.3	11.4	12.1	7.8	7.5	37.8
St. Stephens Bank	57.8	4.4	0.0	0.0	11.8	16.2
Summerside Bank	33.3	2.1	0.0	0.0	12.4	14.5
Union Bank of Halifax	24.1	5.0	34.2	0.0	-17.9	21.3

a = paid-up equity and reserve fund expressed as a percentage of all other liabilities
b = gold, Dominion Notes and deposits to secure note circulation
c = all security holdings plus loans to the Government of Canada and Canadian provincial governments
d = incorporates loans to and from other banks in addition to correspondent and agency balances
e = cash, securities, call loans and net assets with banks

Source: *Canadian Gazette* (Ottawa).

that government policy could have preserved the prosperity of the region with minimal costs to the economy as a whole.[8]

There is a substantial international literature which claims that English-style commercial banks were inappropriate for, and thus inhibited, industrialization.[9] There has been a vigorous debate over the social returns to British foreign investment in the late 19th and early 20th centuries, as well as the hypothesis that the flow of funds overseas was so large because British financial institutions explicitly or implicitly discriminated against local industry.[10] This literature has helped to focus the search for precise mechanisms that would link integration into the Canadian economy with the relative industrial decline of the Maritimes. It has also spawned the hypothesis that the transfers of funds out of the Maritimes resulted from the discriminatory policies of the banks. R.T. Naylor has argued the extreme case that "Maritime underdevelopment and the loss of its financial independence went hand-in-hand".[11] Acheson has suggested that the Maritimes suffered from an absence of institutions prepared to finance large-scale industrialization, and Frost has argued that after 1885 the BNS inhibited development in the Maritimes because it was "reluctant to expand its Maritime business".[12] Clement, citing both Naylor and Acheson, has generalized the argument to conclude that the

---

8   T.W. Acheson, "The National Policy and the Industrialization of the Maritimes, 1880-1910", *Acadiensis*, I, 2 (Spring 1972), pp 3-28, and "The Maritimes and 'Empire Canada'" in David J. Bercuson, ed., *Canada and the Burden of Unity* (Toronto, 1977).

9   In contrast to bankers in Japan and Germany, British bankers did not involve themselves directly in the management and restructuring of large industrial enterprises, confining their activities largely to short-term commercial loans rather than the long-term loans provided by German industrial banks. R. Cameron, *Banking in the Early Stages of Industrialisation: A Study of Comparative Economic History* (New York, 1967), and *Banking and Economic Development: Some Lessons of History* (New York, 1972).

10   Some of the most important studies in this very extensive literature are: A.K. Cairncross, *Home and Foreign Investment 1870-1913* (Cambridge, 1953); P.C. Cottrell, *British Overseas Investment in the Nineteenth Century* (London, 1975); Michael Edelstein, *Overseas Investment in the Age of High Imperialism* (New York, 1982); Herbert Feis, *Europe: The World's Banker, 1815-1914* (New Haven, 1930); B. Elbaum and W. Lazonik, eds., *The Decline of the British Economy* (Oxford, 1986); William P. Kennedy, *Industrial Structure, Capital Markets, and the Origins of British Economic Decline* (Cambridge, 1987).

11   R.T. Naylor, *The History of Canadian Business, Volume 1* (Toronto, 1975), p 150.

12   Acheson, "National Policy"; J.D. Frost 'The 'Nationalization' of the Bank of Nova Scotia, 1880-1910", *Acadiensis*, XII, 1 (Autumn 1982), p. 29.

National Policy stimulated Maritime industry, but that "the ruling financial elite failed to allow its development".[13]

We find these criticisms of the operation of the banking systems in the U.K. and the Maritimes unconvincing on intuitive and evidential grounds. The literature on the Maritimes shares with that on the U.K. a complete absence of systematic microeconomic evidence that the banks acted in other than an efficient manner. Recent research in Canada has actually demonstrated that the industrial sector made considerable use of bank credit, and that because it was often the practice for banks to obtain personal guarantees from firm directors to secure lines of credit, it was not uncommon for industrial firms to obtain loans greater than or equal to the value of the proprietors' fixed and working capital in the firm.[14] And on more general grounds, the demonstrated entrepreneurial ability and success of the largest Maritime banks make it more difficult to understand why they would have been unresponsive to opportunities for making profitable loans to industrialists in the Maritimes or elsewhere in Canada. Given that they were prepared to expend resources on finding profitable business outside the Maritimes, and were very successful in doing so, why should we suppose that these banks neglected potential business in the Maritimes that could surely have been canvassed at lower cost?

Criticisms of the banks often rest implicitly on the fundamental misconception that in the absence of discrimination in bank policy regional deposits and loans will be balanced, so that for the banks to use the "savings" of one region to underwrite lending in another would adversely affect and therefore exploit the "saving" region. This was, of course, one of the fundamental concerns underlying the preference for a unit banking structure in the U.S.,[15] although we now know that even in the 19th century U.S. interbank lending provided a mechanism for transfers to occur.[16] In fact, the great contribution of a banking system to economic development is to provide a clearing mechanism through which a spatial redistribution of claims on and debts to the banking system can be achieved. Payments are made by a firm surrendering ownership of a deposit to another firm, and receipts take the form of the acquisition of a claim on a bank, so that at each branch of a bank deposits are surrendered as payments are made and acquired as payments are received.[17]

---

13   W. Clement, *The Canadian Corporate Elite: An Analysis of Economic Power* (Toronto, 1975), p. 67.

14   L.T. Evans and N.C. Quigley, "Discrimination in Bank Lending Practice: A Test Using Data From the Bank of Nova Scotia 1900-1937", *Canadian Journal of Economics* 23, 1 (February 1990).

15   J.F. Johnson, *The Canadian Banking System* (Washington, 1910), p. 92.

16   J.A. James, *Money and Capital Markets in Postbellum America* (Princeton, 1978).

17   For a discussion see J.A. Galbraith, *The Economics of Banking Operations: A Canadian Study* (Montreal, 1963).

The efficiency of a branch banking system in undertaking these activities is that it internalizes and thus reduces both the costs of assessing claims in different regions and the costs associated with meeting spatial imbalances in payments and receipts. Where the deposits at any branch are insufficient to cover the payments that the branch must make to the rest of the banking system, settlements are made via book entries at the head office of the bank without any physical movement of funds taking place. For each branch this process is limited only by the availability of funds (reserve position) of the bank as a whole and the ability of the branch to generate business that is considered more profitable than the business generated by other branches.

Payments can be made freely by any firm or household up to the limit of the deposits that they hold with the banking system, but can only exceed deposits for any individual customer (and thus for any region in aggregate) as a result of the bank granting credit. The credit allocation function is therefore central to any analysis of whether or not the banks have a purely passive or an active role in shaping the pattern of payments and receipts at any branch. Most claims that the banking system inhibited Maritime economic development argue that spatial disparities between deposits and loans result from discriminatory banking credit allocation policies. R.T. Naylor has argued that Central Canadian financiers destroyed Maritime banks and drained funds out of the region, starving Maritime firms of needed credit and thus causing the industrial decline of the Maritimes, while using the funds to promote commercial and staple-linked activity in Central Canada and the expansion of grain farming in the West.[18] Utilizing branch deposit and loan data as well as correspondence from the BNS, Frost suggests that the very large differential between deposits and loans at branches in the Maritimes supports "Naylor's assertion that the major banks promoted the drainage of capital out of the Maritimes".[19] Regehr, using these data for Western Canada, concludes that for most of the period 1900-39 "the Bank of Nova Scotia received more deposits in western rural communities than it granted in loans. This suggests that western farm complaints about unduly restrictive bank credit policies had some validity".[20]

But if the banks provide an efficient credit market, setting terms for access to loans that fairly evaluate macroeconomic conditions as well as the risks and transactions costs incurred, then we can regard the net balance of deposits and loans at each branch simply as an indicator of the local balance between the demand for credit and the wealth that customers of that branch choose to hold in the form of deposits. Differentials between bank deposits and loans at an in-

18 Naylor, *History of Canadian Business*, p. 111.

19 Frost, "Nationalization", p. 29.

20 T.D. Regehr, "Bankers and Farmers in Western Canada 1900-1931", in J. Foster, ed., *The Developing West* (Edmonton, 1983), p. 311.

dividual branch or in any region may therefore arise as a result of the efficient organization of banking markets, and it is impossible to distinguish between efficient and discriminatory banking policies solely on the basis of deposit and loan data. Any assessment of the broader implications of this transfer of funds depends on whether we think that Maritime entrepreneurs and politicians did not have access to funds on equivalent terms, as well as on how they would have utilized the funds if they had remained in the Maritimes. Such counterfactual assessments may only be made with extreme caution, as David Alexander has noted.[21]

Perhaps more importantly, it is not clear that the implicit prescription for bank management offered by the critics of the major Maritime banks is viable. If a local bank restricts its lending to local commerce and industry, its fate becomes enmeshed with local entrepreneurs. The bank is thus unable to offer its shareholders, note-holders and depositors the lower level of risk that derives from a diverse portfolio of assets. At the same time people resident in the Maritimes were not obliged to hold all of their financial assets in claims on local banks: they increasingly had access to a wider market comprising claims on national and international banks in addition to an international securities market. The viability of local banks therefore depended upon their ability to offer risk-adjusted returns commensurate with their non-local competition. In practice this meant that attempts to support local industry with loans that were larger or cheaper than those available from national and international institutions inevitably resulted in a fall in the risk-adjusted return to depositors and a commensurate withdrawal of funds. Even if it had been possible to restrict the flow of funds out of the Maritimes, it is not clear that this would have increased the rate of economic growth or the level of economic development in the region. If the viability of Maritime firms rested on their ability to obtain credit and capital at subsidized (less than the world) rates, then a policy of financial isolation would have resulted in more industry and employment in the region, but a lower per capita standard of living.

The analysis underlying this result may be made more explicit with the use of a simple diagrammatic representation of the position of a representative bank based in the Maritimes when that region is integrated into a much larger national or international economy. To construct Figure 1 we assume that the bank is able to collect enough information about applicants for credit to order them on the basis of the risk-adjusted return that they offer, so that at any level of lending the bank faces declining marginal returns. The diagram also assumes that the bank has information about the nature of the demand for credit outside the Maritimes, and that because this market is so large compared with the size of the Maritime bank, over the feasible range of supply there exists a

21   David Alexander, *Atlantic Canada and Confederation* (Toronto, 1983), especially
     p. 137.

Figure 1

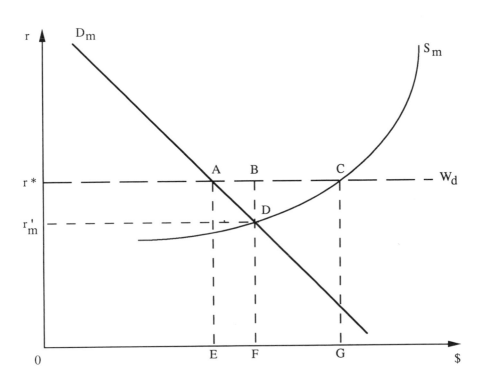

Where: D_m = demand for bank credit in the Maritimes
W_d = demand for bank credit outside the Maritimes
S_m = supply of credit by Maritime bank
r = risk adjusted interest rate

world risk-adjusted interest rate (r*) at which the demand for credit is perfect-ly elastic. For ease of exposition we assume that the profits of the bank are derived from an intermediation commission levied on customers at a fixed rate per dollar of interest charged or paid, so that r* is also the equilibrium rate of return on deposits. The rate of interest paid on deposits determines the funds available for the bank to lend. The shape of the supply schedule is dictated by the assumed existence of alternative channels through which funds can flow into or out of the Maritimes, so that if a bank offers depositors less than r* they will invest their funds elsewhere, while if it offers more than r* it will at-tract deposits from outside the region.

Under these circumstances, if the Maritime bank functions in an integrated national or international market, it will lend E to local businesses and place EG outside the region. Total lending will be G, and this is proportional to the profits of the shareholders in the bank. Because the schedule depicting the demand for credit in the Maritimes extends below r* there will clearly be un-exploited opportunities for making loans in the Maritimes if we understand this to mean borrowers offering a risk-adjusted return > 0, but there are no ap-plications for credit that the bank will wish to satisfy if the opportunity cost provided by the world demand for credit is taken into account. However, if the Maritime bank is required to utilize its available funds by lending only in the Maritimes, lending in the region will increase from E to F, but the total value of deposits/loans will fall to F. In this case the return to depositors must be reduced to r^1_m if the bank is to remain viable, and $r^*BDr^1_m$ represents the direct losses to depositors who place funds with the bank at the lower interest rate. In addition, the area ACD represents the total welfare loss in the region resulting from the lower value of the funds placed with the bank as a result of the policy of financial isolation, and FG is proportional to the profits foregone by shareholders in the bank.

The implications of this model for an assessment of the record of banking in the Maritimes are straightforward and testable. First, we would expect that if the potential growth path in the Maritime Region resulted in a higher demand for bank deposits than for bank loans, the viability of Maritime banks would depend on their ability to lend their surplus funds outside the Maritimes. Second, we would expect that the banks who did not expand their lending base outside the Maritimes would inflict losses on shareholders and/or depositors and be uncompetitive. Third, our model suggests that for any amount of funds deposited with banks in the Maritimes, the risk-adjusted return obtained on the loans will be higher for banks operating in the whole of the Canadian market than for those operating solely in the Maritimes. Thus, we would expect the business of small locally oriented Maritime banks to be more valuable to institutions with the capacity to make loans in national and international centres experiencing rapid growth than to the local shareholders.

Table Three
The Record of Maritime Chartered Banks, 1880-1925[a]

Name	Date at which Failed	Date at which Merged	Buyer	Loss to Shareholders[b] ($000)	Loss to Shareholders[b] (% equity)	Loss to Creditors[c] ($000)	Assets[d] ($000)	Growth Rate[e] 1891-1925
Bank of P.E.I.	1881			.310	187.9	-	1,108	-
Union Bank of P.E.I.		1883	BNS	65	28.6	-	900	-
Maritime Bank	1887			1,083	131.9	801	1,715	-
Pictou Bank	1887			164	65.6	-		-
Summerside Bank		1901	BNB	-	-	-	292	7.86
Commercial Bank		1902	UBH	50.4	12.2	-	1,954	9.41
Halifax Banking Co.		1903	CBC	44.0	4.0	-	6,025	5.16
Exchange Bank		1903	BM	-	-	-	680	2.31
Bank of Yarmouth	1905			335	100.0	-	820	-1.75
Peoples Bank, Halifax		1905	BM	618	42.9	-	6,395	8.87
Merchants Bank, P.E.I.		1906	CBC	83	12.2	-	2,036	10.53
Peoples Bank, N.B.		1907	BM	-	-	-	1,041	1.81
Union Bank, Halifax		1910	RBC	182	6.7	-	25,333	12.69
St. Stephens Bank	1910		BNS	260	100.0	-	802	1.12
Bank of New Brunswick		1913		-	-	-	11,975	5.22
Bank of Nova Scotia							228,866	7.76
Royal Bank of Canada							618,739	12.69

a = Maritime banks are here defined as those with their head office in New Brunswick, Nova Scotia or PEI during this period.

b = The loss to shareholders is as computed by H.C. McLeod, and includes all capital written down during the life of the bank and the shareholders' double liability. Equity includes the amount of the published reserve fund.

c = Losses to creditors are understated to the extent of negotiated settlement of claims at less than 100% of face value.

d = Assets in 1925 or the last year reported.

e = Real annual compound growth rate as a percentage of total assets. Calculations are made for the period July 1891 until July 1925, or the year in which the bank failed or was merged. Constant price estimates were calculated using the GNP deflator reported in A.G. Green and M.C. Urquhart, "New Estimates of Output Growth in Canada", in D. McCalla, ed., *Perspectives on Canadian Economic History* (Toronto, 1987).

Sources: B.H. Beckhart, "The Banking Systems of Canada", in H.P. Willis and B.H. Beckhart, eds., *Foreign Banking Systems* (New York, 1929), pp. 334-9; bank returns as published in the *Canada Gazette* (Ottawa).

Four of the smallest banks achieved real compound growth rates of less than 2.5 per cent per annum after 1891, and two of these, the St. Stephens Bank and the Bank of Yarmouth, inflicted total loss on their shareholders (see Table Three). Only one of the unit banks, the Summerside Bank, achieved moderate growth in the 1890s without loss to its shareholders, and it was so small that it would be inappropriate to attempt to draw any lessons from this experience. Above this level, a number of the Maritime banks achieved rates of growth equal to or greater than that of the BNS. But in most of these institutions the shareholders suffered losses and sold out to larger and more diversified banks, as a part of which their Maritime business was more valuable. The key factor that appears to have differentiated the BNS from these institutions, and which underlay that outstanding record of the RBC, was their earlier and greater commitment to the diversification of both their loan and deposit business in the period after 1880.

Finally, we consider the extent to which evidence on the operations of other types of banks illuminates the record of the chartered banks. The Maritimes also contained a small number of private banks. Because these institutions operated as unincorporated partnerships they could not issue bank notes but were not restricted by the terms of the Bank Act. Neufeld found only six in 1885, three in New Brunswick and three in Nova Scotia, while by 1895 there were only seven.[22] In contrast, in Ontario and Western Canada there was a very rapid expansion of private banking in this period, based on a growth in demand for banking accommodation that was in advance of the establishment of branches of the chartered banks and/or fell outside the range of business that the chartered banks were prepared to do. The record of private banking in the Maritimes therefore provides no support for the view that there were banking opportunities left unexploited by the chartered banks with branches in that region.

In many jurisdictions savings banks have been important financial conduits, usually for government finance but often for mortgage money as well. The process can be observed in many European countries, as well as in New Zealand and in Australia, both before and after the federation of the Australian colonies. Before Confederation the savings banks of the Maritime colonies had behaved in exactly this way. However, at Confederation the savings banks were transferred to the Dominion, and while local Maritime offices remained open, net new deposits were treated as loans to the Dominion Government. The same was true of the postal savings system, to which, as time passed, savings bank deposits were gradually transferred. The sums, furthermore, were not small by comparison with the revenues of the Maritime provincial governments.[23] At Confederation there was $1.4 million on deposit with the

---

22 E.P. Neufeld, *The Financial System of Canada: Its Growth and Development* (Toronto, 1972), ch 5.

23 In 1914-15 the total revenue of the three Maritime governments was only some $4 million. Data are from the *Canada Year Book*, various years.

Dominion savings banks, almost entirely in the Maritimes; by 1887 the figure had peaked at $20 million, and then declined to $15.6 million in 1900; even in 1914, after some loss of competitiveness, deposits were still $13.9 million. In the Post Office savings banks, meanwhile, total deposits rose from $204,000 to $37.5 million in 1900, and to $41.9 million in 1914. By 1900 about one-sixth of the Post Office savings balances, and virtually all of the balances in the Dominion savings banks, were attributable to people resident in the Maritimes. The savings banks therefore do represent a direct channel through which funds from the Maritimes were invested outside the region.

The available evidence relating to the chartered banks and the savings banks clearly suggests that there was a strong demand for low-risk savings instruments in the Maritime Provinces of the type that might have been provided by a "credit mobilier" type of "universal bank" or an investment trust. But without a demand for the long-term credit in which such institutions specialized, it is not clear that any significant amount of lending could have been done in the region.[24] Why, for example, did the financial entrepreneurs of Halifax or Saint John not establish such an institution if there was a need for (and a profit to be made in providing) these services? In this respect anecdotal evidence can certainly be provided in support of the hypothesis of a lack of business rather than a lack of entrepreneurship: for example, financier Max Aitken began his career in the Maritimes, and the Royal Securities Corporation began as a Halifax promotion.

It is therefore difficult to argue convincingly that the Maritimes suffered as a result of the extra-regional integration of the region's banks, whether through the outward extension of the BNS and the RBC, or through the inward extension of other Canadian banks. These extensions widened the area from which funds could be drawn, and raised the average rate of return on bank assets,[25] thus providing higher returns for the very considerable number of people in the Maritimes who were depositors and/or shareholders in the BNS and the RBC. Furthermore, we believe that it is unrealistic to argue that small locally oriented Maritime banks provided any general advantages for that region after the 1880s. They may have added to regional capital accumulation by making more loans available to local entrepreneurs, but it seems likely that any gains resulting from this would have been more than off-

---

24 In Europe "credits mobiliers" began their lives largely as "railway banks", but in the Maritimes, railway finance was in part a matter for Ottawa, and in part for the City of London. On the credit mobilier see Rondo Cameron, *France and the Economic Development of Europe, 1800-1914* (Princeton, 1961), chs. VI, VII. For a general survey of the securities market in the Maritimes see C. Armstrong, "Making a Market: Selling Securities in Atlantic Canada Before World War 1", *Canadian Journal of Economics*, XIII (August 1980), pp. 438-54.

25 In the period from 1885 to 1914 the most profitable branches in the Bank of Nova Scotia network were those outside the Maritimes. See Quigley, "Bank Credit".

set by the lower returns to depositors and shareholders resulting from lower lending rates and/or more bad debts, and the resulting fall in deposits with the banks. Thus, even if there were credit-worthy Maritime industrialists whose entrepreneurial skills were being stifled by the discriminatory policies of the major chartered banks, it is not clear that a policy of financial isolation would have provided material benefits for the region as a whole.

From the turn of the 20th century Canadian bankers began to publicly articulate the view that they had a role in the regional transfer of funds, and that this was central to the integration and economic development of the nation. Sir Edmund Walker of the Canadian Bank of Commerce was widely quoted as saying that his bank "gathers deposits in the quiet unenterprising parts of Ontario, and lends the money in the enterprising localities". After 1910 farmers were assured that loans at Western Canadian branches were in excess of deposits to refute claims of inadequate credit facilities and deflect charges that farmers paid interest rates for bank credit at usurious levels. Walker's statement to the Select Standing Committee on Banking and Commerce that "at a hundred and twenty-two western branches of the Canadian Bank of Commerce...we have farmers' deposits of $2,869,926, and we have loans to farmers amounting to $13,035,784" has been accepted as indicative of the position for the banking system as a whole.[26]

However, the interpretation of the data provided by Walker is not straightforward. The term "farmers' deposits" may indicate that deposits at branches in the major urban centres in the West were not included in the figures provided, while "loans to farmers" may have included the loans made to grain elevator companies. In addition, to accept these data as providing an accurate picture of the position of Western branches within the banking system we need either to know the precise date at which these figures were calculated, or obtain figures averaged over a number of years. Accuracy is especially vital because lending in the West was highly seasonal, especially in respect of the requirements of grain elevator companies. Annual fluctuations in the size and value of the grain harvest would also have been an important determinant of the value of the loans outstanding given that much of the banks' lending to Western farmers must have been secured by grain. ·

We attempt to provide a more systematic and rigorous account of transfers of funds through the Canadian banking system in this period, utilizing deposit and loan data for up to 360 branches of the BNS and up to 1,200 branches of the RBC. These data were obtained from the summary ledgers maintained in the head offices of the two banks, and consist of annual averages of the daily balances in branch deposit and loan accounts. To avoid problems created by the fact that the data are highly sensitive to the particular year being con-

---

26   Select Standing Committee on Banking and Commerce, *Minutes of Proceedings, Evidence etc.* (Ottawa, 1913), p. 484.

sidered, our analysis utilizes five-year averages of the individual branch/year deposit and loan observations. For the BNS, both deposit and loan figures portray the regional diversification of business that occurred in the period 1890-1930 (Table Four and Table Five). In general terms, this meant a decline in the importance of the deposit base provided by branches in Nova Scotia, and in the rest of the Maritimes to some degree, and a dramatic increase in the proportion of deposits collected in Ontario. Jamaica contributed more deposits to the branch network than did Saskatchewan, Alberta and British Columbia combined throughout the period 1892-1926. The lending business had already undergone a substantial diversification by 1892 as a result of the opening of branches in Montreal and Minneapolis, but almost 45 per cent of the loans of the BNS were still made at branches in Nova Scotia in the early 1890s. After 1896 the proportion of loans made in Nova Scotia fell much further, as Ontario, Western Canada and the Hispanic Caribbean absorbed an increasing share of the total loans of the BNS.

The spatial distribution of deposits and loans within the RBC in the early 1920s mirrors to a large degree that of the BNS (Table Six and Table Seven). A major exception in terms of both deposits and loans was in the Caribbean. Jamaica was of little significance for the operations of the RBC, but in the rest of the Caribbean both deposits and loans made up a very significant proportion of total bank business. Thereafter, deposits in the Caribbean declined quickly, in part because of the closure of branches in Cuba, and the proportion of total loans made in this region fell quite dramatically as advances made in Cuba in 1920 were gradually liquidated but not replaced by new loans. This decline was counteracted by a very rapid increase in the proportion of loans placed in Quebec, with less significant increases in Ontario and the U.S. (to take advantage of rising interest rates in the late 1920s).

As might be expected given the distribution of its branches, the RBC drew a much larger proportion of its deposits from the West than did the BNS, and its loans in the West do not display the concentration in Manitoba evident in the latter bank (Table Six and Table Seven). But, in more general terms, the small proportion of total loans made at branches of both banks in Manitoba, Saskatchewan and Alberta is worthy of consideration, especially in view of the contradictory claims about the extent to which the banks made loans to farmers in the West. The branch network of the BNS in the West was too small to provide a basis for any wide generalizations, but in the 1920s the RBC accounted for approximately 30 per cent of the total branches of the chartered banks in this region. The data thus suggests that at least by the 1920s, despite continued immigration and expansion of the cultivated land in Western Canada, and undoubtedly with the exception of loans to elevator companies and pools during the crop-moving season, Western loans were far less significant in the total portfolio of the banks than has commonly been supposed.

Table Four
Regional Distribution of Deposits Within the Bank of Nova Scotia*

	1892-6 (%)	1902-06 (%)	1912-16 (%)	1922-6 (%)
British Columbia	-	0.0	2.2	2.8
Alberta	-	0.6	2.2	1.4
Saskatchewan	-	0.0	1.3	1.9
Manitoba	-	1.9	2.3	3.4
Ontario	-	7.8	23.7	41.0
Quebec	3.5	4.7	4.9	5.9
New Brunswick	17.2	20.5	20.1	12.0
Nova Scotia	64.7	42.2	19.6	11.3
Prince Edward Island	7.4	7.0	4.3	2.1
Newfoundland	2.7	4.2	6.0	5.2
Jamaica	2.2	4.9	8.9	6.2
Hispanic Caribbean	-	0.1	2.4	4.9
U.S./U.K.	2.3	6.0	2.1	1.9
Total ($)	6,433,400	21,103,600	62,287,000	174,578,400

Table Five
Regional Distribution of Loans Within the Bank of Nova Scotia*

	1892-6 (%)	1902-06 (%)	1912-16 (%)	1922-6 (%)
British Columbia	-	0.1	3.1	3.7
Alberta	-	0.6	3.0	1.2
Saskatchewan	-	0.0	1.9	2.0
Manitoba	-	1.3	5.6	6.1
Ontario	-	22.3	28.3	37.0
Quebec	10.6	11.0	10.5	10.8
New Brunswick	12.3	12.4	15.5	9.6
Nova Scotia	44.4	17.7	11.0	6.0
Prince Edward Island	4.4	3.9	1.5	1.5
Newfoundland	1.5	5.8	4.6	2.7
Jamaica	1.0	1.1	2.3	1.4
Hispanic Caribbean	-	0.4	3.4	6.5
U.S./U.K.	25.8	23.4	9.5	11.5
Total ($)	9,623,800	19,172,400	58,389,800	129,587,800

* = averages for five-year periods
Source: Quigley, ''Bank Credit', ch. 6.'

Tables Four to Seven demonstrate that the extension of the business of the BNS and the RBC into Ontario must be interpreted as an extension of the deposit base, as well as the search for an outlet for surplus funds. In fact, the importance of the deposit base provided by Ontario branches to these two banks suggests that, for the banking system as a whole, the generally held view about the Maritimes as the predominant region of net "saving" in Canada in the late 19th and early 20th centuries requires considerable qualification. In 1890 there were many more branches of the Canadian chartered banks in Ontario than in Prince Edward Island, New Brunswick and Nova Scotia combined, and by 1914 there were more than five times as many branches in Ontario than in the Maritimes. Even by 1901, 50 per cent of the bank branches in Nova Scotia were controlled by banks whose operations were confined entirely to the Maritimes, and within these branch networks we would expect deposits and loans to be nearly balanced. And all of the major national banks that had emerged by 1930 had large branch networks in Ontario and Quebec.

These findings also cast some doubt on the proposition that it was "saving" in the Maritimes that underwrote bank loans in the West. In 1901 the BNS had only one western branch, in Winnipeg, and the RBC had none. Only the Union Bank of Halifax, the Bank of Montreal and the Bank of British North America had branch structures which could have facilitated the transfer of funds from the Maritimes to Manitoba, Saskatchewan and Alberta, and none of these had a large network of deposit-collecting branches in the Maritimes. All of the other banks with branch networks in the West in 1900 were based in Ontario and Quebec. It should therefore not be surprising that the BNS and the RBC established large deposit bases in Ontario at the same time that they expanded into the West. For the banking system as a whole, even in 1900, any surplus payments made from Western branches appear to have been more likely balanced by excess deposits at branches in Ontario than branches in the Maritimes.

To examine the extent to which the net regional balance of deposits or loans varied from that for the banks as a whole, the raw figures obtained by subtracting the value of aggregate deposits and loans in each province or region were adjusted for the implicit reserve ratio for each bank and period indicated by the figures for loans to deposits given in Tables Four to Seven.[27] Figure 2 demonstrates that between the years 1892 and 1906, branches of the BNS in the U.S., Quebec and (after 1897) Ontario made net loans in excess of deposits, while in the Maritimes, Jamaica and Newfoundland (in the 1890s) deposits were in excess of loans. In the period 1912-16, branches in the West and British Columbia had loans in excess of deposits by more than the average for the bank as a whole, but only in Manitoba was the volume of funds com-

---

27 The implicit reserve ratio is calculated as (deposits — loans)/deposits for the bank as a whole.

Table Six
Regional Distribution of Deposits Within the Royal Bank of Canada*

	1921-5 (%)	1926-30 (%)	1931-5 (%)
British Columbia	7.4	8.0	7.4
Alberta	3.6	4.5	3.8
Saskatchewan	5.3	6.7	4.7
Manitoba	4.9	5.1	5.0
Ontario	24.9	23.8	27.7
Quebec	14.1	16.6	18.1
New Brunswick	2.9	2.6	2.7
Nova Scotia	7.3	6.2	6.9
Prince Edward Island	0.6	0.5	0.5
Newfoundland	1.0	0.9	1.2
Jamaica	0.7	0.5	0.7
Caribbean*a*	17.4	14.3	11.5
U.S./U.K.	9.9	10.3	9.8
Total ($)	442,174,000	592,376,000	509,457,000

Table Seven
Regional Distribution of Loans Within the Royal Bank of Canada*

	1921-5 (%)	1926-30 (%)	1931-5 (%)
British Columbia	3.8	5.1	4.5
Alberta	4.0	3.8	4.3
Saskatchewan	6.1	3.9	6.4
Manitoba	5.5	3.6	2.5
Ontario	16.3	17.5	20.0
Quebec	14.1	23.1	30.9
New Brunswick	3.9	3.3	4.4
Nova Scotia	5.6	4.0	5.8
Prince Edward Island	0.4	0.3	0.5
Newfoundland	0.6	0.4	0.6
Jamaica	0.7	0.3	0.4
Caribbean*a*	25.4	15.2	7.8
U.S./U.K.	13.6	19.5	11.9
Total ($)	330,974,000	479,338,000	355,024,000

* = averages for five-year periods
a = Caribbean excluding Jamaica
Source: Quigley, "Bank Credit", ch. 6.

parable with that in Ontario and Quebec (Figure 3). By 1922-6 the most notable change in this pattern was that with the acquisition of the business of the Bank of Ottawa, Ontario had a substantially higher proportion of deposits than in the bank as a whole. In addition, branches in Saskatchewan and Alberta both had a ratio of loans to deposits near the average for the Bank as a whole in 1922-6. In both 1912-16 and 1922-6 branches in the Hispanic Caribbean had net loans in excess of the overall ratio, while Jamaica continued to have a very large excess of deposits over loans.

In 1921-5 branches of the RBC in British Columbia, Ontario and Nova Scotia had the highest ratio of deposits to loans in that bank's network, and Ontario retained the position as the province with the greatest excess of deposits over the average for the bank as a whole throughout the period 1921-35 (Figure 4). In New Brunswick, loans made by the RBC exceeded deposits in 1921-5 and 1931-5 when adjusted by the implicit reserve ratio for the bank as a whole, and that was also true for Saskatchewan and Alberta. By 1931-5 the ratio of loans to deposits in the Caribbean (excluding Jamaica) and Europe and the U.S. was less than that for the RBC as a whole, although quite the reverse had been true in the two earlier periods. Fluctuations in the net position of the Western Provinces indicate the importance of the quantity of wheat produced and its price in determining the level of deposits with the banking system. In addition, Figure 4 demonstrates the significance of the increase in loans placed in Quebec after the mid-1920s for the operations of the RBC: by 1931-5 Quebec had the largest net excess of loans over deposits amongst all provinces/regions in which the bank operated.

The major difficulty with aggregate regional analysis such as that conducted in the previous section is that it provides no information at the level of the individual branch. To assess spatial variations in the pattern of net branch deposit and loan balances for the period as a whole, Figures 5 and 6 present pooled results for individual branches in different time periods. The excess of loans or deposits at each branch of the BNS in each year from 1902 to 1926 was calculated (with excess loans as positive numbers and excess deposits as negatives), and the median value for a series of five-year periods, 1902-06, 1907-11, 1912-16, 1917-21, and 1922-6, was obtained. This procedure was repeated for data from the RBC, producing for each branch a median value for the excess of deposits or loans for each of the three periods 1921-5, 1926-30, and 1931-5.[28] Thus for the BNS, each branch contributed up to five branch/period median observations of excess loans or deposits, and for the RBC each branch contributed up to three branch period observations, to the total for each province/region. The data were portrayed graphically (with excess deposits shown as negative values) in a form that indicates the range of observations for the province/region as a whole using the vertical distance of

---

28 Since the implicit reserve ratio was different for each five-year period, Figures 5 and 6 utilize unadjusted data.

The Bank of Nova Scotia, Net Regional Balances of Branch Deposits and Loans
Adjusted for the Implicit Reserve Ratio for the Bank as a Whole
(averages for five-year periods)

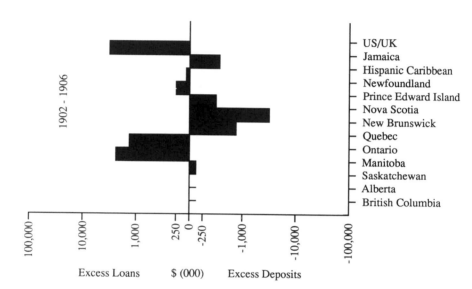

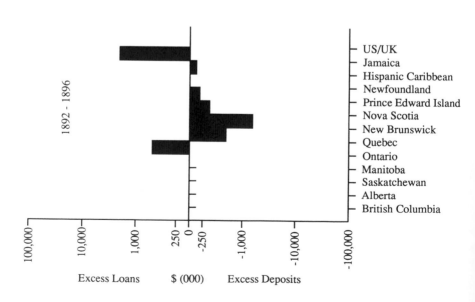

the lines of two different widths to indicate the 50 per cent and 98 per cent ranges of the observations.

The results portrayed in Figures 5 and 6 indicate that at the broadest level, the branch network in each province or region displays a hierarchical structure akin to that for each of the banks as a whole. While the majority of the branches in each province or region had excess deposits, there was also a small number of branches providing credit in excess of local deposits. And of those branches with excess loans, only a very small proportion allocated large amounts of funds (more than $1 million) in excess of local deposits. This we may take as the most fundamental aspect of the regional structure of net branch receipts and payments facilitated by the banking system: within each region as well as in the system as a whole, there was a very large range of net excess deposit and net excess loan positions, but only at a small number of branches did the effective demand from credit-worthy borrowers exceed local deposits by a very large amount.

Within each of the two banks, and within different provinces and regions, there were, of course, important variations. In the BNS more than 75 per cent of the branch/period observations in each province or region fell within the zone of excess deposits, with the exception of Manitoba, the Hispanic Caribbean and Saskatchewan (Figure 5). The pattern in Manitoba reflects the importance of the business of the bank in Winnipeg and the small number of branches in other parts of that province. The observations in the Hispanic Caribbean are in line with evidence that the BNS became established in that region to finance trade between the U.S. and the Caribbean, and except in Cuba after 1920, concentrated its branches in centres where there were opportunities to make commercial loans without constructing a substantial network of deposit-collecting branches.

In both Alberta and Saskatchewan the range of net balances at branches was very small. This might indicate that the lending business of the bank in those two provinces was more evenly spread among the branches, but given earlier evidence cited about the attitude of the BNS to the West, it probably reflects the fact that even in the major centres of these two provinces the bank did not do a large lending business, as well as the difficulties of building up a large deposit-collecting business at branches in that region (Figure 5). The operations of the BNS in both Jamaica and Prince Edward Island were heavily biased towards a net surplus of deposits. This is most noticeable in Jamaica, where the bank had branches at which deposits exceeded loans by up to $6 million on average.

Data for the RBC demonstrate the significance of its greater and (through the banks that it absorbed) longer presence in Western Canada, since there were branches with substantial amounts of both net excess deposits and net excess loans (Figure 6). Nonetheless, compared to the structure of the branch networks of the RBC in Manitoba, Ontario, Quebec, New Brunswick and

Figure 3

The Bank of Nova Scotia, Net Regional Balances of Branch Deposits and Loans
Adjusted for the Implicit Reserve Ratio for the Bank as a Whole
(averages for five-year periods)

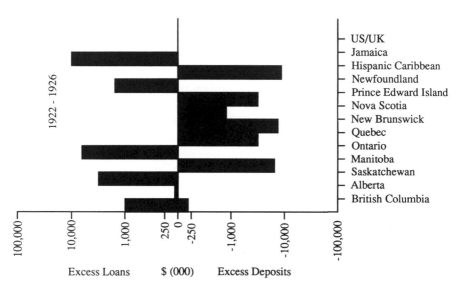

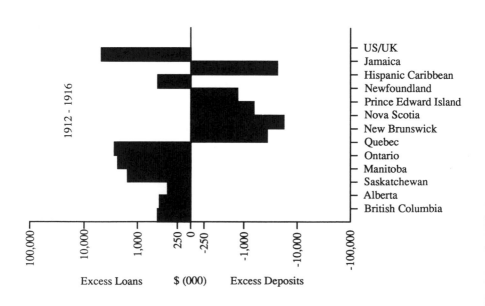

Figure 4

The Royal Bank of Canada, Net Regional Balances of Branch Deposits and Loans
Adjusted for the Implicit Reserve Ratio for the Bank as a Whole
(averages for five-year periods)

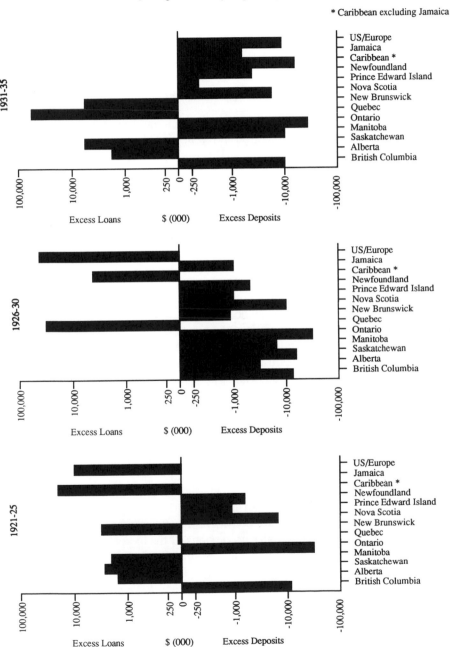

Nova Scotia, the range was small. This might be taken as evidence of relatively large amounts of loans being made at branches in farming communities, but
it should still be stressed that branch deposits exceeded branch loans for 75
per cent of the observations in Saskatchewan and 65 per cent in Alberta. In the
Caribbean outside Jamaica the range of net excess deposits and loans was very
large, demonstrating that the RBC also made large volumes of loans in the
major trading centres of that region, but that it also had (especially in Cuba) a
substantial network of branches where deposits exceeded loans. In Prince Edward Island, but particularly in Newfoundland and British Columbia, a very
high proportion of the branches of the RBC had excess deposits and there
were few centres where large amounts of loans were made above the level of
branch deposits.

These data suggest that the emphasis which has been placed by previous
authors on regional discrimination in the allocatory policies of the banks is
misplaced. In Nova Scotia and New Brunswick the branch networks of both
banks were structured in a pattern which conformed closely to that in Ontario,
Quebec and Manitoba — there were many branches where deposits exceeded
loans and a small number of branches with (often very large) net loan balances. Only in Saskatchewan and Alberta (the region to which funds were
supposedly "drained" from the Maritimes) and in Prince Edward Island were
the branch structures significantly different, and for the former two provinces
the high median values indicate that, in part at least, lending was simply more
widely dispersed, or the demand for monetary assets was lower than in the
other provinces.

This means that in those provinces/regions where loans exceeded deposits
overall, the net balance was primarily a function of the degree to which a
small proportion of the branches made very large amounts of loans in excess
of local deposits. This was true for both banks in each period, and applied
even in Alberta and Saskatchewan, where there were comparatively fewer
centres with large amounts of excess loans. Thus, the data suggest that a
simple hypothesis about regional discrimination is difficult to sustain, unless it
can accommodate the existence of branches with net excess loans in regions
where the aggregate position is an excess of deposits, though investigation of
the extent of hierarchical discrimination seems a worthy subject for further research.

Any formal examination of the hypothesis that the regional pattern of bank
deposits and loans resulted from discrimination in bank credit allocation
policies must begin with careful consideration of the precise specification of
the proposition to be tested. Extreme versions of the hypothesis would suggest
that the banks did not make loans at certain Maritime branches, or did not
make loans to some or all manufacturing firms in the Maritimes. Evidence
presented in this paper clearly establishes a *prima facie* case against this version of the hypothesis because of the existence of Maritime branches with net

Figure 5

The Bank of Nova Scotia, Branch Excess Deposits or Loans
(Branch Medians for five-year periods 1902 - 1926)

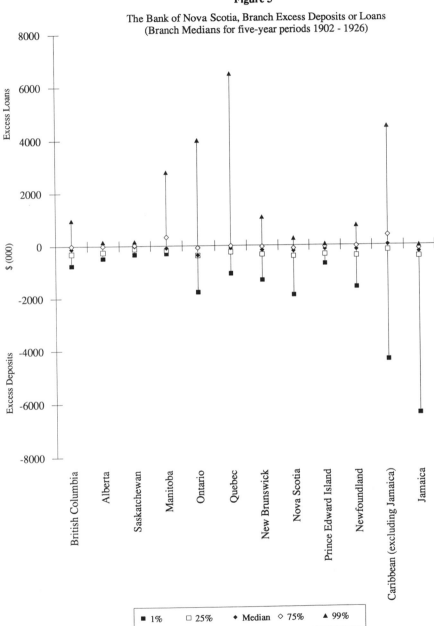

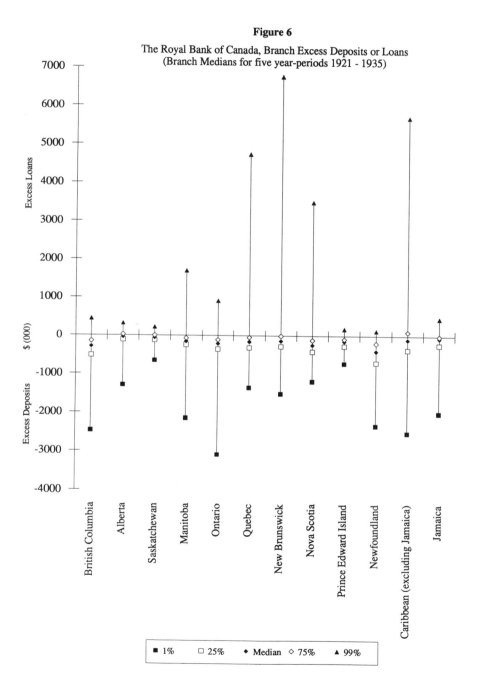

Figure 6

The Royal Bank of Canada, Branch Excess Deposits or Loans
(Branch Medians for five year-periods 1921 - 1935)

loans. However, any definitive test of discrimination that takes the form of exclusion from the credit market requires data on the *ex ante* demand for credit, and this will never be available: any absolute refusal to grant credit would normally be communicated by the branch manager before a formal written application was processed and (if necessary) sent for approval to the regional head office. Consequently, it is not possible to test the hypothesis that worthy applications for credit were refused by the banks on the basis of discrimination.

Our inability to measure the *ex ante* demand for credit assumes much less importance if we attempt to test the more sophisticated version of the discrimination hypothesis that Maritime and industrial firms were systematically provided with less credit than other firms. In our view there is no reason to assume that discrimination only occurs through exclusion from the bank loan market. If there were participants in the credit market who were disadvantaged or the object of systematic discrimination, we would expect that some would be refused credit and that others who actually obtain credit would receive smaller loans (judged against some surrogate measure of legitimate demand for credit such as capital size) than the groups against whom no discrimination was practised. Discrimination may therefore be defined as a significant difference in the size of loans obtained by firms of particular types or in particular locations, and evidence of larger or smaller loans in the Maritimes will suggest whether a prima facie case for the presence of discrimination against borrowers in this region can be established.

In a recent paper Lewis Evans and Neil Quigley[29] used a sample of 460 individual customer loans larger than $25,000 obtained from correspondence of the general manager as a basis for a regression analysis of the hypothesis that Maritime and industrial firms received less credit than firms of other types and in other locations. The sample includes 227 manufacturing firms, 20 per cent of which were primary processing, 152 firms located in the Maritimes and 227 firms in Ontario and Quebec. The results of this analysis provides estimates of the loans obtained by different types of firms in different locations, allowing for the influence of capital size (which is used as the basis for determining legitimate demands for credit).[30] In Table Eight the regression results reported in this paper are expressed as percentages of the loans obtained by observa-

---

29 The discussion and analysis that follows is a summary and reinterpretation of Evans and Quigley, "Discrimination in Bank Lending Practice".

30 The inclusion of a large number of dummy variables means that the estimated model is different for each significant dummy entered into the analysis. For this reason, the general comparisons of loan size in different regions are made for firms other than grain elevators, primary processing and small manufacturing firms, these being the sectoral dummies that generated coefficients significantly different from the model.

tionally equivalent firms in the Maritimes.[31] Table Eight indicates that small firms in Ontario received loans that were only 18 per cent larger than those in the Maritimes, while small firms in Western Canada received loans 12 per cent smaller than in the Maritimes. We do not believe that these differences are significant. Only in Montreal, and for non-manufacturing firms, was the size of loans granted significantly different from that in the Maritimes, and we cannot interpret this as evidence of discrimination against borrowers in the Maritimes unless we are prepared to argue that there was also discrimination against borrowers in Ontario and Toronto.

The finding that loans to large firms in the Maritimes were more than twice as large as loans to identical firms in Ontario or the West is not at variance with the declining relative performance of industrial firms in the Maritimes during the early 20th century, and may in fact be indicative of it. For example, the decline may result from Maritime firms being less able or willing to enter the long-term capital market, which in turn might result from their being less profitable and successful than firms in other regions. The BNS's traditional ties to, and strong market position in, this region may also be important. But whatever the explanation, the finding is contradictory of a suggestion that the relative industrial decline of the Maritimes resulted from banks such as the BNS restricting the availability of credit in the region. Moreover, because the loans made to Western Canadian firms were virtually the same as, or slightly smaller than, those in Ontario our results cannot be interpreted as supporting a hypothesis about the banks using credit to finance Western expansion at the expense of other regions of the country.

We have argued that the general suggestions in the literature about the role of the banking system in the relative industrial decline of the Maritimes are at best highly misleading. First, deposit and loan data collected from banks provide no information about the efficiency of bank activities or about the existence of discrimination. The data analysed in this paper do, however, tell us that the individual branch structure of lending operations was strongly hierarchical in all regions, and that in this respect there appears to have been no difference between the organization of Maritime branches and those in other regions. Second, we have introduced several important qualifications relevant to discussions about transfers of funds out of the Maritimes. It seems likely that Ontario was more important than the Maritimes as a source of surplus deposits for the banking system, but in terms of both the banking and savings bank systems there is little doubt that the Maritimes had net claims on the financial system in this period, or that through a variety of channels sig-

---

31 Because the model is nonlinear in its variables, sensible comparisons of the loans granted to subpopulations of firms can only be made at a given capital size. Given the range over which the capital of the large firms in the sample varies, we have provided comparisons for large firms evaluated at both the average capital size for all firms in addition to the average capital size for large firms.

Table Eight
The Value of Loans Made to Individual Firms by the Bank of Nova Scotia as a Proportion of Loans Made to Individual Firms in the Maritimes[a]

Location	Small Firms[b]	All Firms[c]	Large Firms[c]
Quebec (incl. Montreal)[d]	100%	100%	100%
Montreal[d]	191%	100%	100%
Ontario (incl. Toronto)[d]	118%	40%	33%
Toronto[d]	118%	40%	33%
Western Canada[d]	88%	45%	38%
West. Can. grain elevators	162%	291%	312%
All manufacturing firms[e]	85%	100%	100%
Manuf. firms, Montreal	100%	100%	100%

a = Sample of 460 loans of more than $25,000 made between 1900 and 1937. Values are estimated from a regression of loan size on capital, year and regional/sectoral dummy variables (see Evans and Quigley, "Discrimination in Bank Lending Practice"). Size of Maritime loans is determined at the average capital size for the relevant size subpopulation.

b = Small firms are here defined as those with a capital size of less than $63,000. The average capital size of this sample was $38,930.

c = Because of the sensitivity of the model to significant variations in capital size, we report results for all firms in the sample (average capital size $312,550) and for the large firms in the sample (average capital size $544,410).

d = Includes all firms except grain elevators, primary processing and small manufacturing.

e = Does not include primary processing.

Source: Calculated from Evans and Quigley, "Discrimination in Bank Lending Practice".

nificant amounts of funds from the Maritimes found higher returns outside the region than were available locally. Taking into account the increase in the return to Maritime depositors and shareholders that resulted, we see no reason to assume that the net effect on the wealth of the Maritimes was negative. Third, we have suggested that the available secondary evidence provides no support for the charges of discrimination levelled against the banks. The only systematic data on individual loans yet made available to researchers indicates that the BNS treated its established Maritime customers with a generosity more readily characterized as shoring up the declining Maritime economy than promoting its demise.

Cutting the Pie into Smaller Pieces: Matching Grants and Relief in the Maritime Provinces During the 1930s

Ernest R. Forbes

The Maritimes in the 1930s was for many a grim place to live. The documents give a picture of an often repressive society in which governments were slow to try to bridge the gap between the comfortable and the desperately poor. The three provinces were among the last to adopt such social programmes as old age pensions and mothers' allowances and they were on record as opposing unemployment insurance. They were the meanest of all the provinces in their aid for the unemployed. All levels of government attempted to avoid responsibility for relief, sometimes at the expense of the health and lives of their citizens. The record abounds with examples of elderly and destitute refused assistance, deaf and blind cut off from their schools, seriously ill denied hospitalization, and moral offenders savagely punished.

Maritime governments were unique neither in the nature of their problems nor in their responses to them; they shared in the broad ideological currents of the day.[1] If their attitude towards those in need seemed harsher than governments in other provinces, it was primarily because of their more limited economic resources and their inability to participate effectively in the federal government's relief programmes. The matching grant formulas in the federal programmes would have been fair, if all the provinces had possessed equal wealth. But since their resources varied dramatically, the poorer provinces' had either to commit a much greater percentage of their funds to a given

---

This essay was presented to an Atlantic Canada Studies Conference in 1985 and appeared in *Acadiensis*, XVII, 1 (Autumn 1987). The research for this paper was funded by the Social Sciences and Humanities Research Council of Canada. The author is particularly indebted to Murray Young, Eric Sager and Robert Young for advice and criticism and to Carol Ferguson for research assistance in newspapers.

1   For general perspectives on relief policy see James Struthers, *No Fault of Their Own: Unemployment and the Welfare State 1914-41* (Toronto, 1983); J.H. Thompson with Allen Seager, *Canada, 1922-1939: Decades of Discord* (Toronto, 1985); Christopher Armstrong, *The Politics of Federalism: Ontario's Relations with the Federal Government, 1867-1942* (Toronto, 1981); L.M. Grayson and Michael Bliss, eds., *The Wretched of Canada: Letters to R.B. Bennett* (Toronto, 1971); Michiel Horn, ed., *The Dirty Thirties: Canadians in the Great Depression* (Toronto, 1972); and John Taylor, "Relief from Relief: The Cities' Answer to Depression Dependency", *Journal of Canadian Studies*, XIV, 1 (Spring 1979), pp. 16-23.

programme or to deny to their citizens the benefits conspicuously available elsewhere.[2] In discouraging the expansion of relief programmes at federal-provincial conferences, Maritime governments were expressing the frustration and political embarrassment which the inequities of the relief structure created for them. As the political pressure mounted locally for greater participation in federal relief programmes, they became more adept in cutting their meagre share of the pie into smaller pieces.

This problem was compounded by the poorer provinces' inability to alleviate economic disparity among the municipalities within their borders. As the percentage of uncollected taxes mounted and the proportion of future budgets committed to servicing the municipal debt increased, ratepayers' representatives became increasingly mean in their definition of relief need. With revenues dwindling and debt service charges mushrooming, provincial governments could only urge further restraint. Thus, residents in the poorest municipalities in the poorest provinces became the victims of a process which at two stages reduced the assistance which should have come their way.

The statistics show just how little the Maritimes obtained from the federal relief programmes. Of the total of $463,667,018 which the central government distributed among the provinces from 1930 to 1939, residents of the Maritimes received only $15,151,475 or 3.3 per cent. Calculated on a per capita basis, this works out to just over a third or 33.5 per cent of the national average. If one includes federal relief loans to the provinces of $175,839,121, the Maritimes' share drops to less than a quarter or 23.7 per cent.[3] The disparity in federal funding was also reflected in the smaller amount actually paid the recipients of direct relief. In the winter months, from January to May 1935, for example, the three levels of government spent an average of $2.84 for each relief recipient in the Maritimes, an amount less than one half of the $6.18 spent in the remaining six provinces.[4]

---

2   For surveys of matching grant programmes in Canada see D.V. Smiley, *Conditional Grants and Canadian Federalism* (Toronto, 1963), pp. 1-6 and J.A. Maxwell, *Federal Subsidies to Provincial Governments in Canada* (Cambridge, 1937), part II.

3   Calculated from Department of Finance, "A Summary of Net Loans to Western Provinces under Relief Legislation by Fiscal Years" and "Dominion Relief Expenditures Since September 1930", 13 June 1940, J.L. Ralston Papers, MG27 111, vol. 50, file "Loans to Provinces Gen. (Secret)", Public Archives of Canada [PAC].

4   The monthly rates for those receiving relief in the individual provinces were P.E.I., $1.93; N.S., $4.38; N.B., $1.67; P.Q., $5.40; Ont., $8.07; Man., $6.58; Sask., $3.58; Alb., $6.49; B.C., $6.96. Calculated from J.K. Houston, "An Appreciation of Relief as Related to Economic and Employment Tendencies in Canada", 31 October 1936, Department of Labour Papers, RG27, vol. 2096, file Y 40, PAC.

The contemporary explanation for the discrepancy was the apparent difference in need. The Maritimes required less because they suffered less severely from the Depression. This myth was widely accepted at the time and has persisted in the literature from the period. The myth was partly created by defenders of the region. In the late 1920s politicians, board of trade leaders, and newspapermen embarked upon a campaign to counter the negative image of their economy projected by the earlier Maritimes Rights propaganda and to attract investment in a period of economic expansion.[5] When their tactics appeared to pay dividends in new investment in pulp and paper and in tourist facilities, Maritime leaders met renewed depression by increasing the urgency of their campaign. No group of evangelists could have more zealously proclaimed the message of imminent salvation or more vigorously denounced the sin of unbelief. The Halifax *Herald* greeted the new year of 1930 with a list of reasons for regional optimism and exhorted all Maritimers to keep their faith. The Moncton *Times* stated flatly that "business and labour conditions are better in the Maritimes than in any other part of the country". The Kings County *Record* printed an open letter from the editor of *MacLean's Magazine* congratulating the Maritime people on their new-found prosperity and urging them to maintain their positive approach; "1930 will be what sound thinking makes it". The *Record* itself went on to explain why local industries would not be "retarded by any temporary depression" and in 1931 offered an editorial analyzing the "happy situation in which the Maritimes find themselves". The Ottawa *Journal*, the *Telegraph Journal* noted in the spring of 1930, had stated that "while the rest of us have all become querulous and pessimistic the Maritimes have all become optimists". The Vancouver *Sun* attributed the transformation to the Duncan Report which "has changed the Maritimes from a section of despondency and decadence into a live section of optimism and growth" and hailed the regional defenders as "economic statesmen". By 1932, when the orchestrated optimism of regional leaders had begun to peter out, the impression remained throughout the country that the Maritimes was somehow better off.[6]

The statistics of the period do not support the myth that the Maritimes suffered less from the Depression than did the rest of Canada. Indeed, it was often contradicted in the data compiled for the Rowell-Sirois Commission. But the commission scholars did not confront the myth head on and at times seemed to encourage it. S.A. Saunders, for example, gave the decline in per

---

5   E.R. Forbes, *The Maritime Rights Movement, 1919-1927: A Study in Canadian Regionalism* (Montreal 1979), p. 180.

6   Halifax, *Herald*, 3, 6, 7 January 1930; Moncton *Times*, 2 June 1930; Kings County *Record*, 3 January 1930 and 2 January 1931; Saint John *Telegraph-Journal*, 14 April 1930. See also K.G. Jones, "Response to Regional Disparity in the Maritime Provinces, 1926-1942: A Study of Canadian Intergovernmental Relations", M.A. thesis, University of New Brunswick, 1980, pp. 45-47.

capita income in the Maritimes in the first three years of the Depression as four to five percentage points smaller than in Ontario and Quebec and far behind that of the West.[7] But if one considers the actual figures instead of percentages, which were skewed by the region's incomplete recovery from the recession of the early 1920s, the Maritimes' per capita personal income of $185 in 1933 was only marginally above the Prairies' $181 and very substantially below the Canadian average of $262.[8] The impact of the Depression was more directly indicated by the only complete employment survey of the period. The 1931 Census reported 19 per cent of regular wage-earners not working in the Maritimes on 1 June 1931 compared with 16.6 per cent for Ontario, 16.9 per cent for Quebec and 18.4 per cent for the country as a whole. Only in the devastated West were the numbers higher, ranging from 19.9 per cent in Saskatchewan to 24.7 in British Columbia.[9] Of course, more Maritimers did live in rural areas (62.2 per cent compared with a national average of 47 per cent), where fuel and shelter tended to be cheaper. But the discrepancy in relief granted remains even when one compares urban communities of similar size. A report of relief in ten cities with populations of less than a 100,000, compiled by the Welfare Council of Canada in 1935, showed the average monthly cost per relief recipient for the three Maritime cities, Halifax, Saint John and Sydney, to be $3.77. The average for the other seven was $9.47.[10] The lower cost of living can not explain the discrepancy, since in 1930 the Department of Labour reported that the average weekly cost of food,

---

7   S.A. Saunders, *The Economic History of the Maritime Provinces* (Fredericton 1984), pp. 49-51 and *Report of the Royal Commission on Dominion-Provincial Relations*, (Ottawa 1940), p. 150; W.A. Mackintosh, *The Economic Background of Dominion-Provincial Relations* (Ottawa 1939), pp. 70-1.

8   Dominion Bureau of Statistics, *National Accounts Income and Expenditure 1926-1956* (Ottawa 1958), p. 64.

9   The other provincial figures were Manitoba, 21.4 and Alberta, 21.6. Calculated from *Canada Year Book 1933* (Ottawa, 1933), p. 778.

10   The other cities ranged from a high of $11.47 in Calgary to a low outside the Maritimes of $5.78 in Hull. Calculated from "Relief Trend Report No. 2", Papers of the Canadian Council on Social Development (Before 1935 this was the Canadian Council on Child and Family Welfare), MG28, I10, vol. 125, file 1935-37, PAC. The Halifax entry was compiled from "The Direct Relief Report...Nova Scotia", January 1935, RG27, vol. 2096, file Y 40-0 "Nova Scotia Statistics", PAC. This is not to suggest that amounts paid elsewhere for relief were excessive. Indeed, studies of relief in Ottawa and Montreal argue the contrary. See Judith Roberts-Moore, "Maximum Relief for Minimum Costs: Coping With Unemployment and Relief in Ottawa During the Depression, 1929-1939", M.A. thesis, University of Ottawa, 1980; June MacPherson, "'Brother Can You Spare a Dime?', The Administration of Unemployment Relief in the City of Montreal, 1931-1941", M.A. thesis, Concordia University, 1976.

light, heat and rent in the Maritimes was just 7.4 per cent below the national average.[11] Nor does James Struthers' theory of "less eligibility", *i.e.* the perceived need to keep relief low enough to prevent it from competing with local wages, in itself account for such large gaps in relief levels. New Brunswick's average wage of $3.82 per person per day was 30 per cent below the national average of $5.47, but Nova Scotia's $5.62 was marginally above it.[12] If total relief costs in the Maritimes were reduced by lower wages and cheaper living expenses, they were also raised by the inclusion of destitute elderly and single mothers, who in Ontario and the West were treated separately under old age pension and mothers' allowances programmes.[13]

The striking disparity between the Maritimes and the other regions is explained in large part by the inability of the Maritimes to participate in the federal matching grants on which the relief programmes were based. The process of metropolitan consolidation which led to the concentration of manufacturing, wholesaling and financial institutions in southern Ontario and Quebec also hived much of the taxable resources of the nation within the two central provinces.[14] Ontario and Quebec were the only provinces readily able to match large federal grants for relief. The western provinces were in a weaker position — their need greater, their finances impaired by the Depression and their credit limited by past borrowing and reputations for less than financial orthodoxy. But what the westerners did retain was the confidence that however severe the existing Depression, their ultimate growth was assured. They also believed that, with their increased population and political influence, they would eventually be able to redress injustices in the federal system which discriminated against them. Their problem was to obtain the money to deal with immediate relief needs. This they initially did by borrowing their share of the funds from the federal government in the form of relief loans and, as this source threatened to dry up, by developing a variety of ex-

---

11   The Maritime figure was $19.68 (P.E.I., $19.74; N.B., $19.87; N.S., $19.74) and the Canadian average $21.25. Calculated from Department of Labour, *Prices in Canada and Other Countries 1930* (Ottawa 1931), p. 7.

12   Department of Labour, *Wages and Hours of Labour in Canada 1929, 1934, and 1935* (Ottawa 1936), p. 93; Struthers, *No fault of their Own*, pp. 6-7.

13   Kenneth Bryden, *Old Age Pensions and Policy Making in Canada* (Montreal, 1974), p. 98 and Veronica Strong-Boag, "'Wages for Housework': Mothers' Allowances and the Beginning of Social Security in Canada", *Journal of Canadian Studies*, XIV, 1 (Spring 1979), pp. 24-33.

14   See L.D. McCann, "Metropolitanism and Branch Businesses in the Maritimes, 1881-1931", *Acadiensis*, XIII, 1 (Autumn 1983), pp. 112-25 and T.W. Acheson, "The Maritimes and 'Empire Canada'" in D. Bercuson, ed., *Canada and the Burden of Unity* (Toronto, 1977), pp. 87-114.

pedients to extort more.[15] The Maritimes, though no poorer in circumstances, were much poorer in future prospects. Without the West's option of borrowing against the expectations of future growth, they could only marginally participate in the shared cost relief programmes.

The inverse relationship between poverty or need and the participation in federal relief was also apparent within the Maritime region. New Brunswick's greater problems were reflected in a per capita income figure of $174 and an unemployment rate of 20 per cent compared with Nova Scotia's $202 and 19.6 per cent. Yet Nova Scotia received 15 per cent more on a per capita basis for relief purposes and an additional $3.2 million for their destitute elderly before New Brunswick joined the old age pension programme.[16] The gap appears more severe in the amounts actually given relief recipients. In 1934, for example, recipients in New Brunswick received an average of $2.27 per month compared with $3.72 for those in Nova Scotia or 39 per cent less, while Prince Edward Island whose per capita income was just $133 paid out an average of only $2.21 per recipient.[17]

The onset of the Depression found the three Maritime governments already struggling with problems arising from the matching grants formula. The old age pension scheme by which the federal government paid half the cost of $20 monthly pensions to the needy elderly posed a serious problem for Maritime governments. Already burdened with debt charges as a percentage of revenue far above the national average (26 per cent for Nova Scotia and 28 per cent for New Brunswick compared with 15 per cent for all provinces), they could ill afford a programme which might consume an additional 15 to 20 per cent of annual revenues.[18] Limited finances along with a disproportionate number of

---

15   As Minister of Finance Rhodes' correspondence with the western governments on relief was voluminous. See especially Memoranda dated 30 May and 13 July 1932, Rhodes Papers, MG2, pp. 47947 and 47134, Public Archives of Nova Scotia [PANS]. For British Columbia and Saskatchewan perspectives on relief administration see J.D. Belshaw, "The Administration of Relief to the Unemployed in Vancouver during the Great Depression", M.A. thesis, Simon Fraser University, 1982; Blair Neatby, "The Saskatchewan Relief Commission, 1931-34", in Donald Swainson, ed., *Historical Essays on the Prairie Provinces* (Toronto, 1970); P.H. Brennan, "Public Relief Works in Saskatchewan Cities, 1929-1940", M.A. thesis, University of Regina, 1981; Alma Lawton, "Urban Relief in Saskatchewan during the Years of the Depression, 1930-1939", M.A. thesis, University of Saskatchewan (Saskatoon), 1969.

16   See footnotes 3 and 9 above and W. Eggleston and C.T. Kraft, *Dominion-Provincial Subsidies and Grants* (Ottawa 1939), pp. 104 and 115.

17   P.E.I.'s unemployment rate was 6.8 per cent in 1931.

18   Royal Commission on Dominion-Provincial Relations, Public Accounts Inquiry, *Dominion of Canada...and Provincial Governments: Comparative Statistics of Public Finance* (Ottawa 1939), p. 95; *Final Report of the Commission Appointed to Consider Old Age Pensions* [Fredericton 1930] in New Brunswick Cabinet

potentially eligible aged seemed to put the pension scheme out of reach. Yet the pressure on the governments to establish pensions mounted as national funds were directed to the elderly in Ontario and the four western provinces while denied to those in the Maritimes. The failure to provide old age pensions was a factor in the discontent which almost defeated the Conservative government of E.N. Rhodes in the Nova Scotia election of 1928.[19] In the late 1920s elderly Maritimers sent their often pathetic letters to federal politicians requesting assistance from the national pension scheme, but the latter disclaimed any responsibility and referred them to provincial governments. In the federal election of 1930 Mackenzie King claimed that pensions were a provincial responsibility; the problem was constitutional. Campaigning in the Maritimes, R.B. Bennett gave the constitutional argument short shrift: "I will see to it that old age pensions are paid to every province.... it is a national obligation.... If the Dominion can pay fifty per cent of the Old Age Pensions why cannot it pay 99 per cent?"[20]

After the federal election, the provincial spokesmen cited Bennett's statements as constituting a promise of a new pension scheme and urged the elderly to write to the federal government. As the months passed without any word on the pensions, individual and provincial appeals for federally-funded pensions became increasingly strident.[21] Finally, in the summer of 1931, the long-awaited announcement arrived. But it brought neither a federally administered scheme nor 99 per cent funding for those run by the provinces. The matching grant formula was still intact with the federal government's contribution raised to 75 per cent. For the Maritime provinces this change merely tantalized. Since their revenues were further impaired by the Depression,

---

Papers, RG.... RS29, 1930, Provincial Archives of New Brunswick [PANB]. Prince Edward Island's debt was relatively low at 10 per cent of revenues, but Premier A.C. Saunders estimated that pensions for 20 per cent of those 70 years of age or older would require "about 18% of the total revenue". A.C. Saunders to J.L. Ballon, 7 January 1930, Premier's Office Papers, Provincial Archives of Prince Edward Island [PAPEI]. H.E. Mahon in the "Interim Report of the Commission...to Consider Old Age Pensions" estimated the cost of the pensions in Nova Scotia at $2.2 million at a time when provincial revenues totaled just under $7 million. Appendix no. 31, *Journals of the House of Assembly*, 1929.

19 E.R. Forbes, "The Rise and Fall 1922-33 of the Conservative Party in the Provincial Politics of Nova Scotia", M.A. thesis, Dalhousie University, 1967, pp. 112-4 and 129-30.

20 Yarmouth *Light*, 3 July 1930 (clipping in Ralston Papers, vol. 15). See also E.N. Rhodes' speech in Moncton in the Moncton *Times*, 21 July 1930.

21 See File #13 "Old Age Pensions" in Nova Scotia Provincial Secretary-Treasurer's Papers, RG7, vol. 225, PANS. See J.A. Macdonald to J.S. Gallant, 18 October 1930, J.A. Macdonald Papers, PAPEI.

having to find even a quarter of the cost seemed to leave the pensions as far out of reach as ever.

Nonetheless, as the political pressure for old age pensions continued, the three provinces eventually found a way to introduce them. In 1933 Prince Edward Island led the way. After conversations with the federal bureaucracy, the Islanders decided that, if they could not raise their revenues sufficiently to participate in the federal programme, they could scale down the programme to fit their revenues. Moreover, smaller pensions would conform more closely to their other relief payments. The government set the maximum pension at $15 rather than $20 and developed a means test stricter than those employed in the other provinces. It passed legislation making it obligatory that children provide for their parents. The support of children was given an arbitrary value and added to the theoretical total capital wealth of the individual. This "capital" was assumed to yield an income of 5 per cent per year and if a person's income was calculated to be in excess of $125, the excess was subtracted from the pension. Of the approximately 6000 residents of 70 years or more on the Island, only 1200 were ruled eligible for any portion of the pension. Many of these were simply shifted from the direct relief rolls, for which the province paid 50 per cent or 33 1/3 per cent if they lived in Charlottetown, to the pension rolls for which the province paid just 25 per cent.[22]

It was an astute political move whose advantages were not lost on the Liberal oppositions in Nova Scotia and New Brunswick. In the former Angus L. Macdonald promised old age pensions in the election of 1933 and introduced them soon after taking office. In New Brunswick Allison Dysart made the government's failure to provide old age pensions an issue in the 1935 campaign and established them the next year. The provincial governments were careful to prevent the municipalities from taking advantage of money saved from the care of the elderly to expand relief services. A Nova Scotia spokesman at the Dominion-Provincial conference of 1935 told how the new government had intervened at the municipal level to place its own nominees on local relief committees and boasted that through "rigid administration" and "more stringent regulations" it had reduced the numbers on relief from about 50,000 to about 16,000.[23] In New Brunswick in 1936 Premier Dysart accompanied his pension scheme with an attempt to curb relief at the municipal level. The government persuaded the municipality of Gloucester, for example, to accept a system of relief quotas which reduced the allowance for those on relief to just $.70 a month.[24]

---

22 *Canadian Annual Review*, 1934, p. 268. See also Bryden, *Old Age Pensions and Policy Making in Canada*, pp. 84-97 and 101.

23 Minutes of the Dominion-Provincial Conference, 9 December 1935, Provincial Secretary-Treasurer's Papers, RG7, vol. 231, file 8, PANS.

24 "Report of the Direct Relief Committee", 31 December 1936, Minutes of the Municipal Council of Gloucester, RG18, RS149, PANB.

Moreover, neither province admitted that they were introducing pensions that paid substantially less than other provinces. In New Brunswick, government spokesmen obscured initial complaints with a discussion of means test regulations. Confronted with the opposition's charge that even "almshouse residents" did not receive more than $15, the government suggested that the pensions would rise once the programme became better established.[25] The federal report for 1936-37 listed the average monthly pension paid under the act as $10.58 in Prince Edward island, $13.39 in New Brunswick and $14.49 in Nova Scotia compared with an average of $18.24 in the other six provinces.[26]

The technical education programme was another which taxed the ingenuity of Maritime governments to participate and created additional political problems for them. Nova Scotia, which had pioneered technical education in Canada, had concentrated its expenditures at the university level. The federal act of 1919 was designed to encourage technical programmes in high schools. By 1929 Nova Scotia and Prince Edward Island governments had failed to obtain even half of the federal grant allotted to them.[27] New Brunswick participated more fully, channelling funds into vocational schools in Saint John, Woodstock and Sussex, only to be embarrassed by the federal government's decision to terminate the programme in 1929. Under intense pressure from the municipalities to take over the federal share of funding, New Brunswick urged the Bennett government to resume its contribution.[28] Although federal legislation was passed in 1931 to do so, it was not implemented. In 1930 H.P. Blanchard of Colchester County warned Premier Rhodes to consider carefully the perils of entering another federal programme lest the senior government "back out...and leave the whole 100% on the province as they did with the main highways, technical schools etc".[29]

Given these difficulties, it was not surprising that the three provinces greeted the federal relief programmes of the 1930s with something less than enthusiasm. As early as 1928 the three Maritime premiers voiced their exasperation in response to federal labour minister Peter Heenan's proposal for unemployment insurance. They simply could not, they argued, commit

---

25 *Synoptic Report of the Proceedings of the Legislative Assembly of New Brunswick,* 1937, pp. 23-5 and 1938, p. 8.

26 *Labour Gazette,* XXXVII, 5 (May 1937), p. 513.

27 Janet Guildford, "Coping with De-industrialization: The Nova Scotia Department of Technical Education, 1907-1930", *Acadiensis,* XVI, 2 (Spring 1987), p. 79; and Maxwell, *Federal Subsidies and Provincial Governments in Canada,* p. 211.

28 J.D. Palmer and W.K. Tibert to C.D. Richards, 8 December 1931 and C.D. Richards to F.M. Sclanders, 19 February 1932, NB Cabinet Papers, RG1, RS9, PANB.

29 H.P. Blanchard to E.N. Rhodes, Rhodes Papers, p. 40930, PANS.

provincial funds to a new programme when they were already unable to participate in existing programmes. Rhodes took pains to make clear that their quarrel was not with unemployment insurance, since they were "sympathetic to all modern measures of similar character". J.B.M. Baxter of New Brunswick noted both his province's inability to initiate pensions and the added burden of the "probable withdrawal...of assistance to technical education" in explaining why the proposed unemployment scheme was "utterly impossible" for a province "of such limited means".[30]

The new matching grants programmes of the 1930s again promised to increase the strain on provincial finances, they offered no guarantee of permanency, and they threatened to awaken expectations among municipalities and individuals for a degree of provincial participation which these provinces could not afford. The three provincial governments therefore tried to keep their participation in relief programmes to a minimum. They sought to portray their role as essentially that of intermediaries between the municipalities, who were responsible for relief, and the federal government, which wished to come to their aid. Nova Scotia warned its local governments of the limited nature of its commitment which would end with the termination of federal funds.[31] New Brunswick went further, scaling down the requests for assistance from the municipalities and cutting off its contribution in the summer months.[32] At the Dominion-Provincial conferences Maritime representatives spoke out against further extensions of relief programmes, criticized the other provinces for their extravagance and emphasized the primary responsibility of the municipalities for relief.[33]

The three provinces found more attractive the relief proposals involving highway construction — particularly the trans-Canada highway projects for which the senior government initially paid half of the cost. These offered political patronage, much-needed employment, and progress towards realizing the provinces' strong aspirations for a tourist industry. Indeed, they suggested

---

30 Copies of the three letters, E.N. Rhodes, J.B.M. Baxter and Saunders to Peter Heenan, dated 3 August 1928, are in Rhodes Papers, p. 47338, PANS.

31 Circular letter from R. Gordon to the Nova Scotia municipalities, 21 April 1931, Provincial Secretary-Treasurer's Papers, RG7, vol. 225, file 12, PANS.

32 C.A. Ferguson, "Responses to the Unemployment Problem in Saint John, New Brunswick, 1929-1933", M.A. thesis, University of New Brunswick, 1984, pp. 109-13 and D.P. Lemon, "Public Relief Policy in Moncton: The Depression Years, 1929-1939", M.A. report, University of New Brunswick, 1977, pp. 15-6.

33 See statements by A.P. Paterson, Walter Lea and Mr. Paul in the Minutes of the Dominion-Provincial Conference, 9 December 1935, Provincial Secretary's Papers, RG7, vol. 231, file 8, PANS; Charlottetown *Guardian*, 21 March 1934, quoted in L.J. Cusack, "The Prince Edward Island People and the Great Depression, 1930-1935", M.A. thesis, University of New Brunswick, 1972, p. 135.

another aspect of the provinces' dilemma. Should responsible leaders concentrate scarce resources on the direct relief of individuals while the provincial infrastructure, including roads and electrical development, fell so far behind the rest of the country as to impair future development? Yet, after 1932, the federal government abandoned its highway programmes and shifted to a policy of direct relief because it was less costly.[34] At the nadir of the Depression the provinces were left to complete construction largely with their own resources. They obtained the money for both roads and direct relief by borrowing and, by the end of 1933, debt charges consumed respectively 35 and 55 per cent of Nova Scotia and New Brunswick revenues. The financial problems of New Brunswick, in particular, remained acute throughout the decade as its governments had difficulty in selling bonds and faced tough negotiations with chartered banks.[35]

The relations between the provinces and the municipalities often paralleled those of the provinces and the Dominion. A few of the wealthiest municipalities were able to participate in the federal programmes to the extent that their provincial governments would let them. But the gap in economic resources among the municipalities left the poorest without the finances to obtain more than a fraction of the assistance available. Moreover, like the provinces, the municipalities were already embarrassed by their enforced participation in programmes which took little account of their straitened circumstances.

In Nova Scotia premier Harrington noted in the spring of 1931 that the "financial condition" of some of the Municipalities seemed to be "in very bad shape".[36] Guysborough county, already suffering from rural depopulation, general out-migration and pockets of chronic poverty in the 1920s had no reserves with which to cushion the effects of a new depression on its fishing and lumbering industries. Failing to collect more than 36 per cent of its taxes by the spring of 1931, the municipality found itself unable to pay bank overdrafts and debts to the province. A bitter county clerk protested that the escalation of costs in municipal estimates was due almost exclusively to the items of the budget over which the municipality had no control, including education, care for the insane and the indigent ill, and child welfare. The Hospital Act, in particular, forced the municipality to "pay for every seeming

---

34 E.N. Rhodes to J.F. Fraser, 10 November 1931, Provincial Secretary's Papers, vol. 225, no. 5, PANS.

35 R.W. Gouinlock to P.S. Fielding, 21 May 1937, Premier's Office Papers, PAPEI. See copy of telegram for the Premier of New Brunswick from "the four banks who lend money to that province", in G.T. Towers to J.L. Ralston, 15 April 1940, Department of Finance Papers, RG19 vol. 2697, PAC.

36 G.S. Harrington to John Doull, 17 July 1931, Provincial Secretary-Treasurer's Papers, RG7, vol. 225, PANS.

affliction anybody may imagine he has".[37] Faced with reports of widespread destitution, the county council sought permission to distribute whatever money it did obtain, in the cheapest way, as direct relief.

In New Brunswick the difficulties of the poorest municipalities followed a similar pattern. The northern counties suffered from the problems of the forest industries, especially lumber, and the fisheries. With the closure of sawmills the parish officers of Northumberland county rapidly exceeded the amounts assessed their parishes for assistance to the poor. Their appeals for provincial help brought reminders that the parishes were a municipal responsibility and legislation authorizing the municipalities to borrow to meet parish obligations.[38] The Northumberland Council secured loans to cover their overseers' deficits but carefully assigned responsibility for both principal and interest to the parishes which had incurred them. Early in 1933 the provincial and federal governments recognized the special nature of Northumberland's difficulties by increasing their share of relief in the county to 80 per cent. Even this assistance was not sufficient to keep the county solvent. With an estimated one third of the county requiring relief and tax revenues shrunk to 40 per cent of "normal", the bank cut off credit.[39] The province then provided guarantees for temporary relief loans until the county's new bond issue. But only a portion of the bonds could be sold and by 1934 the long-suffering merchants who were unable to collect the more than $10,000 owing for past relief orders refused further credit.[40] The county's appeal to their famous native son, R.B. Bennett, reporting "large numbers destitute to danger of starvation" brought the standard reply that there was "no contact between Dominion and municipalities". Faced with predictions of "serious disorders imminent", the province finally agreed to make loans to the municipality while accepting its bonds as security.[41] The neighbouring counties of Gloucester and Restigouche were likewise refused bank loans in 1934. Gloucester too had to be bailed out by the province but Restigouche, with a stronger economy, launched a collection drive, resolutely cut back on expenditures and managed to re-establish its credit with the bank.[42]

---

37   J.A. Fulton to John Doull, 2 April 1931, *ibid.*

38   22 George V, 1932, c.6.

39   Minutes of the Municipal Council of Northumberland, 17, 21 January 1933, RG 18, RS153, PANB.

40   *Ibid.*, 13 February 1933.

41   Minutes of the Municipal Council of Northumberland, 17, 18 January 1934; Order in Council, 3 April 1934, New Brunswick Cabinet Papers, PANB.

42   Minutes of the Finance Committee of the Municipality of Gloucester, 4 April 1935, Gloucester County Minutes, PANB; Minutes of the Municipality of Restigouche County, 22 May 1934, RG18, RS155, A1, PANB and "Auditor's Report" in *ibid.*, 1 January 1936.

The New Brunswick municipalities protested what their Union spokesman T.H. Whalen called the province's "continually unloading things on the municipalities". They particularly resented the charges for hospitalization which the province increased during 1931.[43] With so many of their people unable to pay for their health services, the three northern counties appealed to the province to assume the responsibility and became increasingly reluctant to commit the indigent to long term hospitalization.[44] The denial of hospital services, particularly to the victims of tuberculosis, may have been reflected in changes in the provincial death rate. The number of deaths per 100,000 declined throughout the 1920s, leveled out in the early 1930s, and rose again in Gloucester and Northumberland at mid-decade. In the year ending October 1935, deaths from tuberculosis in Gloucester municipality jumped from a previous annual average of less than three to 40 and the following year to 50.[45] In presenting Northumberland's submission before the Rowell-Sirois Commission D.K. Hazen stated that "the Municipality, owing to lack of funds is unwilling to pay the expenses of hospital treatment if it can be avoided and the treatment, therefore, is not generally given in the advanced stages when it is most effective".[46] In 1937 a Red Cross worker from Chatham included in her report to the cabinet a snapshot of a tubercular woman convalescing in a room which had been hastily created for her by neighbours closing in a verandah.[47] A proposal to give health officers the authority to commit indigent patients to hospitals was successfully resisted by the municipalities who required formal approval of admissions by parish representatives. Restigouche also refused to accept doctors' bills not signed by the overseers of the poor.[48]

The position of the parish officers directly responsible for relief was not an enviable one. For a consideration of perhaps $10 a year the poormasters were

---

43   Royal Commission on Dominion-Provincial Relations, Report of Proceedings, 23 May 1938, p. 9069. (Copy in stacks at Harriet Irving Library, UNB).

44   Minutes of the Municipal Council of Gloucester, 20 January 1932; Minutes of the Municipality of Restigouche County, 18 January 1934, PANB.

45   The Annual Reports of the Sub-Health District of Gloucester were included with the county minutes, 31 October 1935 and 31 October 1936. For expenditures on tuberculosis care see *Submission by The Municipality of Gloucester to the Royal Commission on Dominion-Provincial Relations* (April, 1938), p. 15. (Copy in stacks at Harriet Irving Library).

46   Royal Commission on Dominion-Provincial Relations, Report of Proceedings, May 23, 1938, p. 9085.

47   Mrs. E.T. McLean to J.B. McNair, 17 January 1938, New Brunswick Cabinet Papers, PANB.

48   Minutes of the Municipality of Restigouche, 18 January 1935 and 22 January and 17 July 1936 and Minutes of the Municipality of Gloucester, 24 January 1936.

expected to investigate the needs of hundreds or even thousands of relief recipients and take the steps necessary for their survival. During their financial crises, the municipal councils tended to divide whatever money they collected among their most pressing creditors and to distribute what was left among the parishes for relief. When the money ran out, the poormasters often tried to secure loans on their personal credit for which the municipality might eventually take responsibility. On one hand was the constraint imposed by the difficulty of borrowing money and, on the other, the pressure of watching their friends and neighbours go hungry. An investigation of Restigouche finances in 1934 revealed several thousands of dollars in unrecorded liabilities incurred by individual poormasters.[49] It is not surprising that the harried poormasters reacted angrily towards those who inadvertently increased the number of mouths they had to feed. Sentences of nine months to a year became customary for males prosecuted by the poormasters for the crime of bastardy.[50]

The problems of Prince Edward Island were similar to those of the rural municipalities. In the 1920s, the province faced rising expectations in education, roads, health and welfare with hopelessly inelastic revenues and a longstanding tradition of popular resistance to direct taxation. Of greatest urgency was the need to provide better public health services. National anti-tuberculosis campaigns had considerable appeal when upwards of one per cent of the population (estimates ranged from 700 to 1000) were infected by the disease.[51] Pressure from Women's Institutes, Red Cross and other groups for the construction of a sanitarium drove Premier A.C. Saunders to desperate pleas for additional funds from the federal government. As he told the Young Men's Commercial Club in 1928, in resisting their petition for a sanitarium, there are "only two sources of revenue", the federal government and the farmers, and the latter "do not feel disposed to stand for any additional taxes".[52] Specifically Saunders called on the federal politicians for the province's share of additional funds which might come from the general rationalization of provincial subsidies recommended by the Duncan Commission. The King government had used a vague promise of a new investigation to detach Prince Edward Island from the Maritime Rights campaign, but the anticipated settlement failed to materialize. At the beginning of the 1930s A.C. Saunders and his successor, W.M. Lea, diverted appeals for improved services, including higher salaries for teachers and old age pensions, with the

---

49 "Auditor's Report", Minutes of the Municipality of Restigouche, 3 July 1934.

50 J.W. Farth to J.B. McNair, 20 August 1935 and A.W. Bennett to A.J. Leger, 13 March 1931, New Brunswick Cabinet Papers, PANB.

51 A.C. Saunders to Rev. T. Constable, 26 November 1928, Premier's Office Papers, PAPEI.

52 A.C. Saunders to G.S. Buntain, 1 March 1928, *ibid.*

plea that these must await the additional funds from Ottawa.[53] The province did contribute $30,000 to the building of a small sanitarium by volunteer groups, but it obtained a portion of this money by cutting back the assistance previously given to enable blind and deaf children to study in the specialized schools in Halifax.[54]

With the onslaught of another Depression, successive P.E.I. premiers worked to minimize the popular expectation of relief. Relief, they argued, was largely unnecessary for the Island with an economy based on mixed farming and lacking either the large population of industrial unemployed or the drought which afflicted the West. But as the bottom dropped out of the market for Island potatoes and fish these arguments became less convincing.[55] Lacking rural municipalities, the provincial government was responsible for relief outside of the towns, and in a deliberate policy to discourage those seeking relief, it refused to inaugurate new procedures. It merely extended the traditional paupers' list by which indigents were aided at the rate of $5 per family per month after a case had been made for them by local clergymen, doctors or neighbours. It also encouraged volunteer agencies to greater efforts in succoring those in difficulty. In 1932 it did persuade the federal government to pay for a portion of the paupers' list and the customary third for relief administered through the municipality of Charlottetown.[56]

The letters to the premiers documenting individual cases for relief reveal unpleasant features of rural poverty. They tell of farmers lacking seed for crops, of animals slowly starving in their stalls, of children suffering malnutrition, and of a long waiting list for the sanitarium.[57] Moreover, as the Depression worsened, its impact became cumulative and apparently irrevocable. In a 1936 letter to the Dominion commissioner of relief, Prince Edward Island's Deputy Provincial Treasurer, P.S. Fielding, explained that unemployment conditions on the Island had failed to respond to improved markets because "a large proportion of our farming population has ...degenerated into circumstances where the conditions of market have very little effect on their general living conditions. [They]...have reached the stage

---

53 E.R. Forbes, *The Maritime Rights Movement*, pp. 186-7; A.C. Saunders to Agnes Murnaghan, 27 March 1929, and W. Lea to R.B. Bennett, 5 February 1931, Premiers' Office Papers, PAPEI.

54 A.C. Saunders to G.E. Saville, 31 October 1939; G.E. Saville to A.C. Saunders, 28 October 1929, and A.C. Saunders to George Bateman, 29 August 1929, *ibid.*.

55 Cusack, "Prince Edward Island and the Great Depression", ch. 2.

56 J.D. Stewart to Harry Hereford, 9 January 1934, "Direct Relief Files 1935-1941", Records of Dominion-Provincial Affairs, RG21, PAPEI.

57 P.A. Scully to A.C. Saunders, 27 September 1929, and Dr. R.K. Boswell to T. Campbell, 6 February 1939, Premier's Office Papers, PAPEI. "I know you may be tired of such cases", Boswell wrote.

where they are unable to cultivate their land, which has consequently... deteriorated. Stock and equipment have been gradually depleted...during the past winter conditions generally were far more critical than...in any previous season". Two years later an unemployment committee representing churches, labour unions, the Legion, the Free Dispensary and the Fishermen's Loan Board reported "distress and destitution" in Charlottetown and "employment conditions...more serious than at any time since the depression set in".[58]

The direct relief statistics from municipalities reinforce the impression of an inverse correlation between poverty and relief under the matching grants programme. In Nova Scotia one can discern four levels of assistance according to the average monthly payments to relief recipients. The most generous community, Amherst, which before the war boasted more millionaires per capita than any other town or city in Canada, occupies a level by itself.[59] This small manufacturing and commercial centre of about 8,000 maintained almost 2000 people on relief throughout 1933 at an average cost of $5.70 per month.[60] This figure was almost on a par with the national average and more than a quarter above the per recipient contribution of any other Maritime municipality. At a relief conference of Nova Scotian municipalities in 1934, Amherst Mayor Read defended his town's greater largesse by noting that its grant for food worked out to four and a half cents per person per meal for a family of four and invited the other mayors to explain "how anyone can live on less". His challenge was not accepted. Amherst retained and even extended its lead through the remainder of the decade.[61]

Mining towns held three out of four places at the next level. Glace Bay, Springhill, and New Waterford owed their prominence in granting relief less to relative wealth than to the organization and political influence of those demanding assistance. The initial pressure for help came from areas where labour was organized, alert to the funds distributed in industrial centres elsewhere, and determined to obtain their share. Familiar with the co-operative relief activities required by strikes, the leaders of District # 26 United Mine Workers of America co-operated with the Corporation in rationing shifts and with the municipalities in appointing investigating committees to apply for

---

58   P.S. Fielding to Harry Hereford, 6 August 1936, "Direct Relief Files 1935-1941", PAPEI; see resolution and collection of statements dated 11 May 1938 in *ibid.*.

59   Nolan Reilly, "The Growth and Decline of Amherst as a Manufacturing Centre, 1860-1930", a paper delivered to the Sixth Atlantic Studies Conference, May 1985.

60   The monthly "Direct Relief Reports" from Nova Scotia to the Minister of Labour are complete from April 1933 to March 1934 and largely complete from October 1932 until the end of the decade, RG27, vol. 2096, file Y 40-0, PAC.

61   *Proceedings of...the Union of Nova Scotia Municipalities*, 1934, p. 143. For accounts of what it was like to "live on less" see David Frank and Don MacGillivray, eds., *George MacEachern: An Autobiography* (Sydney, 1987), ch. 3.

and distribute what direct relief was available. The town of Glace Bay borrowed $100,000 in 1930-31 and then, with its credit nearly exhausted, required "donations" to the municipality from relief recipients of one-third of their total assistance as an expedient to keep federal and provincial funds flowing.[62] Although required to abandon this practice, the miners were able to force attention from Conservative provincial and federal governments who regarded the industrial centres as critical to their continued political success.[63] Particularly useful at this time was their reputation for radical militancy. A federal investigator of conditions in the mining communities in August 1931 reported that "the Red element" was "showing signs of liveliness" and there was potential for a strike "worse than anything previous in the history of Cape Breton". This report was followed by the announcement of new relief projects by the senior levels of government. The federal government also increased coal and steel tariffs and coal transportation subsidies.[64]

Most other urban centres, Halifax, Trenton, Westville, New Glasgow, Sydney Mines, Truro, Dartmouth, Sydney, and North Sydney, gave relief averaging in the $3.50 to $3.00 range. Last among the towns which paid relief on a twelve month basis were Inverness, Pictou, and Stellarton at close to $2.00 each. Only two rural municipalities paid relief for the 12 month period, Pictou County at $3.07 and Cape Breton County at $2.07. At the bottom level were the remaining 17 municipalities who paid relief on an irregular basis often restricted to the winter period. Guysborough County was one of these. In 1934 it cut off relief in May and did not resume it again until February. A check of Guysborough's relief payments in the peak month of March indicate how erratic and limited its assistance really was, even during the few months it was offered. In 1934 the three levels of government distributed through the municipality $3066 to 2696 people for an average of $1.14 per person. A year later they gave 90 people an average of $2.20 apiece for the month.

On Prince Edward Island the gap was sharp between those receiving provincial aid and those assisted through the municipality of Charlottetown. For February 1935 the average payment for the 6,466 provincial recipients was $1.90 compared to Charlottetown's $3.20 for 2,119 residents of the city. For February 1936 the disparity increased as the respective averages were $2.19 and $5.35. Prince Edward Island's overall figures were reduced by in-

---

62 M.S. Campbell, "Re unemployment situation etc. Sydney, North Sydney, Sydney Mines, New Waterford, Dominion, Glace Bay, Louisburg and Springhill", copy enclosed with H.H. Ward to G.S. Harrington, 18 August 1931, Provincial Secretary-Treasurer's Papers, RG7, vol. 226, #7, PAC.

63 W.J. White, "Left wing Politics and Community: A Study of Glace Bay, 1930-1940", M.A. thesis, Dalhousie University, 1978, pp. 69-77 and 44-7.

64 M.S. Campbell, "Re. unemployment situation etc.".

terruptions in relief, usually during the summer months. The combined average of province and city for the year 1935 was just $1.77.[65]

For New Brunswick more fragmentary data suggests a similar gulf between the stronger and weaker municipalities in the amount paid. In the year ending 31 March 1935, Moncton carried an average 1,344 people at a monthly rate of $3.35, Saint John paid $2.93 to a monthly average of 4761, and Campbellton assisted 507 people at $1.35 a month for two months.[66] In February 1936, Gloucester municipality gave its 12,234 relief recipients an average of $1.14 apiece. February averages for the previous year for Moncton and Saint John were respectively $4.35 and $3.21. In Ontario the average paid each relief recipient for the same month was $8.13.[67]

In New Brunswick the low level of relief given even prevented the province's participation in the national programme for encouraging a return to the land. The talk of a "back-to-the-land" movement initially drew responsive echoes from New Brunswick, whose politicians were conscious of its large tracts of uncleared forests, previous failures to attract immigrants, and an earlier interest in colonization by Acadian spokesmen. In 1930 premier J.B.M. Baxter advised the unemployed to "go back to the land and work it", for as long as one has "land and health" a man will not starve.[68] The province announced a new tri-partite programme to go into effect in March 1932, appointed a board to administer it, and began surveying lands and building roads for the new settlers.[69] But the New Brunswick government apparently failed to consider the terms of the national programme from the prospective of its municipalities. The programme called for each level of government to contribute $200 per family: $400 for building materials, animals and farm

---

65 Copies of monthly relief reports to the Minister of Labour are contained in two boxes of papers entitled "Relief to 1940", PAPEI and in RG27, vol. 2096, file Y 40-1 "Statistics PEI" (First and Second sections), PAC.

66 New Brunswick seemed determined to avoid supplying data which could be used for comparisons in the amounts of relief given. Statistics on three communities for one year is given in Department of Labour Papers, RG27, vol. 2096, file Y40, "Classification of Unemployed", PAC.

67 Report of the Direct Relief Committee to the Municipal Council of Gloucester in Minutes, 31 December 1936, p. 452, PANB. RG 18, RS 149 gives the amount spent on relief for the month. The numbers on relief in New Brunswick municipalities for one month only are contained in the Department of Public Works, RG 14, RS 128, 4/16, PANB. For provincial figures see J.K. Houston, "An Appreciation of Relief", p. 25.

68 Saint John *Telegraph-Journal*, 15 September 1930 and New Brunswick, *Report of the Department of Lands and Mines*, 1930, pp. 53-4.

69 "Agreement...", 17 May 1932, New Brunswick Cabinet Papers, PANB; *Report of the Department of Lands and Mines, 1932*, p. 56.

implements and the remaining $200 to provide additional support over the first two years. In Ontario, at these figures, municipalities might expect to recover their investment in the first two years through a saving of direct relief costs. In Nova Scotia, where the programme was inaugurated for "surplus" miners, it at least suggested the possibility of an eventual break even point.[70] But so much lower were the direct relief totals in New Brunswick that the programme meant only increased costs to the municipalities. Some municipalities were also uneasy about who would be responsible for future relief in the new settlements should they fail to become self-sustaining. New Brunswick municipalities therefore unanimously rejected the scheme. Even Restigouche County, which had rushed to offer Campbellton as a headquarters for the programme, ultimately refused to participate.[71]

It is one of the ironies of the period that the back-to-the-land movement became most popular in a province which could not participate in the national programme. So desperate were many New Brunswickers and so limited their alternatives that they clambered to take out land with only a fraction of the assistance available elsewhere. In 1932 the number of new families setting out each year to carve new farms out of the New Brunswick wilderness rose from about 150 to more than 300 and after 1936 exceeded 600. By 1939 the department of lands and mines, which was responsible for parcelling out the lands, reported a population of 11,165 in several dozens of new settlements concentrated in the northern counties. Quebec with five times the population had 24,666 and Manitoba came a distant third at 5,900.[72]

Despite their heroic efforts in clearing and cultivating land, few of the new settlers managed to become economically independent. The provincial government regularly supplied them with seed, allowed pulp-cutting from their 100 acre claims and, aided by federal grants for the relief of unorganized territories, supplied $4.07 worth of groceries four times a year.[73] In 1935 the province circulated additional cash among the colonists through bonuses for land ploughed and brought under cultivation. In the summer of 1939 a federal department of agriculture analysis of the economic progress of 300 settlers in northern New Brunswick revealed that their average total net worth including

70 Department of Labour, "Report on Nova Scotia's Unemployed", R.B. Bennett Papers, p. 477764, Harriet Irving Library, UNB.

71 Moncton *Transcript*, 17 June 1932: Minutes of the Council of the Municipality of Restigouche, 23 January 1931 and 5 July 1932.

72 New Brunswick, *Report of Department of Lands and Mines*, 1939, p. 120; Department of Labour, "Dominion Unemployment Relief Since 1930" (January 1940), p. 39; see also W.M. Jones, "Relief Land Settlement", in L. Richter, ed., *Canada's Unemployment Problem* (Toronto 1939), pp. 261-95.

73 E.M. Poirier, "The Founding of Allardville Settlement", M.A. report, University of New Brunswick, 1973, p. 21.

cleared land, buildings, farm implements, and personal possessions after an average of 4.2 years on their new holdings amounted to just $578. This was about what they might have received at the outset had they resided in most other provinces. Noting their lack of adequate farm implements, machinery for clearing land and sewing machines for their wives, the investigators concluded that, as a result of insufficient capital, their efforts had been largely wasted.[74]

In August 1934 the federal government officially abandoned the matching grants formula in direct relief for a new programme of grants-in-aid to the provinces. These were to be based on "need and the ability of the province to deal with the problem". The grants, which were fixed in advance and paid regularly at monthly intervals, did help the provinces in planning their programmes. They had limited effect, however, on the distribution of federal assistance since the principal indicator of need was taken to be the money spent by each provinces under the old matching grants system. The timing of the transition was unfortunate for the Maritimes. The new monthly relief grants of $68,000 — $2125 to Prince Edward Island, $2500 to New Brunswick and $40,875 to Nova Scotia — were substantially less than the federal share of relief costs paid to the region for 1933. But unlike the country as a whole, whose relief payents continued to rise during the first half of 1934, those in the Maritimes declined sharply as municipalities ran out of money and provincial governments forced draconian cutbacks in the summer months. In 1933 monthly relief totals varied from $312,422 in February to $164,253 in July. In 1934 the totals were respectively $268,700 and $101,810 for the same two months.[75] Thus, while the new grants-in-aid could be projected as increases over the low summer relief totals,[76] they were in fact reductions of more than one quarter from the *average* monthly direct relief payments by the federal government to the Maritimes through the calendar year of 1933. The federal payments continued with little variation through 1935 and in December of that year provided the base for a 75 per cent increase to all provinces by

---

74 A. Gosselin and G.P. Boucher, *Settlement Problems in Northern New Brunswick* (Ottawa 1944), Canada Department of Agriculture Publication No. 764, pp. 24-9. The settlers had held their claims an average of 4.2 years when the study was made. By this time the provincial department responsible was also beginning to doubt the value of the programme. See Department of Lands and Mines, "A Discussion of Land Settlement in New Brunswick", RG10, RS106, box 42, "Corres, re Reconstruction".

75 Department of Labour, "Dominion Unemployment Relief Since 1930" (January 1940), pp. 97-8, Department of Labour Papers, PAC, RG27, vol. 213 and J.K. Houston, "An Appreciation of Relief", pp. 21-3.

76 See James Struthers, *No Fault of Their Own*, p. 117 and p. 242, n. 43

a newly elected Liberal government. The increase was intended "to enable the provinces to lighten the burden upon the municipalities".[77]

The matching grants mentality persisted, however. In 1936 the King government commissioned Charlotte Whitton of the Canadian Welfare Council to analyze the existing relief structure and to produce recommendations for reform. Whitton, who emphasized the importance of professional social workers in the distribution of relief and was adept at telling King what he wished to hear, counselled against any additional assumption of relief responsibilities by the federal government.[78] The need for expert supervision was implicit in her charge that, under the grants-in-aid system, the provinces were escaping their relief responsibilities. Whitton chose the Maritime provinces as her prime exhibit of provincial delinquency. In nearly half a page of underlined prose, she reviewed past relief statistics on the Maritimes to suggest prosperity (later she referred directly to "prosperous and pleasant little Prince Edward Island") and gave the startling information that the provincial and municipal governments were together paying only 19 per cent of relief costs on the Island, 12 per cent in Nova Scotia, and eight per cent in New Brunswick. Whitton created her dramatic statistics by reference to a period which did not include the winter months in which most Maritime municipalities concentrated their limited payments. Elsewhere her own tables reveal the anomaly that she was presenting. For the year, 1935-36, they show that New Brunswick, Nova Scotia and Prince Edward Island paid respectively 56 per cent, 39 per cent and 68 per cent of their direct relief costs. The provinces may not have been aware of the attack which had been launched against them. Whitton asked that her 300 page study be kept confidential since there were "a few statistics" of which she was not certain.[79]

In next two years the Maritimes tightened their relief offerings still further in a campaign against the "demoralizing effect" of relief and "relief dependency". The federal government provided the incentive by trimming its direct relief payments to the provinces by 15 per cent in April 1936 and another 10 per cent in June. After Whitton's report, total direct relief grants to the provinces were cut by about one third in April and June 1937 and those to the Maritimes by 62.7 per cent.[80] Once again the Maritime governments seem to

---

77 "Dominion Unemployment Relief Since 1930", p. 23.

78 James Struthers, "A Profession in Crisis: Charlotte Whitton and Canadian Social Work in the 1930s", *Canadian Historical Review*, LXII, 2 (June 1981), pp. 169-85.

79 [Charlotte Whitton], "The Organization of Aid to Persons in Distress: Report and Recommendations of the Division on Co-ordination of Aid", March 1937, Department of Labour Papers, RG27, vol. 227, file 617, vol. 2, pp. 65b and 68-9, PAC.

80 Monthly payments to the provinces are given in "Dominion Unemployment Relief Since 1930", pp. 25-7. More comprehensive annual figures which includes money for work projects and drought relief are available in "Dominion Relief Expenditures", J.L. Ralston Papers, PAC. Total federal relief payments to the Maritimes

have been masking adversity in public assertions of optimism. With the return of better economic conditions, they argued, relief was no longer so necessary. New Brunswick went further. In August of 1936 the government of Allison Dysart announced the absolute termination of direct relief in New Brunswick.[81]

There was a certain logic in the government's action. To the degree that its finances would permit, the Dysart government, upon taking office late in 1935, had launched a series of positive programmes including pensions for the aged and the blind and new public works projects.[82] In the poorer municipalities they agreed to pay up to 90 per cent of the cost of the relief of unemployables.[83] The employables thus isolated were expected to find work in expanded highway programmes, a slowly improving forest industry, or by joining the pioneer settlements. The federal cutbacks forced the pace. Rather than undercutting the new programmes to pick up a much larger share of direct relief, the Dysart government apparently decided to reap whatever political and psychological advantage might be derived from posing as the first government in Canada to end "the dole". This decision was easier for New Brunswick than for other provinces since their people received so little in any case, especially during the summer months. Government spokesmen in New Brunswick explained their action as necessary to defend the credit of both provinces and municipalities and to help those dependent on direct relief which was "sapping the morals and initiative of our people".[84] As economic conditions again worsened in 1937, this 'cold turkey' cure caused real suffering even among people who had a very limited acquaintance with "relief

---

dropped from $2.8 million in 1935-36 to $2.5 million in 1936-7 and to $1.4 million in 1938-9. Relief payments to the country as a whole for these years were $79.4 million, $78.0 million and $68.5 million. See also J.R. Rowell, "An Intellectual in Politics: Norman Rogers as an Intellectual and Minister of Labour, 1929-1939", M.A. thesis, Queens' University, 1978, pp. 143-4.

81 Saint John *Telegraph-Journal*, 13 August 1936. For a collection of statements on relief policy by members of the New Brunswick cabinet from May to August 1936 taken from the Saint John *Telegraph-Journal*, see enclosures J.H. Conlon to Marjorie Bradford, 13 April 1937, Canadian Council on Social Development Papers, MG28, I10, vol. 122, file "1937", PAC.

82 Positive views from different perspectives on Dysart's administration are contained in R.M. Tweedie, *On with the Dance: A New Brunswick Memoir, 1935-1950* (Fredericton, 1986), and Patrick Burden, "The New Brunswick Farmer-Labour Union 1937-1941", M.A. thesis, University of New Brunswick, 1983.

83 See New Brunswick Cabinet Papers, 1 December 1936.

84 *Synoptic Report of the Proceedings of the Legislative Assembly of New Brunswick,* 1937, pp. 57 and 131.

dependency". The province did relent sufficiently to provide emergency assistance to the city of Saint John and the northern municipalities during the winters of 1937 and 1938.[85]

With the benefit of hindsight one can criticize Maritime leaders on humanitarian grounds for failing to do more to ameliorate the hard circumstances of their people in the 1930s. Throughout the period they seemed to accept, to grant and to rationalize less than the minimum required by their citizens for physical and economic health. So harsh were their policies in all three provinces, even when compared to those of other governments in the period, that they tempt one to attribute them to some distinct trait of regional character, perhaps arising from a different class configuration or a unique aspect of their political culture. But a close examination of the structure and operations of the relief process in Canada reveals logical reasons for the Maritimes' apparently deviant behaviour. Under the system of conditional matching grants the three provinces were forced to play in a relief game whose rules only allowed the effective participation of wealthier players. The additional pressures and more limited choices faced by Maritime leaders largely explain their more draconian treatment of those requiring assistance.

The study of relief policies in the Maritimes suggests yet another perspective on the cumulative development of regional disparity in Canada. In the 1930s with business stagnant throughout the country, federal funds played an important role in the economic survival of individuals and industries. The Maritime region received during the decade approximately $50 millions less in relief monies from the federal government than they would have had the money simply been distributed on a per capita basis. In the extreme deflation of the mid 1930s such a sum was not insignificant. One can speculate on the role which it might have played in saving individuals from personal bankruptcy, allowing independent commodity producers to maintain their operations within a market economy, or enabling at least some of the pioneer settlements to emerge as productive communities. One might speculate too on the impact of this sum if it had been available to the provincial governments for the health and education of the regional work force and/or maintaining the region's relative level of infrastructure including roads and electricity.[86] It is ironic that, while emerging as the agent of the welfare state in Canada, the federal government, through the inequity of its matching grants formulas, inadvertently became an agent in the development of regional disparity.

---

85 New Brunswick, "Public Accounts", *Journals of the Legislative Assembly,* 1939, pp. 355-6 and A.P. Paterson's report to the Cabinet 20 May 1937, New Brunswick Cabinet Papers.

86 Weaknesses in these areas would later be cited as factors in the consolidation of regional disparity during the 1940s. E.R. Forbes, "Consolidating Disparity: The Maritimes and the Industrialization of Canada during the Second World War", *Acadiensis,* XV, 2 (Spring 1986), pp. 3-27.

Contributors

T.W. Acheson is the Chair of the Department of History at the University of New Brunswick and is the author of *Saint John: the Making of a Colonial Urban Community* (University of Toronto Press, 1985).

Béatrice Craig is an Associate Professor in the Department of History at the University of Ottawa and is the author of several papers published in *Journal of Forest History* and *Histoire sociale/Social History*.

Ken Cruikshank is an Assistant Professor in the Department of History at Trent University and the author of *Close Ties: Railways, Government and the Board of Railway Commissioners, 1851-1933* (McGill-Queen's, 1991).

Ian Drummond is a Professor in the Department of Economics at the University of Toronto and is the author of several books on international monetary history and Canadian economic history.

Lou Evans is the Professor of Economic Theory at the Victoria University of Wellington and the author of numerous papers in the *American Economic Review, Econometrica* and other journals.

E.R. Forbes is a Professor in the Department of History at the University of New Brunswick and is co-editor with D.A. Muise of *The Atlantic Provinces in Confederation* (University of Toronto Press/Acadiensis Press, 1993).

Marilyn Gerriets is a member of the Department of Economics at St. Francis Xavier University. Another of her studies on early industrialization in Nova Scotia has been published recently in *Business History*.

Kris Inwood is an Associate Professor in the Department of Economics at the University of Guelph. He has published many articles on Canadian economic history and is the author of *The Canadian Charcoal Iron Industry, 1870-1914* (Garland, 1986).

Jim Irwin is an Associate Professor in the Department of Economics at Central Michigan University and the author of several papers published in *Agricultural History* and *Explorations in Economic History*.

Alan MacNeil recently completed his doctorate in the Department of History at Queen's University and is the author of several papers published in *Histoire sociale/Social History* and *Canadian Papers in Rural History*.

Greg Marchildon is an Assistant Professor in the School of Advanced International Studies at John Hopkins University and the author of papers in *Business History* and *Essays in the History of Canadian Law*.

D.A. Muise is a member of the History Department at Carleton University and is co-editor with E.R. Forbes of *The Atlantic Provinces in Confederation* (University of Toronto Press/Acadiensis Press, 1993).

Neil Quigley is an Associate Professor in the Department of Economics at the University of Western Ontario and is the author of several papers on financial history in the *Canadian Journal of Economics, Business History Review* and other journals.